Thomas Olden

The Church of Ireland

Thomas Olden

The Church of Ireland

ISBN/EAN: 9783337324254

Printed in Europe, USA, Canada, Australia, Japan

Cover: Foto ©Lupo / pixelio.de

More available books at **www.hansebooks.com**

BY

THOMAS OLDEN, M.A.
MEMBER OF THE ROYAL IRISH ACADEMY; VICAR OF BALLYCLOUGH,
AUTHOR OF
"THE HOLY SCRIPTURES IN IRELAND ONE THOUSAND YEARS AGO."

With Maps.

LONDON:
WELLS GARDNER, DARTON & CO.
2 PATERNOSTER BUILDINGS, E.C.
AND 44 VICTORIA STREET, S.W.
1892

1892.

PREFACE.

WHILE these sheets were passing through the press the Church of Ireland suffered a grievous loss in the death of the learned and accomplished Dr. Reeves, Bishop of Down, Connor, and Dromore, who was without a rival in his acquaintance with the ecclesiastical literature of Ireland. Up to the last, notwithstanding his many engagements, he found time with his usual kindness to read the proofs of this work for me. The essay on S. Patrick (Appendix A.) had not then been reached by the printer, but before any part of the work went to the press I had sent this to the Bishop in manuscript. I felt doubtful as to how he would receive it, as it differs considerably from previous theories on the subject. I was, however, much gratified when he assured me of the pleasure with which he read the argument. I hope it will be found to throw some light on a difficult subject. The Bishop has been taken from us, in the Providence of God, when he could ill be spared, and I deeply regret that it is now not in my power to thank him for the help he so willingly gave me. His works are indispensable to any one who writes on Irish ecclesiastical history, and they will be found frequently quoted in the following pages. Numerous references are also made to the Tripartite Life of S. Patrick, edited by Mr. Whitley Stokes, D.C.L. Oxon., the second volume of which contains all the contemporary documents connected with his history. These are given in the original languages, together with numerous extracts from ancient authors, which illustrate them. The student is thus supplied with all the materials for the investigation of the origins of Irish Christianity in the most convenient form, and edited by one of the first scholars of the age. Formerly they could only be gathered from rare works, many of them not to be found except in large public libraries.

Some of the Lives in the "Dictionary of National Biography" have also been used, and though this may not appear so satisfactory as a reference to the original documents, it really amounts to the same thing, as all articles in the Dictionary are supplied with a summary of the authorities on which they are founded. I had the less hesitation in quoting them, as the Lives in question were written by myself from original sources. The Church History of Rev. R. King, which gives so many important documents, and his able history of the Primacy of Armagh, have been often consulted, together with many other authorities, published and unpublished, the names of most of which will be found at pp. 430, 431.

The first map prefixed shows the early division of Ireland (see p. 118), the churches underlined in red in the southern division being those of the chief ecclesiastics who were present at the Synods of Magh Léne and Whitefield (*ib.*). Those so indicated in the North are the churches of those to whom the Pope-elect and the Roman clergy[1] addressed their letter on the Easter question about 640 (Ussher, Works, iv. 427). The second map exhibits the dioceses as they exist at present, the only difference since disestablishment being that there has been an increase in their number, Clogher having been detached from Armagh, and endowed as a separate bishopric. In the Appendix (A.) will be found some considerations on the dates connected with S. Patrick's history. A few other matters which required to be noticed have also been placed in the Appendix in order not to interrupt the course of the history, and as they were not likely to interest the general reader. I have to acknowledge my obligations to many friends for occasional assistance in this work, among whom I would especially mention Mr. Whitley Stokes, D.C.L.,

---

[1] They were: *Bishops*, Toméné of Armagh, Colman of Clonard, Cronan of Oendruim, Dima of Connor, and Baithen of Taghboyne. *Priests*, Cronan, Abbot of Moville; Ernan, Abbot of Tory Island; Laisrean, Abbot of Ardmicnasca; Scellan, the leper of Armagh; Segene, Abbot of Bangor; and Sarán O'Critain, of Tisaran, whose church was in the South.

LL.D., Professor Ridgeway of Cambridge and Queen's College, Cork, and the Rev. E. Milner-Barry, M.A., of Tunbridge Wells, whose kindness in making extracts I have often put to a severe test.

I will only add that my desire has been to give a faithful presentation of the facts in this history, and to show that the Church through all the changes of the past has retained its historical identity, and is now, as it has ever been, the CHURCH OF IRELAND.

CONTENTS.

	PAGE
I. PRE-CHRISTIAN IRELAND	1
II. THE CONVERSION OF IRELAND—S. PATRICK	9
III. SAINTS OF THE FIRST PERIOD—S. BRIGIT	31
IV. SECOND PERIOD—SAINTS AT HOME	49
V. SECOND AND THIRD PERIODS—SAINTS ABROAD.	
1. GREAT BRITAIN	71
VI. SECOND AND THIRD PERIODS—SAINTS ABROAD.	
2. THE CONTINENT	91
VII. THE CONSTITUTION OF THE CHURCH	110
VIII. ITS EASTERN ORIGIN AND PRIMITIVE CHARACTER	130
IX. THE HIBERNENSIS AND THE IRISH SCHOOLS	146
X. THE DANES—THE ROUND TOWERS	166
XI. KING BRIAN—THE CHRISTIAN DANES	184
XII. STATE OF RELIGION—CHURCH GOVERNMENT	202
XIII. DIOCESAN EPISCOPACY	220
XIV. THE ANGLO-NORMANS AND ADRIAN'S BULL	237
XV. THE ANGLO-NORMAN AND NATIVE CLERGY	257
XVI. THE STATUTE OF KILKENNY	275
XVII. THE REFORMATION	291
XVIII. EDWARD VI. TO JAMES I.	310
XIX. JAMES I. TO CHARLES II.	339

CONTENTS

	PAGE
XX. CHARLES II. TO GEORGE I.	360
XXI. GEORGE I. TO DISESTABLISHMENT . .	381

APPENDIX.

A. S. PATRICK	405
B. THE CELTIC DOGS . . .	420
C. ON THE WORD "CANÓIN"	421
D. LOUGH EIRKÉ . . .	424
E. PARALLEL SAINTS	425
F. A HYMN IN TWO LANGUAGES	426
G. LITURGICAL TERMS	427
H. A POEM ON ROME BY JOHN SCOTUS . . .	429
AUTHORITIES QUOTED	430

HISTORY OF THE CHURCH OF IRELAND.

CHAPTER I.

PRE-CHRISTIAN IRELAND.

THE condition of Ireland in the period immediately preceding the advent of Christianity to its shores so vitally affected the Church founded there that some remarks on the subject are necessary.

The wave of Roman conquest had spent its force on Britain, and though Agricola contemplated the invasion of Ireland, and troops were assembled for the purpose, the design was never carried out. Thus, while Britain was known as "the Roman island," Ireland remained independent, and was termed the "barbarous" or non-Roman island. This immunity from the fate of most European countries had a profound influence on her subsequent history, and it would not, perhaps, be too much to say that some of its effects are perceptible even at the present hour.

In its general aspect the country was densely wooded, and even down to the seventeenth century districts where not a tree is now to be seen were clothed with mighty oaks or the rich vegetation of native shrubs. Tracts of this latter kind were known

A

as "fastnesses" from their difficulty of access, and played an important part in the troubles of the sixteenth and seventeenth centuries.

Unacquainted with Roman civilisation, the Irish had their own tribal institutions, such as those descended to them from their Aryan ancestors, and their own form of heathenism, derived from the same source; but "of the deities of Greece or Rome they had no knowledge, nor had they any Celtic names or designations for them."[1]

It was a country of clans, the members of which derived their name from an ancestor who was regarded in a certain sense as still the head. Thus the clan of O'Neill meant the descendants of Niall of the Nine Hostages, whose achievements were thus always kept in memory. The clans, though independent in reality, acknowledged the authority of an over-king, who in early times resided at Tara; but his rule was nominal, and the population generally were entirely unacquainted with the idea of a central government and executive.

The inhabitants are termed in the "Confession of S. Patrick" Scoti[2] or Scots, and Hiberionaces, the former being the ruling race; and the usual name for Ireland down to the eleventh century is Scotia. But when the colony from Ireland which settled in the West of Scotland in the fifth century formed a kingdom with a monarch of their own, Ireland began to be known as Scotia Major or the Greater Scotland, and the colony as Lesser Scotia, and finally the name became appropriated altogether to Scotland. The Scots of Ireland are regarded as the race otherwise called Milesians,

---

[1] Todd, S. Patrick, 456n.
[2] Said to have been so called from painting or tattooing their bodies (Bollandist's A.A.S.S., Oct. 22, Tom. ix. 656, col. 1).

descendants of Miledh of Spain, who make such a figure in the legendary history of Ireland, as the conquerors of the previous races who inhabited the country. Some of these primitive tribes remained distinct down to historic times; as, for instance, the Firbolgs, who are mentioned in the Life of S. Grellan as occupying a territory in the counties of Roscommon and Galway, and an account is given of the invasion of their territory and their conquest by the people of Oirghialla or Oriel, which embraced the county of Louth. These subjugated races are comprehended under the general term of Hiberionaces, so called from Hiberio,[1] the name by which the country was known, and which has survived that of the Scotic conquerors.

In the Lives of S. Patrick, Druids are frequently mentioned, and the Order of Bards also occupies an important place. The former are represented as engaged in education, as the same class was in Gaul, according to Cæsar. He mentions as one of their tenets the doctrine of the immortality of the soul,[2] and there is reason to believe that this was also held by the Irish Druids, as one of their terms [3] preserved in the "Book of Armagh" implies a similar belief. This must in some degree have facilitated the reception of Christianity among them.

The Bards acted as genealogists and historians as well as poets, and many of them were amongst the

[1] "*Hiberio*, which is also the designation of Ireland in the 'Itinerary of Antonine,' is the Latin form of the native name Eriu. The *b* sounding as *v* gave Iverio (*h* being omitted as not a distinct letter of the Irish alphabet), and by a phonetic law *v* between two vowels disappearing, it became Ierio, Ieriu, and finally Eriu. The modern Erin is the dative case" (Wh. Stokes in M. Müller's "Science of Language," vol. i. p. 275).

[2] De Pell. Gall., vi. s. 14; Strabo, iv. 197.

[3] "The day called *Erdathe* by the Druids, that is, the Day of Judgment of the Lord" (Tripartite, ii. 308, line 8). It is not a loan word from the Greek or Latin, and seems to be a native term.

earliest converts. They were a numerous body, and in the sixth century were supposed to number one-third of the population.

In the popular religion there was no systematic mythology like that of Greece or Rome, but a few deities, whose forms are indistinct and shadowy, are occasionally mentioned, such as Badb, the goddess of war and carnage; Nuadu, a sea-god, the Nodens of Britain; and Brigit, a goddess who is supposed to have had a fire ritual, and who corresponded with the divinity mentioned by Cæsar as having some of the attributes of Minerva.[1] But these were little known to the mass of the people, whose religion consisted in a vague belief in earth-gods,[2] dwelling within the hills of the *Sid*, as their mysterious abodes were called, and whose only objects of worship were stones, trees, and wells. Pillar stones, which were so numerous in many parts of the country, were believed to be inhabited by spirits, as at this day among the Arabs of Palestine.[3] The chief seat of this worship was the Plain of Adoration,[4] where a large idol, called Crom or Cenn Cruaich, stood, which was plated with gold[5] and surrounded by twelve smaller ones covered with brass. It is stated in the "Book of Leinster" that the Irish sacrificed children to this idol :—

"Milk and corn
They used to ask of him urgently,
In return for a third of their offspring.
Great was the horror and the wailing there."[6]

---

[1] "Brigit is certainly connected with the old Celtic goddess-name Brigantia" (Stokes, "Cormac's Glossary," p. 23).
[2] *Dei terreni*, as Latin writers term them. In Irish they were *fir sidhe*, "(fairy) men of the hills ;" *bean sidhe* (Banshee) is the female form.
[3] Lieut. Conder, Heth and Moab, p. 329.
[4] *Magh slecht*, situated near Ballymagauran, in the county of Cavan.
[5] A legendary confirmation of this is, that Tigernmas, a worshipper of the idol, was the first to smelt gold in Ireland (A.F.M., A.D. 3656).
[6] Book of Leinster (Facsimile, 213 *b*).

PRE-CHRISTIAN IRELAND.

The worship of trees was prevalent, as the frequent occurrence of the word *bile*, a sacred tree, in local names attests.[1] Five famous trees are mentioned in the " Book of Leinster."[2] They were the Eo Rossa, a yew-tree; the Eo Mugna, an oak; the Bile Dathi, the Bile Tortain, and the Craeb Uisnig, which were ash-trees. These trees fell or were destroyed in the time of the sons of Aedh Slaine, in the seventh century.[3] This would seem to indicate that the veneration for them finally ceased at that time. When the Eo Rossa, which stood at Drombarna, Co. Monaghan, fell, it was bestowed by S. Molaisse on the saints of Ireland, and it is recorded in the Life of S. Molling[4] of Luachair that he engaged a celebrated artisan, named the Gobán Saer, to construct an oratory for him from the portion assigned to him. But in thus converting this object of pagan worship to a Christian use S. Molling suffered personal injury, which, we are told, an agent of Satan endeavoured to aggravate. The Eo Mugna was felled by the poet Ninnine. It is thus described :—It was a vast tree, the top whereof was as broad as a plain. Thrice a year did it bear fruit, and it remained hidden from the time of the Deluge until the night on which Con of the Hundred-battles was born. Thirty cubits was the girth of that tree, and three hundred cubits its height.[5] Another authority tells us it bore three kinds of fruit every year. First, wondrous apples of great size; secondly, blood-red berries; thirdly, brown-speckled acorns. Of the latter, its produce was nine

---

[1] As *Maghbhile*, Moville; *Rathbhile*, Rathvilly, &c.
[2] Facsimile, pp. 199*b*, 200*a*.
[3] Began to reign A.D. 658.
[4] Dairchell or Molling in "Dictionary of National Biography."
[5] Calendar of Œngus, p. clxxxi., ed. Stokes.

hundred sacks.[1] In the Life of S. Berach [2] we have further evidence that the belief continued in Christian times. He proposed to a Druid who resisted him that a public trial should take place before the judges as to the respective claims of Christianity and heathenism, but the Druid declined unless it were to take place under a tree in which a demon had his residence, whose aid he wished to have.

The worship of wells was in existence in S. Patrick's time, and he found the people worshipping one which was artificially enclosed and covered with a square stone. They believed a Druid was buried beneath the stone, and they called the well the King of Waters.

The population lived within the enclosures commonly known as Danish forts, but which were in existence long before any Danes were heard of in Ireland. In these their houses of timber or wattled-work were placed, surrounded generally by a single rampart, but in the case of royal residences by two or more. Such enclosures, with their primitive houses, became the model of the Irish monastery, and were termed "cities."[3]

The worship of the sun is referred to by S. Patrick as practised in his time, and one of the customs connected with it, and still retained, in Ireland was the lighting of bonfires, once common throughout Europe. The first day of May was known in the Irish language as the day of Beltine, either the fire of Baal, or, as by some interpreted, "the lucky fire." The fires are now transferred to the 23rd of

---

[1] Book of Leinster, 200*a*, lines 15, 16.
[2] Of Cluain Coirpthe, Co. of Roscommon (Boll., Actt S.S., Feb. 15, p. 343*b*).
[3] The forts are called in Irish *Lis*, which is translated *civitas*. Thus, *Loeg-less*, the name of a well at Tara, is translated the "calf of cities." Cæsar calls similar enclosures, with their houses, *oppida*.

June, the eve of S. John the Baptist's day, but originally they seem to have been connected with the summer solstice.[1]

The Elysium of the Irish was on the banks of the Boyne, which was even a more famous river in prehistoric times than at the present day. It was known as the "land of promise," the language of the Old Testament being applied to it after the introduction of Christianity. The territory was described as "the Brugh of the Boyne," in which was situated the plain of Mel, or honey, evidently taken from the account of Canaan as the land flowing with milk and honey.[2]

Communication with the outer world was almost unknown, for though traders touched at some of the ports, the independence of the various tribes made it difficult to travel through the country, and the language was also an obstacle. Roads there are said to have been, and five of them radiated from Tara, the seat of government, but they were only "cuttings"[3] through the woods, which the law required to be periodically cleared of the brushwood and undergrowth which tended to close them up again.[4]

We have here a state of society in which the people were cut off from Western civilisation, and from those objects of interest which occupied the human intellect abroad, as well by their independence of the Roman

---

[1] On the Continent the practice survived the Roman occupation and the Teutonic conquest, which attests the extraordinary vitality of Celtic tradition. In the Bavarian highlands they are known as *sonnen-wend-feuer*, solstice fires, and a capitular of Charlemagne condemns them as a remnant of paganism (Pertz, ili. 17).

[2] But how degraded the idea became when applied to heathen times we may see from the description given of it in Irish literature :—" Admirable is that land. There are three trees there always bearing fruit ; there is one pig there always alive, and another pig ready cooked ; and there is a vessel full of excellent ale " (" Book of Leinster," 246*a*).

[3] *Slighe*, from *sligim*, to cut.

[4] Book of Rights, Introduction, pp. lvi., lx.

Empire as by their want of acquaintance with the Latin language. Their horizon was bounded by the shores of Ireland, and local topics only engaged their attention; nor could their poets find a nobler subject for their greatest epic than the carrying off of a bull.[1]

But when Christianity appeared among them it introduced a wholly new order of ideas. Its spiritual teaching found in them a congenial soil, and the seed sown sprang up with wonderful vigour. With it came also the Latin language, then the common medium of communication throughout Europe, and it became possible for them to make use of the literary treasures of the ancient world. In this point of view the words of the hymn of Fiacc are expressive :—

"Patrick's coming was a help to Ireland,
Which had been shut up."[2]

---

[1] The *Ta:n bo Cualnge*, or Cattle Spoil of Cooley, County of Louth.
[2] Windisch, Wörterbuch, S. V. Fochelim.

CHAPTER II.

THE CONVERSION OF IRELAND—S. PATRICK.

As early as the year 200, while the Roman Empire was still heathen, there were Christians in Britain, and from the year 300 onwards it possessed an organised Church, whose bishops are found attending the Council of Arles, A.D. 314.[1] The vicinity of Ireland and the communication between the two countries made it a matter of certainty that some knowledge, however slight, of Christianity should reach it, apart from any formal mission. There is, therefore, probably some basis of truth in the legends which describe this as actually happening : how Cormac mac Art in the third century refused to be buried with his pagan ancestors ;[2] how the Druids, observing the spread of Christianity, prophesied the triumph of a missionary who should come across the stormy sea.[3] And a wilder legend tells how Connor mac Nessa, who lived in the first century, heard of the death of Christ from the Roman Consul Altus. But the first actual introduction of Christianity appears to have taken place in the south and south-west. Kieran of Saigir, a native of Cape Clear island, whose birth is assigned to A.D. 352, is termed in his Life the " first-born of the saints of Ireland,"[4] and the chieftains of the adjoining territory, who belonged to his mother's family, the

[1] H. and S., vol. i. 4, 7. [2] Petrie, R. Towers, p. 100. [3] Trip., p. 35.
[4] This honour was also claimed subsequently for two of S. Patrick's converts (Todd, p. 344).

"first who believed in the Cross and granted a site for a church."[1] The memory of the saint is still preserved in the island, where the ruins of his church are shown, and the strand, with its pillar-stone inscribed with a cross is called "S. Kieran's Strand." The legend that he foretold the coming of S. Patrick thirty years afterwards indicates that he was believed to have preceded him by that period of time. Farther to the west, in the peninsula of Dingle, are the remains of several churches or oratories, one of which, that of Gallerus, is still perfect. This singular building, the sides of which slope until they meet, and which shows no knowledge of the principle of the arch, is regarded by Dr. Petrie[2] as the work of a Christian people of an earlier date than that usually assigned to S. Patrick. We may, therefore, accept it as highly probable that from some time in the third century "there were British Christians at work in the south of Ireland,"[3] and that Christianity had made some progress there at an early period.

The first historical notice by a foreign authority of a regular mission to Ireland is the statement in the Chronicle of Prosper of Aquitaine that "Palladius was ordained by Pope Celestine, and sent as first bishop to the Scots (Irish), who were believers in Christ."[4] Very few people, it may be presumed, have ever heard of Palladius; and this is natural enough, as little is known about him. According to one account, he built three churches in the county of Wicklow (wooden structures, of course), and then went away, abandoning his mission owing to the opposition he encountered. Another story makes

[1] The Corcalaidhe, Todd, pp., 200, 201.
[2] R. Towers, pp. 131, 132.
[3] Zimmer Keltische Studien, s. 183, who says, "the beginning of the third century," which seems too early. [4] Trip., Appendix, p. 493.

his stay in Ireland only a "few days."[1] His subsequent history is also involved in doubt, one writer telling us he passed over to Scotland, and after labouring for a while, died there; another, that he suffered martyrdom among the Scots (Irish), "as ancient saints relate."[2] He is a shadowy personage, and whatever was his fate, it is clear that his mission was a failure. His obstacle was, the Life of S. Patrick in the "Book of Armagh" tells us, that "no man can receive anything from earth unless it be given him from heaven."[3]

On his abandoning his mission the usual view is that he was succeeded by S. Patrick, who, some add, also owed his mission to Celestine. Here the question is sometimes asked even by those otherwise well informed, Was there ever such a person as S. Patrick? For many appear to regard his connection with Ireland in much the same light as that of S. George with England or S. Andrew with Scotland. Ireland, however, is an exceptional country in many ways, and in none more so than in possessing a patron who is a real personage and the actual missionary by whom the island was converted.

No one can read the evidence which Mr. Whitley Stokes[4] has collected from writers at home and abroad during each of the centuries from the fifth to the thirteenth inclusive without being convinced that he is a strictly historical character. In his case we do not suffer, as in that of Palladius, from a lack of historical materials; on the contrary, their very quantity is embarrassing. They are of two classes, the contemporary documents and the Lives, the earliest of these

[1] The fourth Life in Colgan, quoted in Todd, p. 297.
[2] Todd, pp. 286-298.
[3] John iii. 27. See Hogan, Analecta, p. 25.
[4] Trip., Introduction, pp. cxxix.-cxxxii.

being two centuries later than his time, and described by the editor as "religious romances."

The contemporary records are "S. Patrick's Confession" or "Apologia pro Vita sua," his "Epistle to the Subjects of Coroticus," and his "Irish Hymn;" with the poem of Secundinus or Sechnall, of which he is the theme.[1] No serious doubt has ever been raised as to the genuineness of these documents. They are free from the fables and marvels of the Lives, and in their sobriety of tone and evident truthfulness they breathe the spirit of an early age. As long as we adhere to them there is no difficulty, but they do not go into details as to his history or the conversion of Ireland, and it is only when we turn for information on this point to the Lives that we find how true the words of Dr. Petrie are :—"The history of the propagation of the Gospel in Ireland is involved in obscurities and contradictions."[2]

Seven of these Lives have been published by Colgan,[3] and these, with two documents[4] contained in the "Book of Armagh," form the materials from which, with those already mentioned, it has been endeavoured to write the life of S. Patrick. The general result may be pronounced to be failure. Dr. Lanigan, a learned and acute writer, was unsuccessful. "He succumbed to the difficulties of the task" is the verdict of Dr. Petrie.[5] Dr. Todd, one of the most eminent scholars of the age, some thirty-five years later composed a Memoir of his life and mission, which is also unsatisfactory; but he happily employed his great

[1] All are published in Mr. Stokes' Tripartite, vol. i. p. 48; ii. pp. 357-359.
[2] Dr. Petrie's Tara Hill, p. 86.
[3] Trias Thaumaturga.
[4] The Life by Muirchu Maccu Machtheni, on which see Appendix A., and Tirechan's Collections. The "Book of Armagh" is a compilation of the date A.D. 807. [5] Tara Hill, p. 89.

critical abilities in an examination of the Lives, and pronounced that they were "interpolated to impose on an uncritical and credulous people," and that it was "impossible to reconcile them with the facts of history."[1] Sir S. Ferguson, in a learned and suggestive essay, confirms this, pointing out that they bring S. Patrick into communication with ten generations, which is a simple impossibility.[2]

It is obvious that Lives of S. Patrick composed at the present day on the principle of using these religious romances as though of equal authority with the contemporary records must be unsatisfactory. There is no doubt that they preserve many facts of his history, but no criterion has yet been discovered by which the true can be discriminated from the false, and it is, therefore, absolutely necessary to draw a line between them and the original documents. Two hundred years ago, Tillemont, a critic of the highest ability, stated the case with perfect correctness, and his words may be quoted here:—"The Irish, who have a special veneration for S. Patrick, have not failed to produce many histories of him—more, I believe, than have been written of any other saint. Four original accounts composed by his disciples, they say, are lost, but we have still a great many facts circumstantially related about him. It is possible that many of them are true, but there are also many which are evidently false. Seeing, therefore, that there is no certainty attainable, we prefer, in treating of his history, to rely on his 'Confession,' which is believed to be authentic, and which is truly worthy of him."[3] Following the example of Tillemont, the

[1] Todd, p. 319, note 1, and p. 332.
[2] Transactions of the Royal Irish Academy, December 1885, p. 130.
[3] Memoires pour servir à l'Histoire Ecclesiastique des Six Premiers Siecles, M. de Tillemont ; Paris, 1712. vi. pp. 455-466.

contemporary documents, and particularly the "Confession," are taken as the basis of the notice of S. Patrick in this chapter, supplemented occasionally by any statements in the Lives which throw light on them and are not inconsistent with their spirit. Happily, the contemporary documents afford all the information which is of real interest as regards his early history, the motives which influenced him in undertaking the mission, the nature of his teaching, and his personal character.

The usual view as to the respective positions in point of time of him and Palladius is, that he was the second missionary. But there are good reasons for believing that this is an error, and that S. Patrick was really the first. The question is discussed at length elsewhere,[1] and it will be sufficient now to state that the view maintained here is that he was the Sen Patrick or Patrick senior of the native records; that he preceded Palladius; that he laboured in Ireland during his life, never leaving the country; that the reason his name dropped so much out of sight is, that he could not be connected with the Roman mission; and that in the ninth century, by the blending of the acts of Palladius with his, as some think, or simply by the liberal employment of fiction, the S. Patrick of popular belief, the missionary of Celestine, the Archbishop and Apostle of Ireland, came into existence. Sen Patrick was the author of the "Confession," the "Coroticus Epistle," and the "Irish Hymn;" and also the subject of Secundinus' encomium. He begins his personal narrative by saying he belonged to a Christian family, being the son of a deacon named Calpornius, and the grandson of a presbyter,[2] Odissus.

[1] See Appendix A.
[2] The Hymn of Fiacc represents Odissus as a Deacon.

His father also held the office of decurion or magistrate of a Roman colony. He was born about 373 at Ailclyde,[1] now Dumbarton, according to the "Book of Armagh," and had arrived at the age of sixteen, when he was seized and carried off by pirates from a place called Bannaven Taberniæ, supposed to have been somewhere on the north-west coast of Britain. Torn from his family at a tender age, and sold to a provincial king[2] in the north of Ireland, his hardships were very great. His employment was tending cattle[3] in the woods and on the mountains, and he had painful recollections in after years of the winter's "snow and frost and rain." In his time of trial he had recourse to prayer, and "the love and fear of God grew in him, and his faith became stronger." "Then the Lord brought me," he says, "to a sense of my unbelief, that I might, even at a late period, call my sins to remembrance, and turn with all my heart unto the Lord my God." After six years of bondage he had a dream in which he was told he should escape, and the port was mentioned. Acting on the suggestion, he fled, reached the port,[4] and found a vessel ready to start, but when he sought for a passage the head or supercargo[5] angrily refused him. Returning to his lodging much cast down, he betook himself to his invariable resource of prayer, and before he had finished he heard a loud voice crying out, "Come back, for those men are calling you." Having had an interview with them he was received on board, the vessel sailed, and after a voyage

---

[1] Trip., Introd., pp. cxxxvi.–cxliii. He is said to have been called Sucat and three other names. Patricius, which is not one of them, was well known by the Irish to be only a title. A gloss on the Book of Hymns says it was *nomen graid la Romanu*—the name of a rank among the Romans (part i. p. 12). According to Nennius, he assumed it (*sumpsit*) on his ordination by Amator (Trip., p. 499, line 33).
[2] Stated to be Miliuc, king of North Dalaradia, in the county of Antrim.
[3] *Pecora.*   [4] It is vain to inquire what port this was.
[5] *Gubernator.*

of three days they arrived at port, and landing, set out on a journey of twenty-eight days through a desert. From the moment he reached the ship all the Lives fail us, prodigal as they are of information about miracles and trivial incidents. None of them tells us how he, a fugitive slave, obtained his passage after the supercargo's refusal, nor whither the ship was bound, nor in what direction the journey lay, nor what the desert was. Tillemont thought the port was in Scotland, and Dr. Lanigan suggests Treguier, in Normandy, on the strength of a seventeenth century Breviary which is of no weight. Pursuing the narrative, we shall find that the "Confession" itself probably throws some light on those points. In the course of their journey through the desert they were reduced to extremities from hunger, and the head of the party appealed to Patrick as a Christian to pray for help to his God, who, he had told them, was all-powerful. From this we may gather that he had been trying to convert them to Christianity, especially as, when describing his first interview with them, he says, "I hoped they would come into the faith of Christ." In reply to their request now he says, "Turn in faith to the Lord my God, to whom nothing is impossible, that He may send food into your path even until you are satisfied, for it abounds everywhere to Him." " And by God's help it happened so ; for lo ! a herd of swine appeared in the way before our eyes, and they killed many of them, and halting there two nights, were much refreshed." Now we come to an important passage : " And their dogs had their fill, for many of them had become exhausted, and were left by the wayside dying." What, then, were these Dogs, which, though many were left by the way, still appear to have been numerous ; which were so valuable that the party ran the risk of losing their own lives by starvation to save them, and which he thinks it worth while to mention in such a document as the 'Confession'? Before answering this question it is necessary to mention one or two facts. In that age the "Celtic dogs," as they were termed, were held in the highest esteem in the East for hunting purposes. The wolf-dog or deer-hound was common to Gaul, Britain, and Ireland, and is described in enthusiastic language by Arrian, a Greek author who wrote a treatise on hunting in the second century. They were highly valued at home, and were a monopoly of the Irish kings, as appears from the "Book of Rights."[1] They must have been a source of considerable profit, as a large export trade was carried on in them abroad, and the traders who brought to Ireland the brazen caldrons and other articles of commerce probably took back numbers of them. It would, therefore, appear that the dogs for which the party on this occasion were so solicitous were dogs of commerce, and were on their way to the depôt for sale in the East. If we now return to the embarkation of Patrick, the matter appears much plainer. Refused by the supercargo, the men, that is, the other members of the trading party, called him back. After a conversation they take him on trust (*ex fide*), inasmuch as they find he will be useful to them. He speaks Latin, as the son of a Roman colonist, and this is a convenience to them; and, as the servant of a provincial king, he is familiar with the management of those valuable dogs. There is, therefore, little difficulty in concluding that he gives his services in return for his passage. Arrived at port, the ship is left, and the trading party, with Patrick, set out on their journey. What was the port? In reply to this, the depôt for the trade

[1] For the authorities on this subject see Appendix B.

between the British Islands and the East was the Loire.[1] From this the route lay overland to Narbo and Marseilles. Down the Loire, more than two centuries later, Columbanus was sent under escort to be put on board a vessel bound for Ireland. From Nantes, on the Loire, an active commerce was carried on with Ireland from the earliest time.[2] A voyage of three days with a fair wind would bring a vessel thither from the Irish coast. It is, therefore, in the highest degree probable that this was the route taken. The district through which their land journey lay was desolate, for it had been "devastated by the Quadi, Vandals, Sarmatians, Alains, Gepidae, Heruli, Burgundians, Alemanni, and—oh, supreme calamity!—by the Huns."[3] Gaul was then overgrown with forests, M. de Montalembert tells us, owing to the desertion of the inhabitants. If there were not forest-trees, there was a lower growth of wood—copse-wood, maple, birch, aspen, witch-elm, and thickets of thorn and brambles. These intermediate regions were called "deserts," because the population had abandoned them.[4] Such was the desert in which Patrick and his companions ran the risk of perishing. An exactly similar journey through an African desert is described in a letter from Bishop Smythies to the Archbishop of Canterbury of September 3, 1889:—"Through the devastations of war, we had to walk sixteen days through the forest without meeting a man the whole time. At the time the men's food was almost exhausted, and at that time of the year it is most difficult to get near any game on the march; but by God's good provi-

---

[1] The Greek Trade Routes to Britain, by Professor Ridgeway, *Folk-Lore Journal*, No. 1.   [2] Greith, Geschichte, p. 86.
[3] S. Jerome, quoted by Montalembert, Les Moines, vol. ii. p. 225.
[4] Les Moines d'Occident, vol. ii. pp. 316–318. The School of Lismore, in the county of Waterford, is described as in a desert (*in eremo*), because in the primeval forest ("Codex Salmanticensis," p. 656).

dence I was able to shoot a large antelope, which supplied the men with meat to the end of our journey."

When the party, with their dogs, arrived at the trading station their engagement with Patrick would cease and he would be free. Thus, in the natural course of events, he is found in the South of France, in the vicinity of Arles. Then returning by the same route, or descending the Loire like Columbanus, he would be in the neighbourhood of Tours, and not far from Auxerre. These are the three places mentioned in his Lives, but there is no notice of Lerins, on which Bishop Greith and others dwell so much as his place of education. Its school was, probably, not in existence at this time.[1] There is little doubt that his presence in this part of Gaul, as now described, is the foundation on which is built the huge superstructure of fable about his wanderings in Gaul and the islands of the Tyrrhene Sea. At this time the whole bent of his mind was towards a missionary career, and he would, as a matter of course, avail himself of the opportunities within his reach of fitting himself for it. Amongst the contradictory statements in his Lives are those relating to his studies, some saying he read with German of Auxerre, whose See was supposed to be in Italy; others, that he studied with S. Martin. Muirchu's account is, that he went first to German, and then to S. Martin; but as the latter died eighteen years before German became Bishop of Auxerre, this is out of the question.

Assuming that Patrick was born about 373, and taken captive about 389, he would have escaped and reached Gaul about 395. This being so, he could not have studied with German, but there is no difficulty as to his having been with S. Martin. The proba-

[1] The mention of Lerins by modern writers is due to a conjecture of the Bollandists (Actt S.S., March 17, p. 528), founded on a corrupt reading—Aralanensis—of the Latin name of Arles; but see Trip. ii. 420, note 1, and Addenda, p. 668.

bility of this being the true account is immensely increased by a consideration of the relative positions occupied by German and Martin in Irish tradition. Of the former nothing was known in Ireland, and he is unnoticed, except once in the "Annals of the Four Masters," where he is called S. Patrick's tutor. Martin, on the other hand, was well known; he is referred to three times in the Calendar of Œngus, and four times in the Lebor Brecc Commentary on it; his day was observed in Ireland, and his Gospel was said to have been preserved at Derry; ecclesiastics took his name, or called themselves Mael-Martain (servant of Martin); and the only Life in the "Book of Armagh" besides S. Patrick's is that of S. Martin, by Sulpicius Severus. The story of German's connection with S. Patrick is undoubtedly pure fiction. It is not found in his Life by Constantius, his contemporary, and appears for the first time in the later Life by Eric of Auxerre, who knew nothing of the matter himself, but derived his information from Bishop Marcus,[1] a Briton, of whose character or credibility little is known. The introduction of his name is due to the alteration of the date of S. Patrick's mission, for when he came to be represented as S. Palladius' successor and his date was brought down to A.D. 432, it was evident that S. Martin was too early, as he died in 397 or 401, and therefore German, who was well known in Britain, was brought on the scene as his teacher. Sulpicius describes the Monastery of S. Martin. The greater part of the community, he says, lived in places hollowed out of the side of the mountain; they had all things in common, and wore the coarsest clothing. In such a community a young man like Patrick, evidently of an ardent missionary spirit, would find a ready welcome.

[1] Ussher, Works, vol. xv. p. 9.

The next thing he tells us in his "Confession" is, that after a few years he was in Britain with his parents. This interval would seem to be the time devoted to study in preparation for his mission, and its shortness accounts for the imperfection of his education. A few years would not enable a student, however diligent, to recover the loss of six years passed in slavery at the most important period of his life. On concluding his studies we may assume that he returned to Britain by the usual trade route, and thus once more found himself at home. His parents received him affectionately, and observing the bent of his mind, besought him earnestly, after the trials he had gone through, not to leave them again. With weeping and tears they offered him many worldly inducements, his elders joining with them. But it was all in vain, for even while he slept "it seemed to him it was the island of the Gael he saw before him."[1] In this state of mind he had a dream, in which a man named Victoricus came to him from Ireland with innumerable letters, one of which he gave him, inscribed "The voice of the people of Ireland;"[2] and at the same time he seemed to hear the voice of the dwellers by the Western sea saying, "We entreat thee, holy youth, to come and walk still among us." This finally determined him to go, and he went. But when? We are asked by most of his biographers to believe, that this young man, whose whole soul was on fire with missionary zeal, waited for thirty long years before he went to Ireland; that he put off the enterprise on which his heart was set until age had cooled his ardour and his youthful vigour had departed. To find occupation for him during that time is the great difficulty. Some tell us he was

[1] Trip., Introd., p. xlix.
[2] *Hiberionacum.* The word is significant as representing the bulk of the population, the ruling race being termed the Scoti.

engaged in study; but if so, it is surely strange that he should lament in his "Confession" not only his want of learning, but his want of the opportunities of acquiring it.[1] Others say he wandered aimlessly about Gaul and Italy and the islands of the Tyrrhene Sea; but the simpler way is to confess ingenuously, with his latest biographer, " that where he was during this time we know not."[2]

An argument in favour of this long delay has been drawn from a passage in the "Confession" in which he says "he did not go to Ireland until he was nearly worn out."[3] But the words obviously refer to the severe mental struggle between affection for his parents and what he regarded as a Divine call. His affectionate disposition appears from many passages, and if the conflict between duty and affection convulsed his whole nature and produced physical exhaustion, it would not be surprising. But there is no reason to suppose that any great length of time elapsed between his call, and his proceeding on his mission.[4] It appears to have been at this time that a charge was brought against him by some of his elders, who objected to his consecration on account of a juvenile fault. But the difficulty was removed, and he was duly commissioned for the work. The period of thirty years mentioned on this occasion[5] appears to refer to his age at that time, when, according to the canon of a Gaulish Council, he would be eligible for the episcopate. He seems to have returned to Gaul, with which communication was easy,[6]

[1] Ferguson, p. 131.
[2] S. Patrick, His Life and Teaching, E. J. Newell, M.A., S.P.C.K., p. 37.
[3] *Donec prope deficiebam*, Trip. ii. 365.   [4] Ferguson, p. 91.
[5] *Post annos triginta invenerunt me*, Trip. ii. 365.
[6] "One element of civilisation remained to Cumbria (in which Ailcluyd was situated). The road was open to Gaul," &c. ("Historians of Scotland," by Bishop Forbes, vol. v. p. xxvii.).

and there received consecration from Amator,[1] Bishop of Auxerre, as stated by Muirchu in the "Book of Armagh,"[2] and then to have gone direct to Ireland with a few companions. Such was the origin of a mission which has identified his name for all time with the Church of Ireland. He declares his mission was "from God," who chose him for the work; the Lord commanded him to come; the love of Christ transferred and gave him to the Irish people; and he closes his "Confession" with the solemn words, "I bear witness, in truth and joy of heart before God and His holy angels, that I never had any occasion but the Gospel and its promises to return to that nation from which I at first escaped with difficulty."

The time when S. Patrick's mission took place was A.D. 397, according to Mr. Whitley Stokes,[3] and it is remarkable that the last decade of the fourth century was a period of great mental activity in the church.[4] S. Jerome was writing against Jovinian; Paulinus composing his Christian poetry at Nola; Ambrose and Augustine offering their contributions to the literature of the Church, and Chrysostom had just been raised to the throne of Constantinople. There are several references in the "Confession" to his youthfulness at this time. He is addressed in his dream, "O holy youth!" he says he was in Ireland "from his youth up," and he speaks of this desire to visit his "parents."[5] But much as he desired it, he

[1] Amator was consecrated 388; *d.* 418.
[2] Trip., vol. ii. p. 273. He uses the Gaulish form of the name, Amatorex. But see ibid., p. 506.
[3] Nennius, Historia Britonum (Trip., p. 498), has it 405, eight years later.
[4] The Historians of Scotland, by Bishop Forbes, vol. v. p. xxvii.
[5] Dr. Lanigan, who believed he was sixty years of age when he came to Ireland, is obliged to understand the word *parentes* to mean relations, but when taken in connection with the expressions quoted, this forced interpretation is unnecessary.

could not go, he says, because the Lord "commanded him to be with the Irish people the remainder of his life."[1] It is very clear from his language that he never left the country, and never again beheld the faces of his family or friends.[2] Time does not permit an account of his missionary labours in Ireland, even if they could be satisfactorily deduced from the Lives. They did not extend to the whole of Ireland, a great part of the south not having been visited by him. The "Book of Armagh" brings him as far south as Cashel, but there is no reason to think he visited the counties of Cork, Kerry, Waterford, or Clare. His journey south was but a "flying visit,"[3] according to Professor Zimmer. The evangelising of the south-west is attributed by Dr. Lanigan to Benignus, but on no sufficient grounds. Four bishops belonging to the south are stated to have been in Ireland when S. Patrick came—Kieran, already mentioned, Ailbe, Declan, and Ibar—and an interview is said to have taken place between them and the saint, which resulted in his allowing their dignity and waiving his own claim to their submission. The story was accepted by Ussher and Colgan; but Dr. Todd, arguing from the late dates at which they are said to have flourished, rejected it.[4] Yet, if they are brought down to a late period, it should also be considered that an extremely early date is assigned to their births. The consequence of this is, that they have been represented as living to an extravagant age. Ibar, we are told, was 404 years old;[5] Kieran of Saigir, 360;[6] Ailbe, 181. This prolongation of their lives appears to be the result of an

[1] Trip., p. 370.
[2] Ferguson, p. 100. This disposes of the stories about his sisters having been in Ireland with him. The persons mentioned were probably sisters in the religious sense.
[3] *Ein Ausflug*, Keltische Studien, vol. ii. p. 183.
[4] Todd, pp. 198-221.   [5] Martyrology of Donegal.   [6] Ibid.

attempt to reconcile the fact of their early date with their supposed interview with S. Patrick; for when, by the fictions of the ninth century, he became Celestine's archbishop and apostle, it was deemed proper that their position should be recognised by him. The most recent critic, referring to Dr. Todd's view of the period at which they flourished, says: "I do not desire to be understood as yielding convinced assent to the late date assigned."[1] The Lives of those saints all agree that Ireland was heathen in their time,[2] which harmonises with the early date mentioned. An agreement supposed to have been made between S. Patrick and Ailbe and Declan is given in an Irish stanza, which their respective communities, it is said, were strictly forbidden to translate. It runs thus, according to Dr. Todd's translation:—

> "Humble Ailbe is the Patrick of Munster,
> With all my honour.
> Declan is the Patrick of the Desii;[3]
> The Desii are with Declan for ever."[4]

The more correct reading of the second line is, "And my equal," which brings out the object of the legend more clearly.[5] It purported to be an acknowledgment by the apostle of their equality with himself.

S. Patrick condemns the idolatry of the heathen in his "Confession," and the "Book of Armagh" describes him as visiting the "Plain of Adoration," where the great idol Cenn Cruaich[6] stood with twelve smaller idols around, and aiming a blow at the chief idol with his crozier, the staff of Jesus. The staff never

[1] Ferguson, s. 125.
[2] Ussher, Works, vol. vi. pp. 333-342.
[3] From whom the Barony of Decies, Co. Waterford, derives its name.
[4] Todd, p. 220.
[5] Dr. Todd read *mo gach rath*; but Zeuss ("Gr. Celt.,"2nd. ed., p. 961) prefers *mo co-cruth*, "meus æqualis."
[6] Believed to be the same as the British Pennocrucion (Rhys, "Celtic Britain," p. 300), initial *P* being changed to *C*.

left his hand, but the idol fell aslant, and continued so. It was a moral victory over a declining heathenism. Again, he found them worshipping a well, "honouring it as if it were a god" because they understood a Druid was buried in it; but he removed the cover and convinced them of their error. On founding a congregation it was his custom to bestow some gift on them, such as a bell, a chalice, or a paten, and sometimes a more valuable present, described as "the Books of the Law and the Books of the Gospel."[1] The former expression is explained by another passage in which they are termed the "seven Books of the Law." This was the portion of the Old Testament known as the Heptateuch,[2] or seven books, which was much used in early times, especially in Gaul. It comprised the Pentateuch, with the Books of Joshua and Judges, and sometimes Ruth. This volume was given as a preparation for the entire Old Testament, and it was convenient at a period when to make copies of the whole was laborious. The "four books of the Gospel" was the expression used instead of "the four Gospels" by the early Irish, and conveyed the idea of their unity more distinctly. From the importance attached by him to the Scriptures, of which his "Confession" is a proof, it may have been that he is described as "the man of the enduring language, i.e., the Holy Canon;"[3] in other words, "the man of the Bible." In thus giving

---

[1] The Book of Armagh, in Trip., p. 300.
[2] Ibid., p. 326. See Forcellini, s. v. It is mentioned by Sidonius Apollinaris, A.D. 430 (Migne lviii., Lib. v. Ep. 15); also by Alcuin, Alcimus Avitus, S. Jerome, and Gregory the Great.
[3] Lebor-na-h-Uidhre, in Trip., ii. 566. "It was Christianity, the religion of a Book, which for the first time introduced many of the ruder nations outside the Empire to the art of writing" (Sir H. Maine, "Early History," p. 13). For the Irish use of the word Canon, see Appendix C.

away copies of the Heptateuch he set an example in which he was followed by others. Thus the Irish Life of S. Barré or Finn Barr of Cork states that, when parting from the pupils of his school of Lough Eirkc, at Addergoole, in the Queen's County, he bestowed on some of them the seven Books of the Law and the four Books of the Gospel.[1] It is somewhat remarkable that the only copy of the entire New Testament which has come down to us from the ancient Church is that in the "Book of Armagh," which was believed to have been S. Patrick's, and from which the whole manuscript derived its name, "The Canon or Scripture of S. Patrick." A remarkable dialogue between him and the two daughters of the King of Ireland, who were at school near Rathcroghan, in Connaught, is given in the "Book of Armagh," and is generally accepted as genuine. They eagerly questioned him as to the God whom he worshipped; and eventually, when sufficiently instructed[2] to answer the usual interrogations, they were baptized. A singular part of the story is, that after their baptism they desired to "see Christ face to face." But he told them they "could not, unless they first tasted death,"[3] and unless "they received Christ's body and His blood." "And the girls said, 'Give us the sacrifice, that we may see the Spouse;' then they received the sacrifice, and fell asleep in death." Dr. Todd is not satisfied with Dr. Lanigan's explanation of this as meaning spiritual death, and calls attention to

---

[1] Betha Barra, Royal Irish Academy, M.S. A. 44, folio 113; also the Life of S. Finn Barr in "Dictionary of National Biography." See Appendix D.
[2] The Rev. B. MacCarthy, D.D., on the Stowe Missal, "Trans. Royal Irish Academy," November 1886, appears to think that S. Patrick baptized his converts without previous instruction; but this story evidently implies preliminary teaching.
[3] Rom. vi. 2; Col. iii. 3.

what follows :—"And Patrick put them under one mantle in one bed and their friends bewailed them greatly."[1] But he did not make allowance for the habit of treating figures of speech literally,[2] which runs through all this literature, as we shall see hereafter. When once the expression came to be understood of literal death, all the usual accessories were supplied by the imagination of the writer.

On his journeys he was accompanied by a strong man or "champion," as he is called, Bishop MacCarthenn. One day, after lifting the saint over a difficult place, as he was wont, he groaned aloud, and when questioned as to the reason, complained that he had been "a long time on the path," and he asked St. Patrick to bestow a church on him such as his companions had received. In compliance with his request he placed him at Clogher, giving him as a memorial the *Domnach airgid*, which contained a copy of the Gospels. This manuscript, with its primitive box of yew and the beautifully wrought shrine of later workmanship in which it is enclosed, is in the Library of the Royal Irish Academy in Dublin.[3]

An important element of the success he achieved was the design he constantly kept in view of raising up a native ministry and drawing his followers from the educated classes. One of his earliest converts was Duffack,[4] chief poet of Ireland; and when St. Patrick consulted him as to the "material" for a bishop, that is, a suitable person to consecrate to the office, he proposed his pupil, Fiacc. The conditions were, that he should be "a freeman of good lineage,

---

[1] Trip., i. 103.
[2] In Muirchu's Memoir a lady in the same way dies after baptism, *i.e.*, a death unto sin (Hogan, p. 48.)
[3] See Dr. Petrie's description of it, "Transactions of the Royal Irish Academy," vol. xviii.
[4] Dubhthach maccu Lugair.

without defect, without blemish, whose wealth is not over-little and is not over-much. " I wish a man of one wife, unto whom hath been born only one child."[1] It was to a clergy such as this, possessed of the best education then attainable in Ireland, that the literary position of the Irish Church in the following centuries was, in a great measure, due. The high standard thus set up in the beginning was maintained by their successors.

Towards the close[2] of his career, not at the commencement, as generally supposed, he had the interview with King Laegaire as described with such sensational incidents in the " Book of Armagh." He lit his paschal fire in sight of the palace of Tara on an occasion when no fire but the king's was permitted, and a contest ensued between him and the king and his Druids. It was when in fear of death on that occasion he is said to have composed his hymn known as " The Deers' Cry," one of the oldest compositions in the Irish language. " Notwithstanding some tincture of [heathen] superstition, we find in it the pure and unadulterated truths of Christianity, a firm faith in the protecting providence and power of God; and Christ made all in all."[3]

The Epistle to the Christian subjects of Coroticus or Ceretic,[4] King of Ailclyde, is a remonstrance addressed to that chieftain for having killed or made slaves of some of his converts on the day after their baptism, and is supposed to have been written between 412 and 428. " There breathes, it has been observed, through its reproaches and words of technical objurgation, a lofty sentiment and energy of imagination which would make any prose translation inadequate to its full reproduction."[5]

[1] Hogan, pp. 104, 105.   [2] Todd, pp. 417, 418.   [3] Ibid., p. 432.
[4] Ferguson, p. 116.   [5] Ibid., p. 92.

The "Confession" was written towards the close of his life, and with the intention of explaining his motives in coming to Ireland and giving some facts of his personal history. It displays an acquaintance with the Scriptures which Tillemont notices with surprise, and which could only have been acquired by diligent study. It also contains a summary of his religious opinions after the manner of a creed; but the most complete picture of him as a religious teacher is to be found in the hymn of Secundinus, which was composed during his lifetime and by an eye-witness.[1]

His death took place in A.D. 463,[2] in the eighty-eighth or ninetieth year of his age. A short time previously he had founded Armagh, and there he was buried. His Crozier (the Bachall Isa), his New Testament, and his Bell were preserved there, and became in after-time the title-deeds of his successors. The last two objects are still in existence,[3] and thus serve to connect the present with the remote past. Some canons attributed to him will be noticed hereafter.

High testimony has been borne to the value of his extant writings, on which the foregoing account is chiefly founded. According to Bishop Forbes, "The only historical works which supply any light on the extremely obscure condition of Britain at this time are the two treatises of S. Patrick, the "Confession" and "Letter to Coroticus,"[4] and Sir Samuel Ferguson pronounces them "the oldest documents in British history."[5] As such they occupy a unique position, which entitles them to become the standard by which all later Lives of S. Patrick should be judged.

[1] See Trip., vol. ii. pp. 386-389.
[2] Trip., Introd., p. cxliii.
[3] The Bell is in the Museum of the Royal Irish Academy; "The Book of Armagh" in Trinity College.
[4] The Historians of Scotland, by Bishop Forbes, vol. v. p. 29.
[5] Ferguson 67.

CHAPTER III.

SAINTS OF THE FIRST PERIOD—S. BRIGIT.

A WRITER of the eighth century divides the time from S. Patrick to A.D. 665 into three periods, and describes the difference which the religious character of each presented. The document is entitled "A Catalogue of the Saints of Ireland according to their Different Periods,"[1] and it points to a decline in religion as having taken place after the close of the first, which includes the mission of S. Patrick. The saints of that period are accounted most holy; those of the second very holy; those of the third holy; and they are respectively compared to the sun, the moon, and the stars. It will be convenient to follow this arrangement in treating of the history of the Church between the beginning of the fifth and the middle of the seventh century, not affirming its perfect accuracy as to dates, but regarding it as giving a fair representation of the condition of religion. The "Catalogue" begins thus: "The first order[2] of saints was in the time of Patrick; and then they were all bishops, famous and holy, full of the Holy Ghost, 350 in number, founders of churches. They had one Head—Christ, and one chief—Patrick; they observed one mass, one celebration, one tonsure from ear to ear. They celebrated one Easter on the

[1] First published by Ussher, "Works," vi. 477-479; subsequently by Fleming, "Collectanea Sacra," pp. 430, 431, with some differences.
[2] The word Catholic, which is here in Ussher's copy, is not found in Fleming's.

fourteenth moon after the vernal equinox, and whoever was excommunicated by one church all excommunicated. They rejected not the services and society of women, because, founded on the Rock Christ, they feared not the blast of temptation. All these bishops were sprung from the Romans, Franks, Britons, and Scots."[1] This period terminated at A.D. 543.

From this it appears that those who flourished during the century and a half after the coming of S. Patrick took him as their leader and model. There was complete uniformity in the Church founded by him as to liturgical observance, the Eucharist, the tonsure, and Easter; and they rejected not the services of women, the reason given being that, as true believers, they had no need of such a precaution.[2] That bishops should have been very numerous in Ireland is in accordance with the fact that the nations which were earliest converted had always great numbers. They were sent out by him and his followers without fixed Sees, some of them becoming founders of monasteries; others obtained land and other privileges from the chieftains and petty kings; others again were content to exercise their ministry in monasteries, subject to the jurisdiction of the abbot or *coarb*; and, in general, men of piety and learning were advanced to the order of bishop as a sort of degree.

We need not, however, believe that S. Patrick consecrated "three hundred and fifty bishops, founded seven hundred churches, and ordained five thousand priests."[3] In accordance with the popular belief on this

---

[1] This paragraph is not found in Fleming.
[2] An ancient poem in the Book of Lismore refers to "Folk of severe discipline who served the King of the White Sun; neither children nor wives used to be a hindrance to them: their natures were pure" (Lives, p. 136).
[3] The "Tripartite" makes the number of bishops 370; "The Annals of the Four Masters," 700 (vol. i. p. 157).

SAINTS OF THE FIRST PERIOD: S. BRIGIT. 33

subject is the story of S. Mochta of Louth, a Briton and a disciple of S. Patrick, which represents his "family" or monastic community as having many bishops:—

"No poverty had Mochta, in the burgh of Louth,
Three hundred priests, one hundred bishops, together with him,
Eighty psalm-singing noble youths;
His household, vastest of courses!
Without ploughing, without reaping, without kiln-drying,
Without work, save only reading."[1]

The inference to be drawn from this is, that to the writer of the poem so large a number did not seem improbable. If we were to judge by the system of the present day, when a bishop presides over a diocese, the state of things described would be altogether incredible. But diocesan episcopacy had not then been introduced into Ireland, and bishops being generally unattached, the increase of their number involved no difficulty. In other respects, too, customs prevailed with regard to the order unknown elsewhere. One of these was the association of bishops in groups of seven, who lived together. Six such groups are mentioned in the "Martyrology of Donegal," some of them said to be brothers. Unusual as this seems, it is much surpassed in strangeness by the Litany attributed to Œngus the Culdee,[2] which enumerates one hundred and thirty-eight such associations of seven. Besides these it mentions two parties, each of one hundred and fifty bishops, and two more of three hundred and fifty. It is evident, from these passages, that bishops were believed to have been extremely numerous in early times; and also that the limitations of the order, and the rules by which it was regulated elsewhere, were not in force in Ireland.

A subject of some interest connected with the title

[1] The Lebor Brecc, in Œngus, cxxxii.
[2] Ibid., folio 11a. Book of Leinster (facsimile), 373b, c, d.

of the "Catalogue" referred to is the application of the term saints to these groups of bishops and other similar bodies. In the Litany of Œngus, which is probably of the tenth century, a vast number of persons are so described—priests, deacons, exorcists, leaders, doorkeepers, pilgrims, monks, and others. They are reckoned not only by fifties and hundreds, but sometimes by thousands. For instance, "the 3300 saints with Gerald, bishop, and with the fifty saints of Leyney, in Connaught, who settled at Mayo, of the Saxons;"[1] and the "4000 monks, endued with God's grace," who were under the rule of Comgall at Bangor.[2] On one occasion, when giving details of the Monastery of S. Finn Barr at Lough Irche,[3] the author finishes by giving up the attempt at enumeration, and simply quotes the following stanza:—

> "Remember Lough Irche,
> With its sweet-toned little bell;
> As many as the leaves of the trees
> Are the saints who are therein."[4]

Œngus includes in his Litany not only those born in Ireland, but strangers, Britons, Franks, and Romans; for Ireland, as we have seen in the "Catalogue," was not only native to famous saints, but hospitable. But in what sense were all these saints? The names of multitudes of them are still remembered by the people, and prayer is offered to them at holy well and penitential station and ruined church. The Bollandists have discussed the question with their usual learning, founding their remarks on the 3300 saints who are said to have been with Gerald at Mayo.

"The Irish, they say, would not have been so liberal in canonising dead men in troops[5] whenever they seemed

---

[1] Book of Leinster, 373*b*, lines 59–61. [2] Ibid., c., lines 43–45.
[3] Life of S. Finn Barr, in "Dictionary of National Biography."
[4] Book of Leinster, 373*b*, lines 36–38. On the situation of Lough Irche, see Appendix I. [5] *Turmatim.*

to be somewhat better than usual, if they adhered to the custom of the Universal Church throughout the whole world of giving that honour to martyrs only." Then, after describing the mode in which the title to saintship is ascertained in other cases, they go on :—
"They are to be separately enrolled in the number of saints who are entitled to be invoked, either in obedience to a pontifical decree or by public consent of a Christian people convinced of the sanctity of any one by open and repeated miracles. This reasonable law has been hitherto so little observed by the pious and simple Irish that fully a fifth part of the work of Œngus[1] is composed of parties of saints of that kind who are to be invoked together; and we may justly suspect that those who compiled the Irish Hagiologies were not more circumspect, though they were saints themselves and of early date. We are, therefore, constrained to demand other and weightier proofs of the public and ecclesiastical cultus wont to be given to saints only by the Universal Church. In default of these we cannot accept the title of saint in Irish authors in any other sense than if we found the expressions "of pious memory," or "of happy recollection," or "servant of God" prefixed to the name of any one who died a pious Christian."[2]

From these observations it appears that, as the Irish saints are not entitled to the name by pontifical decree or by papal recognition, they are simply the national saints of the Irish, canonised by the Irish people, and acknowledged by them only, as saints. An instance of such canonisation is found in the Life of Corbmac. He had five brothers, who laboured in different parts of Ireland, to each of whom, it is re-

[1] The Litany before mentioned.
[2] Actt S.S. (Bolland), March 13 (Vita Giraldi), vol. ii. p. 293a, b.

corded in his Life, "the piety of after times assigned celestial honours,"[1] that is, gave them the title of saint. Originally the title was bestowed on all the people of God, as being holy by election and profession, and this was the usage both under the Old Testament dispensation and the New; and it continued to prevail for more than three centuries after Christ. It was somewhat later, however, limited to those who were especially devoted to holy offices or to a holy life, as the clergy and monks and nuns. This latter appears to be the meaning which it bore when the Gospel was first preached in Ireland, and it continued to be the accepted usage throughout the early history of the Irish Church. In consequence of this general use of the term, the Lives in the Irish language, as a rule, never prefix it to any one's name. For instance, in the "Tripartite" and other Lives we find simply Patrick or Columba, but never S. Patrick. The contrary was the usage abroad, and in conformity with it the Roman Calendar of the eighth century scrupulously prefixes the title to every name. It is also given to those found on a marble Calendar of the ninth century published by Cardinal Mai.[2] The reason of the difference appears to be, that the saints of the Roman Catholic Church, being comparatively few and constituting a kind of celestial aristocracy, required some designation by which they could be recognised as members of it. The Irish saints, on the contrary, being rather a democracy and consisting of such vast numbers, the name conveyed no personal distinction, and therefore was not prefixed.

In this great multitude who bore the title we see the reason the Irish claimed for their country the

---

[1] Life of Corbmac, "Dictionary of National Biography."
[2] Smith's Dictionary of Antiquities, s. v., Saint.

honour of being the Island of Saints. An Irish poet of the twelfth century begins his poem by thus addressing his country, "O Virgin Eire, Island of Saints,"[1] and it is said to have been so called from "the innumerable hives of saints at home, and the swarms of them sent abroad into the world,"[2] the allusion being to the monasteries as places where they were prepared for their mission. Nor was it only living saints who imparted sanctity to the island, but their burial-places were regarded in some sense as still inhabited by them, and the ground was consecrated by their presence. The great island of Aran was similarly termed "Aran of the Saints," and the title included the dead as well as the living, for the author of the Life of S. Kieran tells us: "In it there abides a multitude of saintly men, and innumerable saints lie there who are unknown to all save the Almighty;" and the Life of S. Ailbe says: "Great is that island; and it is a land of saints, for no one knows the multitude of saints who are buried there but God alone."[3] The Bollandists are no doubt right in regarding it as merely equivalent to "servant of God." The Irish saints were not regarded as having attained complete felicity. They were not looked on as reigning in heaven. On the contrary, numerous inscriptions on tombstones ask for prayer in their behalf.[4]

During the first period there were many British ecclesiastics in Ireland, some in connection with S. Patrick, others later. Mochta[5] of Louth, already mentioned; Lomman of Trim, with his brother Manis and

---

[1] Giolla Moduda O'Cassidy, A.D. 1143. O'Reilly, Irish Writers, p. lxxxiii. [2] O'Flaherty's Ogygia, p. 21.
[3] O'Flaherty's Iar Connaught, p. 79.
[4] The formula generally used is *oroit do*, "a prayer for;" sometimes contracted to *or. do* or *or. ar.* Petrie's "Christian Inscriptions in the Irish Language," edited by Miss Stokes, vol. ii. p. 179.
[5] d. 543.

others; Doccus;[1] Mel, said to have been a nephew of S. Patrick; and Melchu, Rioch, and other brothers of S. Mel, who were probably brothers in a religious sense. To these must be added Sechnall, who gave his name to Dunshaughlin,[2] and is otherwise known as Secundinus, the author of the poem in praise of S. Patrick; Auxilius, from whom Killossy,[3] in Kildare, was named; and Isserninus, all of whom seem to have been Gauls.[4] Such were some of the workers who assisted S. Patrick or followed him in the preaching of the Gospel in Ireland.

Amongst the earliest fruits of their labours may be reckoned Brigit, the famous Abbess of Kildare, who demands special notice as the first woman who was engaged prominently in the work of the Church. The position of the sex was very low at the time of her birth and for long after. Women took part in battle and fought with great fury, and a painful incident arising from this is said to have led to the introduction of a law[5] forbidding them in future to take part in the conflicts of men. It was introduced by Adamnan, Abbot of Hy, and was due, there is little doubt, to the influence of Brigit and those Christian women who followed her example in devoting their lives to the service of God, and thus elevated their sex in the eyes of their countrymen. A sketch of her life will illustrate this notice of the first period of the Irish Church and give a picture of the state of religion and society at that time.

She was born in 453,[6] her father, Duffack, being a person of good condition; her mother, who belonged to the tribe of Dal Conchobar, in the county of Meath, was the bondmaid of Duffack. Dr. Lanigan will not hear of this, but the whole early history of Brigit,

[1] *d.* 472. [2] *Domnach Sechnaill.* [3] *Cill Ausille.* [4] Lanigan, i. 261.
[5] Termed the "Lex innocentium," Reeves' "Columba," p. 179.
[6] For her history, see her Life in the "Dictionary of National Biography," and the original Irish Life in the "Book of Lismore."

as told in the Irish Life, rests on this fact. It is worthy of notice that in this and other cases there is a difference between the story as told by Colgan and Lanigan from the Latin authorities and as it appears in the simple narrative of the Irish Life. In the former she is a highly educated young lady of noble birth, whose acts are in accordance with the ecclesiastical and social usages of the eighteenth century. In the latter we are carried back to an early age and a primitive state of society, where all is simple, and homely, and peculiar usages religious and social, come into view. Nor in the present case did it appear to the author of the Irish Life that the accident of her birth should lessen our respect for her character and labours.

The relations between Duffack and his bondmaid excited the jealousy of his wife, and he was obliged in consequence to sell her, but he was not allowed by native law[1] to sell her offspring. She was bought by a Druid or wizard, and placed by him at his farm near Faughard, close to Dundalk, and there she gave birth to Brigit. A legend relates that the mother having gone out one day, leaving the child covered up, the neighbours saw the house all ablaze, so that the flame reached from earth to heaven; but when they went to rescue the girl "the fire appeared not." This story, which is told of many other Irish saints, is an application of the appearance to Moses in the desert when the bush burnt with fire but was not consumed. It is one of the many instances in which we observe how much the language and incidents of Scripture were wrought into the daily life of the Irish people and coloured their narratives. As the child grew up "everything her hand was set to, used

[1] "The bishops said, 'Sell the bondmaid, but do not sell the offspring'" ("Lives of Saints from the Book of Lismore," p. 184). Possibly the bishops consulted may have been one of those groups of seven referred to.

to increase and reverence God." She tended the sheep; she cared for the blind; she fed the poor. But after a time a longing seized her to go home to her father, and when this was made known to him he came and took her with him. Here her first care was for her foster-mother, while at the same time she attended to all domestic matters. She tended the swine, herded the sheep, and cooked the dinner; and it is characteristic of her affectionate nature that when a "miserable, greedy hound" came into the house she gave him a considerable part of the dinner. While thus engaged the thought of her mother in bondage frequently came to her mind, and she requested her father's permission to go to her, but he would not consent. Very unhappy at this, and grieving for her mother's sad condition, she at length resolved to go without her father's leave, and she accordingly made her way to Faughard. "Glad was her mother when she saw her, for she was toil-worn and weary." And now Brigit took the dairy in hand, and all prospered. At this time the Druid and his wife came to visit the farm; and though the Irish Life says little directly as to her religious conversation, the result of their visit, through her influence, was that they abandoned heathenism and became Christians. Her success in the conversion of the heathen is expressed in a hymn composed in her praise by Broccan,[1] in which she is said to be "a marvellous ladder for pagans to visit the kingdom of Mary's Son." On becoming a Christian the Druid said to her, "The butter and the cows that thou hast milked I offer to thee. Thou shalt not abide in bondage to me, but serve thou the Lord." Brigit, with that noble indifference to worldly things which her whole history shows, replied, "Take thou

[1] Goidelica, p. 142.

the cows, but give me my mother's freedom." In the end he bestowed both on her, and with characteristic generosity, "she dealt out the cows to the poor and needy," and returned with her mother to her father's house. Once more at home, "whatever of her father's wealth her hands would find or get she used to give to the poor and needy of the Lord." Indignant at this, at length he determined to sell her, for, as the child of his bondmaid, she was his property. He accordingly took her one day in his chariot, at the same time telling her, "It is not for honour or reverence thou art carried in the chariot, but to take thee to be sold, that thou mayest grind at the *quern*[1] of Dunlaing, king of Leinster." Arrived at the king's residence, he left her at the gate in the chariot, and went in to the king. "Wilt thou buy my daughter from me?" he said. The king inquired why he wished to sell her. He replied, she was giving away everything he had. The king desiring to see her, she was brought in, and he asked her why she gave away her father's property, and suggested that if he purchased her she might do the same with his. She replied, "The Virgin's Son knoweth if I had thy power, with all thy wealth and all Leinster, I would give them all to the Lord of the elements." The king then said to her father, "It is not meet for us to deal with this maiden, for her merit before God is higher than ours," and he ordered her to be set free. In this simple story we have a genuine picture of Irish life at an early period. The next thing we hear of her is her solemn dedication to the Lord's service, when, it is said, "the form of ordaining a bishop was read over her by Bishop Mel," a legend

[1] The handmill in use in Ireland. See Matt. xxiv. 41. Ancient Laws of Ireland, vol. iii. pp. 402, 450.

which probably had its origin in her peculiar position at Kildare, to be mentioned presently. Heathenism was still prevalent to a considerable extent in her time, lingering, as elsewhere, long after Christianity had been generally adopted, and Brigit's labours were directed very much to those still outside the pale of the Church. The difficulties of bringing the realities of the invisible world to the understanding of the heathen people are exemplified by another interview which she had with the King of Leinster. Having gone to him on an errand, one of his slaves offered to become a Christian if she would obtain his freedom. She made the request of the king, holding out to him the hope of a heavenly reward. But the pagan monarch could not take in the conception. "The kingdom of heaven," he said, "as I see it not, and as no one knows what it is, I ask not; and a kingdom for my sons I ask not, for I shall not myself be extant, and let each serve his time. But give me long life and victory always over the O'Neills." The great event of her life was the foundation of Kildare. It was a double monastery for men and women, and on this account it seemed to her that a bishop should be included in her staff of ecclesiastics, to consecrate churches and confer orders. For this office she selected Condlaed, who was then living as a hermit, and she engaged him "to govern the church with her in episcopal dignity;" and so he became "the anointed head of all the bishops, and she the most blessed chief of all the virgins." Dr. Lanigan, who, like so many others, failed to see that the Irish was a national Church, with its own peculiar usages, is much perplexed by this part of her history, and endeavours, but in vain, to make it square with the discipline of the Western Church. He will not allow that she appointed the bishop, as "it cannot be supposed that so humble a saint would have arrogated to herself a privilege quite contrary to the canons of the Church."[1] As to the attitude of the Irish to the canons referred to, we shall see hereafter, but it is quite clear from the language[2] of her Life that she appointed Bishop Condlaed, and that he was under her jurisdiction. Two incidents in her life illustrate this. Condlaed had gone to Brittany,[3] and brought back some "transmarine and foreign vestments," which he used on special occasions. But Brigit, always sympathising with distress, and perhaps not caring for foreign innovations, cut them up and made clothes of them for the poor.

On another occasion he expressed a desire to visit Rome, and this was perfectly natural, as he was not only her bishop, but her chief artist, and Rome was then the home of art. He was one of those workers in gold and silver and other metals who have left so many beautiful specimens of ecclesiastical art[4] for the admiration of the present age. On his applying to Brigit for permission she refused to grant it, on which he presumed to set out on his journey without leave, but had only got as far as Dunlavin, in the county of Wicklow, when he was devoured by wolves. This was interpreted as a judgment for his disobedience, because, as a native authority[5] tells us, "he tried to go to Rome in violation of an order of Brigit."

The monastery thus established by Brigit is the

[1] Eccles. Hist. i. 409.   [2] Ibid., "Primum episcopum *elegit*."
[3] Letha is used both to signify Italy and Brittany, the latter being the earlier usage. In the present instance this would seem most probably to be its meaning. See Todd, p. 22.
[4] The collection of the Royal Irish Academy, now transferred to the Museum of Science and Art in Dublin, contains many of these works of art—shrines, bells, pastoral staffs, crosiers, &c., of an early age.
[5] The Lebor Brecc, quoted in Œngus at May 3.

first clear instance of one provided with a monastic bishop under the rule of the head of the institution, and also of a double monastery of men and women, a system which was subsequently imitated on the Continent.[1] A description is given of the church of Kildare by a writer of the ninth century which is of considerable interest, as we have no similar account of any other church in Ireland at that age; and soon after it was written the church and monastery were sacked and burnt by the Danes. The author tells us the bodies of Bishop Condlaed and the holy virgin Brigit are on the right and left of the decorated altar, deposited in monuments adorned with various embellishments of gold and silver, and gems and precious stones, with crowns of gold and silver depending from above. Within the church were three oratories, separated by partitions of planks. One extended along the breadth in the east of the church from one party-wall to the other, and at its extremities were two doors. Through the door at the right the chief prelate entered the sanctuary, accompanied by his regular school and the officiating clergy. Through the other only the abbess, with her virgins and widows. Two other ornamented doorways gave entrance to the members of the general congregation, one to the men, and the other to the women.[2] Such was the provision made by Brigit in pursuance of her perfectly original plan of a double monastery, in which she struck out a line for herself with that independence which is the chief characteristic of the early Irish Church. One of the institutions at Kildare which has attracted much attention is the "perpetual fire" which Giraldus Cambrensis describes as existing

[1] M. Ozanam rather fancifully attributes the chivalry of the French character to this association of the sexes in the Irish monasteries in France. [2] Petrie, Round Towers, pp. 197, 198.

in the twelfth century, when he visited Ireland. At Kildare, in Leinster, he says, celebrated for the glorious Brigit, many miracles have been wrought worthy of memory. Among these the first that occurs is the fire of S. Brigit, which is reported "never to go out," being carefully tended by the nuns and holy women, so that "from the time of the virgin it has continued burning through a long course of years; and although such heaps of wood have been consumed during this long period, there has been no accumulation of ashes."[1]

This fire, which has been generally regarded as unique, was really only a survival of a practice once by no means uncommon. Several other instances are on record, though this is the only one which continued to so late a date as the twelfth century. It was even in existence a century later, when Henry, the Norman Archbishop of Dublin, attempted to extinguish it. It was, however, relit by the Irish, and did not cease altogether until the suppression of the monasteries. In the Life of S. Kieran of Saigir,[2] traditionally regarded as having preceded S. Patrick, we have an account of such a fire, which is described more in detail. On one occasion it was allowed to go out by the carelessness of the person in charge, and there was consternation in the monastery, for it was from this sacred fire all the other fires were kindled. Still more, the weather was cold, and there were visitors in the guest-house. In this emergency S. Kieran went forth, spread abroad his hands and prayed, whereupon a thunderbolt fell, which he wrapped up in his robe and took home, and was thus enabled to rekindle the

[1] The Historical Works of Giraldus Cambrensis, Bohn, p. 96. The Order of Druidical Virgins, who, according to Bishop Greith, had previously kept up the fire in heathen times, had no existence but in his own imagination (Geschichte, p. 166).
[2] Now Seirkieran, near Birr, in the King's County.

fire. In this legend it appears that the fire was believed to have been originally divinely kindled, and it could only be renewed in the same way.[1] There was also a perpetual fire at Inismurray Island, off the coast of Sligo, where, amongst the curious ecclesiastical remains, the Fire House still stands. The natives all aver that here of old burnt a perpetual fire, from whence all the hearths in the island which, from any cause, had become extinguished were rekindled. A flagstone[2] which formed the hearth on which the fire burned was in existence a few years ago, but it was, unfortunately, broken up by the workmen engaged in repairing the ruins. By this act, as Mr. Wakeman observes, archæology has suffered an irreparable loss, as it was the only relic remaining in Ireland of this curious observance.[3] One more instance of these fires should be mentioned. In the cathedral yard of Cloyne, in the county of Cork, are the ruins of a Fire House, which, when measured in 1881,[4] were 26 feet long by 16 feet 7 inches broad, and 2 feet 10 inches thick, the greatest height being then only about 2 feet. It is described on a map of the cemetery made in 1743 as "the Fire House," and was certainly of the same nature as that already described. This primitive usage, which is only connected with the names of the earliest saints, appears to have died out at an early period everywhere but at Kildare. It

---

[1] *Betha Ciarain*, in MS. 23, M. 50, Royal Irish Academy; also the Life of S. Ciaran of Saigir in the "Dictionary of National Biography." This practice, which was of Irish origin, was introduced on the Continent by the missionaries of the eighth century, the sacred fire being obtained by means of a burning glass. It was never observed at Rome, the only parallel being the new fire at Easter in the Greek Church of Jerusalem. Duchesne, "Culte Chretien," pp. 240, 241.

[2] Called *Leac na teinidh*, the flagstone of the fire.

[3] Inismurray, by W. F. Wakeman, "Journal of the Kilkenny Archæological Society," 4th series, vol. vii. pp. 228, 229.

[4] Annals of the Cathedral of Cloyne, by R. Caulfield, LL.D., Cork, 1882, p. 31.

seems to have been of pre-Christian origin, for in primitive times the custom prevailed of having a common fire to which all could resort, and this seems to have been adopted by the Church and connected with religion.

A French writer suggests that the high reputation which S. Brigit enjoyed was due in some measure to her bearing the name of the heathen goddess of the Irish. He is of opinion that this deity was supplanted in Christian times by S. Brigit, and that the Irish of the Middle Ages rendered to her some of the veneration their pagan ancestors were wont to yield to their goddess.[1] But this does not account for the expressions used with regard to her. She is entitled "The Mother of the Lord,"[2] or "one of the Mothers of the Lord." She is "the Queen of the true God,"[3] and therefore "the Queen of Queens."[4]

The explanation of this extravagant language is that it is due to the rivalry between the Irish Church and the propagandists of foreign views. Whatever they said of the Virgin Mary the Irish would affirm of their native saint, and, if possible, outdo it. If they had a Mary the Irish also should have one, and so they said Brigit was "the Mary of the Gael."[5] The "Book of Leinster" contains a list[6] of native and foreign saints who were "of one manner of life," and accordingly are arranged in parallel columns. In this list Brigit is placed on a level with the Virgin Mary, the idea on which the enumeration is founded being that no saint could be superior to those of Ireland. This exaltation of

---

[1] M. de Jubainville, Cycle Mythologique Irlandais, p. 145.
[2] S. Brigit, in "Liber Hymnorum," vol. i. p. 64, note B.
[3] Ibid., pp. 58, 59.   [4] Goidelica, p. 137.
[5] Book of Hymns, p. 64, note B.   [6] See Appendix E.

Brigit into which they were forced, as it were, by the language of their opponents, was an episode in the struggle of the Irish to assert the nationality of their Church, and to prevent its absorption into the Continental Church.

Brigit's death took place in 523; and, as we have seen, she was buried in Kildare, where her remains were enshrined in the ninth century. They are said to have been afterwards transferred to Down, and buried there with the bodies of SS. Patrick and Columba, according to a couplet which has had a very wide circulation from the time of the appearance of the work of Giraldus Cambrensis on the "Topography of Ireland."[1] It is thus translated—

"Patrick, Columba, Brigit, rest in glorious Down,
Lie in one tomb, and consecrate the town."

Yet the verse, though appearing in the printed copies of Cambrensis, was absent from the three manuscripts used by Ussher,[2] and the fact of the burial was denied by the monks of Glastonbury. The story is certainly not free from suspicion, for it would be strange if the remains of Brigit, after being enshrined, were again committed to the earth. There is some reason to believe, as we shall see, that the story was a political device of John De Courcey.[3]

It is evident that we see in Brigit a character of great energy, piety, and courage. She was warmly affectionate, generous, and unselfish, wholly absorbed in the desire to promote the glory of God, especially in the conversion of the heathen and the relief of suffering. Such a personality could not but impress itself on the Irish people, as hers has done in a remarkable manner.

[1] Distinct. iii. cap. xviii.
[2] Ussher, Works, vol. vi. p. 455.   [3] See *infra*, p. 255.

CHAPTER IV.

THE SECOND PERIOD—IRISH SAINTS AT HOME.

THE document already mentioned goes on to describe the state of the Church in the next period :—" In the Second Order of Saints there were few bishops and many presbyters, three hundred in number. The had one Head, our Lord. They had different rites of celebration and different rules of living. They celebrated Easter on the fourteenth moon after the equinox, and had a uniform tonsure from ear to ear. They avoided the society[1] and service of women, and excluded them from their monasteries. This order continued during four reigns, *i.e.*, from 543 to 599. They received a ritual for the celebration of Mass from the holy men of Britain, David, Gildas, and Docus." The comparison of these saints to the moon, while the first were like the sun, indicates a certain degree of inferiority. They are not said to have followed the example of S. Patrick, and their avoidance of the society and service of women is regarded as an evidence that they were weaker in the faith than their predecessors. There appears to have been somewhat in the nature of a reaction at this time, after the swift acceptance of the faith on the preaching of S. Patrick. In the case of the Irish, as in that of their kinsmen the Galatians, the fervour of their faith cooled down, their former super-

[1] *Consortia.*

stitions reasserted their power, and ideas of pagan origin tended to become intermingled with Christianity. Thus, the impulse communicated by the intense zeal and powerful individuality of S. Patrick had to some extent died away, and a new proclamation of Divine truth was needed to restore life to the Church. The Life of Disibod,[1] written in the twelfth century, represents this decline as an apostasy, and the authoress, the Abbess Hildegardis, thus describes it :—"At the time when the holy man was thus governing the people by words and examples, a huge schism and great scandals prevailed in all that country (Ireland). Some rejected the Old and New Testament and denied Christ; others embraced heresies; very many went over to Judaism; some relapsed into paganism; some desired to live, not as becomes men, but like beasts in a base manner; others, in fine, although, from outward decency, they observed some appearance of morality, in reality cared for nothing good."[2] But this account of the matter, drawn up on the Continent by a stranger, is evidently highly coloured. It was derived from materials preserved in the monastery founded by Disibod,[3] and evidently communicated by him. But he was very unpopular at home on account of his moroseness and the extreme asceticism of his mode of life. "He lives, the people said, as though he was not a human being, and he wants us to follow his example."[4] He had eventually to leave Ireland, owing to the hostility of his flock, and we may, therefore, regard the account he gave of his treatment as tinged by feelings of disappointment and annoyance. Some foundation,

---

[1] Flourished A.D. 594-674.   [2] Todd, p. 109.
[3] Disibodenberg, at the confluence of the Nahe and the Glan.
[4] Life of Disibod, in "Dictionary of National Biography."

however, there seems to be for the statement that heathen practices prevailed. S. Columba, in a poem composed on the occasion of his escape over the mountains from Tara, refers to superstitious observances practised at the court of the Christian King Dermot :—

> " Our fate depends not on sneezing,
> Nor on a bird perched on a twig,
> Nor on the root of a knotted tree,
> Nor on the noise of clapping hands.
> Better is He in whom we trust,
> The Father, the One, and the Son."

And again :—

> " I adore not the voice of birds,
> Nor sneezing, nor lots in this world ;
> Nor a boy, nor chance, nor woman ;
> My Druid is Christ the Son of God,
> Christ, Son of Mary, the great Abbot,
> The Father, the Son, and the Holy Ghost."[1]

These were the principal omens and methods of divination in use among the ancient pagans. To restore once more the purity of religion, Ainmire, King of Ireland,[2] first cousin of S. Columba, is said, in the Life of Gildas, to have sent for that saint to Britain entreating him to come to Ireland and restore ecclesiastical order, for almost all the inhabitants of the island had abandoned the Catholic faith. The state of things is exaggerated in order to render the merits of Gildas more conspicuous as a reformer. When he received the communication, his Life tells us, " armed with heavenly weapons he went to Ireland to preach Christ." His coming is recorded in the Welsh Annals, and both the Welsh and Irish Annals notice his death.[3] It was chiefly to the school of S.

---

[1] Todd, p. 122.   [2] Reigned A.D. 568-571.
[3] There is much uncertainty as to who this Gildas was. The name is a corruption of *Giolla De*, "servant of God," and is applied to many persons.

David of Wales that the Irish were indebted for the restoration of religion. The saints, David and Docus, or Cadocus, with whom Gildas is associated, are stated in the history of that time to have been the teachers of the Second Order of Saints, and through them they exercised a powerful influence on religion in Ireland. For those who received their education under them came back to Ireland as reformers, and gathering large bodies of pupils, imparted to them the new impulse they had received. About the same period others from the North of Ireland resorted to Whitherne,[1] or Candida Casa, in Galloway, which also was a famous school. There is ground for supposing that the influence of S. Martin was felt both at S. David's and Whitherne, and thus acted on the Irish Church, with which, we have seen reason to believe, he was already connected through S. Patrick. From these two sources fresh life was introduced into the Church, a constant intercourse was kept up with Scotland and Britain, and from this time we find many ecclesiastics described as "men of the two countries,"[2] or "of the two divisions," in consequence of their having passed some of their time there as well as in Ireland.[3] Renewed as religious life was by the intervention of the British saints, it was nevertheless different in character from that of S. Patrick. We do not hear of remonstrances against heathen practices on the part of the Second Order of Saints such as appear in the "Confession of S. Patrick," and they seem to have tolerated many things which we should have expected them to oppose. The result has been a certain admixture of heathen usages with

---

[1] Skene, Celtic Scotland, vol. ii. p. 45, &c.
[2] *Fer-da-leithe*, or *Fer-da-crich*.
[3] So Berchan, Reeves' "Columba," p. 314, note *n*, and MacCarthenn of Clogher. Nine others bearing this title are in the "Martyrology of Donegal."

Irish Christianity. Dr. O'Donovan attributes this to S. Patrick. "Nothing is clearer," he says, "than that Patrick engrafted Christianity on the Pagan superstitions with so much skill that he won the people over to the Christian religion before they understood the exact difference between the two systems of belief, and much of this half-Pagan, half-Christian religion will be found, not only in the Irish stories of the Middle Ages, but in the superstitions of the peasantry of the present day."[1] This observation, as far as it regards S. Patrick, however, is founded on the interpolated Lives, and derives no support from his genuine writings. On the contrary, the language of the "Confession" with reference to sun-worship and idolatry is quite in a different spirit, as is his denunciation of heathenism and idolatry in his Irish Hymn. It does, however, seem in some degree applicable to the saints of the Second Order, who tolerated such practices as well-worship. We may perhaps assume that, finding themselves unable to cope with these inveterate superstitions, and being unsupported by any external power, they thought it better to temporise, hoping that, under the influence of the preaching of the Gospel, those superstitions would die out. But the course of Irish history did not favour this result, and thus may be accounted for the tinge of paganism which Dr. O'Donovan notices in the religion of the Irish peasantry. Bishop Greith apologises for the line taken by the Second Order of Saints, and explains that "the passage to Christianity was thereby rendered easier, as the Christian cult did not entirely displace the ancient form of worship, but purified and made use of it."[2] "Thus," he says, "the new convert saw in the well in which he was baptized, as afterwards in a

[1] Annals of the Four Masters, vol. i. p. 131. [2] *Geschichte*, s. 166.

font, the holy well by which his fathers had once offered up their prayers." But the well-worship in Ireland, which has survived from heathen times, has nothing to do with baptism, and the only connection it has with Christianity is the substitution of a saint for the Druid of heathen times. One result of this gentle dealing with the native paganism was, that there were no martyrs during the conversion of Ireland. This was brought as a serious charge against the Irish Church by Giraldus Cambrensis in the twelfth century. "It is wonderful," he says, "that in a nation so cruel and bloodthirsty, in which the faith had been planted in very early times and was always very flourishing, there should be no crown of martyrdom for the Church of Christ;"[1] and he regards this as a reproach to the clergy. A complete contrast to the method of Christianising a country thus described is presented by the course pursued in Germany :—
"There the priests were occupied for a long time in destroying every trace of heathenism, in condemning every ancient lay as a work of the devil, in felling sacred trees and abolishing national customs."[2] It is not, therefore, quite accurate for M. Ozanam[3] to say that Christianity has "always treated converted nations with respect as to their religious customs." In his own country, also, heathen practices were suppressed, but by legal means, through the decrees of Councils. Thus the Council of Arles, A.D. 452, ordered that, "if in any diocese any unbeliever either lighted torches or worshipped trees, wells, or stones, or neglected to destroy them, he should be found

---

[1] Giraldus Cambrensis, Bohn, p. 142. Bishop Greith is singularly unfortunate here, both as to his fact and his illustration. "As the hills of Ireland," he says, "are planted with fruitful vines, so the Irish Church is illustrious (*glänzend*) with the red blood of her martyrs" (s. 461).
[2] Max Müller, Chips, vol. i. p. 191.   [3] Œuvres, vol. v. p. 98.

guilty of sacrilege;"[1] the Council of Tours, A.D. 567, ordered those "to be excommunicated who perpetrated at trees, stones, or wells things contrary to the ordinances of the Church.";[2] and the Council of Rouen, A.D. 692, condemned all who practised rites at such places "as though a deity were present there who had power to do them harm or confer benefits upon them."[3] The result has been that well-worship and other heathen practices were extirpated in France at an early period, and the editor of a French periodical expresses his interest in seeing still practised in Ireland a custom which in France was a matter of history. But in both the cases now mentioned those who were active in abolishing the customs were Germans or Franks, of a different race from the Celtic population, with whose ways they had no sympathy. In Ireland there was no such foreign element at that time, nor until the Conquest, when we find a Norman archbishop endeavouring to suppress Brigit's fire.

The saints of this period were chiefly engaged in education. They established schools, which quickly became famous, and the numbers who flocked to them were very great. Bede[4] describes the nobility and middle classes of England as sending their sons to Ireland at this time, either for the purpose of studying the Scriptures or in order to lead a stricter life. All were generously provided by the Irish people with books and teaching, and also maintained gratuitously. Native writers do not take credit for this uncommon hospitality, but it was, nevertheless, one of the most remarkable episodes in European

---

[1] Fergusson, Rude Stone Monuments, pp. 24, 25.
[2] Ibid.   [3] Ibid.
[4] Eccl. Hist., lib. iii. chap. 27.

history. Nor was it only from Great Britain that students flocked to these schools, for all the nations north of the Alps were represented. A foreign writer thus describes one of them:[1]—

> "Now haste Sicambri from the marshy Rhine;
> Bohemians now desert their cold North land;
> Auvergne and Holland, too, add to the tide;
> Forth from Geneva's frowning cliffs they throng.
> Helvetia's youth by Rhone and by Sâone
> Are few: the Western Isle is now their home.
> All these from many lands, by many diverse paths,
> Rivals in pious zeal, seek Lismore's famous seat."

The ambition of every young man on completing his education was to become the founder of a monastery. His first proceeding was to obtain a site, and if he had powerful friends he might succeed in doing so; but it was not easy, for land, that is, arable land, was very scarce, the country being clothed with forests. In most cases the site granted was in a forest, and then the labour of felling the trees was very great. When S. Patrick was on a journey to Ulster he met with some people felling a tree, and his sympathy was aroused by seeing "the blood come through the palms of their hands."[2] All classes among the family or monastic community of the saint engaged in the toil. When Theodore, King of Munster in the eighth century, became a monk at Lismore, he is described as armed with an axe and hatchet, "felling the lordly woods" which surrounded the place on all sides;[3] and so necessary was it to be prepared for such work that we read of a bishop habitually travelling with an axe slung on his back.[4] To avoid this difficulty S. Columba on one occasion placed a church north and south, because large trees stood in the way of its occupying the usual position.[5]

---

[1] B. Moronus on Lismore, Ussher, "Works," vol. vii. p. 30.
[2] Trip., vol. i. p. 221.
[3] Codex Salmanticensis, p. 665.
[4] Ibid., vol. i. p. 137.
[5] Reeves' Columba, p. 397.

The site being obtained and cleared, the monastery was erected of wattled work, the rods being woven between stakes driven into the ground. The first operation being the driving of these, the expression for the erection of such a building came to be " to drive "[1] or plant it. The buildings composing the monastery varied in number, from four[2] in the early period to seven in later times. All were enclosed with a rampart and fosse.

The selection of the site was generally attributed to supernatural guidance in after times. In the Life of S. Fintan it is related that an angel clothed in white met him one day in the wood, and pointed out to him the seven places where his buildings were to be erected, and he accordingly set up crosses in the places indicated.[3] At Hy the number of buildings was six—the church, refectory, kitchen, guest-house, library, and workshop. The monastery thus founded, with its appropriate buildings, was known as the "city"[4] of the saint. If it became a great school and students flocked to it from all quarters, accommodation was found for them by the erection of huts or booths, which were quickly run up, the materials being at hand everywhere in the great woods. There is, therefore, no difficulty on this ground in believing that very large numbers were received at some of these schools. But there was nothing in the least resembling the buildings which are deemed essential to the colleges and universities of modern times. A group of huts such as here described, occupied by a considerable population, was not improperly called a city. The numbers are said to have reached three thousand on some occasions. Bede gives that of

---

[1] *Saidis cli and.* "He sets or plants a stake there" ("Trip.," p. 149, also 158).
[2] Ibid., p. 236.
[3] Life of S. Fintan, "Dict. Nat. Biog."
[4] *Civitas.*

the Welsh Bangor as 2100. When many foreigners attended, they seem to have grouped their huts according to nationality, and therefore we hear of the Saxon Third [1] at Armagh, or, in modern phrase, the Saxon quarter. The food was prepared in large caldrons, after the manner of the schools of the prophets. In the story of the founding of Armagh, King Daire is said to have given S. Patrick one containing six firkins, termed "a marvellous copper caldron from over sea."[2] We cannot suppose that those huts were furnished or afforded much more than shelter from the weather, and as transcribing manuscripts was one of their chief occupations, it seems difficult at first to understand how, in such circumstances, they could write. The Irish antiquary, Duald MacFirbis,[3] appears to supply information on this point, for he speaks of Irish historians writing the history of their country "on their knees," which does not mean in a kneeling position, as the reader might suppose, but with the book supported on one knee crossed over the other—a slow and laborious mode of writing. This primitive custom was not uncommon among writers of the Irish language of the poorer class as late as the middle of the present century.

Besides the buildings of wattled work, there were also some churches of stone,[4] though probably not many. They were of the simplest form, and, according to Mr. Freeman, represented the earliest churches of all, before the Basilicas were Christianised, that is, before the time of Constantine, and therefore before

---

[1] A.F.M., A.D. 1092.
[2] *Æneum mirabilem transmarinum* (Muirchu, in Hogan, p. 46). So Cæsar says of the Britons, *Ære utuntur importato*. Many of these caldrons are in the Museum of the Royal Irish Academy.
[3] O'Curry, MS. Materials, p. 217.
[4] Miss Stokes, Early Christian Architecture.

the apsidal form was introduced, the latter being the usual Roman type. The form of monasteries, from whatever source immediately derived, must ultimately be referred to an Eastern pattern, such as that which Adamnan saw on Mount Tabor.[1]

But whatever may have been the rude simplicity of life in those schools, it was at least peaceful at this early period, and for many a year Ireland was the only spot in Europe where study could be pursued without molestation and under competent teachers. What did it matter to those who crossed the seas to reach her shores, the choice spirits of an age of war and confusion, how rough the hospitality may have been if they gained the object of their lives, the acquisition of knowledge, especially the knowledge of the Scriptures? One of the most celebrated of the founders of monastic schools was S. Finnian.[2] After "reading the Psalms and the ecclesiastical order," he crossed the sea at the age of thirty, and, according to his Irish Life, proceeded to Tours.[3] He is next heard of at S. David's, in Wales, in association with David, Gildas, and Docus. Here he acquired the British language, speaking it as if it were his native tongue. He now wished to visit Rome, but the writer of his Life informs us he was admonished by an angel not to do so. "What would be given thee at Rome will be given thee here, he said, 'arise and renew faith and belief in Ireland after Patrick.'" He founded Clonard[4] about 530, "and is said to have had 3000 pupils there. Amongst them were the company

---

[1] Reeves' Columba, p. 360 note *t*. Ozanam, Œuvres, vol. iv. p. 100.
[2] *D.* 550.
[3] By the Irish called Torinis. The Latin Life substitutes Dairinis, an island in the Bay of Wexford. His visit to Tours is also mentioned in the "Office of S. Finnian."
[4] Cluain Iraird, in the Barony of Moyfenrath, county of Meath.

known as "the twelve apostles [1] of Ireland," and from this circumstance it may have been that he obtained the title of master (or tutor) of the saints of Ireland.

The title given to the twelve ecclesiastics referred to evidently implies some kind of parallel with our Lord's Apostles, and they were probably looked on as laying again the foundations of religion in Ireland. The success of S. Finnian's labours in the restoration of religion was celebrated in a poem which begins—

> "Shone forth the Sun of righteousness,
> Erewhile obscured by clouds." [2]

He died of the pestilence known as the yellow plague, which ravaged the British islands in the middle of the sixth century.[3]

The desire to visit Rome felt by S. Finnian is also noticed in the case of others at this period. The instance of Condlaed has been already mentioned. Another is that of Molua, who came to S. Aidan of Ferns expressing a wish to go on pilgrimage to Rome, but the bishop refused him permission. "Verily," replied Molua, "if I see not Rome I shall soon die." S. Aidan, however, took him up on his chariot, and they were not seen until the following day; but it seemed to Molua that they had been to Rome, and he was as well acquainted with the city as if he had been there.[4] The Life of S. Berach of Kilbarry, county of Roscommon, has a similar story. A disciple of his, named Colman, was so resolved to go there that nothing would induce him to forego his purpose. Finding his resolution immovable, Berach accompanied him part of the way, where

---

[1] They were Kieran of Saigir, Kieran of Clonmacnois, Brendan of Clonfert, Brendan of Birr, Columba of Terryglas, Molaise of Devenish Island, Cainice of Aghabo, Ruadan of Lorrha, Movi of Glasnevin, Senell of Cloninis, and Nennidh of Inismac-Saint.   [2] Todd, p. 101.
[3] Life of S. Finnian, in the "Dictionary of National Biography."
[4] Todd, p. 115.

Kieran another saint, joined Berach in remonstrating with him. He declared, however, that he would not rest till he had seen Rome with his own eyes. Berach then made the sign of the cross over his eyes, whereupon he saw Rome clearly, and was satisfied.[1] Rome, the capital of the world, must have exercised a powerful attraction on the races on the outskirts of the Empire. Apart from its ancient glory, it was now sanctified in their eyes as the burial-place, according to popular belief, of the Apostles SS. Peter and Paul, whose tombs were shown, one on the Via Ostiensis, and the other in the Vatican. Among so religious and inquisitive a people as the Irish, there must have been an eager desire to visit the great city, but it was the policy of the Irish Church, as we have seen, to throw obstacles in the way of this intercourse, and to preserve the native institutions from foreign influence.

Another S. Finnian, of Moville,[2] educated at Whitherne[3] in Galloway, is said in his Life to have been "the first to bring the Gospel to Ireland." This, as we have seen from the action of S. Patrick, cannot be meant literally, and it probably means that he introduced a revised text, which, as the gloss suggests, may have been that of S. Jerome. The Calendar of Œngus[4] notices this in a somewhat obscure passage, which, however, confirms the interpretation suggested. There are several legends connected with this manuscript which show how much it was valued. S. Columba is said to have copied it clandestinely, and

---

[1] Boll. A.A.S.S., Vita Berachi, Feb., xv. p. 345*b*.
[2] Maghbhile, in county of Down.
[3] H. and S., vol. i. 121, note *b*.
[4] The passage is, "A body of red gold with purity, over a sea came he" (p. cxxxvi.). Another reading, *co-recht* instead of *correcht* (p. cxliv.), brings the text more into harmony with the gloss of the Lebor Brecc. It will then run, "A body of red gold with purity, *i.e.*, with the law (purified)." The "law" is then explained in the gloss, "with the Gospel, that is, the new law." See also Todd, p. 104.

when the daylight waned before he had completed his work, his fingers gave forth light and illuminated the page. The establishment of S. Comgall at Bangor, in Ulster, founded A.D. 559, was one of the most important, as well for the great number of pupils as for the distinction of those who were educated there. S. Bernard, speaking of it, says it was "the head of many monasteries, a holy place fruitful in saints, one of whom, named Luan, alone is reputed to have been the founder of one hundred monasteries;" its pupils overspread Ireland and Scotland, and poured over the Continent like a flood.[1] The "Antiphonary of Bangor," now in the Ambrosian Library at Milan, is a noble relic of this great institution. It has been 1200 years absent from Ireland, and the correspondence of its entries with those of the Irish Annals bears most important testimony to the fidelity of the latter. Amongst the hymns which it contains is the following commemorating the abbots who ruled there, and closing with the name of Cronan, who then occupied the office; thus we learn the date at which it was composed, for this abbot died November 6, 691 :—

"The holy valiant deeds of sacred fathers
  Based on the matchless Church of Benchor ;
  The noble deeds of abbots, their number, times, and names
  Of never-ending lustre. Hear, brothers, great their deserts,
  Whom the Lord hath gathered to the mansions of His
     heavenly kingdom.

Christ loved Comgill ; well, too, did he the Lord ;
  He held Beogna dear ; He graced the ruler Aedh ;
  He chose the holy Sillan, a famous teacher of the world,
  Whom the Lord hath gathered to the mansions of His
     heavenly kingdom.

He made Finten accepted, an heir generous renowned ;
  He rendered Maclaisre illustrious, the chief of all abbots ;
  With a sacred torch He enlightened Segene,

[1] Quoted in Lanigan, Ecc. Hist. vol. ii. p. 68.

A great physician of Scripture,
Whom the Lord hath gathered to the mansions of His heavenly
  kingdom.

Bercenus was a distinguished man ; Cumine also had grace ;
Columba a congenial shepherd ; Aidan without complaint ;
Baithene a worthy ruler ; Crotan a chief president,
Whom the Lord hath gathered to the mansions of His heavenly
  kingdom.

To these so excellent succeeded Caman, a man to be beloved by all:
Singing praises to Christ, he now sits on high. That Cronan,
The fifteenth may lay hold on life, the Lord preserve him,
Whom the Lord will gather to the mansions of His heavenly
  kingdom.

The truest merits of these holy abbots,
Meet for Comgill, most exalted, we invoke,
That we may blot out all our offences
Through Jesus Christ, who reigns for ages everlasting." [1]

One of the most famous of the saints of the sixth century was S. Brendan [2] of Clonfert, known as "the Navigator," from his voyage in search of the Promised Land. Born at Tralee, called by Latin writers *Stagnum Li or Littus Li*, he was grandson of Alta, of the race of Ciar, a descendant of Rudraige, from whom the Ciarraighe, or people of Kerry, are descended. Sent first to S. Ita of Killeedy, he became afterwards a pupil of a bishop named Erc, with whom he read "the Canon of the Old and New Testament." At his ordination the words of our Lord (Luke xviii. 29, 30) impressed him deeply, and he resolved to forsake his country and inheritance, beseeching his Heavenly Father to grant him "the mysterious land far from human ken." One night he dreamt that an angel appeared to him and said, "Arise, O Brendan, for God hath given thee what thou soughtest, even the Land of Promise." On this he arose, and going forth alone on the mountain, he looked out and beheld the vast and dim ocean stretching out on every side, and

---

[1] The Antiphonary of Bangor, by Bishop Reeves, p. 11.
[2] Flourished 484-577.

in the distance the Land of Promise, with angels hovering over it. Such was the origin of his voyage, which was made in a wicker vessel covered with hides; "in this," according to his Irish life, "he sailed over the wave-voice of the strong-maned sea, and over the storm of the green-sided waves, and over the mouths of the marvellous, awful, bitter ocean, where they saw the multitude of the furious red-mouthed monsters with abundance of great sea-whales." What truth there may be in the story of his voyages it is difficult to say, but they seem to be founded on a real expedition amongst the Hebrides and the Northern islands. The legend was extremely popular throughout Europe in the Middle Ages, and as early as the eleventh century it was known in France, Spain, and Holland. It was no longer the simple story of his wanderings among the islands, but was expanded, and numerous adventures, some of them from classical sources, worked into it. Schröder traces it in its augmented form to the Lower Rhine,[1] where, probably, some monks of Brendan's order were settled, and first gave it to the world in its Continental form, when it excited intense interest.[2]

Another S. Brendan, of Birr in the King's County, founded a monastery there about 550. He was a disciple of S. Finnian of Clonard, and is described in the Life of that saint as "a prophet in those schools," and also of the saints of Ireland,[3] where there is little doubt we must understand by prophet a preacher of the Gospel. In the Calendar of Œngus he is termed "fair head of Ireland's prophets." A legend represents S. Columba as being aware of his death at the time of its occurrence, though far away from the

[1] Sanct Brandan, Erlangen, 1871. Einleitung, p. xv.
[2] See Life of Brendan of Clonfert, in "Dictionary of National Biography." [3] Lanigan, Eccl. Hist., vol ii. p. 39.

scene. Ordering the sacred service of the Eucharist to be got ready, he is asked how he knew of S. Brendan's death, as no messenger had arrived. "Last night," said Columba, "I saw heaven open and choirs of angels descending to meet the soul of Brendan, and the whole world was illuminated by their brilliant and surpassing radiance."[1]

A picture of the conversion of some heathen in the West of Ireland at this period is given in the Life of S. Caillin of Fenagh, who flourished about 560. The Conmaicne, who were the inhabitants of the Barony of Dunmore, in the county of Galway, finding their tribe too numerous for their territory, "planned a truly horrid fratricide and breach of brotherhood among themselves." This barbarous remedy for the congestion of the population they would have carried out but for the interference of S. Caillin, who undertook to search for more land for them. Arrived, in the course of his expedition, at Breifne,[2] he endeavoured to persuade Fergna, the king, to become a Christian, but he refused to listen, and ordered his son to expel S. Caillin from his kingdom. The prince, Hugh the Dark, proceeding to do so, found the saint and his followers engaged in worship, and instead of driving him away, they became believers. Hugh presented his fortress to S. Caillin, who built a church in it, the ruins of which are still in existence, and the outline of the fortress may be traced.[3] The king then ordered the Druids to banish the Christians, and they were engaged in some heathen rites for this purpose, when Hugh, indignant at their proceedings, was about to attack them, but S. Caillin, in that Christian spirit which contrasts so remarkably with

[1] Life of Brendan of Birr, in the "Dictionary of National Biography."
[2] In the counties of Cavan and Leitrim.
[3] Petrie, Round Towers, p. 444.

the legends of a later period, said, " No, we will not exercise human power on them." On the death of Fergna, Hugh succeeded to the kingdom; but he was dissatisfied with his appearance, being of a dark complexion, and here we have one of those stories which read so oddly in the lives of Irish saints. He requested S. Caillin to produce a change in his appearance which would render him like S. Rioch of Inis-bo-finne. The saint accordingly prayed for him, and in the morning they were found to be exactly alike.[1] The meaning of the story evidently is, that the demeanour of the Irish chieftain underwent a change owing to the influence of Christian teaching. Similar stories are told of S. Patrick,[2] S. Finnchu,[3] and others. This is in accordance with the usual habit of the Irish of taking figurative language literally, and filling in the details according to fancy.

When recognised as the teacher of the tribe, we find S. Caillin bestowing on them a *Cathach* or battle standard to carry in war. It is described as "a hazel cross with the top through the middle." Nothing, perhaps, shows more than the presentation of these objects how the Church was compelled to accommodate itself to the warlike habits of the people, notwithstanding that the message it brought to them was the Gospel of peace. So Grellan[4] of Roscommon presented his crozier to the race of Maine, and assured them that they should never be subdued as long as they held it. "Let the battle standard of the race be my precious crozier," he said, "and they shall never be defeated in battle." The crozier of S. Columba was also used in this way, and known as "victory in

[1] Life of S. Caillin, in "Dictionary of National Biography."
[2] Trip., vol. i. p. 152.
[3] Life of Finnchu, in "Dictionary of National Biography."
[4] Life of S. Grellan, ibid.

SECOND PERIOD: IRISH SAINTS AT HOME. 67

battle."[1] But the most famous of these talismans was the *Cathach* proper of S. Columba, a silver reliquary containing a copy of the Psalms, which is thus described by an Irish author :—" It is the chief relic of Columba in the territory of Cinel Conaill, and it is covered with silver under gold; and it is not lawful to open it; and if it be sent thrice right-hand wise around the army of the Cinel Conaill when they are going to battle, they will return safe with victory. And it is on the breast of a *coarb* (abbot) or cleric, who is, to the best of his power, free from mortal sin, that the *Cathach* should be brought round the army."[2] The work in which this occurs was written in the sixteenth century, and gives expression to the ideas then prevalent. The superstition with regard to the opening of the *Cathach* is evidently of comparatively modern origin, and arose only when the Scriptures contained in it were no longer used for reading. But the pagan usage of going right-hand wise round any object has continued to prevail more or less through all the history of the Irish Church, and may be seen in practice at holy wells in the present day. It was not exclusively Celtic, and appears to have been in use among the Greeks and Romans."[3]

The exclusion of women from the domestic life of the saints of the second period is one of those marks of inferiority referred to in the account of them. It was contrary to the feelings of the Irish, as already mentioned, and seems to have called forth remonstrance from the sex. The legend of S. Canair and S. Senan of Iniscattery Island, immortalised by Moore, seems to have this for its object. When she sought

[1] *Cath. bhuaidh*, Reeves, "Columba," p. 332.
[2] O'Donnell, in Reeves, ibid., p. 249.
[3] On the ceremonial turn called Desiul, by Sir R. Ferguson, "Proc. R.I.A., June 1876."

admission to his island, that she might end her life there, he replied, "Women enter not this island." "How canst thou say that?" she replied. "Christ is no worse than thou. Christ came to redeem women no less than to redeem men. No less did He suffer for the sake of women than for the sake of men. Women have given service and tendance unto Christ and His Apostles. No less than men do women enter the heavenly kingdom. Why, then, shouldst thou not take women to thee in thine island?" To these strong arguments he can only reply, "Thou art stubborn."[1]

The schools appear to have been at their highest degree of prosperity, when it was suddenly interrupted by the great plague which ravaged Europe in the sixth and seventh centuries, and carried off, as is supposed, one-third of the human race. It was known as the yellow plague, and appeared at three different periods —first in 550, and again in a more severe form in 664, when, according to the annalist Tigernach, "abbots and kings innumerable died." The English students at that time in Ireland were carried off in great numbers by it, as we learn from Bede; others were dispersed abroad. A favourite refuge was an island, as described in a poem in the Book of Hymns by a lector[2] of Cork, composed in this period of terror. In the Preface it is said to have been written "to protect his school from the pestilence, when he was on a voyage to a certain island, fleeing from the pestilence till there were nine waves between them and the island, for pestilence does not pass beyond, as the wise tell."[3] The plague appeared for the third time in

---

[1] "Lives from the Book of Lismore," p. 219. [2] Colman ua Cluasaig.
[3] Goidelica, 2nd ed., p. 124. On these visitations, see Reeves' "Columba," pp. 182, 183. It was called the *buidhe chonnaill*, *connall* being the stalk of ripe corn, the yellow colour of which resembled that of the sufferer.

684, acccording to the Annals of Ulster, and again the following year, when a "great mortality of children" is recorded. These seem to have been the orphans of those who died of the plague. Great efforts were made by some of the clergy to save their lives, and it is particularly recorded of Ultan of Ardbraccan that he adopted a singular contrivance for the purpose. It is referred to as follows in the Calendar of Œngus at September : "Greatly play the children round Ultan of Ardbraccan ;" and the Commentary explains that the children were "the babes of the women whom the yellow plague slew," and it goes on to explain why they played around him :—" This was Ultan wont to do : to cut off the cows' teats, and to pour milk into them, and to put them into the children's mouths." [1]

This plague is connected with the subject of overpopulation by the writer of the Life of S. Gerald of Mayo. According to him, there was a scarcity of land in Ireland at this time, that is, of arable land, the greater part of the country being a forest ; and the population having increased, a great difficulty was felt in obtaining land. According to him, an edict was put forth by Dermod and Blathmac, kings of Ireland,[2] that the clergy and laity should assemble, for there was a great famine in the land, because so great was the multitude of people that there was not enough of land for all. Therefore no one was allowed to hold more than nine acres, or seven of arable land, eight of coarse, and nine of wood.[3] In this state of things the seniors advised "that the people should assemble, and fast, and pray to God to reduce the number of the lower class by

[1] Œngus, pp. cxxxvi., cxlii.   [2] A.D. 657.
[3] This regulation is also mentioned in the Preface of the Hymn of S. Colman referred to, but with a slight difference, each man being allowed nine acres of bog, nine of land, and nine of forest.

a pestilence, so that the rest might live in comfort." Ultimately the decision was left to S. Gerald, and S. Fechin, Abbot of Fore (Westmeath). Gerald gave it as his opinion that it was wrong to ask God to take away people by a pestilence, and referred to the feeding of the Israelites in the wilderness, and of the 5000 by our Lord; adding, "Even now, by a few small seeds in the ground, He feeds the human race." Fechin, on the contrary, said regard should be had to the number who prayed, for all the nobles of the land prayed for the removal of the lower class. After this, it is said, an angel of the Lord announced that the great people should die for offering so wicked a prayer, and, accordingly, the two kings and a multitude of nobles and clergy, including S. Fechin himself, were carried off by the yellow plague.[1] The settlement as to the amount of land to be allowed to each family indicates, Sir Henry Maine observes, "the change from a system of collective to a system of restricted enjoyment,"[2] and this in consequence of the increase of population. We may regard this increase as due in some degree at least to the preaching of the Gospel, which at its first acceptance tended to mitigate the tribal wars and lessen the loss of life, as we have seen in the case of Caillin. It is remarkable that the name of Colman, the "peaceful (or dove-like) one," should have been so extensively popular as to have been chosen by no less than 226 Irish saints.[3] And one can hardly attribute this to any other cause than a desire on their part to be regarded as preachers of peace on earth and goodwill to men, while at the same time it was a quiet protest against the warlike habits of the time.

[1] Life of S. Gerald, in "Dictionary of National Biography."
[2] The Early History of Institutions, p. 114, 4th ed., 1885.
[3] Book of Leinster, 366g and 367 a, b, c.

CHAPTER V.

SECOND AND THIRD PERIODS—IRISH SAINTS ABROAD.

1. GREAT BRITAIN.

THE missions of the Irish Church to other lands were so extensive that a separate treatise would be needed to do them justice. The time has not yet come for a full account of all, as the foreign sources of information have not yet been thoroughly examined, but all accounts agree that the exodus from Ireland in the sixth, seventh, and eighth centuries was very great. The movement took in the period in which the Third Order of Saints flourished, and it is, therefore, necessary to give the description of them from the same document which has been already quoted.

"They were holy presbyters and a few bishops, one hundred in number, who dwelt in desert places, and lived on herbs and water and the alms of the faithful. They shunned private property. They had different rules and Masses, and different tonsures, and a different Paschal festival. For some celebrated the Resurrection on the fourteenth moon or sixteenth. They continued until the great plague, A.D. 665." The influences which led to this great movement from Ireland were various. Chief among them was the passion for the ascetic life which took hold of the ecclesiastics of the third period in a remarkable manner, when the example of the Egyptian hermits[1] was eagerly imitated. To remove far from human society and dwell in solitude, given up to meditation on Divine things, was their great object. Sometimes they would put off from shore in their frail vessels covered with hides, and reaching the open sea, draw in their oars and suffer the wind to waft them they cared not whither. Sometimes they retired to the depths of the forest, and taking up their abode in a hollow tree, or forming a rough shelter of branches, dwelt there, living on roots and water, and becoming so familiar with the wild animals that the birds are said to have perched on their hands. To the sympathetic and imaginative spirit of one of them,[2] it seemed as though the branches and leaves of the trees sang sweet songs to him and celestial music alleviated the severity of his life. But this temper was unsuited to the practical business of life, and, when an ecclesiastic of this class had to deal with the errors and failings of mankind he found himself unsuccessful, and preferred to go abroad and serve God in other lands. There he could live as he desired, and the very qualities which caused him to be disliked at home would attract the admiration and regard of the heathen and half-heathen populations abroad.

Another reason for the outpouring of Irish missionaries was the very large numbers of ecclesiastics. Trained in the Holy Scriptures and fitted for the clerical life in the numerous monastic schools, and abounding in zeal, there was no adequate field of labour for them at home.

When the comparatively small population of Ire-

---

[1] An account of their settlements in the Egyptian deserts was accessible in the Dialogues of Sulpicius Severus in the "Book of Armagh."
[2] S. Kevin of Glendalough. See "Dictionary of National Biography."

land in the seventh and eighth centuries is considered, it seems strange that there could have been so many as to warrant S. Bernard's comparison of them to a flood, or Aldhelm's account of them as coming to England in fleets. The explanation of this is to be found in a law of the Brehon Code, in which, among the rights of the Church, it is declared that "every first birth of every human couple, the mother being a lawful wife," belonged to the Church; and if there were eleven or more children, of whom not less than ten were sons, the Church was entitled to demand another son.[1] This was evidently taken from the Mosaic law,[2] by which the first-born of the Israelites were given to Aaron and his successors. "Rights such as these were never," as the editors observe, "claimed as against the whole body of the laity by any other Christian Church in Europe." The Church, on her part, was bound to teach the child thus claimed, and as there were no exemptions, all classes of society, from kings' sons downwards, were found in the monastic schools. The object aimed at seems to have been to train up ecclesiastics, and such was the state of society and the unsettled habits of the people, that it might well seem that a Christian life was almost impossible except in the peaceful society of such a community. One of the difficulties of carrying out such a law was the probability of a youth becoming dissatisfied with the life and giving up his studies. There was no supreme executive[3] to enforce the law and compel him to remain, and the object was, therefore, sought to be attained by other means. He might be deterred by learning the serious con-

---

[1] Senchus Mor (Brehon Laws), vol. iii., p. 57.   [2] Num. xviii. 15.
[3] Sir H. Maine discusses the sanctions of the Brehon Law, and concludes that in heathen times they must have been supernatural, as we see here they were under Christianity.

sequences of abandoning the religious life. This appears to be the motive of the historical romance, the Life of Kellach, son of Eoghan Bel, King of Connaught. He had been placed, in accordance with this law, as a student in Clonmacnois, under S. Kieran. But his father was mortally wounded in battle, and having no other son old enough to succeed him, advised his chieftains to ask S. Kieran to permit the young prince to leave the monastery and become king. Kieran refused, and Kellach, yielding to the persuasions of the chieftains, left clandestinely, and in consequence was cursed by the saint. After a time the rude life of the laity palled on him, and he repented of his act. Returning to the monastery, he was received by S. Kieran and permitted to resume his studies, became eminent for sanctity, and was forgiven by the saint. But the curse could not be recalled, and the story recounts the various incidents which eventually led up to his violent death.[1] The curse, however, had no further operation, and his salvation was not affected by it. The same impression was intended to be conveyed by an anecdote in the Life of S. Fintan (or Munnu). Dimma, a chieftain in the county of Wexford, had two sons, one of whom was placed with Fintan at Taghmon, the other under Cuan at Airbre. Going to visit them accompanied by his chieftains, he found the son who was under Cuan's charge dressed in purple, with a quiver of purple arrows,[2] his writing-tablet bound with brass slung over his shoulder, and wearing shoes embroidered with gold and bound with brass. The other, on the contrary, was with some boys walking

---

[1] Lebar Brecc (Facsimile), pp. 272*b*–277*a*, and Actt. S.S. Boll., May 1, p. 104, to which my attention was originally drawn by Bishop Reeves.

[2] This is one of the few mentions of archery in Irish literature.

in front of the waggons chanting psalms aloud, dressed in a mantle of black undyed wool, a short white tunic edged with black, and common shoes. The king was displeased at his mean apparel, and remonstrated with Fintan. But the saint assured him that the well-dressed youth would meet with a violent death, whereas the other would eventually be a sage, a scribe, a bishop, and an anchorite, and would go to heaven.[1]

The result of the law, thus enforced as far as possible by the aid of supernatural terrors, was the training of a vast number of ecclesiastics, by whom the army of missionaries was constantly recruited.

A further cause of the movement we are considering was the great plague, which has been already referred to. A general flight took place from Ireland at that period, and swelled the numbers who went abroad from higher motives.

The earliest missionary who went forth from Ireland was Colum Cillé, more generally known as Columba. He, with Patrick and Brigit, is accounted one of the patrons of Ireland, and for this reason, and because of his great and successful labours, he demands a particular notice. His career belongs both to Scotland and Ireland, and his countrymen were proud of him, as diffusing abroad the light of the Gospel, which he had learned in his native land. In allusion to this, a legend tells us that S. Finnian saw in vision two moons arising in the sky, one of gold, the other of silver. The silver moon was S. Kieran of Clonmacnois; but the moon of gold, which rose in the North of Ireland and lighted Ireland, Scotland, and the West of England with its radiance,

---

[1] Codex Salmanticensis, p. 405, London, 1888, and Life of S. Fintan, in "Dictionary of National Biography;" Law of Fosterage, Senchus Mor, vol. ii. p. 148, 149; Haddan and Stubbs, vol. ii., pt. ii., p. 331.

was Colum Cillé.[1] He was born at Gartan, in Donegal, in A.D. 521, and being closely related to the reigning families of both Ireland and Scotland he occupied a position of commanding influence, without reference to his talents, energy, and religious zeal. When of fit age he was placed successively under the charge of the two Finnians, and then of Movi at Glasnevin, who soon after died of the yellow plague which caused the dispersion of the school.

He began his career by founding the Monastery of Derry at the age of twenty-five, and he subsequently established one at Durrow, the importance of which is noticed by Bede. His great activity and energy, together with his connection with the royal family, led to his being mixed up with political matters, and he incurred some censure. This seems to have influenced him to move away from immediate contact with those entanglements. Ireland evidently afforded no scope for his immense energy and zeal. Accordingly, he passed over to Scotland with twelve companions in 563, being then in the forty-second year of his age, and with the consent of the Scottish king, his relative, occupied the island of Hy, now called Iona. It was on the border of the territories of the Picts and the Scots, a colony of Christians, who, under stress of famine,[2] had emigrated from Ireland previously, giving to their new home the name of Dalriada, after their former territory. The conversion of the Picts, the dwellers in the wilderness, was the noble object that fired his imagination and inspired

---

[1] Colum Cillé, or Colum (also Columb) of the Church. When the diminutive is added it becomes Colum-án (Colman), of whom 226 are enumerated in the "Book of Leinster." When Colomb, the other form of the name, is so treated it becomes Columb-án (Columbán), or with the Latin termination, Columbanus. Once more, with a prefix and another suffix, it is Mo-cholum-og (Mocholmog), five of whom are in the "Martyrology of Donegal."

[2] Lebar Brecc, p. 238*d*, col. 2, line 16.

his zeal. In later times it came to be believed that he was sentenced to banishment, but his biographer, Adamnan, knew nothing of it. In pursuance of his mission he traversed every part of the Pictish territory. All the country north of the Grampians, that is, nearly all modern Scotland, was visited by him, and his marvellous energy was only equalled by the undaunted courage with which he penetrated the remotest haunts of the heathen people. Embarking in his frail coracle covered with hides, he faced the stormy seas which beat upon the western isles to bear to them the message of the Cross.

The work of his which was most fruitful in its ultimate results was the establishment of the Monastery of Hy, which was for so long the citadel of Christianity in Northern Europe, when it was almost swept away by the barbarian invasions. On the death of Conall, lord of Scottish Dalriada, he was succeeded by Aidan, his first cousin, who, to strengthen his position, sought consecration at the hands of S. Columba. After some objection he complied, "ordaining and bestowing his benediction on Aidan."[1] This rite, now performed for the first time in Western Europe, was borrowed, like so many other practices of the Irish, from the East,[2] where the Greek emperors were so inaugurated. M. de Montalembert[3] says the event took place at Iona, and that Aidan was inaugurated "on a great stone called the 'stone of Destiny.'" The stone, he adds, was removed to the Castle of Dunstaffnage, then to Scone, and finally to Westminster, where it is now beneath the coronation

---

[1] Dr. Killen, Eccl. Hist., vol. i. p. 36, thinks the ceremony of inaugurating a king the same as the conferring of Holy Orders, and draws what he regards as an argument for Presbyterian ordination from this incident. [2] H. and S., vol. ii. p. 108.

[3] Les Moines d'Occident, vol. iii. p. 197; Paris, 1866.

chair. He gives no authority, and there is nothing
of all this in Adamnan's Life of S. Columba, and it is
a safe remark of Dr. O'Conors's, that "when the 'stone
of Destiny' was carried [from Ireland] to North Britain
is not certain." Dr. Petrie did not believe it [1] to be
the coronation stone, nor does Mr. Skene; and Shake-
speare seems to have been of the same mind when he
made Richmond describe Richard III. as

"A base, foul stone made precious by the foil
Of England's chair, where he is falsely set." [2]

An important event in Columba's life was his attend-
ance at the Convention of Drumceatt, at which some
differences between the Scottish colony and the parent
Government were arranged. S. Columba was received
by the assembly with great distinction, a musical performance [3] forming part of the proceedings. He was
so much elated by this that Baithin, afterwards his
successor, quoted a passage from S. Basil [4] to abate
his pride. After twenty-two years more of incessant
activity in the supervision of his various establish-
ments in Ireland and Scotland, and in the quiet work
of transcribing the Scriptures, which was the occupation of the closing days of his life, he passed away
by a peaceful and happy death in his own church at
Iona, on his knees before the altar, and with the words
of prayer on his lips. So ended a noble career, and
thus calmly did the great soldier pass to his rest.
His mission inspired the zeal of others who joined
him in his labours; amongst these were Ernán, Lug-
neus, Baithin, Findchan, Cailtan, and Diuni. About

[1] The stone is known in Irish tradition as the Lia Fail, but there is
no authority for translating it "the stone of Destiny." Dr. Keating has
it "the stone of Failias," an imaginary town in Denmark from which
it came.
[2] Richard III., Act v. sc. 3.   [3] Termed *aidbse*.
[4] The passage may have been the following : "Virtue consists in aiming at humility and abhorring the swelling of pride."

the same time came from Ireland Moluog of Lismore, in Argyll, and afterwards, in A.D. 600, Congan, in 617 Donnan of Egg, and in 671 Maelruba of Applecross,[1] who, each in his own district, carried out the work begun by their great forerunner.

The going forth of Columba was due entirely to his own missionary zeal, but the later mission to England, which now claims our attention, owed its origin to an application from that country for Christian teaching.

Oswy, over-king of Northumberland, had been an exile in Ireland, where he received the Christian faith and was baptized. On subsequently returning to England to occupy the throne in A.D. 634, he made a request to the elders of Ireland that a bishop should be sent to him for the purpose of establishing a mission to his heathen subjects. His kingdom extended as far north as Edinburgh, and included, besides Northumberland, the present counties of Cumberland, Westmoreland, Lancashire, Yorkshire, and the bishopric of Durham. Previously nominally Christianised by Paulinus, the Roman missionary, it had relapsed into paganism on the death of King Edwin in 627.

Such was its condition when Aidan was sent from Iona in response to the king's appeal and began his labours there. His first proceeding was to set up a monastery after the Irish fashion at Lindisfarne, and here were the headquarters of his mission for the seventeen years during which it lasted. On his death in 651 Finan succeeded him. He also was from Iona, the great missionary centre of the Irish Church, and his zeal and devotion were worthy of its high reputation. To him was due the conversion of the East Saxons, embracing Essex, Middlesex, and

[1] The situation of this was first identified by Bishop Reeves.

half of Hertfordshire; and also the extensive kingdom of Mercia, occupying the centre of England from Derby to Oxfordshire, and from Hereford to Bedfordshire. Finan was succeeded by Colman, who was not inferior to his predecessors, and on the close of his mission in 664 the position may be thus described. Wessex was under a bishop ordained in Gaul, but in communion with the British bishops; Sussex was still heathen; Kent and East Anglia only, were in communion with Rome and Canterbury. So that sixty-eight years after Augustine, and in the time of his successor, there remained only those two counties as the fruits of his mission, the whole of the rest of England except Wessex and Sussex being in full communion with the Irish Church. All this was effected within the space of thirty years by the three Irish bishops and their assistants. It is, therefore, a mistake to give Augustine the credit of the conversion of England. His work was not permanent, as appears from the relapse of the people of Essex, East Anglia, and even Kent.

"Aidan and Finán," says Archbishop Ussher, "deserve to be honoured by the English nation with as venerable a remembrance as Austin the monk and his followers."[1] "Truth requires us to declare," says Bishop Wordsworth, "that S. Austin from Italy ought not to be called the Apostle of England, and much less the Apostle of Scotland, but that title ought to be given to S. Columba and his followers from the Irish school of Iona."[2]

The Irish mission to England came abruptly to a close owing to the differences between the Irish and Roman Churches on the subject of Easter,[3] as

[1] Ussher, Works, vol. iv. p. 357.
[2] Wordsworth, Occasional Sermons, p. 81. [3] Bede, Book v. chap. 20.

well as on matters of ritual. The Irish observed Easter on the Sunday between the fourteenth and twentieth of the moon, which was originally the general practice, and they determined the moon by the ancient cycle of eighty-four years usually attributed to Sulpicius Severus, but really of earlier date. This had been their usage from the period of the conversion of Ireland, but the Frankish invasion of Gaul and the Saxon occupation of the East of England placed a barrier of heathenism between them and the Continent, which cut off intercourse with it for a century and a half. During that period many changes were made at Rome. A new cycle of 532 years was invented; and this being afterwards set aside, another of nineteen succeeded. The limits of Easter were also changed, and were now the 15th and 21st. While these alterations were going on abroad the Irish Church was perfecting its internal organisation unaffected by external influence, and thus, when the mission of Augustine to Britain brought the Roman clergy in contact with the Irish, they found them differing in many points from themselves and resolute in maintaining their own views. And they were sustained by their Church at home in their opposition to what they regarded as innovations on primitive practice which were pressed on them by the Roman missionaries. Bitter feelings were exhibited on both sides, and Laurence, Archbishop of Canterbury, in a letter to the Irish written A.D. 605, complained that an Irish bishop had refused to eat under the same roof with him. The dispute culminated in a Synod held in A.D. 634 at Streanashalch, near Whitby, in Yorkshire. On the Irish side were Colman, Bishop of Lindisfarne, supported by his clergy, and Bishop Cedd of Essex, with the Abbess Hilda.

F

On the other were Bishop Agilberct, with four priests, one of whom was Wilfrid, a trained controversialist. At the outset it was evident that Colman was at a disadvantage, as he spoke in Irish and had to use an interpreter, while King Oswy and his son, who were joint-presidents, were both favourable to the Roman system.

The ground taken by Colman was, that he received his observance of Easter from his elders, by whom he had been commissioned; all his forefathers, men beloved of God, had observed it; it was the custom of S. John, the beloved disciple of our Lord, and the Churches of the East. Wilfrid claimed to have on his side the Universal Church; his Easter was instituted by S. Peter, to whom our Lord had given the keys of the kingdom of Heaven. This latter statement caught the ear of the king, who asked Colman was this so, and could he show any similar promise to Columba? Colman admitted that the words were spoken to S. Peter, and being unable to show that any like communication was made to Columba, the king decided in Wilfrid's favour. In doing so he alleged that he was afraid the keeper of the keys might not admit him into heaven if he displeased him. The barbarian king may have believed that there was an actual gate and key, but whether he did or not, the result was a foregone conclusion, for the reasons stated. It does not appear whether Colman offered any interpretation of the words, "Thou art Peter," &c. He might have thought it useless to prolong the discussion, otherwise he would have had no difficulty in showing what the interpretation was which the Irish divines placed on the text. Thus in the Book of Hymns belonging to the eleventh or twelfth century the following is found: "When it is said, Thou art Peter, &c., it is interpreted Peter confessing [Christ] (Matt. xvi. 16). Whosoever, therefore, will enter into the kingdom of Heaven must acknowledge God by faith, like Peter."[1] So also Dungal, "the famous Irishman," appointed master of the school of Pavia by Charles the Bald: "On this rock, therefore, which thou hast confessed I will build my Church. For the rock was Christ, the foundation on which Peter himself was built, for other foundation can no man lay than that is laid which is Jesus Christ."[2] The Irish school seem to have taken their interpretation from Origen, whose views were much regarded in Ireland.[3] "If any one," he says, "confess when flesh and blood have not revealed it unto him, but our Father in Heaven, he too shall obtain the promised blessings, as the letter of the Gospel saith indeed to the great S. Peter, but as its spirit teacheth to every man who hath become like what that great Peter was."[4]

Colman's reference to S. John and the Churches of the East had a certain amount of truth in it, inasmuch as the Eastern Church, like the Irish, observed Easter on the fourteenth day of the moon, if it was Sunday, whereas in the Roman Church the earliest day was the fifteenth. S. John was an especial favourite with the Irish, who spoke of him as "John of the bosom," from his reclining on our Lord's breast. When his Gospel was transcribed they used the finest vellum and took the greatest pains with the

---

[1] Liber Hymnorum, part i. p. 12.
[2] Migne Patrologia, cv. col. 507. So also the "Codex Maelbrigte," by Bishop Reeves, p. 22, and the gloss on verse 3 of the Hymn of Cummean Fota, "Liber Hymnorum," part i. p. 73. Dungal (flourished 811–827) was termed "Præcipuus Scotorum."
[3] See the Würzburgh Glosses at Romans xiii. 3, and Kanonensammlung, Einleitung, p. xxi.
[4] Farrar's "Life of Christ," vol. ii. p. 16, 15th edition.

text. The celebrated John Scotus, contrasting him with S. Peter, expresses this feeling: "Most high soared Peter when he said, 'Thou art the Son of the living God;' but he went higher who understood that that same Christ was God of God before all time—the spiritual-winged, swift-flying, God-seeing S. John."[1]

"Colman, on the conclusion of the Conference," Bede tells us, "perceiving that his doctrine was rejected and his sect despised, took with him such as cared to follow him, and would not comply with the Catholic Easter and coronal tonsure, and went back to Ireland." He adds that the number who accompanied him was about thirty English and all his own followers. With this party he withdrew first to Iona, from which he had originally come, and then to Inis-bo-fin, a small island off the coast of Galway. It was a great sacrifice thus to abandon the work into which he had thrown himself with all the enthusiasm of his nature. The ceaseless round of services at Lindisfarne; the missionary journeys; the preaching, teaching, transcribing and illuminating books, and all the manifold occupations of a flourishing mission—all were given up at the call of duty. The wrench was great, but he could not bring himself to surrender the rights of his Church at the bidding of strangers.

Wilfrid, his opponent, eventually became archbishop in his room, and so pursued the remaining adherents of the Irish Church that those of Irish birth were obliged either to accept the new system or leave the country.[2] It has already been mentioned that at the time of the Synod nearly the whole of England was in communion with the Church of Ireland, and it must excite surprise to hear that only

---

[1] *Church Quarterly Review*, July 9, 1882.
[2] Bede, Eccl. Hist., iii. chap. 28, p. 140.

thirty Englishmen cast in their lot with S. Colman and his party—teachers, so loved and valued as they were, who had educated[1] a whole generation of Englishmen.

But there is reason to believe that there was subsequently a very large emigration of Englishmen who sympathised with the Irish. The Life of S. Gerald of Mayo, a composition which has been much criticised for its anachronisms, nevertheless has preserved many curious facts connected with this period. According to it, Gerald, with three brothers, Balan, Berikert, and Hubritan, and a sister, left England after the defeat of Colman and came over to Ireland with a great many followers. They first landed in Connaught, at the mouth of the Shannon, afterwards proceeded to the River Moy, and finally obtained a settlement in Mayo. Gerald built a church, called by him "the Church of the Pilgrims,"[2] in allusion to their being strangers, and also Gerald's Church. He had been Abbot of Winchester, according to one account, and the number who came with him and followed him is said to have been three thousand. Dr. Lanigan[3] ridicules the story, but the matter cannot be dismissed in that off-hand way, for most of the facts are corroborated by the local traditions of the places in Ireland where the "pilgrims" settled. Balan took up his abode in the county of Galway, and with him a colony of West Saxons from the neighbourhood of Winchester. The district in which they settled was known in Irish records as "the Saxons' abode,"[4] which is still the name of a prebend in the diocese of Tuam. Berikert is the patron

---

[1] "Imbuebantur præceptoribus Scottis parvuli Anglorum" (Bede, Eccl. Hist., iii. 3).
[2] *Cill n-ailither*, or *Tempoll Garailt* (Petrie, Round Towers, p. 144).
[3] Eccl. Hist., iii. 167.   [4] *Tech Saxan.*

saint of Tullylease, in the north-west of the county
of Cork, where his tombstone, with an inscription of
the ninth century, still stands. This place was called,
from his party, "the Saxon territory."[1] Hubritan
and his followers settled in the neighbourhood of
Kinsale, in the county of Cork, where the parish of
Tisaxon,[2] "the Saxons' abode," still bears witness
to his residence there; and the adjoining parish of
Kilbrittain,[3] across the River Bandon, is probably
named from him. There were also, according to
local tradition, sisters. Of these Lassair is still remembered at Cillasaragh, near Boherboy, in the county
of Cork; Latiern at Cullen, in the north of the same
county; and another, known merely as the "yellow-
haired maiden,"[4] at Drumtariffe, in the county of
Cork, and Killeedy, in the county of Limerick, where
a church still bears her name. The Life of S. Gerald
describes the party as brothers, but when we take the
dates into consideration, it is evident that they must
have been brothers only in a religious sense, for Colman
died in 675; Gerald, according to Ussher, in 697;
Berikert in 839 ("Four Masters"). Thus an interval
of 142 years separates Gerald from Berikert, and
therefore they could not be brothers[5] in the literal
sense. It seems evident that successive parties left
England, for the "Book of Ballymote"[6] states that at
the end of the seventh century there were one hundred
Saxon saints in Mayo under Gerald, and the Litany
of Œngus has an invocation of the 3300 saints with

[1] *Tuath Saxan.* These places were first identified by Bishop Reeves.
[2] According to the Calendar of Œngus, clxxxi., he settled in *Ui-echach*, a district including Kinsale.
[3] Perhaps *Cill*[*Hu*]*britain*.   [4] *Ingen buidhe.*
[5] So much were the terms brother and sister used by the Irish solely in a religious sense, that in order to express the blood relationship it became necessary to say "real brother" or "real sister." Thus *brathai* became *derbhrathair*, and *siur*, *derbhshiur*, which are the terms now in use.   [6] Facsimile, p. 233*b*, line 3.

Gerald the bishop, and with the fifty saints of Leyney in Connaught, who are interred at Mayo of the Saxons.[1] The emigrants had friends in the West Saxon district, who supplied them with funds and kept up a constant communication with them. Gerald divided his monks into three parties, one of which he sent to England to obtain sustenance for the brethren labouring in Ireland; from which it appears that deputations to England to collect funds are not a modern institution, as might be supposed.[2]

After the defeat at Whitby the general adoption of the Roman Easter was only a question of time. The South of Ireland accepted it about 650, influenced by the letter of Pope Honorius to the Irish. The North of Ireland resisted until 703, when they were induced by Adamnan to conform. The Picts held out until 710, and South Wales till 802.

The emigration of these ancient Pilgrim Fathers naturally dropped out of notice in after times when the Roman system was generally adopted. The subject would be unpopular, and hence few allusions are found to the circumstances in Irish literature. It is, however, an interesting evidence of the attachment of the English to their teachers, and it illustrates the strong feelings called forth by this contest, in which the liberties of the Irish Church were felt to be at stake.

Amongst the others who laboured in England, one of the most remarkable was Fursa, who died A.D. 650. " From his boyhood he gave his attention to the reading of the Holy Scriptures and monastic discipline." After pursuing his studies for some time he went to the South of Ireland to visit his relatives, and " by his discourse to sow the spiritual seed of the sacred Word

---

[1] Book of Leinster, p. 373*h*, 59.
[2] The Life of Gerald, in " Dictionary of National Biography."

among them." It was here that he had the first of the strange visions which were placed on record shortly after his death. One day, when overtaken by weakness, he lost all feeling, darkness came over him, and he was carried into the nearest house like a dead man. While in this state he seemed to descry four hands extended from above to him by two angels, who, holding him by the arms, flew beneath him with snow-white pinions. The hands, which were under the wings (Deut. xxiii. 27), sustained him on either side, and he appeared to see angelic forms through the darkness. Ascending still higher, he beheld the faces of holy angels shining with marvellous brilliance, but nothing corporeal could be seen beyond this effulgence. A third shining angel bearing a snow-white shield and a sword of dazzling splendour now advanced before him. These three bright inhabitants of heaven, by the rustling of their wings, the soft music of their hymns, and their lovely aspect, had a soothing effect on him. For they sang, one taking the lead, "The saints shall go from virtue to virtue; the God of gods shall be seen in Zion" (Ps. lxxxiii. 8 : Vulgate). Then one of the celestial band commanded the angel who preceded Fursa to restore him to his body. Soon after, the colour began to return to his face, the angelic voices ceased, and the words of the bystanders became audible, and he returned, as it were, to life.

On the third day after this, at midnight, darkness again overshadowed him, his feet grew cold and rigid, and becoming insensible, he again heard dreadful voices of a great multitude crying and urging him to go forth. Then he saw the aforesaid two angels and the armed angel standing at his head, and heard the soft music of their hymns. Raising him up, they bore him aloft, and he heard the cries and lamentations of demons. They fought, but he could only see terrible and shadowy forms through the gloom. They shot fiery arrows at him and his guardians, which the armed angel received on his shield (Eph. vi. 16). Then an argument took place between the demons accusing and the angels defending him; and the story proceeds: "He was told to behold the world, and looking down from above, he saw a dark valley beneath, in which burned four fires. When asked what these were he was unable to tell, and was then informed that these were the fires which would set fire to and consume the world. They were the fires of falsehood, cupidity, discord, and impiety. Shortly after, the evil spirits vanished, and he saw glorious light and heard soft music. Two holy men, whom he recognised, then told him to go back to the world for a time and preach to all that vengeance was at hand. The end of the world, however, was not to be yet, but the human race was to be afflicted by famine and dreadful plagues." These visions, which occurred about 627, are evidently connected with the time of general terror, caused by the different appearances of the great plague already referred to.[1] The general flight of the population, the disturbance of society, and the panic caused by the devastations of this terrible scourge unhinged the minds of many, and, acting on a highly sensitive temperament, were, at least to some extent, the cause of his visions. They seem also consistent with a cataleptic seizure. For ten years "he preached the Word of God without respect of persons," proclaiming in earnest language the judgments of the Lord against sin. Eventually, wearied by the crowds who gathered round him, he left Ireland with a few companions, and crossing over to

[1] P. 68.

England, arrived in East Anglia, where he was hospitally received by King Sigebert. There he established the Monastery of Cnobersburgh or Burgcastle, in Suffolk, on a plot of land granted by the king; but he retired himself to a hermitage.

The effect of his preaching appears to have been overpowering. Bede tells of the agitation of a monk who, when giving an account of his sermon, broke out into a profuse perspiration from mere terror, though it was the severest season of the year and he was thinly clad. One cannot doubt that this eloquence was effective in awakening ideas of religion in the sluggish minds of the Saxons of East Anglia.[1]

[1] Codex Salmanticensis, p. 77, London, 1888; Bede's Eccl. Hist., lib. iii. cap. 19.

CHAPTER VI.

SECOND AND THIRD PERIODS—IRISH SAINTS ABROAD.

2. THE CONTINENT.

RELIGION at this time was at its lowest ebb on the Continent of Europe, according to the Life of Deicola. Throughout almost all Gaul and Germany, the author says, the fervour of religion had grown cold, not only among the secular clergy, but even in the monasteries. There, where formerly, in the words of Jeremiah, the stars gave forth their light, increasing negligence prevailed. Sarcely one could be found who was fervent in the spirit. The irruption of the barbarian races into Western Europe, which had wrought this evil to the Church, had also left heathen populations in many districts to whom the Gospel had not yet been preached, and whom the Church, in its impoverished and depressed condition, was unable to evangelise. In this state of things, the writer above quoted goes on, the Lord Jesus Christ, grieving for His Church, neglected and almost destroyed by the sloth and ignorance of priests and bishops, caused a most brilliant light from Ireland, the blessed Columbanus, to appear on the frontiers of Gaul. Columbanus, to whom the new religious life of the Continent owed so much, had been educated at Bangor,[1] in Ulster, under

[1] There were three Bangors—Bangor Maur, on the Menai; Bangor yscoed, where the monks were slaughtered A.D. 613; and Bangor in Ulster, the mother of the former two.

Comgall, the master of so many saints. Leaving Ireland with twelve companions about A.D. 590, he passed over to England, and after a short delay continued his journey to France, and directing his course to the north-east, reached the wild forest-clad district of the Vosges. On his way he had an interview with Laurence, one of Augustine's clergy, and afterwards Archbishop of Canterbury. The meeting was a memorable one : on one side was the representative of the Roman Church whose mission it was to assist in the conversion of England and to advance the authority of Rome ; on the other was the Irish abbot, the representative of the Irish Church, going forth on a similar errand to France, and with the intention of carrying out there, as far as possible, the system of the Irish Church. On that occasion, as the letter of Laurence and others preserved by Bede informs us, the differences between the Churches came under review, and Columbanus must have learned the attitude which he might expect the French clergy to assume to his. Whether on this account or not, he made choice of a district in which he would be likely to experience little interference. It has been observed that the missionaries to the Continent who came from the northern part of Britain, from Ireland and from Scotland, where the monastery was the centre of Church life and bishops were subordinate to abbots, preferred to labour in countries where heathen races of German extraction dwelt. Amongst them they at once erected monasteries and evangelised the territory, setting up the same institutions as at home. It was different with the Saxon missionaries from the South of England, who selected Southern Germany, where the institutions were in harmony with their own and no friction was likely to occur.[1] The party of missionaries settled first at Anegray, and soon attracted so many followers that Columbanus was enabled to establish his first monastery at Luxeuil, in the densest part of the forest, about eight miles from Anegray. The unworldly and devoted lives of the party produced a deep impression on the rude inhabitants. The solemnisation of divine offices, St. Bernard says, was kept up by companies, who relieved each other in succession, so that not for one moment, day or night, was there an intermission of their devotion. Soon it became necessary to establish other monasteries to accommodate the numbers who joined them. One of these was Fontaines, so called from the many springs there. This, according to Mabillon,[2] is the first instance of priories or small monasteries subject to the chief monastery and its abbots, as colonies are to the mother-country. His observation is applicable to the Church on the Continent, but it is not correct as a general statement, as the arrangement was common in the Church of Ireland, from which, as in this instance, it was introduced abroad. Columbanus continued to follow the Irish custom as to Easter, and notwithstanding the remoteness of his position, he experienced much hostility from the French bishops. In self-defence he wrote several letters, one to a French Synod, and another to Gregory I., whose interference he requested in the matter, telling him at the same time that the "Western Churches" (*i.e.*, those of Britain and Ireland) would not agree to anything contrary to the authority of S. Jerome. Further troubled on the same burning question of Easter, he wrote pointing out to the Pope that Polycarp and Pope Anicetus had

---

[1] Wasserschleben, Kanonensammlung, Einleitung, 2nd ed. p. xliii.
[2] Annal. Benedict., lib. viii. sec. ii.

agreed to differ on this question, and in conclusion he claimed the right of the Irish to observe their own laws according to the regulation of the 150 fathers of the Council of Constantinople.[1] The further continuance of the controversy was probably prevented by the troubles in which Columbanus was involved by his remonstrance with Thierry, King of Burgundy, for his immorality. The king, stirred up by his mother Brunehaut, was induced to expel Columbanus from his kingdom, and in order to make sure of his departure he sent him down the Loire under escort to Nantes, and there had him placed on board a vessel bound for Ireland. The vessel, however, being driven on shore, Columbanus was free, and making his way to the residence of a friendly prince, was by him conducted to the Rhine at his own desire. Ascending the river he reached the canton of Zug, and subsequently passing on to the Lake of Constance, founded the Monastery of Bregenz. Thierry, having subsequently extended his dominions by conquest, now became ruler of Bregenz, and Columbanus, fearing the intrigues of the unprincipled Brunehaut, deemed it prudent once more to remove. His first thought was to begin a mission to the Slavic race, who occupied the present territory of Venice, but he decided that the time was not come for this. He therefore directed his steps to the Lombard territory, in North Italy, and crossing the Alps, probably by the St. Gothard, he reached Milan in A.D. 612. He was well received by King Agilulf, and in the following year founded the monastery of Bobbio, in Italy, thirty-seven miles north-east of Genoa. While in Italy he engaged in the Arian controversy, and wrote a letter to Boniface IV. in which he comments severely on Pope

---

[1] The second Canon of the First General Council of Constantinople.

Vigilius. In his letters to the Popes, particularly that to Boniface, he is liberal of complimentary phrases, and some passages have been dwelt on as affording support to modern views as to Papal authority. The late Professor Kelly[1] of Maynooth, however, says, "He cannot be cited as a witness of the Ultramontane opinion of the Pope's infallibility;" nor can he, indeed, be considered as going further than giving expression to a high respect for the Pope as the head of the Church of the Roman Empire. The importance of his labours is not to be estimated merely by the institutions he himself established, but also by the stimulus communicated by them and the numerous foundations they gave rise to. Not far from Luxeuil a few years after we find Remiremont, a double monastery, after the example of S. Brigit's at Kildare. Somewhat to the south, on the Haute-Saône, Lure was founded by Dichuil, or Deicola, one of his disciples. From this central cluster southwards to the Lake of Geneva, and north and north-west as far as the Channel and the North Sea, from the Seine to the Scheldt, monasteries arose, looking to Luxeuil as their authoritative model and guide. Continual reinforcements from Ireland recruited their numbers and kept alive their zeal. The eloquence of Columbanus was as fervid as his missionary zeal, and no one can read his letter to Boniface IV. without admiring the fertility of his imagination. Metaphors and figures of speech crowd on one another so swiftly and in such profusion that utterance seems to fail him. Very powerful must have been the effect of his burning eloquence on the rude pagans whom he addressed. "If any one," says Cardinal Baronius, "likes to compare him to the prophet Elias, I shall not object."

In his Latin poetry we have abundant evidence of

[1] Dissertations on Irish Church History, p. 265.

his scholarship. Several pieces [1] of his have been preserved, and one is disposed to wonder how, amidst his many labours, he found time for this indulgence. "It seems," Mr. Haddan observes, "like a link between the past and the present to find Columbanus (and others) relaxing from cares and serious thoughts into Latin verse. Familiarity with Latin classics as well as with the Fathers, both Greek and Latin, shows itself in all the 'Scottish' (Irish) writers."[2] The standpoint of Columbanus as regards the Church of the Empire is sufficiently indicated by the claim he makes on behalf of the Irish Church, as a non-Roman Church, to observe its own usages, and the statement that they will take the Pope's advice if it agrees with S. Jerome's views, but not otherwise.

In his letter to Boniface he attributes the dignity of Rome to its possession, as was believed, of the bodies of S. Peter and S. Paul: "On account of these two apostles of Christ . . . you are in a manner heavenly, if the expression may be used, and Rome is the head of the Churches of the world, saving the singular prerogative of the place of the Lord's resurrection"[3] (*i.e.*, Jerusalem). The Irish have a profound respect for the burial-places of the dead : how much deeper would be their veneration when the dead were the chief apostles of the Lord ! Such was the view in which they habitually regarded Rome, and a singular evidence of this remains in the old Irish language, where the word Rome is found as a familiar term for any burial-place. The full expression is "a Rome of burial,"[4] but generally simply

---

[1] Ussher, Works, vol. iv. pp. 210-220.
[2] Remains p. 275, note. See a curious poem in Latin and Irish, of unknown authorship, in Appendix F.
[3] King, Ch. Hist., iii. 953.
[4] *Róm adnaicthi* ("Goidelica," p. 163).

"a Rome." In this sense, Bardsey Island[1] was so named, and the writer of the life of Aelgar gives as the chief reason of its sanctity, that "the bodies of twenty thousand saints lie there, some of them confessors, others martyrs." So the two saints commemorated by Œngus at October 23 are said to have had "Babylon for their *rome* or burial-place."[2] In later times, when Rome came to be regarded as having other claims on the Irish, this primitive usage was abandoned. It is worthy of notice that the two apostles were in early times always associated with Rome by the Irish, as in the passage from Columbanus. So Caelbe or Nem, of Arran, who was fabled to have been Pope of Rome, is termed "the successor of Peter and Paul."[3] In modern times S. Paul is seldom mentioned in this connection. Through them Rome was the head[4] of the Churches of the world; but the exception of Jerusalem indicates the character of the honour here referred to, and clearly shows that the idea of supremacy is entirely absent from the comparison.

Among the treasures of the library of Bobbio, now at Milan, two are of special interest to Irishmen— the Antiphonary of Bangor, already referred to, and the Commentary of Columbanus on the Psalms. The former, written, it is supposed, a little after 680, is a Book of Anthems compiled for the community of Bangor. It is a most venerable memorial of that famous school, with which, no doubt, Columbanus kept up his connection long after he had left Ireland. The Com-

---

[1] Off the coast of Caernarvon. It was termed Roma Britanniæ. Ussher, Works, vi. 44.
[2] Calendar of Œngus at October 28, p. clii., also note on September 12, p. cxlv.; "Lives from the Book of Lismore," p. 63, line 2111.
[3] Book of Leinster, p. 373, *comarba Petair is Poil*.
[4] The term "head" is still in use among the peasantry to express dignity but not jurisdiction; as, *e.g.*, the head doctor of any town means the most eminent physician.

mentary on the Psalms was at one time attributed to S. Jerome, but it is now allowed to be by Columbanus. It affords evidence of learning uncommon at the period. The author was evidently unacquainted with Hebrew, or at least only knew a few words; but he frequently quotes Greek, and he must have had an exact acquaintance with the different versions of the Bible, as he frequently notes variations in the margin by the formula, "a different interpretation," or "a different reading."[1] The best authorities[2] ascribe the manuscript to the eighth century. It abounds in old Irish glosses or explanations, which are of extreme value to the student of the language. These are ascribed to the following century by the same authorities.[3]

Columbanus was a born leader of men, and inspired his followers with his own enthusiasm. One of these was S. Gall, who evangelised north-east Switzerland and Alemannia or Baden, and has given his name to one of the cantons. He preached with great earnestness, and on one occasion enforced his denunciation of idolatry by sweeping the heathen idols from the altar of the Church in which they had been placed, and flinging them into the lake. His success may be attributed in a large measure to his having acquired the language of the people. Columbanus was probably too advanced in life when he went to the continent to learn a new language; but the great pains that S. Gall and the junior members of the party bestowed on the study may be judged from the vocabularies[4] which are

---

[1] *Debe tintuda: Debe canoine.*   [2] Muratori, Peyron, and Zeuss.
[3] See an article on this MS. by Chevalier Nigra in the Revue Celtique, vol. i. p. 60 *seq*. It is now in course of publication by that eminent scholar, Signor Ascoli, "Il Codice Irlandese dell' Ambrosiana." Roma 1888. Two vols. have already appeared.
[4] They have been published by Lachmann, "Spic. Ling. Franc.," 1825, p. 1; by Greith, "Spicilegium Vaticanum," 1838, pp. 35-45; by Hattemar, "Denkmal," pp. 5-14. The following are specimens of

still preserved in the library of S. Gall, containing lists in which old high German terms are placed in parallel columns with their Latin equivalents. The words are such as are used in the ordinary intercourse of life, and it seems strange at first sight to find amongst them maritime terms which might seem to be unnecessary in an inland country like Switzerland. But their presence is accounted for by the circumstance that the Irish were constantly travelling backwards and forwards to Ireland, and had therefore occasion to use them. So famous were they as travellers that the word "pilgrim" had become the technical term for an Irishman.[1] The vocabularies are contained in small hand-books, and are very much of the same character as those used by the modern insular tourist who endeavours to make himself understood on the continent. One of them is attributed to S. Gall himself, and bears internal evidence of being as old as the beginning of the ninth century. Another companion of Columbanus was Deicola or Dichuil, who was one of the community of Luxeuil, and on the expulsion of his master set out with some others to accompany him into exile. After travelling a few miles, finding himself unequal to the journey, he entreated to be allowed to stay behind and retire to some solitude. Columbanus, with warm expressions of affection, reluctantly consented, at the same time comforting him with words of Scripture.[2]

Deicola, thus left alone, and forbidden by his master to return to Luxeuil, sought the depths of the forest, and while diligent in prayer and religious observances, wandered day after day through the wilderness look-

the words: *Obethe*, for German *Haupt* (head); *Elfe*, for German *Hilfe* (help); *Guas Guildo*, for *was willst du*. I am indebted to his Grace the Archbishop of Dublin for directing my attention to these vocabularies.
[1] Wasserschleben, einleitung xlvi.   [2] Ps. cxxviii. 5.

ing for a place to settle in. One day he came on the unusual sight of a man, who turned out to be a swineherd. The sudden appearance of Deicola startled the man; tall of stature, dressed in Irish fashion, and carrying a heavy staff, the herdsman was much alarmed at his approach. "The outward appearance of the Irish pilgrims," as a foreign writer observes, " was most striking, and the more so as they were still in the habit of painting their eyelids, which reminds us of the ancient Britons and their painted bodies. Their whole outfit consisted of a *Cambata* or pilgrim's staff, a leathern water-bottle, a wallet, and (what was to them their greatest treasure) a case containing some relics."[1] The swineherd anxiously inquired who he was. Deicola replied, "Do not fear; I am a stranger, and my occupation is that of a monk." Reassured by this, he entered into a conversation with Deicola, who desired to know of a suitable spot to settle in. The swineherd suggested a place called Luthra, afterwards known as Lure, which was situated in the forest, and surrounded by streams and marshes, and there he took up his abode. Not far off was a little church, where a monk[2] officiated at certain times. Thither Deicola resorted for prayer in secret, not wishing to be "seen of men," and choosing the night especially for his visits. The doors were closed against him, but he found means of opening them. The windows were stopped with briars and thorns, but still he made his way in. We have here a picture of the relations between the Irish missionaries and the degenerate French clergy of the period. The priest complained angrily of Deicola. "There is a foreign monk living in the wood," he said, "who uses some kind of in-

---

[1] Wattenbach, translated and annotated by Bishop Reeves. Ulster Journal of Archæology, vol. vii. p. 233.
[2] *Miles Christi*, as he is termed.

cantations, and comes here in the middle of the night to say his prayers. I call God to witness, if I find him there again, I will have him beaten and driven away." The prayers of the Irishman were, in the eyes of the Frenchman, no better than incantations. But the people, who admired the extraordinary mortification of Deicola's life, thus passed with no shelter but the woods, replied, " If such virtue is from God, we cannot forbid it; but if he is an impostor, we will drive him away." Deicola persevered, and in the end overcame all opposition, and obtaining a grant of the site on which he had settled, founded the monastery of Lure,[1] near Besançon, which became famous in after years.

Farther east, at Salzburgh, in the Tyrol, on the frontiers of Bavaria and Austria, we find, though at a later period, Fergil or Vergil, who was originally Abbot of Aghabo, in the Queen's County, according to the "Annals of the Four Masters."[2] Leaving Ireland in 745, with the intention of making a pilgrimage to the Holy Land, he arrived in France, and was received with honour by Pepin, who afterwards recommended him to Otilo, Duke of Bavaria. There he became Abbot of S. Peters at Salzburgh, and when occupying that position, came into collision with Archbishop Boniface, who has been termed the Apostle of Germany. He had ordered Vergil to rebaptize a person, because the priest who performed the ceremony had used ungrammatical Latin in doing so. Vergil held that this did not invalidate the baptism, and he refused to repeat the rite. Boniface appealed to the Pope, but the Pope took the same view as Vergil, and decided in his favour.

It was not long, however, before another cause of dispute arose between them, for the nationality, the

---
[1] Life of Deicola, in "Dictionary of National Biography."
[2] Annals of the Four Masters, A.D. 784 (correctly, 789). For his history, see Canisius, Ant. Lect., tom. iii. p. ii.

Church, and the training of the two men were entirely different, and Boniface was unable to endure the liberty of thought which Vergil and other Irishmen claimed. The new subject of controversy was the teaching of Vergil on the sphericity of the earth. This had been the general belief of the ancients; but S. Augustine having pronounced the earth to be a plane surface, his opinion outweighed that of the scientists, and became the orthodox view of the Roman divines of the period. The Irish teachers, however, had little respect for mere authority, and Vergil boldly asserted his view in opposition to the popular belief. Boniface was shocked, and at the same time probably not sorry at having a more plausible ground than before for appealing to the Pope. The Pope in reply tells him if Vergil taught such a doctrine as that there was another world and other people beneath the earth, to call a council and expel him from the Church.[1] It does not appear whether the conclusion drawn from his teaching as to the second human race was that of the Pope or of Boniface, but at any rate the former adopted it as a legitimate deduction from the doctrine of the Antipodes.[2] The fact is, that Vergil, as his title, "the Geometer," indicates, was an eminent mathematician. He was a man of genius, while neither Zachary nor Boniface, who were followers of the traditional belief of the time, understood the subject, or were competent to discuss it. "The idea," as Dr. Lanigan says, "was new to Boniface; for in those times geographical and philosophical learning was not as much cultivated in other parts of the West as in Ireland.

---

[1] Ussher, Works, vol. vi. p. 464.
[2] It is ridiculous to say, as Dr. Bellesheim does, that "perhaps" Vergil regarded the earth not as a sphere, but as a flat disk.—*Geschichte der Katholischen Kirche in Irland*, vol. i. p. 255.

His mode of stating that opinion might have misled a Pope even more learned than Zachary, and induced him to think that Vergil held there was a second species of men inhabiting another world distinct from the earth."[1] After occupying the position of Abbot of S. Peter's for two years, he was appointed to the Bishopric of Salzburgh by King Pepin after the death of Boniface, or by Pope Stephen in conjunction with the King, according to Dr. Lanigan. No incident in his life has caused more perplexity than the circumstance of his "concealing his orders" during his tenure of the abbacy, and having had a "bishop of his own" to perform episcopal functions. Dr. Todd[2] thought it was his priesthood he concealed; but there could have been no connection between his concealing his priesthood and having a bishop of his own to confer orders, for if he had no higher order than the priesthood, whether it was concealed or not, he would have required the bishop. But Dr. Todd's view is untenable, because it is distinctly said he was a bishop before he left Ireland.[3]

Another writer,[4] treating the matter from a presbyterian point of view, thinks it was his "power of ordaining" he concealed, his modesty not permitting him to exercise his right as a presbyter abroad. For this reason he employed a bishop. But the expression is not his "power of ordination," but simply his "ordination."[5] And it would surely be an abandonment of presbyterian principles to have had "a bishop of his own" to confer orders. The latest writer on the Irish Church thinks it safer to pass over the incident alto-

---

[1] Lanigan, Eccl. Hist., iii. 185. [2] S. Patrick, pp. 65-67.
[3] Ussher, vol. iv. p. 462. [4] Dr. Killen, vol. i. p. 96, *note*.
[5] Dissimulata ordinatione ferme duorum annorum spatiis habuit secum episcopum comitantem de patria nomine Dobda ad persolvendum episcopale officium. Mabillon, Actt SS., tom. iv. p. 280.

gether in his voluminous work without any reference to the discussions on the subject. This is certainly not fair to his readers, who are entitled to expect full information from him. His account of that part of Vergil's life is as follows : "Already before 748, the year of Otilo's death, he was appointed Bishop of Salzburgh, and governed the diocese in Irish fashion for twenty-two years as abbot-bishop, while the pontifical duties were performed by his suffragan bishop, Dodogrecus, who is also called a Greek and an Irishman."[1] Here is a series of blunders, for he was not abbot-bishop of Salzburgh, he had no suffragan, and there was no such person as Dodogrecus. The incident of the concealment of his orders and his having a bishop of his own can only be explained by a reference to the constitution of the Irish Church, which, as will be seen presently, was wholly different from that of the continent. The real meaning of Vergil's action appears from a comparison of other instances. In Adamnan's Life of S. Columba, a case of this kind is mentioned which occurred when he was at Iona. An Irish bishop named Cronan, who came to visit the saint, endeavoured from humility as much as possible to conceal himself, that none might know him to be a bishop; but he could not escape the penetration of the saint. For on the next Lord's day, having been invited by S. Columba to consecrate according to custom the Body of Christ, he calls the saint that they might break the bread of the Lord together, as if they had been both presbyters. The saint then approaching the altar, suddenly looked into his face and thus addressed him: "May Christ bless thee, brother. Break thou this bread alone with episcopal rite; we know now that thou art a bishop."

[1] Bellesheim, *Geschichte*, vol. i. p. 255.

Wherefore didst thou attempt to conceal thyself until now?"[1] Here the bishop was influenced by humility. Another instance is that of Disibod.[2] Though a bishop in Ireland, yet from the time he had to leave his country until the day of his death "he never celebrated the Eucharist after the order appointed for bishops, but according to the usage of poor presbyters." The motive for concealment in this case, as in that of Vergil's, was different from that of Cronan. The two former were heads of great monasteries, situated in a country where diocesan episcopacy was established; and if they were recognised as bishops while in that position, governing a large body of ecclesiastics, it would be contrary to the rule that there could be only one bishop in a city, and they would seem to be rivals to the bishop of the diocese. Hence it was advisable that they should act simply as presbyters, leaving the necessary episcopal duties of the monastery to be performed by one of their monks, according to Irish custom. This official being in a subordinate capacity, and under the orders of the abbot, and having no jurisdiction, would not in any way conflict with the authority of the diocesan.

Dr. Bellesheim in the passage quoted confuses Vergil's tenure of the abbey with the bishopric of Salzburgh, for it was before his appointment to the latter that his bishop (who is *not* termed a suffragan) acted for him. After his elevation to the See of Salzburgh there could have been no more concealment, and the bishop referred to, being no longer needed, was appointed Abbot of Chiemsee. Dr. Bellesheim contradicts Mabillon when he says that his "suffragan bishop," as he terms him, acted for Vergil during

---

[1] Reeves' Adamnan, p. 85.
[2] Life in "Dictionary of National Biography."

twenty-two years, for the period during which he concealed his orders was very short (almost two years). In Dodogrecus we have an old error exhibiting its vitality. Dobdagrecus, as Ussher has it, was taken by him to mean "Dobda, the Greek," whereas it is merely a Latinised form of *Dubh-da-crich*, Dubh of the two countries, a name, as already mentioned, indicating that he was a travelled Irishman.

Towards the close of his life, Vergil made a personal visitation of the scenes of his missionary labour, in order to eradicate the remains of idolatry and confirm the people in the faith. The extent of territory over which his oversight reached may be judged from his having travelled beyond Carinthia, and through the intervening territories to Slavonia, and on to the confluence of the Drave and Danube. He was received everywhere with respect and esteem, and shortly afterwards returning to Salzburgh, died on November 27, 785, after an episcopate of thirty years. He combined in a remarkable degree the qualities of the student and the man of action. As to his reputed canonisation by Gregory IX.[1] in 1233, whatever foundation there may be for it, he must have been previously recognised as a saint by the Irish, for he is so entitled in the "Book of Leinster,"[2] transcribed a hundred years earlier.

The ruins of the monastery of Disibodenberg may be seen at the confluence of the Nahe and the Glan affluents of the Rhine, about two miles south-east of Creuznach. It was founded by Disibod, who was born at the close of the sixth century.[3] Leaving Ireland under the circumstances already mentioned,[4] he wandered for ten years about the continent. At length, crossing the river Glan, he perceived a lofty hill

---

[1] Harris's Ware, Writers, p. 49.
[2] P. 348, a.
[3] Flourished 594-674.
[4] See p. 50.

clothed with forest. Ascending this, and weary of his wandering life, he sat down, and addressing his companions, said, "Here shall be my rest." Here he made a shelter for himself on the eastern slope of the mountain, and lived an austere and painful life as a hermit, he and his companions living on roots and herbs. His dress was the same as that he wore when leaving Ireland, of coarse material, and his food was scarcely sufficient to sustain life, for, as the writer of his history says, "He had ever in his thoughts the example of the blessed Paul,[1] the hermit, who with his followers preferred to live in woods rather than in cities." The tidings of his strange life soon spread abroad, and many came to visit him. He had been a diligent student of the native language since his arrival in Germany, and now he was able to speak to his visitors "the word of life and salvation." When his community was finally established, the monks occupied a range of huts, in Irish fashion, on the brow of the declivity, while he dwelt in his cell lower down, and apart from them. The reason assigned for this is that they followed the rule of S. Benedict, while he, living according to the much severer Egyptian manner, did not wish to have a contrast drawn to the disadvantage of his brethren.

Some continental writers have questioned his right to the title of bishop, because the Abbess Hildegardis terms him an "anchorite and a solitary," and Rabanus Maurus calls him a "Confessor." Foreign writers, judging from their own usages, did not understand that in the Irish Church those to whom those terms are applied were often bishops. He is, however, styled bishop by Hildegardis, and by Marianus Scotus. He is also represented on a bronze plate discovered in

---

[1] He lived in the Thebaid early in the third century, and is by some termed the founder of the hermit life.

the seventeenth century as wearing a crown, the episcopal head-dress in Ireland and the Eastern Church.[1]

Such were a few of the Irish labourers abroad. Their deep religious feeling, their unworldliness and zeal, and their eloquence, fitted them eminently for the work to which they were called in the providence of God. To them was mainly due the restoration of Christianity and civilisation throughout the Roman Empire of the West.

Here the Irish race presents a remarkable contrast to other Celtic populations, for none of the latter sent forth missionaries to any non-Celtic people. Cumbria, Wales, and Cornwall, as well as Brittany, were Christian at an early period, but they were not stirred[2] by the same enthusiasm for the conversion of the barbarian races. It may have been that, in the absence of the law which so greatly augmented the numbers of the Irish clergy, they had few to spare for such an undertaking. But whatever the cause, to the Irish alone belongs the honour of that great work which for so many ages rendered the name of their country famous throughout Europe.

But their office was that of pioneers. Inured to hardship, accustomed to the coarsest dress and the simplest food, they had fewer wants than the new races among whom they ministered, and by the austerity of their lives they attracted them to the profession, at least, of Christianity. But they were unable to organise their converts because the Church system they brought from Ireland was only adapted to that country and its institutions, and could not be transferred. So it came to pass that when the Anglo-Saxon missionaries, such as Boniface, appeared on the scene, the star of the Irish began to wane. For those men brought with them the organisation of the Church of the Empire,

---

[1] Life of Disibod, in the "Dictionary of National Biography."
[2] H. and S., i. 154, *n.*

communicated by Augustine and his successors, with its orderly subordination of ranks and settled government. The races converted by the Irish were organised by the Anglo-Saxons, and became members of the continental system. The Irish monasteries abroad ceased to be supplied from home with Irish monks, and passed into foreign hands, and by degrees the Irish mission came to an end. An important factor in the elimination of the Irish element from the Continental Church was persecution. The Irish themselves never advocated or used persecution in any shape or form, being in this respect, as in some others, in harmony with modern ideas. But they were not treated in the same spirit. Wilfrid's action with regard to Colman at Whitby has been mentioned, and his subsequent proceedings against those who continued to follow the Irish customs. Boniface, Bishop of Mentz, is another instance, for having had a quarrel with an Irish cleric named Clement, he complained of him to Pope Zachary. He said he rejected the canons of the Church, and alleged that, "though he had two sons born in adultery, he could still be a Christian bishop," and so on; this latter charge meaning only that Clement was a married man with a family. In writing to the Pope he includes another Irishman, and says: "I entreat your apostolic authority against them, that by your order these two heretics may be cast into prison if you think right, and that no one may speak to them or hold communion with them."[1] In the same year, 745, Zachary held a council at Rome, which ordered Clement to be deprived of the priesthood and anathematised, with all who agreed with him. This was the turning of the tide. Thenceforth Irish opinion lay under suspicion in the Continental Church.

[1] Ussher, vol. iv. pp. 457-460.

CHAPTER VII.

CONSTITUTION OF THE CHURCH.

WHATEVER the form of Church government with which S. Patrick was acquainted, or whatever Irish ecclesiastics of later times may have seen elsewhere, had little influence in determining the organisation of the Irish Church. Its constitution grew out of the circumstances in which it was placed. The case was exactly parallel to that of the Church of the Empire, whose external polity and government were influenced by those of the civil power, and which in its arrangements followed in general the divisions of the Empire.[1] In Ireland the same principle manifested itself in a different way: the Church, as a living force, there also adapted itself to the civil polity, and as this was altogether unlike the Imperial Government, so was the constitution of the Irish Church different from that of the Empire.[2]

In consequence of the tribal constitution already described,[3] and the absence of a central government and executive, there were no great officials representing an imperial authority as in other countries, nor were there any cities to become centres of civilisation. The form which the Church assumed on the conversion of Ireland was to a large extent determined by this condition of society.

[1] Bingham, Origines, vol. iii. chap. i. London, 1840: Smith and Cheetham's "Dictionary of Christian Antiquities," Art. Notitia.
[2] Senchus Mor., Brehon Laws, vol. iii., preface, p. lxxvi.
[3] Chapter I.

At a very early period monasteries were founded, each of which was in fact a spiritual clan, the head of which was the Coarb,[1] or heir of the original founder, whose name was thus perpetuated during the existence of the monastery.

The narrative of the foundation of the Church of Trim, given in the "Book of Armagh," is the earliest illustration of this.

Felim, son of the King of Ireland, dedicated all his territory and possessions at Trim,[2] in the county of Meath, together with all his substance and also his clan, to Patrick and his own son Fortchern. In consequence of this there was a twofold succession kept up at Trim; a lay succession of chieftains, and a clerical succession of Coarbs, both belonging to the same family. As the lay chieftains succeeded each other in hereditary descent from father to son, so the Coarbs had their spiritual descendants, who were also of Felim's clan.[3]

The same system prevailed in almost every abbey of early importance in Ireland, and for many generations the Coarbs of S. Comgall of Bangor were lineal descendants of the family from whom the endowment in land had been originally derived. The mode of succession was regulated by native law, the free election of an abbot by his monks, as elsewhere, being unknown in Ireland. Whenever a vacancy occurred it was filled by a member of the founder's kin, if a suitable person could be found in the direct line. If not, one was chosen from a collateral branch. The saint who founded the monastery might be of the same tribe as the chieftain who granted the land, and in this

---

[1] *Comarba* (*hæres*), a title given to the heads of the chief monasteries.
[2] *Ath Truim.* The Ford of the Elder Tree.
[3] Todd, pp. 150-154, who borrows from Bishop Reeves' paper in the Proceedings of the Royal Irish Academy.

case the matter was simple. But it might happen that he belonged to a different tribe, and then the succession was often retained by the tribe to which he belonged, and the Coarbs were supplied from its members. In this case the two families connected with the succession were different. The rule then was that the tribe of the saint provided the Coarb as long as it could furnish a suitable person; when it failed to do so, the rights of the tribe of the land came into force.[1]

It is unnecessary to pursue the account of those extremely minute regulations, except to mention that every possible case was provided for, and when all ordinary sources[2] failed it was lawful to appoint "a pilgrim of God."

Such was the elaborate system of succession worked out by the Irish legal authorities, and laid down in the Brehon Law. It differed altogether from that which prevailed elsewhere in Europe in recognising the hereditary principle in Church appointments. How it was looked on by the Continental Church we learn from S. Bernard, whose knowledge of it was derived from the Irish abbot, Congan.[3] In his Life of Malachi he says: "There had been introduced by the diabolical ambition of certain people of noble rank, a scandalous usage whereby the Holy See (Armagh) came to be obtained by hereditary succession. For they would allow no person to be promoted to the bishoprick, except such as were of their own tribe and family. Nor was it

---

[1] The Ancient Laws of Ireland, vol. iii. pp. 31–79.
[2] Amongst those were the *Annoit* Church, *i.e.*, where the patron saint was educated, or his relics kept; or a mother Church from which the original founder came. The *Dalta* Church founded by a member of the same community, and the *Compairche* Church, under the tutelage of the same saint.
[3] Ussher, Works, vol. iv. p. 548.

for any short period that this execrable succession had continued, nearly fifteen generations having been already exhausted in this course of iniquity."[1] He goes on to refer to some abuses which prevailed, owing no doubt to the Danish troubles and the general disorganisation of society arising from them. But in the foregoing passage it will be observed it is the principle, not the abuse, of hereditary succession he condemns. He seems to have thought the case of Armagh singular, whereas it was only an instance of a general law governing the succession of all Coarbs in the Irish Church.

The law defined the respective rights of the clergy and laity; the former were entitled to tithes, first fruits, and firstlings.[2] The law of firstlings as applied to the laity has been already noticed. Tithes appear to have been demanded from the holders of Church lands, but they were not generally paid in Ireland, as S. Bernard informs us;[3] and Pope Alexander makes the same statement in his bull addressed to Henry II. The mention of them in the Brehon Law must therefore be regarded merely as the assertion of an abstract right. They are not noticed in the Annals until A.D. 1152, when the Four Masters record that at a synod held at Kells in that year under Cardinal Paparo, tithes were ordered to be "received punctually." Notwithstanding this, and though the cardinal enjoined it by his apostolical authority, yet in this point Dr. Lanigan tells us he was very badly obeyed.[4] In fact, according to the Annals of Lough Cé, they were not paid (regularly?) until the reign of Cathal Crobderg, who died in 1224, more than fifty years after the Norman conquest. The introduction of them was

[1] King, "Primacy," p. 23.
[2] Senchus Mor, iii. p. lvii.
[3] Reeves' "Antiquities," p. 254.
[4] Eccles. Hist., iv. 146.

part of the policy of bringing the Church into line with that of the Continent, and any payments previously made must have been purely voluntary, as there was no power to enforce them while Ireland was an independent country.

Corresponding with the rights of the Church as thus defined were those of the laity. If they fulfil their duties towards the Church it is bound to perform for them " the offices of baptism, communion, and requiem," and " offering from every church to every person after his proper belief, with the recital of the Word of God to all who listen to it and keep it."[1] The laity were required also to devote "every seventh day in the year to the service of God." This observance of the Lord's Day, in pursuance of what was known as the *Cáin* or law of Sunday, is frequently mentioned in the Lives of Irish saints. In the "Tripartite" it is said that, "from Vespers on Sunday night until the third hour on Monday, Patrick used not to go out of the place where he was staying."[2] "Once when he was resting on the Lord's Day near the sea he heard a tumultuous noise of heathens, who were toiling in forming a *rath*. S. Patrick, calling them, ordered them not to work on the Lord's Day. But as they disobeyed his command, the sea broke in and destroyed their work."[3] His example of resting on that day seems to have been generally followed. In the Life of Kellach it is related that Guaire, King of Connaught, ordered him to come to him at noon on Saturday. Kellach replied, "It is Vesper-time now, and I will not violate the Lord's Day. . . . I will go to him on Monday if he wishes."[4] S. Colman Ela,

---
[1] Senchus Mor, iii. 57.
[2] Trip., vol. i. p. 125. On the practice of treating Saturday night as part of Sunday. See Reeves' "Columba," p. 230, note *d*.
[3] Ibid., vol. ii. p. 289.
[4] Life of Cellach in "Dictionary of National Biography."

when passing the Lord's Day at the house of Edan, son of Oengus, saw a man splitting wood on the pavement, and commanded him to desist, as it was the Lord's Day.[1] An evidence of the popular feeling on the subject is afforded by the quaint legend entitled "The Adventures of Leihin." Two members of the community of Clonmacnois were sent out in a boat to cut bulrushes on the bank of the Shannon, for the use of the monastery. Just when they had filled their boat, and were about to return, they heard the distant sound of the bell of the monastery summoning the clergy to Vespers. It was Saturday evening, which, as mentioned, according to the usage of the Irish Church, was reckoned the beginning of Sunday. They determined, therefore, not to leave the place until Monday morning, one expressing his feelings in a poem which gives many strange reasons for the observance of Sunday.

"The voice of Clone's sweet bell I hear, and Sunday now has come,
I will not move till it is past, then will I seek my home.
It is God's appointed day to be observed on earth,
When the King of the Apostles and Mary had their birth.
On it was born the Baptist who preached in Judah's land,
And on it he in Jordan was baptized by heavenly hand.
On Sunday Christ from Hades the captives led away,
On Sunday too by God's decree shall be the Judgment day."[2]

The story goes on to describe their sufferings in an open boat during the fearful night of frost, snow, and tempest which ensued, and the many inquiries they made as to whether any living being ever remembered such a night. All this was meant to enhance the merit of their observance of the day, and to deepen the impression of its sanctity.

An important provision of the Brehon Law re-

---

[1] Life of Colman Ela, in "Dictionary of National Biography."
[2] *Eachtra Leihin*, MS. 23, G. 20, p. 380, Royal Irish Academy.

garding the Church was that all the members of the community, that is, all connected with or subject to the monastery, and forming what was called its "family," down to the lowest grade, were held to be free men. "The enslaved shall be freed, and the plebeian exalted through the Orders of the Church, and by performing penitential service to God. For the Lord is accessible, He will not refuse any kind of man after belief among either the free or plebeian tribes; so likewise is the Church open for every person who goes under rule."[1] In a country where slavery existed, and certain tribes, descendants of conquered races, were termed "enslaved," such a law must have greatly augmented the numbers of the adherents of Christianity.

When a founder established several monasteries in different parts of the country they constituted his *Parochia* or "Diocese," the word being employed in quite a different meaning from the ordinary one. In this peculiar usage it had nothing to do with a definite territory, and thus many "Dioceses" were intermingled, the word referring to institutions only.

The Coarb of a monastery might be a bishop or a presbyter. In the case of the Columbian monasteries he was always a presbyter, S. Columba himself never having passed beyond that order. But each monastery or group of monasteries had a resident bishop, whose duty it was to confer orders, consecrate churches, and perform other episcopal offices. He was under the orders of the Coarb, and only acted when directed by him. The Church of Ireland thus organised presented a striking contrast to that of the Empire, for a bishop in the position described had no jurisdiction, no diocese committed to his charge, and no authority in the

[1] Ancient Laws, iii. p.33.

monastery. His duties were exclusively spiritual. Yet he was an indispensable official, and no monastery was complete without a provision for the performance of episcopal duties. It might happen, except in Columbian monasteries, that the Coarb himself was a bishop, as in the case of Vergil of Salzburgh, or, if he was not, the Scribe occasionally held the office, and a second monastic bishop became unnecessary.

It requires a little effort to realise a condition of things in which the powers of order and jurisdiction were divorced, and the bishop only retained the former. Yet the two are quite distinct, and may be separated as they were in this system.[1] From this it will be seen that Diocesan Episcopacy did not exist in the early Church, and no attempt was made to introduce it until the Synod of Rathbreasil in 1118, which proposed a division of Ireland into dioceses. There were, in fact, neither dioceses, in the ordinary sense, nor parishes, until the twelfth century.[2] The true heads of the Church were the Coarbs, and instead of the compact organisation of the Diocesan system, with its subordination of ranks, there were groups of independent monasteries presenting a close parallel to the native clans.

The Coarbs of the principal monasteries formed a council, who debated questions and spoke the voice of the Church. In the discussions with regard to Easter they were frequently consulted, and S. Colman of Lindisfarne, when refusing to abandon the Irish Easter, speaks of them as his elders, for whom he expresses a profound respect. An example of such a council is the synod held at Magh Léné, in the King's County, at which Cummian was present, and argued on behalf of the Roman Easter. He mentions

[1] Lanigan, Eccl. Hist., ii. 255.   [2] King, "Primacy," p. 25.

in his letter[1] to Segéné, Abbot of Iona, amongst those present, the Coarbs of Ailbe of Emly, of Kieran of Clonmacnois, of Brendan of Birr, of Nessan of Inis-mac Saint, and of Lughaidh of Teernacreeve, in Westmeath. Another similar assembly was held shortly afterwards at Whitefield, near Carlow, at which the principal authorities were Molaise or Laisrian, Abbot of Leighlin, and Fintan or Munnu, of Taghmon, the latter being the defender of the Irish usage.

These were assemblies from the southern division of Ireland, and it is worthy of notice that the important question of Easter was not discussed at a general council of the kingdom. The difficulty in the way of such an arrangement was the divergence of opinion between the North and South of Ireland, and this seems to have had its root in a difference of character between the populations of the two sections of the country. From a very early period a division of Ireland into two "Halves," as they were called, existed. This was traditionally believed to have been made by Conn, of the hundred battles, and Eoghan-mor, otherwise known as Mogh Nuadat, in A.D. 166.[2] The North was in consequence known as Conn's Half (*Leth Chuinn*), the South as Mogh's Half (*Leth Mhogha*), the line of division being a series of gravel hills, extending from Dublin to Clarin Bridge, in the County of Galway.[3] Whatever the origin of the partition may have been, it represented a real difference of character and disposition, which was as perceptible in the twelfth century, when Giraldus Cambrensis wrote his history of the conquest of Ireland, as it is to-day. He is not always an impartial witness, as he had a thorough dislike to the Irish. But

---

[1] Ussher, iv. 442.   [2] According to the Annals of Tigernach.
[3] Called the Eiscir Riada. See Map No. 1, in which the places above-mentioned are underlined in red.

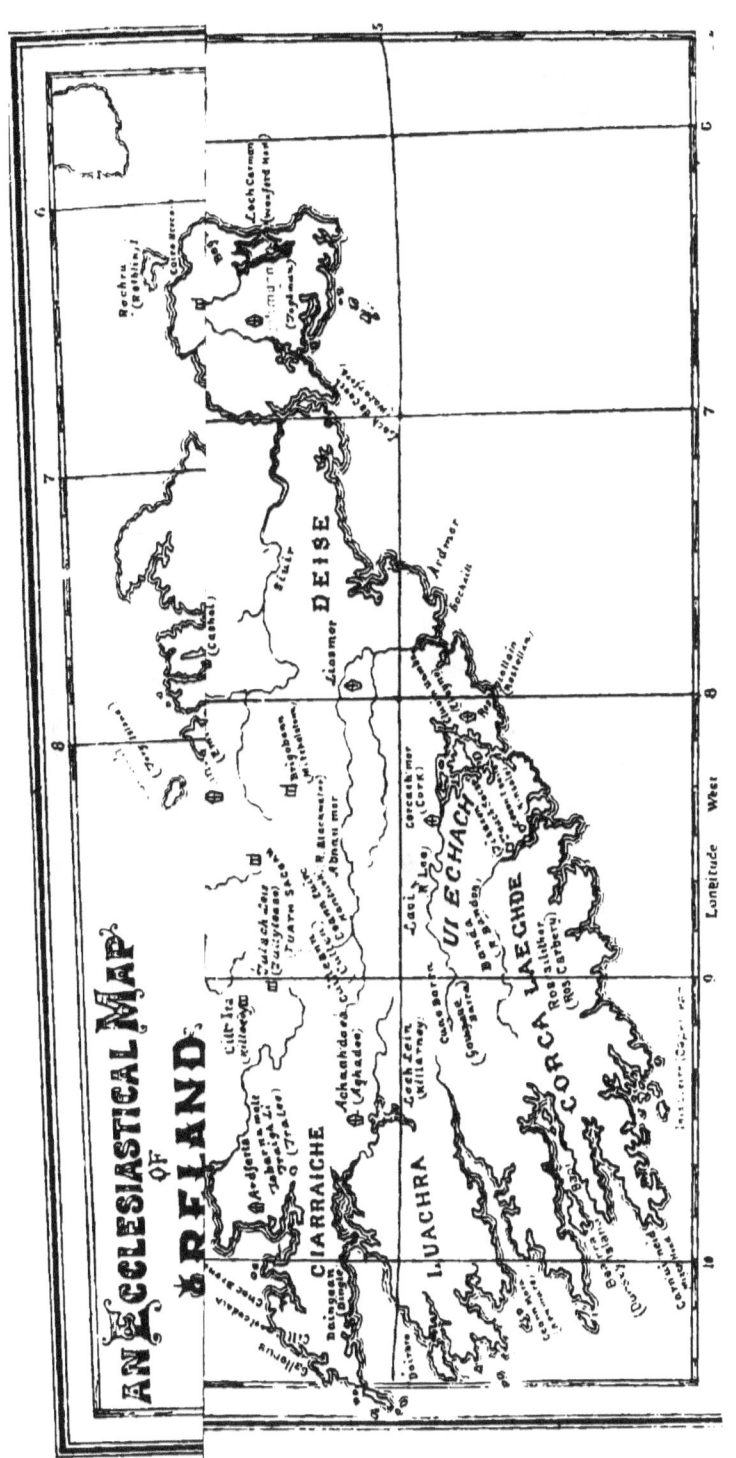

bearing this in mind, and allowing for the dark colours he puts in, his description of the North and South has some truth in it. "We find," he says, "the people of the North of Ireland were always warlike, while those of the South were subtle and crafty. The one coveted glory, the other was steeped in falsehood; the one trusted to their arms, the other to their arts; the one was full of courage, the other of deceit."[1] Perhaps the suavity and politeness of the South seemed to him to verge on deceit; but what politeness does not demand some hypocrisy? He appears to attribute a good deal to the difference of climate. The same dissimilarity of character emerges in the life of Finnchu, where an invasion of the South by the Northern forces is described. "The Munstermen flinch from the fight in horror of the children of Niall, and because of the abundance of their heroes and their accoutrements."[2] They had previously "entrusted themselves to their saints to win the victory from the children of Niall," a source of confidence not altogether out of harmony with the feelings of the South to-day.

In consequence of the stronger national sentiment of the North, it resisted conformity with the New Easter, as it was termed, much longer than the South, and several councils were held there at a later period than those before referred to for the discussion of the question. Between 692–697 one was held, at which Adamnan, Abbot of Hy, was present. It was convened by Flann Febla, Abbot of Armagh, at Derry or Raphoe, and was attended by forty bishops or abbots, amongst whom were Aedh, Bishop of Sletty; Colga, Abbot of Lusk; Mosacer, Abbot; Killen, Abbot of

---

[1] Giraldus Cambrensis, Bohn, p. 186.
[2] Lives, Book of Lismore, p. 243, 244.

Saigir; Mochonna, Abbot of Derry; and Echbert, an Englishman. Though there was no difference of rank among the Coarbs, except what was derived from personal eminence or advanced age and experience, yet a certain pre-eminence was assigned to Armagh from a very early period, as the seat of S. Patrick, the Apostle of Ireland. It was at first merely one of honour, but the idea in after times assumed a more definite form, and became one of jurisdiction as well as dignity.

The succession of Coarbs, whether in Armagh or elsewhere, did not necessarily involve a succession of bishops, as they might be either presbyters or bishops; and it often happened that, though the succession of abbots never failed, there were frequent breaks in the Episcopal line. Not that it is likely that the compass of a modern bishopric was ever without some one monastic establishment which had a bishop, but that the succession was not uninterruptedly preserved in any one monastery, even in that one which, by some accident, came to be the cathedral of the diocese.[1]

Hence catalogues of successive bishops of Irish sees from their founder to the present day must be illusive. The truth is, as Dr. Todd states, that there was no such thing. The names handed down to us as successors of S. Patrick are many of them called abbots, some are called bishops as well as abbots, some are styled bishops only, and some Coarbs of S. Patrick. But there is nothing in this last title to indicate whether the personage so designated was a bishop, a priest, or a layman.[2]

The advocates of Presbyterianism sometimes claim the Irish Church as favouring their views, but its whole history is opposed to this. The confession of

[1] Reeves' "Antiquities," p. 136.   [2] Todd, p. 172.

S. Patrick distinguishes the three orders of bishops, priests, and deacons. And when Aidan and Colman were sent forth from Hy on their mission to England, it was deemed essential that they should be consecrated bishops before entering on the work. The legend of S. Columba's ordination[1] by Bishop Etchen proves that the distinction of bishops and priests was well known when it was written. The concealment of orders in the instances already referred to is a decisive evidence on the point. Not only was the Episcopal order regarded as superior to that of Presbyter, but in the canons of an Irish synod it is treated as combining in itself the seven orders. They are enumerated as those of presbyter, deacon, subdeacon, lector, exorcist, and ostiarius; all these the bishop combines in his own person, being also himself one of them.[2] The question is really not one for argument.

That the clergy were permitted to marry is capable of abundant proof. The mention by S. Patrick of his clerical parentage is well known. The account of the consecration of Fiacc, Bishop of Sletty, as given in the "Book of Armagh," represents S. Patrick as inquiring for a suitable person to appoint a bishop, and laying down as a qualification that he must be "the husband of one wife to whom hath not been born save one child;" and the synod attributed to him, Auxilius, and Isserninus gives directions as to the dress of a clergyman's wife. These canons in their present form are assigned[3] to the eighth century, and therefore go to prove that clerical marriage was usual three centuries later than his time. Still more important is it that the Brehon Laws assume the existence of both

---

[1] Todd, p. 71.
[2] Wasserschleben, Kanonensammlung, Einleitung, lii., liii., and lib. xlii., cap. 22.
[3] H. and S., vol. ii. part ii. p. 328.

married and unmarried clergy. Amongst the provisions relating to ecclesiastics we find that if a bishop should fall into sin, a different penalty is prescribed in the case of the married and the celibate. If the offender is a bishop of one wife, he may recover his grade or position by performing penance within three days, but if he is a celibate he cannot recover it at all.[1] This continued to be the law of the Irish Church down to 1172, when it was brought into conformity with the Roman, as then existing in England, by the Synod of Cashel, and the canon law became binding on it, that is, in theory. How foreign to the traditions of the Irish Church the decree of the Synod on this subject was may be inferred from the "Book of Leinster." That manuscript, written in the middle of the twelfth century, contains two curious lists, one being that of sons[2] of Irish saints, of whom the names and parentage of 189 are given; the other of the daughters[3] of Irish saints, of whom 102 are named. The author of those lists could not possibly have had any idea that there was the least impropriety in saints marrying.

But even after that period numerous instances of the primitive usage are still to be found. Thus, in the time of Pope Gregory IX. (1227–1241), the Bishop of Connor makes humble information that the see being vacant he was elected by the canons, being "the son of a priest, and begotten in priesthood;"[4] and being overcome by the urgency of the canons, he consented, and at the time of his confirmation declared falsely[5] that he was begotten in lawful matrimony, and was then consecrated and held the bishopric five years. Under these circumstances he is ordered to resign.

---

[1] Senchus Mor, i. 55.   [2] P. 369, c 24, d, e, f 44.   [3] 370, a 1.
[4] *Filium sacerdotis et sacerdotio genitum.* Theiner, "Vetera Monumenta Hibernorum," &c., Romæ, 1864. Letter lxx., p. 28.
[5] Falsely according to canon law, but truly according to Irish law.

It will be observed that the canons, who must have known his history, urged him to accept the office, but the new authorities made him resign.

The view of the Irish theologians was fully in accordance with the Brehon Law. We find it stated in the Würzburgh Glosses, as, for instance, on 1 Corinthians vii. 25. " He did not say, let every one abide in celibacy, whether he is able or not. Question, What did he say? The answer is not difficult. He said, 'He that is able to receive it, let him receive it' (Matt. xix. 12)." The preference, however, was given to celibacy, as we find by the gloss on verse 28 of the same chapter. " He manifests here the difference between marriage and celibacy, for when of marriage it is said, ver. 36, 'he sinneth not,' of the celibate he says he doeth well. And when he says of marriage he doeth well, he says of the celibate, 'he doeth better.'"[1]

M. de Montalembert is therefore in error in stating that "it is now clearly shown that in the Celtic Church the deacons and priests never strayed from the Roman doctrine of celibacy."[2] It is strange that there should be such unwillingness to admit a historical fact, but efforts are frequently made to conceal it. The late Professor O'Curry, in his lectures at the Catholic University, having occasion to refer to "Conn of the poor," an eminent member of the community at Clonmacnois, informed his audience that Conn was a "lay religious."[3] But this well-known Irish scholar must have been aware that Conn was Bishop[4] of Clonmacnois, and that he was a married man. Not only was this bishop a married man, but his father, grandfather,

[1] Holy Scriptures in Ireland, S.P.C.K., 1888, pp. 56, 57.
[2] Quoted in Haddan's "Remains," p. 209.
[3] Manuscript Materials, p. 184.
[4] Chronicon Scotorum, Roll's ed., p. 209.

and great-grandfather, all of whom were in holy orders, were married men.[1] His son was Coarb of Clonmacnois, and his son again occupied the same office. The learned Dr. O'Conor also does not hesitate to mistranslate two entries[2] in the Annals of Tigernach in order to disguise the fact of clerical marriage. But so far were the Irish from seeing anything wrong in the marriage of the clergy, that the Brehon Laws seem even to contemplate the possibility of the Pope being a married man. Referring to the relative rank of bishops, they state, "The highest bishop is the Bishop of Peter's Church, because it is under his subjection the chiefs of Rome are; and they are not under the subjection of any one who has not virginity, or repentance, or *lawful espousal*.[3]

It seems to have been an approach to Diocesan Episcopacy when bishops began to be appointed to tribes, as mentioned in the "Lebar Brecc." "There was to be a chief bishop for every chief tribe in Ireland, for ordaining ecclesiastics and for consecrating churches; for soul-friendship to princes and superiors and ordained persons; for hallowing and blessing their children after baptism; for directing the labours of every Church, and boys and girls to reading and piety. For, unless the boys read at every time, the whole Church will perish, and there will be no belief but black heathenism in the land of Erin."[4]

In the absence of the parochial system, we find the clergy travelling through the country in twos and threes, and when a promising youth was met with, engaging him, if possible, to return with them and receive instruction. An instance of this occurs in

---

[1] Annals of the Four Masters, A.D. 1022, 1031, 1056, 1079, 1103, 1128.
[2] Annals of Tigernach, A.D. 798. Annals of Ulster, 1077, 1095.
[3] Senchus Mor., vol. iv., Preface, p. 218.
[4] Lebar Brecc., quoted in "Tripartite," Preface, p. clxxxii.

the "Life of S. Finn Barr of Cork." Two clerics passing his father's house, turned in and were hospitably received. Observing that his son was a boy of special intelligence,[1] they asked to be allowed to take him with them, and the parents consenting, they took him to Leinster, and he ultimately became a founder of monasteries and a saint.[2]

The exposing of children born in sin was frequent, and many celebrated Irish saints, thus cast out in infancy, owed their lives to being rescued by the clergy from death by exposure or from wild beasts. The taint of their birth was never regarded in Ireland as an objection, nor did it lessen the veneration of the people for them. Cumin the Tall, Bishop of Clonfert, "a learned preacher of the Word of God," derived his name from the basket (*cumin*) in which he was placed by those who cast him out.[3] Molua Mac Ochai, of Clonfert Mulloe in Ossory, is said to have been so called from being carried under his armpit (*oche*) by a monk, who found him in a brake of rushes.[4] Sometimes these infants were "cast on the Church," as it is termed, a practice referred to in the "Book of Armagh."[5] These, if cast on the Church without the knowledge of the abbot, became the slaves of the Church.[6]

In addition to the revenue from the resources already mentioned, which were voluntary, the Church also possessed land, consisting of grants made from time to time by chieftains or kings. In the Lives of Irish saints such gifts are frequently referred to as granted on the conversion of the owner to Christianity.

[1] *Elegantem puerum.*
[2] Life of S. Finn Barr, "Dictionary of National Biography," 1864.
[3] Calendar of Œngus, p. clxix. [4] Ibid., p. cxxviii.
[5] In the Book of the Angel, "Tripartite," p. 355.
[6] Wasserschleben, Einleitung, p. liv.

To many of these lands the privilege of sanctuary was attached, and the place in which one might take refuge from his enemies in case of danger was defined by certain marks. This was a valuable privilege amongst a people who were so constantly engaged in deadly quarrels. These asylums were called Termons,[1] and sometimes gave their name to the whole establishment.

In addition to the lands which were the property of the Church, there was also a tribute collected in certain districts by the representatives of well-known saints. The custom was for the Coarb to make a circuit in the district where the memory of the saint was held in esteem, carrying with him the *Minna*, or sacred objects belonging to the saint, such as his bell, or crozier, or gospel, which were regarded as his titledeeds. Thus authorised, he levied contributions from the churches and people. This was called "the Law [2] of the saint." In A.D. 727 the Law of Adamnan is mentioned; in 744, the Law of Kieran of Clonmacnois; in 756, 777, the Law of Columcille.[3] In process of time the Law of Patrick superseded them all, and the Primacy of Armagh became generally acknowledged throughout Ireland. The collection of such taxes was not always effected without difficulty, as may be judged from a story told in the "Book of Leinster." S. Semplan of Terryglas and a party of clerics came to the land of Cronin of Licnasinnach on business. Dermod was cleaning the flag bridge at his door, and had a shovel in his hand. His dog ran at the party and tore the saint, whereupon the saint struck the dog. Then Dermod struck the saint with his shovel

---

[1] From the Latin *terminus*. Ten of these are mentioned in the "Annals of the Four Masters." See Index.
[2] *Lex*, or, in Irish, *cain* and *riar*.   [3] King, "Primacy," p. 31.

and broke the *menistir*[1] of S. Colum, which he carried on his back. This being reported to the Coarb, S. Laichtin, he laid the case before the Prince of Idrone (County of Carlow), who sentenced Dermod to pay the legal penalty of seven *cumals*.[2] The fine was duly paid to the Coarb, who handed it to the Airchinnech, and so the matter ended.[3] From this little glimpse of Church life in the seventh century, it appears that the law in this case was duly carried out, and the clergy protected in the performance of their duty. S. Laichtin, at that time Coarb of Terryglas, died A.D. 622. The Airchinnech, or Erenach, as he is sometimes called, was the official of the monastery who attended to matters of business; he was the hereditary warden of the Church, and looked after the farms and other property, but was subject to the orders of the Coarb. The fine imposed on this occasion was that ordered by the "Ancient Laws"[4] when the person injured was a celibate clergyman.

The seclusion of the Irish Church, after the time of S. Patrick, has been already noticed. It was shared by the British Church, then confined to Wales, and both Churches thus came to have many peculiarities in common. But though generally one in doctrine and practice, the British Church was differently constituted from the Irish. Britain had been for four centuries connected with the Imperial Government, and the idea of a centralised authority had become impressed on the minds of the people. Mr. Skene, speaking of "the great legacies of Rome to

---

[1] *Menister*, from *ministerium*, the box containing the mirna or relics, which, as belonging to the original founder, Colum Mac Criffan, were regarded with great veneration.
[2] A *cumal*, originally a bondmaid, was the unit of value, and equivalent to three cows.
[3] Book of Leinster, p. 353.
[4] Ancient Laws of Ireland, vol. iv. p. 365.

Britain," mentions "the idea of monarchy and the centralisation of authority."[1] With such ideas as these the system of Diocesan Episcopacy was in harmony, and hence Britain seems never to have had any other kind of Church government,[2] whereas Ireland, as we have seen, never possessed it until the twelfth century. The Churches were therefore quite distinct in outward form. Columbanus terms them "the Western Churches," classing them apart from what we now speak of as the Eastern and Western Churches.

The Irish Church again was subdivided into three[3] sections by the native authorities. These were Ireland, Scotland, and Mann. For the Christian settlement of Argyle was an Irish colony, and continued for a considerable time subject to the Irish kings, and Mann was generally regarded as belonging to Ireland.

The Church, thus organised after its peculiar national fashion, was the solitary instance in the West of a Church outside the Empire. In the East there were many, such as those of India, Ethiopia, and others, whose national customs differed from those of the Church of the Empire, as appears from the Canon of Constantinople already noticed.

It is important that its organisation should be distinctly recognised, as it was its independent national character which excited the surprise of the Roman ecclesiastical authorities after the mission of S. Augustine. This seemed to them an unlawful deviation from Roman usage, and hence it became their constant aim to bring it into conformity with their own by a pressure applied with increasing strength as the

---

[1] Celtic Scotland, vol. i. p. 121. [2] H. and S., vol. i. p. 143.
[3] Annals of the Four Masters, p. 978.

Church abroad grew in power, while that of Ireland was gradually becoming weaker in consequence of the Danish inroads. The conflict of rival theories of Church government and varying practices carried on for centuries arrested the natural development of the Irish Church, which at one time threatened to be a formidable rival to the Church on the Continent of Europe. What direction that development might have taken it is now impossible to say, for the Church of Rome, after long effort, was ultimately successful in overcoming the national opposition. The result, however, was not finally attained until she was enabled to add to persuasion and diplomacy the more effectual argument of physical force, represented by Henry II. and his armed hosts.[1]

[1] Reeves' "Antiquities," p. 255.

CHAPTER VIII.

ITS EASTERN ORIGIN AND PRIMITIVE CHARACTER.

THAT Christianity reached Britain originally not from Rome but from the East, was first stated by the Centuriators of Magdeburgh [1] in the sixteenth century, and has since been maintained by many authorities. Ireland is usually included in the statement, and Mr. Fergusson, chiefly on architectural grounds, holds that "everything points to an intimate connection of that country with the further East, and tends to prove that its early Christianity and religious forms were derived from Greece by some of the more southerly commercial routes which at that period seem to have abutted on Ireland."[2] But it has been recently held that there was little difference between the mode in which Britain was Christianised and other European countries, for as the Church of Rome was originally Greek, as we see from S. Paul's Epistle to the Romans, one Greek Church may be supposed to be in most respects the same as another. No doubt, as has been said, all Christianity originated in the East, and gradually reached the West. But it makes a considerable difference whether it passed westward through the capital of the Empire, or arrived by way of the remote province of Southern Gaul. Rome, so

[1] Wasserschleben, "Kanonensammlung," Zweite Auflage, Einleitung, p. xxi.
[2] I. Fergusson, "Illustrated Handbook of Architecture," London, 1885, vol. ii. p. 915.

long the seat of empire, would naturally, to a great degree, impress its own character on the Christianity which it transmitted, whereas a provincial community would have no such power, and would pass it on much as it received it. Further, it is necessary to distinguish between the relative positions occupied by Britain and Ireland in this respect. Britain was part of the Empire, and the constitution of its Church, as we have seen, followed that of the Empire. Its bishops were present at foreign councils, at Sardica, 347; Milan, 355; Ariminum, 359, where three of them received the allowance granted by the Roman Emperor. In Ireland it was very different, for the country was wholly unconnected with Rome; its Church was differently organised; its bishops attended no foreign councils; and it is antecedently probable that it received its Christianity from the East through Gaul, for S. Patrick several times alludes to his friends in Gaul but never mentions Rome, and Sir S. Ferguson, referring to Probus' life of S. Patrick, says, "Few can rise from a perusal of it without the persuasion that some apostolic missionary of the Irish did some time in the fourth or beginning of the fifth century sojourn for purposes of ecclesiastical training in those regions bordering the Tyrrhene Sea, on the southern shore of Gaul."[1] The people in that region were a colony from Asia Minor, and Polycarp, its first bishop, came directly from thence, bringing Irenæus with him. Under those circumstances the Church must have retained its oriental character for a considerable time, and passed on the doctrines and practices of the East with very slight, if any, change. It was during this period that its connection with Ireland, through S. Patrick and his companions, took place. Ire-

[1] Transactions of Royal Irish Academy, December 1885, p. 126.

land, unacquainted with European civilisation, was virgin soil, and the seed of this oriental form of Christianity sown in it soon grew up true to its character. The seclusion of the country immediately after from all European influence for a century and a half gave time for the form of the Irish Church to be permanently fixed and interwoven with the native institutions. Thus was produced a special type of Christianity, which the authorities endeavoured to preserve by interdicting the clergy from visiting Rome. One consequence of this origin was that the Irish clergy always looked to the East, feeling that their Church had its source there, as well as attracted to it by intellectual sympathy, due to the affinity between the Hellenic and Celtic minds.[1] In the conference at Whitby, although S. Colman did not, as it is sometimes supposed, assert the Eastern origin of his Church, yet the Irish, in claiming S. John as their leader, while their opponents looked to S. Peter, defined their position, one side looking to the East and the other to the West.

The Rev. F. E. Warren[2] gives some of the evidence for the Eastern origin, and its cumulative force is considerable. He notices the groups of seven[3] churches, suggesting at once the seven churches of Asia. The smallness of those churches reminded Mr. Fergusson of those of Mount Athos and Asia Minor, where a great number are grouped together, seven being the favourite number. The style of ornament in Irish manuscripts resembles that of Syria and Egypt, the delineation of birds and animals being after the manner of Egyptian fresco painting. In some the

---

[1] Mullinger's "Schools of Charles the Great," p. 119.
[2] Liturgy, &c. of the Celtic Church, pp. 46-57.
[3] Optatus of Milevi mentions seven synagogues on Mount Zion. Lib. iii. p. 62. Paris, 1631.

written letters depend from the line above, as in Greek writing instead of resting on the line beneath. The stamped leather satchels in which the Irish enclosed their books are so exactly like those of Egypt that, placed side by side, they cannot be distinguished from each other. The hanging of books on pegs in these satchels was just as in the Egyptian monasteries visited by Mr. Curzon. So many coincidences immensely strengthen the theory of the Eastern origin of the Irish Church. To them may be added the arrangement of Irish monasteries, which was in accordance with the Eastern pattern, such as Adamnan describes the monastery on Mount Tabor, in which were numerous cells and churches, the whole surrounded by a wall.[1]

Again the Eastern practice of laying up water at Epiphany is mentioned in the life of S. Colman Ela. He had directed the steward to furnish supplies for the festival; the official replied that he had abundance of spring water, but nothing else. We evidently have here a reference to the custom mentioned as follows by Chrysostom:—"In the solemnity in memory of our Saviour's baptism, by which He sanctified the nature of water, they were used at midnight to carry home water from the Church and lay it up, where," he adds, "it would remain as fresh and uncorrupt for one, two, or three years as if it was immediately drawn out of any fountain."[2]

Practices not necessarily connected with Christianity also point to an intercourse with the East. S. Finnchu of Brigown, in the county of Cork, was in the habit of suspending himself by the armpits from iron hooks projecting from the roof of his cell,[3] which

[1] Reeves' "Columba," p. 360.
[2] Bingham, "Origines," London, 1840, vii. 82.
[3] Life of Finnchu, "Dictionary of National Biography."

seems to have been an attempt under difficulties to imitate the Indian fakir, who suspends himself by a hook fixed in his flesh. S. Ita of Killeedy, in the county of Limerick, applied a stag beetle to her side and encouraged it to burrow into her flesh,[1] a practice still prevalent among the natives of India, where the beetle is enclosed in half the shell of a cocoanut, and thus confined is bound to the side by a sash.[2] The prophetic smile of the Irish saint has also its Indian parallel.[3]

These strange practices from the far East, belonging to a later period than the founding of the Church, were probably imported by Irish travellers, who, in the course of their wanderings, visited the remotest parts of the East. In the Geography of Dicuil, written in the ninth century, we have an account of an Irish monk personally conducting a party of tourists to Egypt and the Holy Land; and one of the numerous S. Colmans obtained the title of "the Cimmerian Wanderer," from his familiarity with the coasts of the Black Sea. Nor should the visits of Egyptian monks to Ireland be left out of consideration, as having an important bearing on this question.[4] But not to dwell further on this, it would seem that while an Eastern character was impressed on the Irish Church at its foundation, new ideas and practices of the same sort subsequently found their way into it through intercourse with the East, and tended to keep alive its peculiarities. The Churches of the Continent, in their remote origin Eastern also, were not isolated like the Church of Ireland. On the contrary, they were exposed to the constant action of Western thought,

---

[1] Calendar of Œngus, Jan. 15, p. xxxiv.
[2] Ibid., Gloss., Index, p. cclxxix.
[3] Lives of saints, "Book of Lismore," Preface, p. 306.
[4] Petrie, "Round Towers," p. 136.

and accordingly, as successive waves of change in doctrine, ritual, and practice passed over them, the traces of their Eastern origin were gradually obliterated.

The Church of Britain, it has been stated, "was established probably on the oldest direct tradition from Judea,"[1] and the same observation applies to the Church of Ireland, which is thus a witness to a primitive form of Christianity. The most striking feature in the Irish Church is the attention paid to the Scriptures, and the reputation its schools enjoyed for their interpretation, which attracted students from England and the Continent. Receiving Christianity and the Latin language together, and every congregation being supplied, as we have seen, with a copy of the Scriptures, their first reading-book may be said to have been the Bible. Hence their attention was concentrated on it exclusively. It was not as abroad, where a pagan literature and mythology occupied the ground before Christianity appeared. In Ireland the Scriptures had a clear stage, and engaged for a long time the whole attention of the people. They entered into their legislation, they were employed in their legends, and they coloured their daily life almost as much as amongst the Puritans of modern times. The legends already referred to point to a scarcity of correct copies, and the profound interest excited by the arrival of a new manuscript, such as

---

[1] Lappenberg, "History of England," vol. i. p. 134. A survival of Eastern usage is the monogram, IHS., supposed by some at the present day to be the initial letters of the words "Iesus Hominum Salvator" (Jesus the Saviour of men). But the old Irish were well aware that they are the three first letters of the (Greek) name of Jesus, IHCOTC, —the second letter being the long *e* of the Greek alphabet. In the glossary attributed to Cormac, King and Bishop of Cashel, and written at the close of the ninth century, is the following entry: "IHC. = Iησους, Irish *Isu*, Jesus: in this term the Saviour's name is found." Cormac's Glossary by Whitley Stokes, Irish Archæological Society, 1868, p. 92.

that brought by S. Finnian of Moville. They were solicitous for the purity of the text, as we learn from the legend of Maelsuthain O'Carroll, "chief doctor of the Western world in his time," as the "Four Masters" term him. He was charged with interpolating the canon (*i.e.*, the Bible), and Michael the Archangel announced to three of his pupils (who were in heaven) that, "he was to be sent to hell for ever for this and other sins." When the souls of the pupils appeared to him in the form of doves, and announced the sentence, he repented and said, "I will put no sense of my own into the canon, but such as I shall find in the divine books."

The primitive character of the Church should naturally appear in the lives of the clergy of this period, but unfortunately none of them are earlier than the eleventh century, and they are therefore removed by a long interval from the age in which the subjects of them lived. They are, in fact, religious romances, though preserving many facts of the saints' careers, but coloured by the ideas of their own time.[1] The Bollandist editors complain of them. "When you find," they say, "many of the miracles common to all Irish saints, it is difficult to give credence to them. For instance, it is told of many an Irish saint that he was baptized by an angel, when a boy his future sanctity was foretold, he lived as a hermit in a hollow tree, he flogged a woman who was too forward in her attentions to him, and he had a marvellous control over animals."[2] These are the stock miracles with which the hagiographers of a later time decorated the lives of the saints, and which serve to cast sus-

---

[1] See the remarks of Dr. O'Donovan on the perversion of S. Molling's history, by his mediæval biographer. "Annals of the Four Masters," vol. i. p. 298, note.
[2] Boll., Actt SS. Vit. Dairchell, June 17, tom. iii. p. 406.

picion on them. Very different in style are the authentic utterances of the men themselves, of which a few specimens have come down to us. That they are so few is a subject of regret but not of surprise, considering the immense destruction of documents during the Danish period.

Of special interest is a passage from one of the lectures of S. Comgall,[1] the head of the great monastery of Bangor, in Ulster, whose praise is celebrated by S. Bernard, for the number and eminence of his pupils. He was the tutor of Columbanus, who in his second Instruction thus refers to him, giving an extract from his lecture: "I presume not to lay down principles of mine own littleness, seeking the authority of an abler teacher, namely, the most enlightened and comprehensive teaching of Faustus (*i.e.*, Comgall),[1] from whose words I most appropriately select a few for the commencement of my work, inasmuch as it was by these same precepts of which I desire to speak that he instructed me, unworthy as I am, while under his direction, and thus in age, in worthiness and knowledge my superior, let him first speak, and, as it were, in advance of me, assail the ignorant and slothful. His words are: 'If the cultivator of the land and husbandman, when preparing the soil to commit to it the seed, does not consider his work all done when he has broken up the earth with a strong share, and by the action of the plough has reduced the stubborn soil, but further endeavours to cleanse the ground of unfruitful weeds, to clear it of injurious rubbish, and to pluck up by the root the spreading shoots of thorns and brambles, fully persuaded that his land will never produce a good crop until it be reclaimed from mis-

[1] Flor., pp. 512-601.
[2] This is a Latin translation of Comgall, according to the custom of the period.

chievous plants, applying to himself the words of the prophet, "Break up your fallow ground and sow not among thorns" (Jer. iv. 3), how much more does it behove us who believe the hope of our fruits to be laid up, not on earth, but in heaven, to cleanse from vicious passions the field of our heart, and not suppose we have done enough when we subdue the ground of our bodies by the labour of fasting and watching, unless we primarily study to correct our vices and reform our morals.'"[1] It is interesting to notice that Columbanus was a disciple of S. Comgall, who was a contemporary of S. Columba. S. Gall, again, was a disciple of Columbanus, and thus the teaching of S. Columba descended to S. Gall, and was communicated to the Swiss by him.

Columbanus[2] gives an account of his own views in his letter to the Pope. "All we Irish," he says, "are disciples of S. Peter and S. Paul, and of all the disciples who wrote the divine Canon (*i.e.*, the Bible) under the guidance of the Holy Ghost : we are all Irishmen, the remotest inhabitants of the world : we receive nothing beyond the teaching of the evangelists and apostles : not one of us has been a heretic, or a Jew, or a schismatic, but the Catholic faith is preserved among us intact, as it was originally handed down by you—I mean the successors of the apostles."[3] He has left a collection of thoughts briefly expressed which he terms his Monosticha,[4] and which he no doubt intended as maxims for the guidance of his followers. A few of them will give an idea of their general character. No. 7 is, "Live trusting in God and following the precepts of Christ." 12. "Most excellent is a mind robed in the love of Christ."

[1] Bishop Reeves. "Antiphonary of Bangor," p. 7.
[2] *Fl.* A.D. 559-615.
[3] Lanigan, "Eccl. Hist.," ii. 294.   [4] Μονόστιχα, or single verses.

17. "Let the good words of salvation always sound in thy lips." 42. "Seek not thine own, but the things of Christ, thou who lovest Him." 64. "Faith alone shall be rewarded with the pure gift of faith."[1]

A few words of S. Molua[2] of Clonfert Mulloe have been preserved. Knowing that the time of his departure was near at hand, and his monks being assembled before him, he commended to them the divine precepts, and among other things he said, "Where there is constancy in the divine service there will be religion, but the end of true religion is eternal life. . . . Attend always to prayer in the morning, then to reading, and afterwards work until evening, having regard to the works of God and other necessary duties." Bede tell us of Aidan, Bishop of Lindisfarne, "No other object occupied his heart, his adoration, and his discourses than the redemption of mankind by the Passion, Resurrection, and Ascension into heaven of the Mediator between God and man, the man Christ Jesus."

Mr. Warren traces the Irish liturgies to an Ephesine[3] source, in accordance with the Eastern origin of the Church, but no service-book of the period has come down to us. The earliest is the Stowe Missal, which is assigned to the eleventh century, when Roman influence was in the ascendant in the Irish Church. Yet some information may be gathered from it and others of a later date bearing on the subject. Communion in both kinds was then practised, and therefore must have been at an earlier date; and it has been inferred from some rubrics that it was administered in both species simultaneously, as in the

---

[1] Paræneticorum Veterum, Pars I. (M. Goldastus).   [2] Died 605.
[3] This has been contested, but unsuccessfully, by the Abbé Duchesne, "Origines du Culte Chrétien," Paris, 1889.

Greek Church. While the people were communicating a hymn was sung, beginning, "Come, ye saints, take the body of Christ, drinking His holy blood by which you were redeemed." This hymn, which is preserved in the Antiphonary of Bangor, is peculiar to the Irish Church, no trace of it being found elsewhere. In the Life of S. Molling[1] of Luachair it is related that one day when preparing for Mass a dreadful-looking leper came to him and besought him for the chalice of the altar. Remembering at once the word of the Lord, "I will have mercy and not sacrifice," he administered the chalice to him. The Lord then miraculously supplied him with another. Any one who compares the magnificent Ardagh chalice, in the collection of the Royal Irish Academy, with the smaller ones placed with it, will easily see that it belonged to a time when communion in both kinds was in use. Water was mingled with the wine, or, as expressed in the Stowe Missal, "wine was added to the water,"[2] with the object of symbolising the union of the divine and human natures in Christ. Whether there was a daily celebration at this period we have no evidence; but in the ninth century, when the Würzburgh Glosses were written, it was usual, and the comment on Ephesians i. 7 refers to "the spiritual[3] blood which is offered every day upon the altar."

A peculiarity of the Irish Church was the custom of joint consecration by two priests, no similar practice existing in any other country or at any other time. To consecrate singly was the prerogative of bishops, or of individual priests specially

[1] Boll., Act Sanct., Junii 17, tom. iii. 4c6.
[2] Stowe Missal, Trans. Royal Irish Academy, Nov. 1886, p. 246.
[3] *In fuil spirtaldi.* Compare the post-communion Collect, "the spiritual food of the most precious Body and Blood of Thy Son." So also the Collect for S. Patrick's Day in the Drummond Corpus and Rosslyn Missals.

selected and empowered to consecrate on account of their sanctity or eminence. Connected with the communion was the use of the *culebadh*, or ecclesiastical fan, a custom derived from the East. Several of these fans are mentioned, but always in connection with Irish saints of the earliest date. They also appear in the illuminations of the "Book of Kells."

Baptism was performed by immersion, which was threefold, as we learn from the Würzburgh Gloss on Colossians ii. 14. "Three waves pass over us in baptism, because He was three days in the sepulchre." Then followed the anointing of the forehead and the investing with a white robe. This is referred to in the epistle to the subjects of Coroticus, where S. Patrick complains of the outrage committed on "some neophytes while still in their white robes, the day after they had been anointed with chrism, and while it was yet visible on their foreheads." Connected with baptism was the rite called the Pedilavium or " ceremonial washing of the feet after baptism," founded on S. John, chap. xiii. 4-7. This rite is not found in any Roman office, though it is common to those of the early Gallican Church.

A story is told by Benedict Abbas, at A.D. 1171, in relating the proceedings of the Synod of Cashel, that in the case of the baptism of the child of a rich man, it was plunged three times in milk instead of water. Dr. Lanigan calls this nonsense, and says no such practice existed in Ireland ; yet that there was some ground for it appears from the Life of S. Brigit in the "Book of Lismore." It is said that on her birth the child was bathed [1] in milk immediately, and it is explained, "this

---

[1] *Ronigset*, "they washed (her)," corresponds with the Latin *lavo*, as applied to baptism, *e.g.*, "balneum ubi infantes lavantur." Smith, "Dict. Christ. Antiq.," i. 174. A baptistery at Tullylease in the county of Cork, is called *Poll Laveir*, "the Pool of the *Laver*."

was in accordance with Brigit's merit, even with the brightness and sheen of her chastity."[1] As though milk was more honourable than water for so famous a saint.

It has been held by a recent writer that S. Patrick baptized his converts in great numbers without the preliminary teaching usually given to catechumens in the Continental Church.[2] But this view can scarcely be reconciled with the account of the baptism of the king's daughters. The ceremony in that case was not performed until they could answer the usual baptismal interrogatories, which necessarily required instruction. "Meet is the order," says the Tripartite Life of S. Patrick, "teaching before baptism, for it cannot be that the body should receive the sacrament of baptism, unless the soul first receives the verity of faith."[3] There is little doubt that the numbers said to have been baptized by S. Patrick are exaggerated, as the population of Ireland must have been small at that time. In the Würzburgh Glosses the instruction given before and after baptism is referred to in the gloss on 1 Cor. iv. 15. "Preaching before baptism and teaching after."

In the same commentary "perfect ones[4] who attend at baptism" are mentioned, that is, who were qualified to act as sponsors. A similar name[5] was given to them in the Greek Church, and they seem to have been baptized and instructed Christians, and probably communicants. On one occasion we find S. Brigit acting in this capacity, and "holding the child for baptism."[6] A fee was usually paid at baptism, at least in Munster, by the appointment of Œngus, son of Nadfraech, who was King of Munster at the close of the fifth century.

[1] Lives from the Book of Lismore, p. 184.
[2] On the Stowe Missal, by Rev. B. M'Carthy, D.D., Trans. R. I. A., Sept. 1886, pp. 160-184. The word "catechumen" occurs in Irish.
[3] Trip., p. 164. [4] *Ais foirbthe*, on 1 Cor. iv. 15.
[5] Τέλειοι, Bingham, vol. i. pp. 34, 39.
[6] Calendar of Œngus, p. lxxiii.

He ordered a *screpall*,[1] equivalent to three pence, to be paid; but in some cases a larger sum was given, probably according to the wealth of the parents, for at the baptism of S. Finnchu of Brigown, seven golden pennies[2] were paid to S. Ailbe, who performed the ceremony. The fee was abolished by the Synod of Kells, held under Cardinal Paparo, A.D. 1152.

The subordinate position of the bishops has already been noticed, and the severance of the powers of order and jurisdiction in their case. It only remains to add here that consecration was generally performed by a single bishop,[3] a custom which, though uncanonical, was not invalid.

A peculiar formula in the conferring of a blessing occurs in the life of S. Flannan of Killaloe. His father, King Theodore, having become a monk under S. Colman or Mocholmog, was one day ordered by the saint to go on an expedition to bring some murderers to justice. "I will not go," he replied, "unless you bless me and my posterity according to the manner of the ancient fathers." Colman consenting, Theodore prostrated himself on the ground, and the saint, measuring seven feet by his side, "as if representing the seven gifts of the Spirit," said, "Seven famous kings of your blood shall reign over all Ireland, but thou shalt go to heaven."[4]

The primitive character of the early Church is shown by the vernacular terms in use, as distinguished from those belonging to a later period, when the usages of the Latin Church began to prevail. Those in early use are for the most part translations from the Greek,

[1] The scruple was equal to 24 grs.
[2] Life of Finnchu of Brigown in "Lives from the Book of Lismore," p. 232.
[3] Tripartite, Introduction, p. clxxxi. In 1725 Pope Benedict XIII. is said to have sanctioned it. Killen, ii. 235.
[4] Codex Salmanticensis, p. 959.

or of purely native origin, but the later terms are nearly in all cases loan words. Amongst the former are the words for Gospel, Monastery, Church, Chapel, Bishop, Priest, Eucharist, Paten, Fan (Ecclesiastical), &c.[1]

In framing these, the Irish were either unacquainted with or indifferent to those employed by the Latin Church, and acted for themselves.

The native institutions, amidst which the Church of Ireland grew up, exercised a powerful influence on the habits of thought of the clergy. They were noted abroad for their freedom of speculation and their indifference to authority—a tone of mind due, as already observed, to the absence of an imperial government. Hence they disregarded the councils of the Church, as in the controversy between Clement and Boniface of Mentz. Their view seems to have been that of Bishop Burnet, that all those held during the Empire were "National Synods, to which the Christians of Persia, India, and Ethiopia were not subject,"[2] as they were beyond the frontiers of the Empire. The Irish being in the same position claimed similar rights.

The mission of Augustine to England in 590 brought the Roman clergy into immediate contact with the Irish labouring there, and the efforts of the foreign ecclesiastics to introduce their system were successful in the case of some Irish divines who accepted their teaching, the most eminent of whom was Cummian, a man of considerable learning. Thenceforth there were two systems in conflict within the country, and it is possible from the middle of the seventh century onward to quote passages favourable to Roman ideas, as, for instance, in Cummian's letter[3] written on his conversion, while the bulk of the nation and clergy long

---

[1] See Appendix C.   [2] On Article xxxiv.
[3] Ussher, Works, iv. 402.

continued immovably attached to their ancient ways, and steadfastly resisted the increasing pressure of Rome. Bishop Greith, however, affirms in an unhesitating manner that it was "from Rome, the source of religion, that Ireland undoubtedly derived her faith."[1] But when he proceeds to establish his position, all his authorities are found to be subsequent to the mission of Augustine, and represent the section of the Church which was favourable to the new ideas. If we omit the letter of Cummian,[2] the earliest evidence he brings forward belongs to the eighth century.[3] It is idle to quote authorities of so late a date, when contemporary documents three centuries earlier are in existence which do not support his view. This is one of the many difficulties in the way of the theory of a Roman origin, while the efforts of the authorities to prevent the clergy from visiting Rome add emphasis to them. The earliest communication of a Pope with Ireland is the letter of Honorius, A.D. 634, in which he makes no allusion to any previous intercourse, and, as we have seen, in the time of Archbishop Laurence nothing was known at Rome of the Church of Ireland. When we review the foregoing facts, we gather that the Church received a primitive form of Christianity from the East; had its own Church government and organisation, which were absolutely unique; was famous for the Scriptures; had its own ritual, both in baptism and the holy communion, with features unknown to the Continental Church; and had its own ecclesiastical terminology. In short, it stood apart in the West as an independent National Church.

[1] Geschichte, p. 112.   [2] Chapter ix. p. 153.
[3] The canons attributed to Patrick Auxilius and Isserninus belong to the eighth century (H. & S., vol. ii. part ii. p. 331), Eric and Bishop Marcus to the ninth, the Calendar of Œngus to the tenth, Marianus Scotus to the eleventh.

CHAPTER IX.

THE HIBERNENSIS AND THE IRISH SCHOOLS.

IN the century preceding the Danish inroads, the effect of the intercourse with the Continent is more and more evident in the history of the Irish Church. The studies of the clergy were extended to writers of the East and West, with whom they were previously unacquainted, and they acquired a knowledge of the decisions of councils and the decrees of popes. One result of this was the formation of the large collection of Canons, as they are termed, known by the name of the "Hibernensis," which was first published in 1874, and a second edition in 1885.[1] This has been attributed to two Irishmen, Cucuimne and Ruiben,[2] who flourished in the eighth century, and by whom it was compiled in the monastery of Dairinis, in the Bay of Wexford. Very little is known of either. The death of Cucuimne is entered in the "Annals of the Four Masters," at p. 742, where he is described as "a choice scholar;" and a verse, said to be Adamnan's composition, is quoted with reference to him:—"Cucuimne read the authors half through; the other half of his career he abandoned for his hags." To which he replies:

[1] H. Wasserschleben, "Die Irische Kanonensammlung," Zweite Auflage. Leipzig, 1885.
[2] "Hibernensis," by H. Bradshaw. Macmillan, 1885. He gathers the two names from an entry in one manuscript, which runs thus:— "Huc usq: Ruben et Cucuminae et du rinis." Wasserschleben, however, is not satisfied that they were the authors, as they are only mentioned in one manuscript, which belongs to the tenth century, and the text is corrupt ("Kanonensammlung," Nachtragen, lxii. *note*).

"Cucuimne read the authors half through; in the other half which remains he will read till he becomes an adept.[1] The meaning of the charge brought against him was, according to Dr. O'Donovan, merely that he was a married man.[2] This, at the time the dialogue was composed, had come to be looked on as a declension by those imbued with Roman ideas, of whom Adamnan was one. Ruiben died, according to the "Four Masters," in 720. He was the son of Brocan of Tehelly, in the parish of Durrow, in the north of the Queen's County, and is described in the "Annals of Clonmacnois" as a "good preacher and divine." Whether these were the authors of the "Collection" or not, it appears to have been drawn up for the Irish Church, and afterwards supplemented and expanded in the north of England and in Brittany, where, from the number of existing manuscripts, it seems to have been extensively used. The editor mentions ten manuscripts in which it is contained. These are of various dates, from the eighth century to the eleventh, the earliest being that transcribed at Cambray between 763–790. The passages of Scripture quoted in it are nearly five hundred in number, more than two-thirds of them being from the Old Testament. They are very often applied in the way of adaptation without regard to their original meaning. Thus, the legislation with respect to the cities of refuge (Numbers xxxv.) is applied to the churches which were Termons or asylums.[3] The ordinance of the jubilee (Leviticus xxv.) is

[1] Annals of the Four Masters, p. 742, compared with "Goidelica," 2nd edit., p. 97.
[2] The language about Cucuimne's wife is quite in Adamnan's style, as we see in his "Life of S. Columba," where he describes a married clergyman who was rich and held in esteem, as dying "in lectulo cum meretrice." Reeves' Adamnan, p. 75.
[3] Kanonensammlung, Liber xxviii.

applied in quite the opposite sense to the original, for, instead of the land returning to the owner after fifty years, the lapse of that period secured the right of the possessor by prescription.[1] The laws regarding the rights of kings (Deut. xvii.) are applied to abbots, termed in the Irish Annals "princes."[2] The version of Scripture used appears to be S. Jerome's Vulgate, but many of the texts quoted have not been identified. The term "Canons," applied to the collection, is not to be understood as though they were passed by a synod or council. They are only a compilation for the guidance and information of the clergy in cases of difficulty, and derived from all available sources.[3] Among the authorities quoted are Greek, Latin, and Gaulish Councils, "the Ancient Laws of the Church," Papal decrees, and all the principal writers of the East and West. Extracts are given from Irish and Roman synods, but in numerous cases the sources of the passages given are wrongly indicated. The authors did not consult the original authorities, but used, it seems, compilations made in England and Wales. There are indications of a knowledge of Greek,[4] as a synod of Gregory of Nazianzus is quoted, and a Greek name for monks is used in a canon which is also found in the second synod,[5] attributed to S. Patrick, where they are called Vactroperiti,[6] "carriers

---

[1] Lib. xxxvi.   [2] Lib. xxxvii.
[3] The extracts are numerous from Origen, Jerome, Augustine, Isidore, Gregory Romanus, Gregory Nazianzus, Basil, Lactantius, Ambrose, Faustus, Eucherius, Martin, Theophilus, Pelagius, Andreas, Cassian, Gennadius, Johannes Metropolitanus, "The Recognitions of Clement," "The Apocryphal Epistle of Clement to James," Eusebius' "Eccles. History" (translation), "History of Paul Orosius," "The Chronicle of Isidore of Seville," "Lives of Egyptian Fathers," "Jerome on Egyptian Monks," &c.
[4] On the Knowledge of Greek, see Professor Stokes' "Ireland and the Celtic Church."
[5] Canon xvii., H. and S., vol. ii. part ii., p. 335.
[6] Correctly *Bactroperatæ*, from βάκτρον and πήρα. The description

of staff and wallet," a term used in a contemptuous sense by S. Jerome. The Collection does not, therefore, represent the actual condition of the Irish Church at the time it was drawn up, but a combination of native and foreign usages. Amongst the latter, which have no reference to Ireland, is Book lix., on "The guiding of barbarians." This is a canon of a British synod,[1] and relates to the incursions of the Saxons, when they needed guides to lead them to the places they desired to plunder. In other passages we observe the design of introducing foreign practices in opposition to those of the native Church. An instance of this is the canon attributed to S. Patrick,[2] which directs that any cleric whose hair is not shorn in Roman fashion should be excommunicated, and stigmatises the Irish fashion as being derived from Simon Magus, and first introduced into Ireland by the swineherd of King Leogaire, for which a discourse of S. Patrick is given as authority. But we know from Bede and other sources that the Irish tonsure had not ceased to be the national custom until the time of Adamnan, 704, nor was the Roman tonsure introduced at Hy until 718. It is obvious, therefore, that S. Patrick cannot have been the author of this canon, nor of the "discourse" alluded to. It is manifestly due to foreign influence. The native usage of consecration by a single bishop was deemed irregular by foreign authorities, and this Collection accordingly quotes in opposition to it the ancient statutes of the Church, and also Isidore, who insists on the necessity of three bishops.[3]

of S. Molling collecting alms for his monastery illustrates this. "He carried two wallets, one on his back and the other on his breast, and in his hand he held his tutor's staff; thus did he go around." Betha Molling MS., Bibliotheque Royale, Brussels, p. 45*a*.
[1] Luci Victoriæ.
[2] Book lii. cap. 6 and 7; see also H. and S., ii. 328.
[3] Lib. i. caps. 4, 5.

Nevertheless, the Irish adhered to their own practice, and we find Archbishops Anselm and Lanfranc complaining of it as late as the twelfth century.[1]

The "casting of children on the Church" is the subject of another book,[2] and it is laid down that whoever does this without the knowledge of the abbot, if the church is one where a bishop is buried, or is present, must do penance for three and a half years. But if it is a small church, and there is no bishop there, the penance is reduced to a year and a half. The name of Basilica is said to be given to certain churches because kings (Basileis) only were buried there, "for other men were either cremated or buried under a cairn."[3] This could not be intended for Ireland, as the Basilica, with its semicircular apse, was quite unknown there; and it is held by some that the type of Church belonging to the earliest period in Ireland was that in use before the conversion of Constantine. After that, when Christianity became the religion of the Roman empire, the Basilicas or law courts were converted into churches.[4]

A canon attributed to S. Patrick orders that whoever steals money either in a church or monastery where martyrs or saints are buried, must be punished as the lot shall decide, either by having his hand or foot cut off, or by being imprisoned and performing whatever penance the elders shall decide.[5]

The independent position of the Church as regards the secular powers appears from the numerous passages quoted from the Old and New Testament on the duties of kings. One passage (Deuteronomy xvii. 17) forbids polygamy, and a synod is referred to which

---

[1] Ussher, iv.; Epistles 27, 35, 36.
[2] Lib. xlii. caps. 22, 24.   [3] Lib. xliv. cap. 20.
[4] Freeman, "History of Architecture," p. 196.
[5] Lib. xxix. cap. 7.

would appear to shew that polygamy was not easily eradicated.[1]

The enactment of the Brehon Law with regard to clerics sinning appears also among these canons, and a judgment attributed to Augustine permits such a person, when penitent, only to baptize, administer the communion to the sick, and attend at the altar. An Irish synod further ordered him into exile, and there to minister under the hand of the abbot; but the Irish, it adds, "interpret this more humanely on account of the scarcity of priests," and order that after penance such persons may be consecrated by imposition of hands, and serve in silence until their death, under the seal of penance doing nothing of their own will.[2] The scarcity here referred to could hardly have been in Ireland, and was probably in Northumbria, where every worker was required in the Irish mission to the Saxons. An instance of sending into exile is the story of MacCuill, who intended to kill S. Patrick, and accordingly was supposed to have been sentenced by the saint. "Go," he said, "unarmed to the sea, and pass quickly from Ireland, taking nothing with you except a few clothes, and eating and drinking nothing of the fruit of this island; and when you come to the sea, fasten your feet with an iron fetter, and throw the key into the sea, and enter a vessel of one hide without oar or rudder; and whatever land the wind and the waves waft you to, by divine providence there dwell and carry out the divine commands."[3] A canon which has given rise to much discussion is that attributed to S. Patrick, which orders that, "If any questions arise in this island let them be referred to the Apostolic See."[4] A longer one of similar import is found in

[1] Lib. xxv. cap. 6. In the Life of Finnchu we read of a King of Leinster who had two wives.   [2] Lib. xi. caps. 2, 3.   [3] Trip., p. 288.
[4] Kanonensammlung, Lib. xx. cap. 5; also Ussher, iv. 330, note.

the "Book of Armagh," which is thus given by Archbishop Ussher: "Whensoever any cause that is very difficult and unknown to all the judges of the Scottish nations shall arise . . . it is rightly to be referred to the See of the Archbishop of the Irish (to wit, Patrick), and to the examination[1] of the prelate thereof. But if there by him and his wise men a cause of this nature cannot easily be made up, we have decreed it shall be sent to the See Apostolic; that is to say, to the chair of the Apostle Peter, which hath the authority of the city of Rome.[2]

The relation between these Canons is uncertain. Dr. Lanigan, who assumed that the shorter was the genuine Canon of S. Patrick, considered that in the "Book of Armagh" as an expansion of it.[3] The German editor, on the other hand, believes it to be an extract from the Armagh Canon.[4] They seem to be of about the same date, the latter being assigned to the eighth century,[5] while the earliest text[6] of the Hibernensis belongs also to that century (763–790): that is, three centuries after S. Patrick, or, if the authorship of Cucuimne and Ruiben is accepted, about two centuries and a half.

It has been shown by Dr. Lanigan that the Armagh Canon is not S. Patrick's, and it is in the highest degree improbable that the one in Hibernensis can be his. For there is no mention of Rome or the Apostolic See in any of S. Patrick's writings. Nor could the protracted controversy about Easter have taken place if this Canon was known and accepted by the Irish Church as his. Moreover, Cummian, in his

---

[1] *Examinationem.* O'Curry, who undertakes to correct! Ussher translates this, "jurisdiction," MS. Materials, p. 611.
[2] Ussher, Works, iv. 330.   [3] Eccl. Hist., ii. 391.
[4] Wasserchleben, Einleitung, s. xxxv.
[5] H. and S., vol. ii. part ii. p. 332, note.
[6] Wasserschleben, s. xxx.

THE HIBERNENSIS AND THE IRISH SCHOOLS. 153

letter to Segéné, Abbot of Hy, on the Easter question, would not have quoted the decree of Sardica,[1] in which Rome is referred to as the capital[2] of the world, if he had known this Canon, which takes the higher ground of its being the Apostolic See.

To sum up, it appears that the Canon of the Hibernensis was unknown in 610, when Laurence and Columbanus had their interview, for the Churches at that time knew nothing of each other. It was unknown in 634, when Cummian wrote his letter. And it was plainly unknown in 664, at the Conference of Whitby, or so acute a controversialist as Wilfrid would not have failed to terminate the discussion by bringing forward the direction of the great apostle to refer the matter to Rome.

The earliest manuscript of the Hibernensis in which it is contained was transcribed, as we have seen, between 763–790, not in Ireland but at Cambray. The date of origin of the Canon is therefore between 664 and 790; or, if we accept the authorship of Cucuimne, it will lie between 664–715.

Both it and the Armagh Canon are evidently to be referred to the innovating party in the Church who were endeavouring to introduce Roman ideas, and in order to facilitate their reception, made use[3] of the honoured name of S. Patrick.

The mode of "enquiry into causes"[4] prescribed in the Irish Church is laid down in the Collection, and

---

[1] Ussher, Works, iv. 442. It also occurs in two MSS. of the Hibernensis, Lib. xx. cap. 3, note *e*.

[2] *Caput urbium.* Dr. Bellesheim, with his usual lamentable inaccuracy, says Cummian referred to the "Head of the Churches" (vol. i. s. 182) *dem haupt der Kirchen*, and also that the Synod of Magh Léné acted in compliance with the Canon of Armagh, which of course was never mentioned, not being then in existence. O'Curry, also taking no notice of Dr. Lanigan's conclusive arguments, asserts that this Canon is genuine.

[3] Kanonensammlung, p. 40. [4] Lib. xix.

has no reference to Rome. Recourse was first to be had to the twenty-two books of the Old Testament, the four Evangelists, and the Epistles. Then the Hagiographa was to be consulted, and if the question could not be thus decided, Catholic histories; next, the Canons of the Apostolic See, then the examples of the saints. If all these sources do not afford a solution of the difficulty, the elders[1] of the province are to be assembled. This is the final court of appeal, and the promise of our Lord is claimed for it (Matt. xxviii. 20). Cummian's course, as stated in his letter,[2] seems to have been exactly in accordance with this, supplemented in his case by the Canon of Sardica. Many other Canons in the Collection are of foreign origin, and opposed to Irish usages, such as that forbidding the marriage of those wearing a religious habit; and the fifteen chapters of another book[3] relating to martyrdom, of which the Irish Church had no experience. From the foregoing facts it appears that the authors, who were Irishmen, whether those named or not, had imbibed foreign ideas, and endeavoured to introduce them into Ireland. Adamnan and others were also busily engaged in urging the Roman calculation of Easter on the North of Ireland, as well as other foreign practices. We see in these Canons the influence which acted on the Irish Church, gradually assimilating it to Rome, and preparing the way for its final subjection when political circumstances were favourable.

Amongst those who remained in Ireland and attained eminence as educators of youth was Colchu, Reader or Head Master[4] of the great School of Clonmacnois,[5] founded by S. Kieran in 549. Our chief information about Colchu is derived from a letter addressed to him

[1] Founded on Deut. xxxii. 7. [2] Ussher, iv. 432, &c. [3] Lib. xlix.
[4] *Fer Leighinn.*
[5] Situated on the Shannon, in the King's County.

by Alcuin, the preceptor and confidential adviser of Charlemagne, and one of the most eminent scholars of the Middle Ages.

The letter, dated by Archbishop Ussher, A.D. 794, is addressed "To Colchu, the Chief Scribe, and Master of the Scots" (Irish). The office of the scribe was so honourable in those days that the title was frequently bestowed to enhance the importance of an abbot or bishop. Alcuin's language implies the highest respect. He speaks of him as his "blessed master and pious father," and of himself as a humble Levite; and seems still to feel himself a pupil, as he had been at one time. Charlemagne welcomed Irishmen to his court, finding them valuable helpers in his projects for the extension of education, and Clonmacnois, then famous as a great religious centre, seems to have been one of the sources from which he drew his supply of teachers. Alcuin, in telling Colchu some news which would interest him, says: "I, thy son, and Joseph thy servant, and all thy friends who are with us, serve the Lord in prosperity." He also sends a present of money from the Emperor and himself to certain monasteries and hermits. The amount was considerable, two hundred silver sicli,[1] equivalent to about £11 or £12 of our money. Who would have supposed that the great Emperor would have concerned himself with the welfare of Colchu and the School of Clonmacnois, far away in the barbarous island? His having done so is evidence of the high esteem in which both were held on the Continent in that age. Very little on the subject of doctrine is found in Irish ecclesiastical literature, but in Colchu's case we have an exception. The community or "family" of Clon-

[1] The siclus or sigal was equal to the Irish screpall of 21 grs. It has been mistaken by some for the Jewish shekel.

macnois had a difference with another body of divines on the subject of doctrine, and Colchu was appointed their representative in the discussion which ensued. We are not informed what the question was, but S. Paul's views on it were in debate, and Colchu, who had taken him as his "special master and patron in the spirit as well as in the letter," was admitted to have silenced his opponents. In consequence of this, the story went that S. Paul appeared to him in person, relieved him of the books he was carrying, and bore them home for him.[1]

Many Irishmen of learning sought employment abroad, and found no difficulty in obtaining it. Two of these appeared at the court of Charlemagne in the year 772, and their arrival and reception are thus described in a work written in the following century by a monk of S. Gall, believed to have been Notker Balbulus, or the Stammerer. "When the illustrious Charles," he says, "began to reign alone in the Western parts of the world, and literature was everywhere almost forgotten, and the worship of the true Godhead was accordingly feeble, it happened that two Scots of Ireland came over with some British merchants to the shores of France, men incomparably skilled in human learning and the Holy Scriptures. As they produced no merchandise for sale, they used to proclaim to the crowds flocking to purchase, 'If any one is desirous of wisdom, let him come to us and receive it, for we have it to sell.' They repeated this declaration so often that an account of them was conveyed either by their admirers or by those who thought them insane to the King Charles, who being a lover, and very desirous of wisdom, had them conducted with all expedition before him, and asked

[1] Life of Colchu, "Dictionary of National Biography."

them if they truly possessed wisdom, as reported to him. They answered that they did, and were ready in the name of the Lord to communicate it to such as would seek it worthily. On inquiring of them what compensation they would expect for it, they replied that they required nothing more than convenient situations, ingenuous minds, and, as being in a foreign country, to be supplied with food and raiment. Charles having heard their proposals, and being filled with great joy, at first kept both of them with himself for a short time. After some interval, when obliged to proceed on a military expedition, he ordered one of them, whose name was Clemens, to remain in France, entrusting to his care a great number of boys, not only of the highest noblesse, but likewise of the middling and lower ranks of society, who were by his orders provided with victuals and suitable habitations. The other, by name Albinus, he directed to Italy, and assigned to him the monastery of S. Augustin near Pavia, that those who chose to do so might resort to him for instruction."[1] Clement became a teacher in the palace school, and it has quite a modern sound to hear that competitive examinations were the rule there. He, with the Englishman Alcuin, and the Frenchman Theodulf, were the active agents in the restoration of learning, which was one of the great achievements of Charlemagne's reign. They were, as Mr. Hallam observes, "the true paladins that repaired to his court." Another Irishman, who is known only as a man of letters, was Dicuil, who was born about 755, some thirty years later than Vergil. He was not a man of learning, nor a profound thinker, nor an eminent writer, but an honest

---

[1] De Gestis Caroli Magni, written between 884-888, and dedicated to Charles the Fat (Haddan's "Remains," p. 281).

compiler of such knowledge as he could acquire in a dark age, and he may be regarded as a representative of the average literary Irishman of the eighth century. His title to notice rests on his work, "The Survey of the World." He composed it A.D. 825, and apparently towards the close of his life. "When the seed wheat," he says, "is hidden beneath the soil, and the labour is over, and the night draws on, the oxen are permitted to rest." It is highly probable that Dicuil was one of Charlemagne's band of teachers, from the familiarity his writings show with the events of that period abroad,[1] and his work was evidently intended for the instruction of the Frankish youth. It is composed of two parts—one purporting to give the measurement of the (Roman) world,[2] the other being a compilation from the Roman geographers. The valuable part of his work is the original information it contains, which is of the highest interest, and entitles him to our indulgence for his failings in other matters. Amongst the latter must be reckoned the title of his book, "The Survey of the World," for, being but an indifferent Latin scholar, he mistook the meaning[3] of a poem describing a revision of the map of the empire. The two commissioners—one of whom was the draughtsman, while the other put in the colours—were mistaken by him for two surveyors, who performed the remarkable operation of surveying the empire in "a few months," whereas the actual survey occupied thirty-two years.

He describes a visit by a party of Irish travellers to Egypt, personally conducted by a monk named Fidelis, who explained the different sites, and told

[1] He gives a curious account of the elephant sent to Charlemagne by Haroun al Raschid.
[2] De Mensura Orbis. Letronne, Paris, 1814.
[3] See Tabula Itineraria Peutingeriana. C. Mannertus, Lipsiæ, 1824.

them the stories current in that age. The Pyramids were supposed to be the barns built by Joseph in preparation for the years of famine; and amongst the sights which they were anxious to see were the tracks of Pharaoh's chariot-wheels, but they had no opportunity, owing to the objections of the sailors.

He mentions that thirty years before, some ecclesiastics visited Thule, supposed to be Iceland, and saw the sun, instead of setting, disappear for a short time behind a hill—" yet even for that short time there is no darkness at all, but one can do anything he wishes, as if the sun was shining." He also describes the frozen sea one day's journey to the north of the island. As the voyage referred to took place thirty years before the date of his work, it could not have been later than 795, which is sixty-five years earlier than the date usually assigned for the discovery of the island. A Northern chronicle [1] confirms Dicuil's story, stating that, before the Norwegians occupied it, Christians had arrived there who came from the West by sea, and who left behind them " Irish books, bells, and other things."

These contributions to the history of a very obscure period impart a value to the work of Dicuil, to which it is not entitled by its intrinsic merits.

A foreign writer [2] laments that we only know of the education imparted in the Irish schools just when they had almost ceased to exist, and when their last pupils had nearly all emigrated to the Continent, in consequence of the inroads of the Norsemen. Two treatises, however, have come down to us with which he was unacquainted, but which afford some information on the subject. One is a Commentary on S. Paul's

[1] The Landnamabok.
[2] De Jubainville, Introd., Celt. Lit., pp. 379-382.

Epistles in the old Irish language; the other the Geography of MacCosse, used in the school of Ross Ailithir, now Ross Carbery, in the county of Cork. The Commentary is preserved in the library of Würzburgh,[1] where it has lain for a thousand years.[2] Irish pilgrims frequented the town in the eleventh and twelfth centuries, and this manuscript appears to have been left there by one of them. Had it remained in Ireland it would in all probability have shared the fate of the countless volumes which were destroyed by the Danes, or perished by damp or neglect. The glosses forming the Commentary are written between the lines and round the margin of the pages in minute handwriting, and so much contracted that one must sympathise with the students. They are in the Irish language of the eighth or the beginning of the ninth century, according to high authority,[3] though a later writer[4] thinks they may belong to the following century. The Commentary affords evidence that the training of the Irish schools was by no means narrow. The theology of the East as well as the West is represented in it, and several interpretations are given of difficult texts, sometimes as many as five. Between these the pupil had to make his choice, and the habit thus acquired of looking at a subject from different points of view was an important mental discipline, and conduced to independence of thought. The authors quote Pelagius, Jerome, Augustine, Origen, Gregory the Great, and Isidore of Seville. Pelagius,

---

[1] Situated on the Main, 140 miles north-west of Munich.
[2] It was published first by Professor Zimmer, Glossæ Hibernicæ, Berlin, 1881; by Whitley Stokes, D.C.L., with a literal version, Hertford, 1887; and selections, with a translation by Rev. T. Olden, Society for Promoting Christian Knowledge, 1889.
[3] Zeuss, "Grammatica Celtica," 2nd edit., Pref., p. xxiv.
[4] Signor Ascoli, "Il Codice Irlandese dell' Ambrosiana," Prefazione, p. ix.

who was the most famous heresiarch of his age, was energetically opposed by Jerome and Augustine, and both he and Origen were condemned by several councils. Nevertheless, he is quoted by name in this Commentary forty-two times, but S. Jerome only three. Yet the authors of the work were not Pelagians; they used his notes, but carefully avoided his errors. The fact of Pelagius' Commentary having been attributed both to Gelasius and S. Jerome is, as Bishop Lightfoot observes, a high testimony to its merits. A few extracts from the glosses will give the reader some idea of the teaching of the Irish schools.

1 Thess. v. 23. "I pray God your whole spirit, soul, and body be preserved blameless." *Spirit*—that is, the primary part of the soul by which we understand; or (2) the Holy Ghost, *i.e.*, as it has been imparted to us." These were the views held by the theologians of Alexandria and Antioch respectively. They are here summed up in brief form, but they were probably further explained orally.

1 Cor. xii. 9. "To another faith by the same Spirit; to another the gifts of healing by the same Spirit." *Gifts of healing*—"that he may cure the sick as physicians do (Pelagius), or (2) it means performing miracles of healing." In the former view here mentioned the healing art in all its branches is regarded as the gift of the Holy Spirit to man. And when we reflect on the diminution of human suffering through medical science, and especially by the use of anæsthetics, it would seem that there is much to be said for it.

1 Tim. ii. 4. "Who will have all men to be saved, and come to the knowledge of the truth." *All men to be saved.* Question? why are not all men saved if He desires it, for the Psalmist says, "He hath

L

done whatsoever He hath pleased" (Ps. cxv. 3). The answer is not difficult, because no one is constrained against his will; or (2) a part is put for the whole, for there is no race or language in the world of which some one was not saved; or (3) it was those only whom He desired to save, that He did save; *i.e.*, "who will have all men to be saved," that is, Augustine says, "as much as to say no one can be saved except whom He wills." The first interpretation is that of Pelagius, the second from Primasius, and the third from Augustine. Such is the impartiality of the authors of this Commentary.

The word "prophecy" is usually understood of preaching, as in 1 Cor. xiv. 32. The spirits of the prophets are subject to the prophets. *Prophets*—"some say that the Holy Spirit who was in the prophets of the Old Testament was subjected to the prophets of the New, that is, to the apostles. But this is not true; for it is not of prophets he treats here, but of preachers." Many Irish saints are termed prophets, though no prophecies are recorded of them; and it is highly probable that the name was given to them originally as preachers of the Gospel. The error of regarding all so termed, as foredicting the future was congenial to the nature of the Irish, who have been always disposed to welcome the spurious [1] prophecies put forth from time to time.

1 Cor. xiv. 26. "Hath a revelation." The comment is "memory," that is, "the revealing of mysteries." At first sight this does not appear easy to understand, but it is of great interest as affording an insight into the extent of the studies of Irish theologians, for we have here a reference to Plato's theory of *anamnesis* [2] or Memory. His account of knowledge was, that it

---

[1] O'Curry, "Manuscript Materials," p. 410.
[2] "Dialogues of Plato." Jowett, Oxford 1871. vol. i. p. 269.

was the recalling to mind what had been learnt in a previous state of existence, and the commentary represents a combination of this theory with Christian teaching, the recovery of the lost knowledge being in this case aided by the spiritual illumination of the Corinthian to whom mysteries were thus revealed. This illustrates the observation of Mosheim with regard to the contrast between the Latin and Irish theologians in this century. The former were content to collect testimonies out of the fathers, but "among the Irish only, some discerning ones employed philosophy which was abhorred by others, in the explanation of religious doctrines!"[1] From these instances it will be seen that the Irish students were taught to think for themselves, and had the opportunity of becoming acquainted with the speculations of the great thinkers of the past.

Turning now to secular studies, the geography[2] of Ross Ailithir gives some information as to the knowledge imparted on that subject. It is in the Irish language and in metrical form, no doubt to facilitate its commission to memory. Beginning with Asia, it gives the boundaries of the different countries, with an occasional characteristic of people or territory. These probably formed the heads of oral lectures, and when the magnet, the diamond, and the pearl are mentioned, the students probably heard of the diamond mines of Bengal, from which, according to Gibbon, the Romans were supplied, or of the pearl fishery of Ceylon. The following is the account of India, paradise being supposed as usual in the middle ages to lie in the east of Asia:—

---

[1] Mosheim, ii. 159, Soames' ed., 1841.
[2] "The Geography of Ross Ailithir, with a translation by Rev. T. Olden," Proceedings of the Royal Irish Academy, No. xxxvii. The original is contained in the "Book of Leinster," pp. 135, 136, of the facsimile published by the Royal Irish Academy.

IX.

" From that land to the river Indus westward
Is India great and proud :
From the north, from the Hindoo Coosh,
To the strait of the Mare rubrum [Red Sea].

X.

Known is its excellence on every side,
Its magnets and its diamonds ;
Its pearls, its gold dust,
Its gold, and its carbuncles.

XI.

Its unicorns of fierce habit,
Its soft and balmy breezes ;
Its elephants of mighty strength,
Its two harvests in one year."

Passing over several countries we come to the following :—

" Chaldea and Babylon the strong
Are conspicuous between Arabia
And the plain of Shinar northwards,
Wherein was built Nimrod's tower."

The belief that Nimrod was the builder of the tower of Babel is derived from Josephus, and the form of his name in the Irish (viz. Nebruaid) is that of the Septuagint. This tradition is also found in Dante.[1]

" Nimrod, I saw ;
At foot of the stupendous work he stood,
As if bewilder'd, looking on the crowd
Leagued in his proud attempt on Sennaar's plain.

XIX.

Palestina, the glorious land,
There are the sons of Jacob,
To the south the vigorous Nabatheans
And the lands of the Saracens."

The later Roman writers applied the name Saracen

---

[1] Purgatorio xii. 34. Bacchus was also called Nebrodes, and has been identified with Nimrod (Hoffman's Lexicon Univers., s. v. Nimrod).

to all the tribes; but this author, who distinguishes them from the Nabatheans, followed the earlier account of Ptolemy, in whose time they were a small tribe between Palestine and Egypt.

One more extract will be sufficient :—

> "Land of Alaunia, where is a burning fire,
> From the Caspian Sea to the Palus Mæotis [Azoff]
> Known are their tribes West and East,
> A fair-haired people."

Petroleum has only become generally known in Europe of recent years, but here we find it referred to in the tenth century, for the phenomenon here mentioned (the burning-fire) is undoubtedly that known as the "eternal fires" of Baku on the Caspian, now attracting so much notice. According to the last edition of the *Encyclopædia Britannica*, the earliest mention of this district elsewhere is in the Arabian writer, Masudi, in the tenth century. The Irish were therefore well informed on matters which one might have supposed to be outside the range of their knowledge.

The schools which taught as now described gave a tone to the Church which it long retained, as one uniting with theology the best culture then attainable.

CHAPTER X.

THE DANES: THE ROUND TOWERS.

DURING the period of which we have been hitherto treating, Ireland alone of European countries had no experience of foreign invasion. No enemy from abroad had descended upon her shores and all her difficulties were purely domestic. But now a disastrous change was about to take place, for just before the opening of the ninth century began those inroads of the Norsemen, which were the source of so many calamities to Ireland, and caused more deadly injury to religion and society than anywhere else in Europe. Their first descent was in 795, when they landed on the little island of Lambay, off the coast of Dublin, and sacked the monastery. Various causes have been assigned for the outpouring of these formidable adventurers from their Northern seas. One, no doubt, was the position of their country. With a barren soil and a wintry sky it yielded them but a precarious subsistence, and the tidings of the abundance elsewhere drew them forth to seek their fortunes in more favoured lands. The love of adventure, too, was strong in a race inured from childhood to battling with the elements in their stormy seas. An Irish poet, entering into their feelings, describes the Norse warrior as rejoicing in the storm :—

"Bitter in sooth is the wind to-night,
Rousing the wrath of the white-haired sea,
For smooth sea-sailing hath no delight
For Norroway's sons so bold and free."[1]

---
[1] Miss Stokes, "Early Christian Architecture," p. 95.

And lastly, must be taken into account as a powerful motive a vindictive feeling against Christianity. For the cruel persecution of the Saxons by which Charlemagne ensured their outward conformity to Christianity, in defiance of the principles of the Gospel, had raised up a host of enemies to the Christian name among those Northern people, who sympathised with them. Taking into account those considerations, the fury of their inroads and the havoc they wrought are no longer matter of surprise. Ireland is a country peculiarly exposed to such a danger. The numerous harbours afford a safe anchorage. The coast is indented by creeks and estuaries which run far inland, and the broad waterway of the Shannon gives access to the heart of the country, which thus lies open in every part. The original invaders were Scandinavians,[1] or "Fair Gentiles," as they were termed. They were succeeded about fifty years after by the "Black Gentiles," or Danes, with whom they were often in conflict; but towards the close of the "Viking age" both races seem to have coalesced, and native writers do not distinguish between them. The term Lochlann is used of both, a word which seems to have a resemblance to Viking.[2] Many details, chiefly relating to the South of Ireland, are given in the work of a native author, composed in the eleventh century, and termed "The Wars of the Irish with the Foreigners."[3] It is a long record of plunder and devastation, lasting, with a brief interval of forty years,

---

[1] Mr. H. Bradley (Academy, June 28, 1890) has pointed out that the true form of this name is Scadinavia, the present spelling being due to the current text of Pliny. Hence it is probable that the Balscaden in Fingal, as well as that in Howth, is "the town of the Scandinavians," and not of "Herrings," as popularly believed.

[2] *Loch* is used of a bay, and *Viking* also is from *Vik*, a bay.

[3] *Cogadh Gaidhil re Gallaibh*, edited by Rev. J. H. Todd, D.D. (Rolls Series).

for more than two centuries. Apart from mere plunder, they acted with a settled purpose in their inroads. "The writings and the books in every Church and in every sanctuary were burned and thrown into the water by the plunderers from the beginning [of their inroads] to the end of them."[1] The repeated attacks on the same establishment at short intervals could not have been merely for plunder, as it is impossible to suppose they could have found fresh treasures on every occasion. In 832 Armagh was attacked three times in one month, and again in 839, 850, 873, 876, 890, 893, 895, 898, 914, 919, 926, 931, 943, 995, 1012, 1016. This would appear to have been with the intention of completely destroying it as a centre of religious influence. Extraordinary courage and perseverance were shown by the occupants in restoring their buildings after the storm had passed by. They were deeply attached to those sites, hallowed by the memories of famous saints whose bodies lay in the cemetery. But ultimately they were compelled to abandon them, all hope of restoring the past being lost. To recount the Danish inroads would be merely to repeat over and over again the same tale of ruin and destruction. But one period deserves special notice, when Turgesius attempted to establish a Danish kingdom, and to set up his national heathenism. Assuming "the sovereignty of all the foreigners of Ireland," he occupied the North, and in connection with the royal fleet, which accompanied him, three other fleets appeared in different directions. One anchored in Lough Neagh, another in the Bay of Dundalk, and a third ascending the Shannon took up a position in Lough Ree. Having attacked and taken Armagh after three assaults, he "usurped the

[1] Wars of the Irish and Foreigners, p. 139.

office of Coarb," assuming spiritual as well as temporal authority. He next proceeded to the conquest of Meath and Connaught, and for this purpose joined his fleet at Lough Ree, the great expanse of the Shannon, near Athlone. In this position he was within reach of the monasteries and churches on both banks. Accordingly, he sacked Clonmacnois, Lorrha, Terryglas, the seven churches of Iniscaltra, and all the churches in Lough Derg. His ultimate purpose was evident when he placed his wife Ota at Clonmacnois, then second only to Armagh in importance as an ecclesiastical centre. She seems to have acted as a kind of priestess of the Northern heathenism, for "she used to give her oracular answers[1] from the altar of the principal church there." When Turgesius assumed the Coarbship of Armagh, the rightful owner, Forannán, fled, taking with him the possessions constituting the title-deeds of the See. He took refuge at Cluain Comarda, now Patrick's Well, in the county of Limerick; but his retreat was discovered by the Limerick Danes, who sent a party to capture him. He was taken prisoner and carried off, and "the shrine of S. Patrick was broken by them." This was in 845, and in the same year Turgesius' career came to an end, and with it the last effort to establish heathenism in Ireland. He was taken prisoner by Malachi, King of Ireland, and drowned in Lough Owel, near Mullingar, his usurpation having lasted four years. The memory of the sufferings of the people during the domination of the Norsemen has scarcely yet died out, and the opening words of the history of those wars, though written at a late period, represent the popular feeling. "There was an astonishing and awfully great oppres-

---

[1] Not "audiences," as it has been rendered.

sion over all Erin throughout its breadth by powerful azure gentiles, and fierce hard-hearted Danars ... for the space of 200 years, according to some authorities."[1] And with reference to their anti-Christian character, the author says: "They ravaged her chieftainries, and her privileged churches, and her sanctuaries; and they rent her shrines, and her reliquaries, and her books. They demolished her beautiful ornamented temples, for neither veneration, nor honour, nor mercy for Termonn, nor protection for church or sanctuary, for God or man, was felt by this furious, ferocious, pagan, ruthless, wrathful people."[2] The state of things here described closely resembles the domination of the Turks over the Eastern Church in past ages, and the result was similar in the degradation and demoralisation of the people. The saints of Ireland, Dr. Keating tells us, were prophesying evil in consequence of the pride of the chieftains and the lawlessness resulting from the Danish invasions.

But it would have been impossible for the foreign invaders to have caused all this ruin had not the dissensions of the Irish chieftains aided them. Some of these engaged in conflicts for power, being ecclesiastics as well as chieftains. Felim, son of Criffan, who was King of Munster as well as Abbot and Bishop of Cashel, had no hesitation in plundering the churches of the North of Ireland, and putting the monks and clergy to the sword, in pursuance of his design of becoming supreme king, a claim which they seem to have opposed. An entry in the "Annals of the Four Masters," A.D. 832, relates to him: "A great number of the family of Clonmacnois were slain by Felim, son of Criffan, King of Cashel, and all their

---

[1] Wars of the Irish, p. 3.
[2] Ibid., pp. 41, 42. See Ussher, Works, iv. 479, 480.

Termonn was burnt by him to the doors of the church." In like manner did he treat the community of Durrow. But in the previous year he had already burnt the Termonn of Clonmacnois, and he repeated the sacrilege for the third time in 844. Shortly after this, being attacked by illness, his conscience smote him for his treatment of churches and ecclesiastics, and he attributed the complaint he suffered from to S. Kieran, who, he thought, pursued him and gave him a thrust with his crozier. Notwithstanding his cruelties and depredations, his death is thus recorded by the "Four Masters" at A.D. 845: "Felim, son of Criffan, King, Anchorite, and Scribe, the best of the Irish in his time, died on August 18, of his internal wound, through the miracle of God and Kieran;" and they quote with approbation a poetical lament on his death, in which the Irish are said to be sorrowful for him, as "a prince so generous never again shall be born,"[1] which shows a strange indifference to his unchristian proceedings. The feeling of reverence for sacred persons and buildings had evidently much declined, owing in some measure to the example of the Norsemen, and the immunity from the divine vengeance which they enjoyed in their inroads. When the saint was supposed to preside and watch over his church, and to avenge any insult to it, there was little fear of outrage. But when it became evident that sanctuaries might be violated and yet no punishment ensue, a revulsion of feeling took place. The "Four Masters," relating the plundering of Armagh by the Danes, A.D. 891, when the church and oratory were partially destroyed, quote a verse of poetry: "Pity, O Patrick, that thy prayers did not stay the foreigners with their axes when striking thy oratory."

[1] Annals of the Four Masters, vol. i. p. 473.

This pathetic lamentation expresses surprise as well as sorrow that the patron could no longer be relied on by "the family" of Armagh to protect them from the invader. The disorganisation of society appears from the Annals, where it is recorded that King Malachi, in 845, demolished an island fortress on Lough Ramor, near Virginia, county of Cavan, which was occupied by "a great crowd of sons of death (malefactors), who were plundering the districts at the instigation of the foreigners." Thus it appears that in addition to the Danes there was a native banditti, who imitated the tactics of the foreigners, and established themselves in fortified islands, from which they issued on their expeditions.

The state of anarchy into which Ireland had fallen caused the educated classes to turn their eyes to the Continent, where they could live and work without fear under the protection of the Frankish kings. And so another and later exodus took place from Ireland. Eric of Auxerre, who flourished in the ninth century, referring to it, speaks of "almost all Ireland despising the perils of the sea, and passing over to our shores with her crowd of philosophers.[1] For whosoever among them is most experienced determines on emigrating, that he may work in the service of our truly wise Solomon." Amongst those who left Ireland at this time was Dungal.[2] We owe our knowledge of him, as in the case of so many other celebrated Irishmen, to foreign writers, no mention of him occurring in Irish literature. He is chiefly celebrated as the writer of a letter to Charlemagne on an astronomical question. It was believed that two eclipses of the sun visible in Europe had happened in the same year, and the emperor applied to the abbot of S. Denis at Paris for

---

[1] Haddan's Remains, p. 285. [2] Flourished 811-827.

an explanation. The abbot referred the matter to Dungal, as the most competent authority, and he discussed it in a treatise of much learning. Notwithstanding the general acceptance of the Ptolemaic system at this period, Dungal seems to have held opinions hardly consistent with it. For speaking of the so-called fixed stars which were believed to be immovably attached to the firmament, he says: "Others whose statement is nearer the truth affirm that these also have a proper motion, but on account of the immense time they take to accomplish their revolutions and the shortness of human life, their movements cannot be discerned by observations."[1] About the year 820 Dungal was head of the large school of Pavia, and in a capitular of Lothair, published in 823, the youth from Milan and ten other cities are ordered to repair to Pavia and place themselves under his instruction. He has been regarded as a controversialist, and the writer of a long essay in reply to Claudius, Bishop of Turin. Claudius attracted much notice by condemning pilgrimages to Rome and the veneration of images, and is said to have cast out the images and crosses from the churches, whereat "there arose a cry through all the Frankish territories that he was introducing a new religion." The reply, attributed to Dungal, defends those practices. Muratori, however, doubts that this was the same Dungal, as there were many of the name. The essay is chiefly composed of extracts from Church hymns, and seems unlike the work of a scientific thinker. Some epistles of his to Alcuin are extant, and an acrostic, addressed to Hildoald, for, like Columbanus, he seems to have had a taste for that kind of composition. He bequeathed his library

[1] Life of Dungal, "Dictionary of National Biography."

to the Monastery of Bobbio, where he ended his days amongst his countrymen and friends.[1]

But the most famous of those voluntary exiles [2] who were induced by the unhappy condition of Ireland to leave home and friends was a layman, John Scotus Erigena, who appeared in France in the reign of Charles the Bald, some time before 847, and became the close companion and friend of the king, who enjoyed his wit [3] while he admired his genius and learning. Mr. Hallam "considers him one of the two really considerable men in the republic of letters who appeared from the sixth to the middle of the eleventh century." [4] His scholarship was conspicuous in that age, and when he translated the work of the so-called Dionysius the Areopagite from the Greek at the request of Charles, it excited astonishment that a barbarian from the ends of the earth should be so learned. Dionysius was supposed to be the Areopagite mentioned in Acts xvii. 34, and also Archbishop of Paris, a fiction due to the Abbot of S. Denis, and generally believed in the middle ages. Scotus quotes freely from the Greek and Latin fathers, from Origen, Gregory of Nyssa, Gregory of Nazianzus, and Basil, as well as from Augustine and Ambrose.

He cites Plato and Aristotle, quotes Syriac, and often refers to Hebrew. His philosophical opinions and speculations have been discussed by a long array

---

[1] Dungal, in "Dictionary of National Biography."

[2] Mr. Mullinger ("Schools of Charles the Great," p. 174) attributes the migration of those Irishmen to "penury and love of change and adventure ;" but William of Malmesbury says John went away because of warlike troubles, "*concrepantibus undique bellorum fragoribus.*"

[3] Charles on one occasion gave him three fishes, two large and one small, and told him to divide them with the clergy, two large men ; but he gave them the small fish and kept the two large himself, explaining to the king that it was fair: "Here are two big and one small (fish) ; there are two big and one small (man)."

[4] Literature of Europe, vol. iii. p. 335, 5'h ed.

of authors[1] down to recent times, and are a subject of permanent interest. He holds an unique position in the middle ages as the last of the Alexandrians and the first of the Schoolmen. His philosophy is oriental in character, and is said[2] to have been drawn from writers who were acquainted with Indian thought. The charge of pantheism has been brought against him, and though Mr. Hallam considers it unfounded, later writers[3] do not acquit him of it. It is characteristic of his early training that he held reason to be prior to authority in the order of nature, disparaging the latter after the manner of the Irish[4] generally. He even identifies reason with religion in one place.

Two of his works, that on the Division of nature and the treatise on the Procession of the Holy Ghost, are more in accordance with the teaching of the Eastern than of the Latin Church. He frequently praises the former, as though nearly all wisdom was to be sought from it. At this time Photius, the Patriarch of Constantinople, and his clergy, were anticipating the schism which subsequently ensued with the Church of Rome, and knowing Scotus' influence with Charles, they paid court to him, and endeavoured to draw him to their side, as the most popular and influential politician of the day. From the tone and character of his writings it is not surprising to hear that they did not meet with the approval of the Roman pontiff, and Nicholas I. complained to Charles that Scotus had published

---

[1] Amongst them Schlegel, Guizot, and Cousin may be mentioned.
[2] Migne, Patrologia, tom. 121, 122, sec. 9, p. 15.
[3] See an able article on Scotus in the *Quarterly Review* for July 1882.
[4] Some doubt has been expressed by one or two as to his nationality, and he has even been claimed as a Scotchman. But the Florentine and Darmstadt MSS. give his name as *Eriu-gena*, which makes it quite clear, *Eriu* being the old form of the name of Ireland. Migne, as before, Proem. xxii.

his translation of Dionysius without his apostolic sanction, and he requested the king to remove him from Paris, lest he should "mix tares with the wheat, and so distribute poisoned food." His work on the Division of nature was condemned to the fire by Pope Honorius in the thirteenth century, and two hundred years later, when printed in England, it was placed in the index of prohibited books.

The opinions of Gottescalk on predestination having excited much discussion at this time, Scotus was applied to, and wrote in refutation of them. He and Ratramn also were requested by King Charles to refute the views of Paschasius Radbert on the Lord's Supper. The work of Scotus is supposed by some to be lost, though others believe it to be the same as that attributed to Ratramn. Berengarius, in 1049, adopted his view, maintaining that the bread and wine are not converted into the body and blood of Christ, but are merely emblematic of them.[1]

Pope Leo IX. condemned Berengarius, and ordered his works to be committed to the flames, with that which was believed to be Scotus'. In the long persecution endured by Berengarius he showed an extraordinary fortitude in maintaining his opinions, though compelled three times to retract them.[2] Nor did the influence of Scotus' work cease there, for a translation of part of it is found in the Saxon homilies of Aelfric, in the tenth century, which were known to Ridley and Cranmer. The earliest English edition in black letter was published in 1560 by Bernhard, the friend and attendant of Latimer, in accordance with the last

---

[1] Mosheim, iii. 380.
[2] Readers will remember Coleridge's poem on his last words:—

"No more 'twixt conscience staggering and the Pope,
Soon shall I now before my God appear," &c.
—"Poetical Works," vol. ii. p. 79, London, 1840.

injunctions of Ridley as given in the martyr's letters.[1] Thus it would appear that the writings of the famous Irishman were not without influence on the English Reformation. The editor of his works laments that "he did not use his great endowments for the benefit of the Church;" and he certainly showed the opposite tendency in the poem[2] prefixed to his translation of Dionysius.

Amongst those who remained at home the most remarkable person at the close of the ninth century was Cormac Mac Cuillenan, King of Cashel, who united in his person many offices, being not only a king, but "a bishop, an anchorite, a scribe, and a profoundly learned scholar in the Scotic (Irish) tongue."[3] He is said to have been the compiler of the Saltair of Cashel, or rather the continuer of it to his own time. This work was carried further by King Brian, and in the account of his edition of it the nature of its contents is mentioned. "King Brian, seeing into what rudeness the kingdom was fallen . . . assembled together all the nobility of the kingdom, and caused them to compose a book containing all the inhabitations, events, and septs that lived in this land from the first peopling . . . until that present time, which book they caused to be called by the name of the Psalter of Cashel." A considerable part of this work is contained in a manuscript in the Bodleian Library,[4] Oxford. He was also concerned in the authorship of the enlarged edition of the "Book of Rights," which was attributed, in its original form, to Benean or Benignus, successor of S. Patrick at Armagh. This curious work gives an account of the rights of

---

[1] Massingberd's "History of the Reformation," 4th edit.
[2] See Appendix II.   [3] Annals of the Four Masters, p. 903.
[4] Book of Rights, Introduction, p. xxiv.

M

the monarchs of all Ireland, and the revenues payable to them by the principal kings of the several provinces, and of the stipends paid by the monarch to the inferior kings for their services. It also treats of the rights of each of the provincial kings, and the revenues payable to them from the inferior kings of the districts or tribes subsidiary to them, and of the stipends paid by the superior to the inferior provincial kings for their services.[1] Cormac's literary activity is further shown by the glossary of difficult Irish words and their derivations, composed by him and still extant. This is believed to have been compiled from the interlined glossary or explanations of rare words contained in the Saltair of Cashel, and it shows considerable acquaintance with Greek and Latin, from which he attempts to derive many Irish words, though not always successfully.[2] It would have been happy for him if he had been in a position to pursue such peaceful labours, but his twofold character of bishop-king involved him in warfare, and the possession of temporal power led to his death. He was killed at the battle of Ballaghmoon,[3] A.D. 903, in the south of the county of Kildare, fought by him against the united forces of the King of Ireland and those of Leinster and Connaught, in which six thousand men fell. The beautiful stone-roofed church on the Rock of Cashel, called Cormac's Chapel, which, according to Dr. Petrie, is one of the most curious and perfect churches in the Norman style in the British Empire, has been ascribed to him.[4] But this is an error, as the builder was Cormac M'Carthy,[5] who lived two

---

[1] Book of Rights, Introduction, p. vi.
[2] It was edited by Mr. Whitley Stokes, in the Irish Archæological Society, 1868.   [3] *Bealagh Mughna*, Mughain's pass or road.
[4] Ireland and the Celtic Church, 2nd edit., p. 219.
[5] Annals of Inisfallen, at 1127 and 1138.

centuries later, and happened to be also King of Munster, and bishop, which naturally led to some confusion, as he was not so well known as Mac Cuillenan. The consecration of the church is mentioned in the "Annals of the Four Masters," at 1134: "The church, which was built by Cormac, the grandson of Carthach, King of Cashel, was consecrated by a synod of the clergy of Ireland." This remarkable building is now in charge of the Board of Public Works as a national monument, and its preservation is thus permanently secured.

About the middle of this century the first mention of Round Towers occurs in the Annals. Speculations as to the origin and use of these buildings were of the wildest character in the pre-scientific days of Irish archæology. They were said to have been built by the Danes, who were more given to destroying than to building. Others carried back their date to a more remote antiquity, and attributed them to the Phœnicians, though there is no proof whatever that they knew anything about this island. Then, as to their uses: they were fire-temples, or places from which Druidical festivals were proclaimed, as to-day by the Muezzin in Mahometan countries; or astronomical observatories; or anchorite towers, in which a hermit lived; or a stylite or column saint, after the Eastern fashion, occupied them; or they were penitential prisons, or belfries, or keeps for defence, or beacons, or used as watch-towers. Such were the various and conflicting accounts of the Round Towers given by ingenious theorists, regardless of, or unacquainted with, the historical evidence, which is the only secure foundation for any satisfactory conclusion.

The bell-house or belfry[1] has been proved by Dr.

[1] *Cloictheach* or *clogas*.

Petrie to be of Christian origin, and he has shown them to have been used both as belfries, as keeps or castles, and occasionally as watch-towers. The native name implies that the bell was the chief object of care. Thus, in the "Annals of the Four Masters," at A.D. 1020, we read of "the Bell-house with its bells," and the extraordinary veneration entertained for the bells of famous saints[1] serves to explain how they came to give the buildings their name. Their origin is to be referred to the Danish inroads, which rendered it of the highest importance that there should be some place of safety at hand in which the chief ecclesiastics could take refuge, and place their bells, books, and other requisites for divine service in safety. "Till the invasions of the Norsemen," Miss Stokes observes, "the Irish ecclesiastic possessed his church and school in comparative peace, and the wall that encircled the group of cells and oratories which formed his monastery was deemed security enough for him, as for the Egyptian monk in his Laura. But in the year 800 all was changed. The attempted colonisation by a Pagan invader, resolved to extirpate the Christianity which he found there, and to establish his national heathenism, called forth the resistant spirit of the Irish monk, who protected his humble cell by means of the lofty tower."[2] The situation of the towers along the coast and in the valleys of the rivers most accessible to the enemy is an evidence that those who felt first and longest the brunt of the heathen attack were the first to resort to this means of defence. The earliest is that of Tomgraney, in the county of Clare, erected in 965 by Cormac O'Cillene, who was also the builder of the church at Clonmacnois, where another tower of the

[1] Chap. xii. p. 207.
[2] Early Christian Architecture of Ireland, p. 105.

same kind was begun the same year. A great church-building movement took place just about this time, between 996 and 1008. To this and the two following centuries the erection of the Round Towers is assigned. But whence was the idea derived of this kind of building, so difficult to take by assault or to set on fire, and absolutely impregnable to those not provided with regular means of besieging them, which no party making a sudden inroad could be? "Though the abbey and all its buildings blazed around, the tower disregarded the fury of its flames; its extreme height, its isolated position, and diminutive doorway elevated so many feet above the ground, placed it beyond the reach of the destroyer."[1] Such a tower, with its several chambers, could accommodate from forty to eighty persons, who would generally be the aged or infirm. In answer to the question of the origin of these towers we have to look across to France, where a similar class of buildings existed at an early period. One of the first forms of Campanile in Italy was a tall cylindrical tower with a conical roof, and many instances of such structures in Ravenna, Switzerland, and France prove that it was not uncommon abroad in the eleventh century. It was owing to the advance of architecture, and the preference for designs admitting of more ornament, that it was superseded by other forms. Ireland, as we have seen, was in close communication with France in the reign of Charlemagne and his immediate successors, and both countries suffered at the same time, and in the same way, from the Danish inroads. In France, towers were raised to protect the churches in the valleys of the Loire and the Seine from their attacks, and from thence Irish ecclesiastics, those "men of the two countries" who passed backwards

[1] Petrie, "Round Towers," p. 373.

and forwards, brought the suggestion to Ireland, where it soon bore fruit. Towers were raised wherever the Northmen visited at an early period—that is, in the places affording the easiest access, and the best prospect of plunder. The form of the French towers shews Eastern influence, and this has been traced to the influx of artists, chiefly painters and sculptors, who took refuge in Italy and the West from the severe measures adopted by the Emperor Leo against the worshippers of images. His decrees against images deprived the artists of their employment, and Charlemagne, glad of their arrival in his dominions, took them into his service. To this immigration of foreigners from the East has been attributed the peculiar form of the towers built at that time, which resembled the Eastern cylindrical pillar.

Those French towers have long since given place to more ornate structures, but in Ireland the type still remains, and bears witness to a state of things long past and elsewhere forgotten. Illuminated manuscripts of the tenth and eleventh centuries preserve the forms of them as the artists of that day saw them in France, and we know from them whence our Round Towers were derived. It was the earliest and simplest form which reached Ireland, and became the model which was imitated with so much fidelity by the Irish ecclesiastics. At the beginning of the present century, 118 of them were said to exist in Ireland, and these, with 22 foreign examples, bring the total number up to 140.

In the seventy-six towers still remaining, different styles are discernible, the earlier being much inferior to those of later date. Many of the earliest have fallen, partly, it would seem, owing to their having been most persistently attacked by the Northmen, and also perhaps from the inexperience of the builders, as considerable technical knowledge was necessary in erecting such lofty and slender buildings, and great care was needed to select a proper foundation for them.

"From these noble monuments the historian of Christian art and architecture may learn something of the works of a time the remains of which have been swept away elsewhere; and it may yet be seen, as in the case of her institutions, customs, faith, and forms of art, so in architecture, Ireland points to origins of noble things."[1]

[1] Miss Stokes, p. 111.

CHAPTER XI.

KING BRIAN: THE CHRISTIAN DANES.

THE disorganisation of society, and the injurious effects to religion resulting from it, are manifest in the history of the tenth century. The Danes continued to destroy churches and monasteries. In 926 Kildare was attacked by those of Waterford, and afterwards by a party from Dublin; and again in 927, 928. In the year 926 the Irish of the North gained a victory over them, and slew 800. They retaliated by attacking and plundering Armagh on the festival of S. Martin in 932. In 935 Clonmacnois was sacked as well as Mungret, and many other places. In 941 they were defeated by Callaghan of Cashel, at the head of the Munster forces, with the loss of 2000 men. In 944 Congal the Second, King of Ireland, took Dublin, sacked and burnt the town, and exterminated the Danish inhabitants. This partial account of the occurrences of only eighteen years will be sufficient to enable the reader to understand how fatal to religion such a state of society must have been. The exodus to the Continent naturally continued, depriving the country of nearly all who were eminent for piety or learning, and drawing them off to labour in foreign fields—a sad contrast to the time when students from abroad resorted to Ireland as the peaceful home of literature.

One of those who sought the Continent at this

time was Forannán,[1] who may be taken as a type of
his class. The clan to which he belonged occupied
a plain[2] near Clonmel, not far from Waterford.
Living in the vicinity of that Danish city, and continually exposed to inroads, his thoughts turned to
the Continent, where so many of his countrymen
had preceded him. At Wassor, on the Meuse, in
the modern Belgium, was a monastery over which
Macallen, an Irishman, presided. Forannán, aware
of this, and brooding over his troubles at home,
dreamt of the peaceful life of his brethren by the
Meuse. Taking this for a divine intimation, he
collected twelve companions, the usual retinue of an
Irish missionary, and made his way thither in the
year 969, and eventually became Abbot, enjoying the
high esteem of the Emperor of Germany. In this
manner the Church at home was deprived of nearly
all its leaders, and sank lower and lower in learning,
intelligence, and spiritual force. The Danes continued their inroads on churches and monasteries, but
their original ferocity had now begun to be somewhat
modified. Instead of indiscriminately slaughtering
their captives, as at an earlier period, they had learned
that it was more advantageous to hold them to ransom,
and therefore it became the practice to treat them
well. Self-interest, in the first instance, acted as a
restraint, and gradually led to a diminution of the loss
of life which characterised their early inroads. An
instance of this is recorded in the "Annals of the
Four Masters," at the year 962. "Kildare was
plundered by the foreigners, and a great number of
seniors and ecclesiastics were taken prisoners there."
They were all ransomed subsequently, as a later

[1] Life in "Dictionary of Nat'onal Biography."
[2] The plain of Magh Feimin.

entry relates, by a chieftain named Niall. The exact number thus rescued is not given, but it is said to have been large enough to fill "the great house of Brigit and the Oratory."

Another and more important change in their mode of life was the adoption of Christianity by the Danish inhabitants of Dublin, which took place in the year 948.[1] The profession of the Christian faith by a population nurtured in heathen superstition and a debased morality, must be to a great extent merely external, and the Danes were no exception to this rule. Two years after their conversion to Christianity they burnt the Round Tower of Slane, as recorded by the "Four Masters," "with all its relics and distinguished persons, together with the lector of Slane," and what, perhaps, was esteemed the most serious loss of all, "the crozier of the patron saint, and the bell."[2] In the following year, Godfrey, son of Sitric, with the Danes of Dublin, having established a camp at Kells in the county of Meath, plundered seven of the chief monasteries in the neighbourhood, carrying off 3000 captives, besides gold, silver, raiment, wealth, and goods of every description.[3] Notwithstanding these proceedings, their formal adoption of Christianity was an indication that the tide was turning, and that in the contest between the creeds heathenism was to be worsted.

There was no longer any question of the introduction of heathen rites, or the delivery of heathen oracles from the altars of Christian churches, but by a gradual process the invaders were to be absorbed by the inherent power of Christian truth. Towards the close of their rule a great effort was made by

[1] Lanigan, Eccl. Hist., vol. i. p. 75.
[2] Annals of the Four Masters, A.D. 948, note *a*; true date, 950.
[3] Ibid., A.D. 949.

them to effect the complete conquest of Munster, and the native accounts, after describing the arrival of reinforcements to augment the strength of their forces, give the following description of the oppressive exactions to which the population were subjected at this time : " There was a king from among the foreigners over every territory, a chief over every chieftaincy, an abbot over every church, a steward over every village, and a soldier in every house, so that none of the men of Erin had power even to give the milk of his cow, or so much as a clutch of eggs of one hen, in succour to the aged or a friend, but was forced to preserve them for the foreigner."[1]

But it seemed at length that the end was at hand, and that the country, under a powerful native sovereign, was about to enjoy repose and recover some of its ancient glory. The great Munster sept of the Dal Cais was at this time under the leadership of two brothers, Mahon and Brian, and such was the extremity to which they were reduced by the Danish power that they crossed the Shannon, and taking refuge among the woods of Clare, carried on a guerilla warfare with the enemy. Worn out with the hardships of the contest, Mahon submitted and made peace ; but when he endeavoured to persuade Brian to do the same, he fiercely replied that it was "hereditary for him to die like his ancestors, but not to submit." The courage of his tribe was roused by his words: they took the field, and the great victory of Sulchoit, near the town of Tipperary, broke the Danish power in Munster. This splendid achievement raised the Dal Cais at once to a position of high influence, and at the same time excited the jealousy of the kindred sept, the Eoganachts

[1] Wars of the Irish, p. 49.

of Cashel, who claimed the right of alternate succession to the throne of Munster. Influenced by this feeling, two chieftains of this race conspired with the Danes to murder Mahon, then King of Munster. He was induced by some stratagem to place himself in the power of the chieftains referred to, but before doing so took the precaution of obtaining a safe-conduct from the Coarb of S. Finn Barr and his clergy, some of whom also attended him. As further security he carried suspended round his neck the sacred gospel of S. Finn Barr. Thus safeguarded, as he believed, he proceeded with the escort sent to accompany him, but on their arrival at a spot[1] already indicated by their employers, the guard turned on him to slay him. Seeing his death inevitable, his first thought was for the gospel which he carried. Fearing it should be defiled by his blood, he took it off hastily, flung it to the nearest ecclesiastic, and then met his fate with manly courage. The "flashing of the swords" made known to the conspirators that the deed was done, and by Danish hands, for they alone used steel swords at that time. It was impossible that this entire disregard for Christian ideas and objects of reverence should not affect the Irish people and weaken their attachment to religion, when they observed that no divine vengeance followed the desecration of sacred things. Alliances and intermarriages with Danish families also lowered the moral tone of the chieftains by familiarising them with heathen habits. The crime thus planned and carried out in the case of Mahon only made room for a far more able and powerful ruler in Brian, who now succeeded to the throne, and after taking swift vengeance on the con-

[1] The road over the hill of Knockaroura, near Mallow, seems to have been the scene of the murder, which was witnessed by one of the conspirators from Rahan, hard by.

spirators, rose step by step, until in 1002 he became undisputed King of Ireland. A great leader, an able administrator, a just and pious ruler, he stands out among the nominal sovereigns of Ireland a real king of men. His government was wise and firm, and his special aim was to repair the injury which religion had suffered from the Danish rule. "By him," says the native author already referred to, "were erected noble churches and sanctuaries." In this are included Round Towers, of which he built or repaired many.

He is generally known as Brian Borumha (Boru), as he belonged to the division of the Dal Cais known as the Dal Cais Borumha,[1] so called apparently from a village of that name situated in their territory. The popular view is that he derived his title from the Borumha Laigheann, a tribute said to have been imposed by the sovereigns of Ireland on the Kings of Leinster in prehistoric times, but remitted in the seventh century at the intercession of S. Molling. Brian is supposed to have reimposed it, but there is no proof whatever of this. The legendary account [2] of this tribute represents it as consisting, amongst other property, of 150 couples of men and women slaves, and 150 maidens, one of whom should be the King of Leinster's daughter, who were also to be made slaves. It is grotesque to suppose a pious Christian monarch of the eleventh century imposing such a tribute. But if the material edifices needed rebuilding, the spiritual

---

[1] Wars of the Irish, Introduction, p. cvi.
[2] Annals of the Four Masters, A.D. 106, note *y*. The story is that Tuathal, King of Ireland, had two daughters, one of whom was married to the King of Leinster, who being told he had not chosen the most attractive, shut her up in a secret chamber, reported that she was dead, and proposed for and was married to the other. The newly-married wife unexpectedly met her sister, and fell dead on the spot. As a punishment, the Kings of Leinster were compelled to pay this tribute.

condition of the Church was in equal need of help. The manuscripts of the Scriptures, transcribed with so much care, the service-books from which they ministered in the churches, were no longer in existence; the clergy themselves were far away labouring in foreign lands. To remedy these evils Brian "sent professors and masters to teach wisdom and knowledge, and to buy books beyond the sea and the great ocean, because the writings and the books in every church and sanctuary were burnt and thrown into the water by the plunderers from the beginning to the end (of their inroads). And Brian himself gave the price of learning and the price of books to every one separately who went on that service."[1] He was thirty-eight years King of Munster and fifteen Sovereign of Ireland, until his death at the battle of Clontarf, in the seventy-third year of his age. That victory was won on April 23, 1014, when the famous raven banner wrought by magic spells, and supposed to bring victory to the host over which it fluttered, went down before the standard of the cross. The contest was regarded by the Northern Annalists as one between heathenism and Christianity, and dark forebodings filled the breasts of the Danish warriors. One by one they refused to bear the raven banner, and at last Earl Sigurd had to take it himself, accepting his fate as the last hero of a beaten creed. Brian was, strictly speaking, a usurper, having no right by Irish custom to the throne of Ireland, and the Northern writers do not recognise him. During the period of his reign they consider Malachi as still the lawful sovereign, and it was in accordance with this view that, on the death of Brian, Malachi, who had been deposed, resumed the sovereignty.

Notwithstanding the great defeat of Clontarf, the

[1] Wars of the Irish, p. 139.

Danes still remained a power in the country. Their settlements were not disturbed, but they found it expedient thenceforth to devote themselves to the arts of peace, and Christianity continued to make progress among them. The reign of Brian was not long enough to permit the reduction of the independent chieftains to permanent obedience, and his eldest son having fallen with him at Clontarf, there was no representative of the family to take up the sceptre. From that date to the Anglo-Norman invasion the state of Ireland was one of anarchy. The old rule by which the house of O'Neill enjoyed the sovereign authority had been broken through, and now every provincial king might aim at the throne. Hence a state of disorder supervened, which, following on the Danish inroads, reduced the population to the state of barbarism in which they were found by the Anglo-Normans.

Amidst the vicissitudes through which the country had passed, the peculiar constitution of the Church remained unaltered, though in doctrine and practice it was more or less influenced by foreign ideas, as we shall see. But now the Continental system of Church government at length obtained some footing there, through the conversion of the Danes. They were of kindred race with the Normans, who had just conquered England; and it was natural that their sympathies should be with them rather than with the Irish, who had been so long their enemies, and whose habits of life were so different. The Normans had embraced Christianity in the previous century, and were in communion with the Roman Church. Hence when the Irish Danes adopted Christianity, they desired to have an organisation like that which existed in England. Accordingly, when Dunan or Donat, an

Easterling or Ostman, was made "high bishop,"[1] as it is termed, in 1038, the city of Dublin was assigned to him as a diocese, his jurisdiction being confined to the space within the walls. By this arrangement they showed their disregard of the Irish system, for Dublin was already provided with a native clergy, and an Abbot of Dublin, who was also a bishop, is mentioned in the Annals as early as 785. Dunan was the first bishop in Ireland who possessed diocesan jurisdiction, limited as it was. But he was still in communion with the native Church, and as yet no foreign authority was recognised in Ireland. The prelates of the Church of England, however, already had in view the subjugation of the Irish Church, and Lanfranc, the Italian Archbishop of Canterbury, in a Synod held at Winchester in 1072, put forward a claim to jurisdiction over Ireland, as well as England and Scotland, on the ground of a passage supposed to be found in Bede's "Ecclesiastical History of the Anglo-Saxons." But Ussher[2] has shown that there is nothing in Bede to warrant it, and Giraldus Cambrenses in the twelfth century expressly repudiated the claim. The chief event in Dunan's life[3] was the foundation of the Church of the Holy Trinity, now Christ Church Cathedral, or, more properly, its endowment and reorganisation in accordance with the views of the Danish community. For it appears from an inquisition held in the reign of Richard II. that a Church had been "founded and endowed there by divers Irishmen, whose names are unknown, time out of mind, and long before the conquest of Ireland." Sitric, the Danish King of Dublin, now endowed it

---

[1] *Ardeasbog*, erroneously translated "archbishop" by Dr. O'Donovan; but see Todd, "Life of S. Patrick," p. 16.
[2] Ussher, Works, iv. 567. Lanigan, Eccl. Hist., iii. 464-468.
[3] Dunan, in "Dictionary of National Biography."

with the lands of Baldoyle, Raheny, and Portrane, all lying in the Danish district adjoining Dublin. This new foundation of the Holy Trinity took place between 1038–1042, and the site is described in the Black Book of Christ Church as "the *voltæ* or arches founded by the Danes before the arrival of S. Patrick in Ireland;" and it is added, "S. Patrick celebrated mass in an arch or vault since known by his name." This supposed connection of the Danes with S. Patrick is referred to in a poem contained in the "Book of Rights,"[1] describing their conversion by him, and even giving the name of the king who reigned at the time :—

> "He who was king of hardy Ath-Cliath [Dublin]
> When Patrick came from the North
> Was Alpin, son of Eolathach,
> Of the race of Donald-duv-davach."

Jocelyn, in his Life of S. Patrick, also gives an account of his visit to Dublin, and informs us that the city derived its name from Dublinia, the daughter of this King Alpin. But the king and his daughter[2] are imaginary personages. The story is, in fact, one of those fictions of which the ninth and following centuries were so prolific, and which had for their object to reconcile the Irish to the introduction of the foreign system of Church government. "It was probably circulated," Dr. O'Donovan says, "when the Christian Danes refused to submit to the ecclesiastical jurisdiction of Armagh, and when it was found useful by the Danish party to have it believed that their ancestors were settled in Dublin as early as the fifth

---

[1] The Book of Rights, Dublin, 1847, pp. 224–232.
[2] The Irish name for Dublin is *Baile atha Cliath*, "the town of the ford of hurdles," but as there were other places so named, the word *Duibhlinne*, "of the dark pool," was added to distinguish it, and eventually became the name of the metropolis. The Danes called it Dyfflin, which fairly represents the pronunciation of the word.

century, and converted to Christianity by S. Patrick."[1] The claim to jurisdiction made by Lanfranc had probably some influence with the Danes of Dublin, for on the death of Dunan in 1074, his successor, Patrick, who was elected by the clergy and people of Dublin, was sent to him by Gothric, the Danish king. In the letter which Patrick carried the Danes of Dublin offer him "due obedience," and request him to consecrate Patrick, stating that their object was that he "might be able under the divine authority to preside over them regularly"—an expression in which there is evident allusion to the Irish system, which was regarded by Lanfranc and his successor, Anselm, as highly irregular. Patrick was duly consecrated in S. Paul's Cathedral, having made a solemn profession, in which, after dwelling on the duty of obedience, he says:—

"Reverend Father Lanfranc, Primate of Britain[2] and Archbishop of the holy Church of Canterbury, I, Patrick, elected as prelate to govern Dublin, the metropolis of Ireland, do offer thee this charter of my profession, and I promise to comply with thee and thy successors in all things relating to the Christian religion."

Patrick, on his return to Ireland, brought with him letters from Lanfranc to Gothric and to Turlough, whom he flatters with the title of "the magnificent King of Ireland." This acceptance of the jurisdiction of Canterbury by the Danish king and people of Dublin was the first step in the introduction of the Roman system into Ireland. Thenceforward an agent in the Roman interest held a post of dignity there, and though he was the bishop of a foreign community, and had no

---

[1] Book of Rights, Preface, p. xii.
[2] *Britanniarum*, that is, primate of the two Britains—Britannia superior, the mountainous district of the north and west, and Britannia inferior, the rest of the island. See the *Quarterly Review*, April 1885. The term had nothing to do with Ireland.

influence beyond the walls of the city, his presence afforded an excuse for interfering in ecclesiastical affairs. This prepared the way for the eventual success of the untiring efforts made by the English prelates to reduce the Irish Church to conformity with the Church of England. Passing from Dublin, where Diocesan Episcopacy was now regularly established, to Waterford, another Danish city, we find a presbyter named Malchus, who had been a monk in Winchester, was sent[1] to Anselm, Archbishop of Canterbury, in 1096, with a letter requesting that he might be consecrated bishop of the town. The letter was signed by Murtough,[2] who assumes the title of King of Ireland; Dermod, called Duke, who was Murtough's brother; Bishop Donald,[3] also one of the Dal Cais; Idunan,[4] Bishop of Meath; Samuel,[5] Bishop of Dublin, and Ferdomnach, Bishop of Kildare. Malchus, whose training[6] fitted him to introduce the new system into Ireland, thus owed his appointment to Murtough. He was consecrated, and became the first diocesan bishop of Waterford. Coming now to Limerick, we find Gille,[7] sometimes called Gillebert, placed there as bishop by Murtough in 1106. He was the friend and correspondent

[1] In the "Annals of the Four Masters" he appears at 1135 as Maoilisa O'h-Ainmire, Bishop of Portlairge (Waterford), and chief senior of the Gael. His name was Latinised Malchus.
[2] Muircheartach Mor, son of Turlough, and great-grandson of Brian.
[3] In the "Four Masters," at 1098, he is described as "Domhnall ua O'h-Enni, head of the wisdom and piety of the Gael, fountain of the charity of the West of Europe."
[4] In the "Four Masters," at 1117, Maelmuire ua Dunain, chief Bishop of Munster; probably a mistake, as he belonged to the North.
[5] Samuel O'h-Angli, successor to Donat.
[6] He had an opportunity at Winchester of becoming acquainted with the Church system then in force in England.
[7] He is not mentioned by the "Four Masters," but the "Chronicon Scotorum" gives his death at 1145. "Gille, Bishop of Luimnech quievit." Keating and Colgan term him *Gilla easpuic*, "servant of the bishop," *i.e.*, of Rome, with reference to his Legatine office. The Anglicised form of the name is Gillespie. The surname MacGilla-espuic occurs in the "Four Masters."

of Anselm, whose acquaintance he had made at Rouen, and he is remarkable as the first who held the office of Papal legate in Ireland. Whether he was a Dane or not is uncertain. If he was Abbot of Bangor, as Dr. Lanigan thought possible, it was very likely that he was an Irishman. But the passage from Keating, as quoted by Lynch, to which he refers,[1] does not occur in the original Irish, and seems to have been an invention of Lynch's.

In these transactions we find the O'Briens, heads of the great sept of the Dal Cais, taking a prominent part and actively promoting the movement to assimilate the two Churches. They recognised the superior order and regularity of the system then in force in England as contrasted with the native Church government, now disorganised and weakened. The kingdom over which they ruled included within its limits the three Danish cities of Dublin, Waterford, and Limerick; and now, by their influence, there was settled in each of these towns an agent prepared to carry out the changes they desired. But the Church of Ireland, as a body, took no part in the movement. The name of the primate does not appear, nor those of the Northern clergy. The Coarb of Armagh at this time was Dubdalethe III., who had been Lector, and succeeded in 1049 on the death of Awley.[2] He was the author of some Annals, which have not come down to us, but are quoted in the "Annals of Ulster" and the "Four Masters." He is said to have been the first in Ireland to use the Christian era. At this time flourished Tigernach, Coarb of Clonmacnois, the most trustworthy and ill-used of Irish chroniclers.[3]

[1] Eccl. Hist., iv. 25.
[2] *Amalgaid*, whose daughter, according to the "Annals of Ulster," was married to the Prince of Orier, "Annals of the Four Masters," vol. ii. p. 291, note.
[3] Stokes, "Tripartite," Introduction, p. cxxvii. On the authorities used by him see "Annals of the Four Masters," A.D. 1088, note *o*.

He is remarkable for his candour in admitting that all the monuments of the Scots (Irish) until Cimbaeth were uncertain, and as that monarch flourished about 300 B.C., most people will be of opinion that he allows them a very respectable antiquity. Nevertheless, Professor O'Curry is dissatisfied with so late a beginning for Irish history, and has a long discussion on the subject, in which he suggests that the passage may be an interpolation. But it is questionable whether any native statements regarding the period antecedent to the conversion of Ireland can be treated as strictly historical. The best authorities [1] are of opinion that the population in general were unacquainted with letters before that period, and therefore it is unlikely that there were any records.

Amongst those who passed over to the Continent at this time, the most eminent was Marianus Scotus, or Marianus the Irishman, the author of a celebrated chronicle.[2] He passed ten years as an *inclusus* or immured hermit at Fulda, from 1059 to 1069, and afterwards pursued the same mode of life at Mentz, until his death in 1082. He relates that when at Fulda he was enclosed in the chamber which his countryman, Anmchadh, had tenanted a few years before, where also he was buried; and that he daily said mass standing over the feet of the deceased, beside whose grave his own lay open, occupying, as it probably did, nearly a fourth of the whole space allotted for his abode in life, and serving as a perpetual memento of the still narrower home to which he was hastening.[3] This most strange of lives was

---

[1] Professor Atkinson on Irish Lexicography, p. 31. Compare Stokes, "Tripartite," Introduction, p. cliii.
[2] His name in Irish form is *Maelbrigde*.
[3] Memoir of the Church of S. Duilech, by Bishop Reeves. Proceedings of the Royal Irish Academy, April 11, 1859.

regulated by a fixed order, and is thus described. "The abode of an *inclusus* should be built of stone, measuring twelve feet in length and as many in breadth. It should have three windows—one facing the choir, through which he may receive the body of Christ; another at the opposite side, through which he may receive his food; and a third to admit light, but which should always be filled with glass or horn. . . . He should be provided with three articles, namely, a jar, a towel, and a cup. After tierce (the third Canonical hour), he is to lay the jar and cup outside the window and then close it. About noon he is to come over and see whether his dinner be there. If it be he is to sit down at the window and eat and drink. When he has done, whatever remains is to be left outside for any one who may choose to remove it, and he is to take no thought for the morrow. But if it should happen that he has nothing for his dinner, he must not omit to return his accustomed thanks to God, though he is to remain without food till the following day. In winter, if the severity of the weather require it, he may, with his pastor's licence, wear a woolly cloak, because he is not allowed to have any fire except what his candle produces. He is to be provided with a cotton pallet and a bolster. On Monday, Wednesday, and Friday he is to fast on bread and water. On the other days he may eat one lenten dish, and pears or apples, if he has any. On Sundays and the principal festivals he may use milk. He is to observe silence; between noon and evening he may speak if he wishes. Every day he must repeat *Our Father* fifty times at seven different periods, and the *Come, Holy Spirit*, having special regard to the honour of the blessed Virgin Mary and all saints, and to the relief of souls. If he knows the Psalter let him repeat a Nocturn every day, but if not, 300 *Our Father's*."[1] Such hermitages were popularly known in Ireland as Anker Houses, or Anchorite habitations, and in the Irish language, "the Stone of the Anchorite,"[2] and the occupant was known as "the Man in the Stone." How vivid must have been the realities of the unseen world to such men as these, or those others who kept their lonely vigil on the storm-swept rock of the Skelligs, supporting life no one knows how, and cut off from human society sometimes for months together.

Notwithstanding the long-continued rule of the Danes, and the trials through which the country had passed, the arts continued to flourish. The long struggle which the Irish maintained did not materially paralyse their energies; and not only architecture, but the arts of metal work and sculpture, reached their highest perfection in the period between the tenth and twelfth centuries.[3] Foreign art had not yet come in to modify and supersede the peculiar and original work of the Irish artists. The ecclesiastical architecture of Ireland was a development from the rude pagan style which the first missionaries found in existence. The early isolation of Ireland for so long a period, which has already been referred to, gave time for the growth of a native art, which gradually advanced until it reached its highest example in Cormac's Chapel, on the Rock of Cashel. Churches of the fifth or sixth century are no longer to be found in England, Wales, or Cornwall, but in Ireland they are numerous, and side by side with them the buildings of pagan origin from which the design was derived. Thus it affords a field of study in which may be examined the most primitive ecclesiastical buildings

[1] Reeves, as before, p. 10.   [2] *Cloch angcoire.*
[3] Miss Stokes, "Early Christian Architecture in Ireland," p. 127.

existing in Europe at the present day. The pagan fortresses which still exist on the west and south-west coast of Ireland, with walls from 12 to 18 feet, and sometimes 20 feet high, enclose within their area what are called bee-hive huts, of which many examples are still to be seen. In these the inhabitants dwelt, protected from sudden assault by the external rampart. On the conversion of the chieftain to Christianity it frequently happened that he bestowed his fort on the saint, who then adapted it as a monastery. On the summit of the almost inaccessible island off the south coast of Kerry, known as the Great Skellig, is such a wall or cashel,[1] as it is termed. "It is astonishing," Lord Dunraven says,[2] "to conceive the courage and skill of the builders of this fine wall, placed as it is on the very edge of the precipice, at a vast height above the sea, with no standing ground outside the wall from which the builders could have worked." The bee-hive huts are dry built, and of the same type as the *clocháns*, or houses within the pagan fort of Dunbec in Kerry. In order to form the roof the stones overlap from about half the height of the top, so as to form a dome outside. What determines these to be Christian structures is a cross of six white quartz pebbles let into the wall over the doorway, which contrasts with the dark colour of the rest of the wall. These structures are exactly like the pagan huts; but there are also two oratories, which show an adaptation to Christian uses, for instead of being circular they are rectangular in ground plan; they lie east and west, have a door at the west end, and a small window at the east end opposite to it, and a small platform raised above the level of the floor at

[1] The popular pronunciation of castle (or castellum).
[2] Notes on Irish Architecture, vol. i. p. 28.

the east end for an altar. Such is the primitive church referred to in the prophecy ascribed to the Druids before the coming of S. Patrick :—

> "The Tailchen[1] shall come over the stormy sea,
> His mantle hole-headed, his staff crook-headed,
> His table in the east of his house.
> All his household shall answer him, Amen, Amen."

A more advanced type is the oratory of Gallerus, which, though built without mortar and roofed in the same primitive fashion, is as perfect as the day it was built—according to Dr. Petrie, some fifteen centuries ago. From this early type they proceeded to the erection of larger churches, still covered with stone; and in order to support the great weight, they invented the double roof which excited the admiration of Mr. Fergusson. If they had been allowed to continue to work out this style, "they would," he says, "have avoided the greatest fault of Gothic architecture."[2]

When communication was re-opened with the Continent in the beginning of the seventh century, foreign ideas began to influence Irish architecture, and ultimately from a combination of both the Irish Romanesque came into existence, of which Cormac's Chapel is the noblest example.

In the department of metal work, the crozier of this Cormac, who was king as well as bishop, is a fine example of the skill of the artist. It is described by Dr. Petrie, who believed it to be a specimen of native art, but it has since been ascertained to be Limoges work and not Irish, but it illustrates the influence of the Continent at this time. It may, perhaps, as a work of art, Dr. Petrie says, challenge a comparison with any Christian monument of the same class and age now remaining in Europe.[3]

[1] *i.e.*, "The tonsured one," Tripartite, ii. 449.
[2] History of Architecture, vol. ii. 232.   [3] Round Towers, 310, 311.

CHAPTER XII.

STATE OF RELIGION: CHURCH GOVERNMENT.

THE close of the Danish period by the battle of Clontarf offers an opportunity for a review of the condition of religion and literature, and of ascertaining how much survived after the long night of oppression through which the country had passed, and the general wreck of native institutions. The number of manuscripts produced by the industry of the great army of scribes must have been immense, yet we have seen that King Brian found his measures for the promotion of learning hampered for want of books, and he was under the necessity of importing them from abroad, such had been the systematic destruction of them. But as soon as it became certain that Danish inroads were over, and the country began to enjoy some degree of repose, a literary revival immediately took place. The scattered remains of the early literature were collected and transcribed for preservation, and thus were formed those great compilations which form our chief examples of the Irish language. The earliest of these is the "Book of Hymns," compiled at the end of the eleventh or beginning of the twelfth century;[1] the "Book of the Dun Cow,"[2] transcribed before 1106; the "Book of Leinster," before 1163; the "Speckled Book,"[3]

---

[1] This collection contains hymns in the Irish language ascribed to SS. Patrick, Fiacc, Colman a lector of Cork; Ninine, Ultan, Broccan, Sanctain, Dallán Forgaill, Adamnan, and Mael Isu. See Goidelica, pp. 121-175. Two fasciculi of this were published by Dr. Todd.

[2] *Lebar na h-Uidhre.*   [3] *Lebar Brecc.*

and the "Book of Ballymote," at the close of the fourteenth century; and the "Book of Lecan," at the end of the fifteenth.[1] Hence it appears that there was a continuous activity as soon as the external pressure was removed; and it has been estimated that the manuscript material thus produced would, if printed, fill more than a thousand octavo volumes. But in the long interval of nearly three centuries which elapsed between the beginning of the Danish troubles and the compilation of the "Book of Hymns," many changes had taken place in the language. Not only had the meaning of some words altered, but that of others was entirely forgotten. An instance of the former is the word employed in the Würzburgh glosses to denote faith,[2] as in the expression, "faith without love," in the gloss on 1 Cor. xiii. 2. At a later period it came to signify mortification of the flesh, and in this sense it is used thirteen times in the poem of Cumin of Connor. He applies it to S. Patrick's fasting from Shrove Tuesday to Easter; to Fechin's lying unclothed in his cell; to Fursa singing psalms in a well as cold as snow; to Kevin standing a whole year in his cell, and to Brendan in the following stanza :—

> "Brenainn loves constant piety [*crabaid*].
> According to synod and congregation,
> Seven years on a whale's back he spent.
> It was a difficult mode of piety."[3]

The entire change of meaning is an evidence of a change of religious views, especially as all the writers referred to were ecclesiastics.

Another word whose signification underwent a change was that rendered *prophet*,[4] which, as we have

---

[1] All these, except the "Book of Hymns" and that of Lecan, have been published in facsimile by the Royal Irish Academy.
[2] *Crabud*.   [3] Martyrology of Donegal, p. 131.
[4] *Faidh*, the Latin *vates*.

seen, meant a preacher of the Gospel in the Wurzburgh glosses, and in that sense was applied to many ecclesiastics. But at a later period it came to be used exclusively of one who foretold future events. Originally only four persons were believed to possess the gift of prophecy, and Giraldus Cambrensis enumerates them in the twelfth century, and also the "Martyrology of Donegal," which gives the following stanza :—

> "The four prophets of the fine Gaels,
> Better of it the country whence they came,
> Columcille, Molling the perfect,
> Brenainn of Birr and Berchán."[1]

The number was subsequently vastly enlarged by the addition of all those to whom the term in its original sense was applied,[2] and predictions were invented[3] for them.

Not only was the meaning of some words changed, but that of others was quite forgotten, as in the case of the name of the ecclesiastical fan.[4] The Four Masters, who were eminent Irish scholars, not knowing its meaning, divide it into two words, which accordingly Dr. O'Donovan translates, not being aware of the mistake. The fan, which was used at the Holy Communion in the Eastern Church to drive away flies, was adopted in the Western Church. But it soon went out of use, being unnecessary in a cold climate, and hence it is only mentioned in the case of the earliest Irish ecclesiastics. When it was no longer employed in divine service, the name only survived in manuscripts, and when these were destroyed during the

---

[1] Martyrology of Donegal, December 4, p. 236. Giraldus has S. Patrick instead of Brenainn.

[2] Amongst these were Condlaed, Brigit, Maurán, Colman mac Lenini, Cu Temhin, Corbmac, Beg mac De, Ita, Eoghan of Ardstraw, Finnchu, &c.

[3] See O'Currey's dissertation on these spurious prophecies, "Manuscript Materials," pp. 382-434. [4] *Culebadh.*

Danish troubles it was entirely forgotten. It has been recently recovered,[1] owing to the publication on the Continent of some Irish glosses found in a foreign library.

When the very words connected with religion had changed their meaning or were forgotten, it was evident that a serious change had taken place in the Church. It emerged from the Danish period in a much deteriorated condition, from the united effects of the long deprival of education, and association with the heathen foreigners. Superstitions of various kinds began to crowd out true religion, and were evidently more congenial to a society which had fallen away so far from the high standard of its youth.

One of these, apparently of heathen origin, was the belief that saints retained in their tombs some kind of life. In one of the lives of S. Patrick published by Colgan is a story of a boy who was playing with his hoop near the supposed grave of the saint at Saul, in the county of Down, when it fell down through a chink into the interior of the grave. The boy having put in his hand to recover his plaything, was unable to withdraw it. In this emergency Bishop Loarne, who lived at Bright, not far off, was sent for, and when he arrived he addressed S. Patrick, saying, "Why, O elder, dost thou hold the child's hand?"[2] So when S. Columba made his union with a dead saint, Cianan of Duleek, Columba put his hand half-way through the side of the tomb, and the buried saint put out his hand half-way to meet him. "And they make their union in that wise."[3]

From this belief arose the habit of speaking of a buried saint in the present tense, as in the story of S. Patrick, which refers to the city "where Bishop Loarne *is*," though the life was written many centuries

[1] "On the Culebadh," by Rev. T. Olden, Proc. R.I.A., April 1885.
[2] Vita iv. cap. 37.   [3] Oengus, p. clxxi.

later. The learned Colgan was led astray by this expression, and took it to mean that the saint was alive at the time of the writer—a mistake which caused great confusion, and induced him to antedate many lives by treating them as the genuine composition of the saints whose names they bear. This is now recognised as a misapprehension. Connected with this belief was the greater importance which some burial-grounds acquired from being the place where eminent saints were buried. They were supposed to have obtained special privileges for all who were interred there. S. Fintan (Munnu) of Taghmon obtained the favour that every one interred in the burial-ground which he had marked out with his own hand should inherit eternal life,[1] and, moreover, whoever should be buried within the limits of his Termonn, and within hearing of the sound of his bell, "should not have hell shut upon him."

Enda of Arran, among other requests which he obtained from God, gained the privilege that every contrite person who chose burial with him (*i.e.,* in his burial-ground) should not have the mouth of hell shut upon him.[2] The Bollandists explain this to mean "that he should not undergo the pains of purgatory, or should not be detained long in them;" but this is to read into the story the ideas of a later period.

It was believed also that the prayers of the saints who occupied the same burial-ground were advantageous to those who were interred there.

The bells of saints became objects of superstition from their connection with the saint, and hence the care with which they were enclosed in the beautiful shrines of which so many examples have come down

---

[1] Fintan (Munnu), in "Dictionary of National Biography."
[2] Enda, in "Dictionary of National Biography."

to us. The most celebrated of these was the Bell of S. Patrick, known as the Bell of the Will, which there is little doubt was that used by him, and after his death left to Armagh, the church of his especial regard. It is said in the "Annals of Ulster" to have been taken from his tomb sixty years after his death by S. Columcille. At an early period it became a *cathach*, or battler, and its sanctity constantly increased, until in the eleventh century we read in the "Annals of Ulster" of a warlike expedition made on its account, in which a chieftain carried off 1200 cows and a multitude of captives "in revenge for the violation of the Bell of the Will."[1]

At the close of the eleventh century the King of Ireland and the Coarb of Armagh united in providing for it a costly shrine, which bears an inscription recording, amongst other things, the names of the keepers of the shrine. These were the O'Mulhollands,[2] who held lands by hereditary tenure for the performance of that duty. The bell is quadrilateral, and formed of two plates of sheet iron, bent over so as to meet, and fastened together by iron rivets, and bronzed, apparently by being dipped in liquid bronze. Its power is celebrated in a poem attributed to S. Columcille, though of a much later age :—

> "Two hundred kings without doubt,
> With their famous troops,
> The bell of the mild cleric shall kill.
> O king of glory, with it is my love.
>
> . . . . .
>
> Lewy, son of Leary the furious,
> Who ruined Erin in his time ;
> This is the Bell that killed him.
> O king of the Psalms, with thee is my love."

---

[1] There were two other Bells of S. Patrick—the *Finn faidheach*, or sweet-sounding, and *clog timchill*, the Bell of the Circuit.

[2] Ua-Maelchalland. On this bell, see a paper by Bishop Reeves, Transactions of the Royal Irish Academy, vol. xxvii., Part I.

S. Mochaemog had a bell given him by S. Ita, who told him it would give forth no sound until in the course of his travels he came to the place where his resurrection should be, that is, the site of his future church and monastery. It would then ring out clearly. And so it happened, for Mochaemog, though he had the tempting offer of the king's fort, surrounded by fertile lands, passed on until he reached a desert spot, and there his bell announced that he was to settle.[1] In the life of Finnchu, a similar occurrence indicated the site of his monastery. The Bell of S. Caillin of Fenagh was not only used as a font for baptisms, but also as a minister of vengeance, for if any king (*i.e.* chieftain) objected to pay S. Caillin's tribute, the "Bell of the Kings," as it was called, came into operation; and "if the attendants of *Clog-na-righ*[2] shall legitimately fast against him, striking the bell in the proper place, there will be loss of food, and hunger, and sickness, and diseases, and war, and depredations in his country, or some other kind of vengeance shall fall upon him." Superstitions as to the virtues of the saint's crozier also were widely prevalent in this century. The most famous of these was the *Bachall Isa*, or crozier of S. Patrick, preserved at Armagh for many centuries, and believed to have been given to S. Patrick by our Lord Himself. Every saint who was a bishop or an abbot possessed one, and as they were generally preserved in their churches they became the subjects of many legends. Hence writers of this period adorn the lives of the saints of whom they treat with marvellous achievements wrought by their *Bachalls*.[3] They tell us how S.

---

[1] Mochaemog, in "Dictionary of National Biography."
[2] Its Irish name. S. Caillin, in "Dictionary of National Biography."
[3] From the Latin *Baculus*.

Fursa had only to send his crozier to a sick person, when he was immediately cured: how S. Fiacre, when he wished to make a fosse round his monastery, merely drew his crozier along the ground, which opened before it. And when Finnchu marched right-hand wise round the army, bearing his crozier, he ensured victory for his side.

Of actual change of doctrine in the Church generally, except with regard to the Invocation of Saints, which is found in the Litany of Œngus, in the tenth century, there does not seem to be much evidence at this period. The Tripartite life, which may be assumed to represent the theological ideas of the eleventh century, refers to Baptism, the Eucharist, Confirmation, Penance, Matrimony, and Holy Orders, but there is nothing to indicate that any but the first two were accounted sacraments.[1] Auricular Confession[2] is not mentioned in it nor in the "Book of Armagh," nor is "Extreme Unction," the first instance of which is that of Bishop Domnall, A.D. 1105.[3] A slight trace of the cultus of the Virgin is found, but it is not fully developed until the twelfth century, when it appears in a poem from the Lebar Brecc.[4] Communion in both kinds was still practised. The use of colour in the Church was unchanged, white only being mentioned in the Irish Canons, though purple, which was in use in the Gallican Church in the sixth century, may have also been adopted in Ireland, where it was known.

While superstitions were increasingly prevalent as social confusion and disorder continued, the Holy Scriptures nevertheless retained their pre-eminent position, at least in theory. The following passage

[1] Trip., Introd., p. clxiii.   [2] Ibid., Introd., p. clxiv.
[3] Lives, Book of Lismore, Introd., p. cvii.
[4] Trip., p. clxv. See *supra*, p. 47.

from the Irish of the fourteenth century, three hundred years later, when doctrines had certainly changed, expresses the traditional feelings of the Irish regarding them even then:—

"One of the noble gifts of the Holy Spirit is the divine Scripture, whereby every ignorance is enlightened, and every earthly sadness comforted; whereby every spiritual light is kindled, and every weakness strengthened. For it is through the Holy Scriptures that heresies and schisms are cast forth from the Church, that every quarrel and dissent is pacified. In it is found perfect counsel and fitting instruction by each and every degree of the Church. For the divine Scripture is a mother and a gentle nurse to all the faithful ones who meditate and consider it, and who are nurtured until they are chosen sons of God through its counsel. For the Wisdom bountifully distributes to her sons many savours of the sweet liquor and the pleasures of the spiritual food, whereby they are continually inebriated and gladdened."[1] Somewhat later the reverence for Scripture assumed a perverted form, when copies belonging to early saints came to be regarded as talismans.

About this time, probably, grew up the habit of attributing virtue to the recital of the poem of a famous saint, which was therefore called a *Luirech* or armour. Examples are the poem of Gildas,[2] and that of Columcille,[3] but the most celebrated was the Luirech Phadruig, viz., the Irish Hymn of S. Patrick (see p. 29). Of this it is said:[4] "It is a religious armour to protect the body and soul against demons and men and vices.

---

[1] Lebar Brecc, p. 201*b*, line 9. Trip., i. clxii.
[2] Lebar Brecc, p. 241, col. 2.   [3] Ibid., p. 262, col. 2.
[4] Tara Hill, p. 56. This hymn is sometimes erroneously termed "S. Patrick's Breastplate," but the Irish used Luirech, though derived from Lorica, in the sense of armour.

Every person who sings it every day with all his attention on God shall not have demons appearing to his face," &c.

The foregoing facts will sufficiently indicate the change which passed over the Irish Church owing to the causes already mentioned, and how far it had moved away from its early position. Archbishop Lanfranc when he exhibited an interest in it, and offered the benefit of his advice, does not concern himself with any of the superstitious practices referred to. He was only pained to observe many things done "contrary to the prohibition of the sacred canons."

In his letter to King Turlough he refers to the desertion of wives, and the marrying of others who were in the prohibited degrees of consanguinity; Episcopal consecration by a single bishop, the omission of chrism at baptism, and the acceptance of money for conferring Holy Orders. The desertion of wives, however, was not peculiar to Ireland, but was frequent among the Anglo-Saxons,[1] as well as the Scots of Britain. The rules as to consanguinity laid down in the canon law were not recognised in the Irish Church, which in this and some other respects was mainly guided by the Mosaic law.[2] Consecration by a single bishop was always regarded as valid though irregular, and Pope Gregory expressly sanctioned it in the case of Augustine. It seems to have been practised in the Irish Church from the first.[3] The use of chrism in baptism was the practice of the Irish Church, and is noticed in the second epistle of S. Patrick. The Stowe Missal even orders three separate acts of unction,[4] and also mentions the white garment or veil worn by the newly baptized. It was, however,

[1] Ussher, Works, iv. 493, note.   [2] Lanigan, iii. 497.
[3] See the consecration of Fiacc, Hogan, pp. 105, 106.
[4] Warren, p. 66.

not always easy to obtain oil, and in the eighth century we find Alcuin, then at the court of Charlemagne, sending a present of some to Colchu at Clonmacnois, because "at that time hardly any could be found in Britain." It is highly probable that while the Danes were devastating the country, the difficulty of obtaining it caused the practice of unction to fall into disuse. But, as Dr. Lanigan truly observes, it was never an essential part of baptism. A more serious matter was the acceptance of fees for conferring Holy Orders. This was altogether contrary to the practice of S. Patrick, who in his Confession calls the Irish people to witness that he ordained clergy without charge.[1] The abuse was not confined to Ireland, as the frequent denunciations of it by foreign councils from the fourth century onwards prove. Lanfranc advises Turlough to call a council of bishops and others with his chiefs, and to correct these irregularities. He appears to have acted on this advice, and afterwards sent Bishop Patrick to report the result to Lanfranc; but the Bishop never arrived, having been shipwrecked on October 10, 1084. Towards the close of the century we find Anselm in correspondence with the Irish bishops and King Murtough on Church matters. He advises the bishops, if any difficult questions arise which they cannot determine, that they should consult him. Murtough was on friendly terms with him and Henry I. of England, and the communications he received from so distinguished a source no doubt stimulated him to persevere in the course of action he had entered on for the advancement of religion. In 1101[2] he held a convention at Cashel "of the chief laity and clergy, with Bishop O'Dunan as president, when he made over Cashel of

---

[1] Confession, Trip., p. 372 (8–12).   [2] Annals of the Four Masters.

the Kings to the religious of Ireland free of rent," a grant, the annalist says, such as king never before made. Anselm also corresponded with his friend Gille of Limerick, whom he urged to abolish the erroneous practices which prevailed, mentioning consecration by a single bishop, and the location of bishops "where they ought not to be," referring probably to the groups of seven bishops. His desire was, as Dr. Lanigan says, that he should substitute the "Roman usage" for the Irish, and this he immediately took steps to do. His first proceeding was to compile a treatise concerning the ecclesiastical use or form of service, which he dedicated to the Irish clergy, having been urged, he says, by several of them to write it. The object of this work was that "those divers and schismatical orders wherewith in a manner almost all Ireland was deluded, might give place to one Catholic and Roman office."[1] The orders referred to were the ancient liturgies which existed in Ireland from the introduction of Christianity. As early as the time of the second order of saints, A.D. 543–599, there were different masses[2] or liturgies in Ireland in addition to that of S. Patrick,[3] and though efforts had been made at an early period to obtain uniformity in this matter as well as in Easter, they were unsuccessful. In the course of time modifications were introduced from the Roman liturgy which some of the clergy, in the South at least, were acquainted with. An instance of this is the Donald O' h-Enni referred to in Chapter XI. as concerned with King Murtough in sending Patrick for

[1] Ussher, Works, iv. 274.
[2] The word mass was used not only of the Eucharist but of any service. Ussher, vol. i. p. 136.
[3] In the "Annals of the Four Masters," 1126, is mentioned one who was "learned in the Order of Patrick," which Dr. O'Donovan thought was a code of laws; but *Ord* is the Latin *Ordo*, an office of prayer with its rubrics.

consecration to England. It is stated in the "Annals of the Four Masters," at A.D. 1098, that he was "a doctor in both orders (or liturgies), Roman and Irish." Several such liturgies as those referred to by Gille have been preserved, two of which, the Stowe and Drummond Missals, were in existence when he wrote, and may have been amongst those referred to by him.

The Stowe Missal proves that the Roman Canon was in partial use in Ireland when it was written, but interwoven with passages from the Ambrosian, Gallican, and Mozarabic rites. The reproach of schismatical applied to these services by Gille was unfounded, and he was evidently, as Dr. Lanigan says, but a shallow theologian. The differences between them and the Roman were really very slight, but they assumed extraordinary importance in the eyes of the legate, who could not understand how any Church could presume to differ from Rome. A peculiar feature of the Irish liturgies was the number of collects they contained; another was the form of words by which the Lord's Prayer was introduced. In the Roman liturgy this never varies, but in the Irish several forms are used, though never the Roman. Further, the benediction was given in the Eastern manner; that is to say, the first, second, and fourth fingers were extended, and the third was closed down upon the extremity of the thumb, over the palm of the hand. In the Roman mode, thumb, middle finger, and forefinger are extended, and the third and fourth fingers are bent. The services both at the altar and in the choir were choral, but the music was not the Roman chant in its Gregorian or any other form.[1] Mabillon and Dr. O'Connor regard it as Oriental in its character.

[1] On this subject cf. Rev. F. E. Warren's "Liturgy and Ritual of the Celtic Church."

The most important step towards the introduction of the diocesan system adopted by the legate was the holding of the Synod of Rathbreasil, in which a plan for the whole kingdom was drawn up. There has been much discussion as to the identity of this synod, which is not mentioned in the Annals, and is only found in Keating, who took it from the lost "Book of Clonenagh." The Rev. R. King [1] thought it was the same as that of Fiadh mac Aenghusa, but this is a mistake, for Keating expressly distinguishes them, and they differed not only in place, time, and composition, but in the objects for which they were summoned. Rathbreasil was situated near Mountrath, in the Queen's County, while Fiadh mac Aenghusa was near Usney,[2] in Westmeath. The assembly at the latter was convened in 1111 [3] by King Murtough and the nobles of Ireland, and was presided over by Cellach (Celsus), Coarb of S. Patrick, in association with Bishop O'Dunan, fifty bishops, three hundred priests, and a great number of students, and the object of its meeting was to promote "order and good conduct among all, both laity and clergy." Keating does not term it a synod, but a general assembly,[4] and it seems to have been rather a parliament. No ecclesiastical changes are mentioned in connection with it. The Synod of Rathbreasil, on the other hand, was a Church synod in which no layman of influence attended. It was presided over by Gille, the Papal Legate, the other dignitaries being Celsus, the Coarb of S. Patrick, who here occupies a subordinate place, and Maelisa O' h-Ainmire, otherwise Malchus, termed

---

[1] Primacy, pp. 81-85.
[2] Annals of Lough Cé., vol. i. p. 10. These Annals were not published when Rev. R. King wrote his valuable treatise.
[3] Annals of the Four Masters, 1107.
[4] *Comdail coitcenn.*

by Keating Archbishop of Cashel, but more correctly Bishop of Waterford. The absence of O'Dunan's name is explained by Keating's statement that he died in 1117, in the interval between the synods. In accordance with this, the date 1118 is usually assigned to the Synod of Rathbreasil. It was the first ecclesiastical assembly presided over by a Papal Legate, and the first to close its proceedings with an anathema. For until the Roman system began to be accepted in Ireland, the Church never persecuted opinion, and all through its early history was as tolerant as any Church of the nineteenth century. The Synod of Usney, which has sometimes been confused with the others, was a local gathering held at the place of that name, in the county of Westmeath. The only account of it we have is preserved in the "Chronicon Scotorum," which assigns it to 1107, and states that it was attended by the King of Meath, Bishop O'Kelly, the Abbot of Clonmacnois, and the congregation of S. Kieran. The object of the synod was to settle a dispute regarding the parishes of Meath, and the result of its deliberations was that they were divided between the Bishop of Clonard and the Bishop of Clonmacnois.[1] Gilla Christ O'Maeileoin, Abbot of Clonmacnois, who was the author of the Chronicon, naturally regarded the synod as an important one, having been concerned in it himself, and as it conduced to the peace of the community. But it is also of much interest, as indicating the tendency to Diocesan Episcopacy then exhibiting itself in Ireland, especially as it took place some years before the complete scheme for Ireland was brought forward at Rathbreasil. That

---

[1] The Synod of Fiadh mac Aenghusa was held in the same neighbourhood as that of Usney, which has probably caused it to be confused with it.

synod was the most important of all, if we regard the magnitude of the change proposed in the ecclesiastical government of Ireland. The country was divided into twenty-four dioceses, with two archbishoprics, after the example of the Church of England, and the boundaries of the dioceses were set forth. Two more bishoprics were subsequently added for Meath, one of them, Clonard, being that already mentioned by the Synod of Usney, the other was Duleek. The other sees were: in Ulster[1]—Clogher, Ardstraw, Derry, Connor, Down; in Connaught—Tuam, Clonfert, Cong, Killala, Ardcarn (in Roscommon); in Munster—Lismore or Waterford, Cork, Ardfert, Limerick, Killaloe, Emly; in Leinster—Kilkenny, Leighlin, Kildare, Glendalough, and Ferns or Wexford. The archbishoprics were Armagh and Cashel.

It will be observed that this enumeration differs considerably from that of the present sees, and even when the names are the same they are far from always representing the same districts. Thus, for instance, the diocese of Cork is described as extending from Cork to *Carn-ui-Neid*, *i.e.*, the Mizen Head, and from the Southern[2] Avonmore, *i.e.*, the Blackwater, to the sea.[3] This would include a large part of the diocese of Cloyne.

Another very important enactment of this synod transferred the endowments of the churches to the bishops. "It was at this synod that the churches

---

[1] Ozanam derives Ulster from Ulys(sis)-ter(ra), "the land of Ulysses," which is, at any rate, complimentary to the North, if not quite correct.

[2] So called to distinguish it from the Northern Blackwater, in the county of Tyrone.

[3] In the Irish Life of S. Finn Barr of Cork it is stated that three districts of Munster were granted to him. They were: from the Blackwater to the Lee; from the Lee to the Bandon; and from the Bandon to Cape Clear and *Baoi Bhearra* or Dursey Island. *Betha Barra*, MS. A 44, Royal Irish Academy, p. 110, &c.

of Ireland were given over completely to the bishops without reservation of rent or control over them for any temporal ruler for ever." By means of these endowments some provision, however inadequate, was made for the bishops to enable them to support their dignity in the new position they were about to occupy. The scheme thus laid down seems to have been only partially carried out, and it needed further efforts on the part of those who were urging on the change, before Diocesan Episcopacy was regularly established. The holding of the three assemblies now referred to bespoke the religious activity of the period, and the anxious desire of the authorities in Church and State to provide a remedy for the evils resulting from the long-continued oppression of the heathen invaders. Thinking men had foreseen those consequences. "The saints of Ireland," Keating says, "foretold that calamities would befall Ireland from the pride of the chieftains, and the lawlessness arising from the oppression of the Northmen." With reference to this, S. Patrick was said to have had a vision, in which all Ireland was filled with fiery light, then the mountains only were on fire, and finally he saw lights in the valleys. Jocelyn, a monk of Furness, in his Life of S. Patrick, written under the auspices of John De Courcey, the conqueror of Down, says different interpretations were proposed of this vision by the Irish and the English. The Irish view was that during the denomination of Gurmund[1] and Turgesius, when the saints took refuge in dens and caves of the earth, many practices contrary to ecclesiastical propriety were introduced into Ireland, and new sacraments were framed by ignorant prelates contrary to the form [appointed by] the divine law.

[1] See Giraldus Cambrensis, Distinct III., chap. xxxviii.-xl.

And they assert that the light from the north, which after a long struggle banished the darkness, was Celsus, Archbishop of Armagh, or Malachy, first Bishop of Down and then of Armagh, who restored Ireland to a state of obedience to the Christian law. The English, on the contrary, say that the light was to be ascribed to their advent, for then the Church by its own admission was improved, religion was planted and extended, and the sacraments of the Church and the rules of the Christian law were observed with more fitting rites. He does not undertake to decide the question. The story is in accordance with the view here maintained of the changes for the worse which religion underwent during the Danish period, and the line afterwards taken by the English as Church reformers was grounded on it as it supplied a plausible excuse for the Anglo-Norman invasion.[1]

[1] Ussher, vol. vi. p. 480.

CHAPTER XIII.

DIOCESAN EPISCOPACY.

IN the period at which we have now arrived, Armagh becomes the centre of important events. Although there were no dioceses, in the usual acceptation of the word, before the twelfth century in Ireland, and therefore no metropolitans, nevertheless Armagh was accorded a certain pre-eminence from early times. The abbot was the Coarb or successor of S. Patrick, deriving his spiritual inheritance from the apostle of Ireland. He inaugurated the chief sovereigns, and his mediation was of greatest weight in staying the civil wars constantly arising among the princes. It was, as S. Bernard says, "The see in which S. Patrick when alive presided, and in which after death his remains repose." By virtue of his position the Coarb acquired the right of visitation in other parts of Ireland. In 793 Dubdalethe, who was Coarb, made a circuit of Munster, and obtained his demand. In 1022 another Coarb visited that province, and in 1069 and 1095 similar visitations took place. In 1107 Celsus[1] visited Munster, and subsequently Meath and Connaught.

From that time till 1172 numerous notices occur in the annals of such visitations. Substantial contributions were received on those occasions. Thus Celsus obtained "a full tribute," by which is meant "seven cows, seven sheep, and half an ounce of silver from

[1] *Cellach*, but termed Celsus by S. Bernard, a name used here as more convenient.

every cantred in Munster, besides many jewels." King Brian further granted certain privileges to the Coarb in 1004, by a charter which was entered in the "Book of Armagh" by his secretary in his presence, and is still to be seen in that venerable manuscript.[1] By this instrument the Kings of Cashel were enjoined to render certain dues to Armagh, the pre-eminence of which was thus acknowledged by the South. The canon of the ninth century in the "Book of Armagh" before referred to directs difficult causes to be "carried to the chair of the Archbishop of the Irish, that is, of S. Patrick, and to the examination of its prelate." The pre-eminence of which this was an indication was to receive its fitting accompaniment in the elevation of the Coarb to the dignity of archbishop. The first instance is that of Celsus, who, in the course of his visitation of Munster, "assumed the degree of noble bishop at the request of the men of Ireland,"[2] or, as otherwise expressed, he became archbishop by taking orders at the request of the men of Ireland.[3] In the exercise of his metropolitan office he founded a second archbishopric at Cashel, thus making it evident that the Church of Ireland was still absolutely independent, and did not need to consult any external authority in making her ecclesiastical arrangements. In the distracted state of the country his authority was of great use in making peace between contending chieftains.

Thus in 1126 "a great storm of war raged throughout Ireland," which drew Celsus away from Armagh for a year and a month, during which he was engaged in making a truce of one year between Connaught and Munster. His zealous efforts were by no means unattended with risk, and in the year last mentioned he

---

[1] O'Curry, "Manuscript Materials," p. 653.
[2] Annals of the Four Masters, 1106.   [3] Annals of Ulster.

and his party were set upon and some of them killed, including one of his own clergy, by O'Ruark, Chief of Brefny, in the county of Cavan. This treatment of the Coarb of S. Patrick excited the greatest horror in the mind of the annalist, who declares that there is no safety in Ireland thenceforth until this evil deed is avenged by God and man.

On the death of the last Danish Bishop of Dublin, Samuel O' h-Aingli, in 1121, Celsus assumed the bishopric of Dublin "by the choice of the Irish and foreigners."[1] This appears to have been an attempt on the part of some of the inhabitants to withdraw Dublin from its dependence on Canterbury, but for the time it was unsuccessful, and the Danish inhabitants who were concerned in it could not have been many, for the majority of the burgesses and clergy representing the Danish interest elected Gregory, and sent him to England to Ralph, Archbishop of Canterbury, by whom he was consecrated at Lambeth on October 2, 1121. On this occasion they inform the Archbishop that the bishops of Ireland were very indignant with them for taking this course, especially the bishop who dwelt at Armagh.[2] But the feeling of the Church in general was opposed to the connection with Canterbury, and Gregory having subsequently become Archbishop of Dublin, it wholly ceased.

The death of Celsus took place in 1129 at Ardpatrick, in the county of Limerick, in the fiftieth year of his age. The Four Masters term him "Archbishop of the West of Europe, and the only person who was obeyed by natives and foreigners, laity and clergy." Such expressions are of frequent occurrence in the eleventh and twelfth centuries. In 1020 a Coarb of S. Patrick is said to be head of the clergy of all

---

[1] Annals of the Four Masters, 1121.   [2] Ussher, Works, iv. 328.

the north-west of Europe, and Flood of the dignity of the Western world. At 1034 the lector of Clonmacnois is described as "chief sage of the west of the world;" and at 1040 an anchorite is said to be "head of the West of Europe for piety and wisdom."[1] The annalists do not regard their Church as confined merely to Ireland. They entertain a high sense of its dignity and importance, and with their love for it as the national Church were mingled the memories of its illustrious history, and its long roll of famous saints. From Ireland, as they knew, were drawn the members who kept up the special character of their institutions abroad, and it was to Ireland they returned to appeal for funds to build their monasteries and churches and carry on their work.

The early age of twenty-five, at which Celsus became primate, tended to render him susceptible of the influence of Gille, and as Gille was a correspondent of Anselm, the influence of the Church of England was thus brought to bear on the Irish Church. It was probably in consequence of this that Celsus accepted an inferior position at the Synod of Rathbreasil, where the papal legate presided, and thus showed his readiness to accept the Roman system. Towards the close of his life, feeling his death near, he took the bold step of nominating a successor in disregard of native usage, and for that important office he designated Malachi O'Morgair,[2] enjoining it especially on the two Kings of Munster, Cormac Mac Carthy and Connor O'Brien, to see his wishes carried out. Those princes were both men of piety, according to the standard of the time, the former having already shown his liberality by the erection of Cormac's chapel and two other churches. Connor

---

[1] "Annals of the Four Masters," at those dates.
[2] *Maolmaodhog O'Morgair.*

O'Brien, King of the Dal Cais and of two provinces of Munster, was likewise a builder of churches, and obtained the name of Draggle-tail,[1] from having his clothes soiled with mortar when superintending the workmen. He also took an interest in the Irish monasteries abroad, and contributed generously to the refounding of the Church of S. Peter at Ratisbon, a deputation from that town composed of Irish monks having visited him to ask for assistance.[2]

Malachi, who was thus designated for the primacy, occupies an important position in the history of the Church of Ireland. He enjoyed the friendship of S. Bernard of Clairvaux, who has left a life of him, from which we learn much which native writers omit to relate, and we also see how the Church of Ireland was looked on by an intelligent foreigner. He never visited Ireland himself, but as Malachi was twice at Clairvaux and eventually died there, he had opportunities of learning from him the history and condition of the Church.

Malachi, born in 1095, was the son of Murin O'Morgair, "Archlector[3] of Armagh and of all the West of Europe." At an early age he gave evidence of piety, and in due time was placed under the charge of Ivar O'Hagan, the founder of the Abbey Church of S. Peter, and S. Paul at Armagh, who afterwards died on his pilgrimage to Rome. The dedication[4] of this church and his journey to Rome sufficiently prove that Malachi's earliest impressions derived from his tutor must have been favourable to the Roman system. Soon after

[1] *Slapar-salach*. See O'Brien's Irish Dictionary, s. v.
[2] This monastery was known as "Weigh S. Peter's," or consecrated S. Peter's. Another was afterwards dedicated to S. James, and contributions for the purpose were obtained in Ireland by Christian or Gilla Christ. This became the parent of many monastic colonies of Irish, and S. Peter's was affiliated to it. Bishop Reeves' note on Wattenbach, Ulster Journal, vol. vii. p. 244.
[3] Dr. Lanigan does not like this instance of clerical marriage.
[4] The early Irish only dedicated their churches to native saints.

his ordination Celsus made him his vicar, and S. Bernard tells us his efforts were mainly directed to establishing in all the Churches "the Apostolic sanctions and particularly the usages of the Holy Church of Rome." Amongst these was the Roman method of chanting the canonical hours. Another change was that regarding the confession of sins. In the Irish Church it had been voluntary, but now the Roman usage was urged by Malachi; and also as to marriage within the prohibited degrees, the Irish having taken the Levitical law for their guide, and some even holding it lawful for a man to marry the widow of his deceased brother.[1]

In 1123, finding himself insufficiently acquainted with the Roman system, he proceeded to Lismore, then the great religious school of the South, and placed himself under the instruction of the aged Malchus, who, as we have seen, was trained in Winchester. While at Lismore, Cormac MacCarthy, having been deposed from his kingdom, took refuge in the monastery, and a friendship grew up between him and Malachi. It was on this occasion that Cormac is said to have taken holy orders,[2] like some of his predecessors. He stayed at Lismore four years, and it was during this period that Celsus completed the important work of newly roofing the great stone[3] church of Armagh.

One hundred and thirty years before "Armagh was burned by lightning, both houses, churches, and round tower,"[4] and ever since the church had lain

---

[1] Lanigan, iv. 69.
[2] The expression used in regard to this (Annals of Inisfallen, 1127) is *bachall do ghabhail*, to receive the tonsure, which appears to mean his ordination (Lismore Lives, see Irish Index, s. v. *bachall*). There is also a verb *bachall*, which means to tonsure (Trip., Irish Index, s. v.).
[3] *In daimliag mor*, so called because churches built of stone were then rare in Ireland.
[4] Annals of the Four Masters, 995.

unroofed, a melancholy proof of the condition of the country. Malachi was now recalled to Ulster by Celsus, and here his first design was to restore the famous monastery of Bangor, from which so many eminent men had gone forth in the flourishing days of the Church. But to revive its glories was now impossible. The state of society to which it belonged had passed away, and a new order of things was drawing near. After a brief trial he abandoned the undertaking, and in A.D. 1127, after much pressure, accepted the bishopric of Connor, one of the dioceses defined by the Synod of Rathbreasil, of which he became the first bishop. S. Bernard describes the people as utterly barbarous; "they were without moral principle, savage in their rites, impious as regards the faith, Christians only in name. They paid no tithes nor first-fruits; they neither contracted lawful marriage nor went to confession, and penance was unknown." Such is his account of the flock entrusted to Malachi's care. The picture is drawn in gloomy colours; but deviations from Roman usage are mixed up with moral offences in such a way as to show that they excited as much, if not greater, horror in his mind, and the suspicion arises that the dark background is put in with a view to bring out in clearer relief the zealous labours of Malachi. And so S. Bernard goes on to describe the result: "The barbaric (*i.e.*, native) laws were abolished, those of Rome introduced; the usages of the Church were adopted in all directions, those of a contrary character abandoned," and a general change in the moral character of the people took place. In the midst of this busy life his death took place in 1129 at Ardpatrick, in the county of Limerick, where the See of Armagh anciently had property. S. Bernard says the Holy See (Armagh) had been occupied by members of the same family for nearly fifteen generations, or more than two hundred years—that is, from the death of Maelbrigid in 926 to the appointment of Malachi in 1113; and that before the time of Celsus eight of these Coarbs were married, and without orders, yet still men of education. This was an abuse of the right of appointment belonging to those families, but the lay Coarbs do not appear to have usurped the duties of ecclesiastics. Those they delegated to officials connected with the monastery, and, as far as personal character is concerned, they seem to have been men of blameless lives. The Annals, in noticing them, never express any condemnation, always treating them as good men. It may have been that in those troubled times a layman who could defend the rights and possessions of his monastery was deemed no unsuitable head for the institution. It was nevertheless an abuse, and S. Bernard's strong language is excusable, except when he includes in his condemnation the hereditary rights of the family from which the Coarbs were taken, and their marriage. His words must be taken with a qualification as those of one who was unable to understand that any Church order could be allowable which was not in conformity with that of the Continental Church. The news of the death of Celsus quickly reached Armagh, notwithstanding the distance, and Murtough MacDonnell succeeded immediately, according to native law, three days only intervening between the two events. Malachi also was a claimant to the Primacy, but however willing he may have been to urge his claim, he was not in a position to do so, for the year following Celsus' death, Connor O'Loughlin devastated Dalaradia,[1] the chief town of which was

---

[1] The eastern part of Ulster.

Connor, and Malachi had to take refuge in the South of Ireland. It is supposed, and apparently with reason, that this raid was due in a great measure to the unpopularity of his reforms, which, touching the question of land, probably excited strong feelings among the chieftains.

He fled to Iveragh, a barony in the south-west of Kerry, where the king, Cormac MacCarthy, received him and his brethren hospitably. He was now pressed by Malchus and Gille, who were not far distant, to claim the Coarbship, but he shrank from the undertaking. He believed that the numbers and influence of the family who possessed the hereditary right, together with the long prescription of two hundred years, created an insuperable difficulty in his way. Overcome at length by their urgency, he consented to act in part of the Diocese of Armagh, and the "Annals of the Four Masters" record that in 1132 he "sat in the Coarbship of Patrick at the request of the clergy of Ireland." Nevertheless, he did not venture within the city during the lifetime of Murtough. On the death of that prelate in 1134 he was succeeded by Niall, son of Hugh, in accordance with the native law.

Here the strange fact demands notice that while the Four Masters describe Murtough's death as "the victory of martyrdom and penance," that is, the death of the righteous, S. Bernard gives quite an opposite account. "Murtough," he says, "while alive, had made provision for this end (*i.e.*, Niall's appointment) against his own soul, to have for his heir one in whom, when he left this world to be damned, he might yet continue to add to his deeds of damnation, for this was one of the same damned progeny, a kinsman of his." And Niall is described with rather an indifferent play upon words as "a blackish being (Nigellus), yea, one of the very blackest." This is a spirit of sectarianism alien to that of the Irish Church, but in harmony with the anathema pronounced by the council presided over by the legate Gille. It is evident that S. Bernard's history of these matters is coloured by prejudice, and requires to be corrected by reference to the native annals.

The death of Murtough opened the way for a more vigorous assertion of Malachi's claim. He was now supported, S. Bernard says, by the king, the bishops, and the faithful of the land, who assembled to escort him. It was not, however, any of the Northern kings who sustained him, for they were by no means favourable to the innovation, but O'Brien and MacCarthy, who had received Celsus' dying injunctions. Both kings led a great expedition to the North in 1134, their army being composed of the forces of Munster, Leinster, and Meath, with a large contingent of Danes, and there is little doubt that one of the chief objects[1] of the expedition was to instal Malachi by force. They accomplished this, but as the act was opposed to the popular feeling, he was in some danger, and it was necessary for him to have what would now be termed in Ireland police protection by day and night while in Armagh. Niall, on this usurpation, left the town, taking with him two of the *minna* or sacred treasures of the Church, the "Book of Armagh," and the Staff of Jesus, the possessor of which was regarded by immemorial usage as the rightful Coarb. It was of the utmost importance to Malachi, in view of the popular feeling, to acquire possession of these, but he only succeeded in doing so with regard to the latter, Niall having been obliged to surrender it, according to Dr.

[1] King, "Primacy," p. 97.

Lanigan. The Four Masters, however, give a different account of the matter. They state that Malachi purchased the Bachall Isa, which was the most highly valued by the people. This can only mean that he bribed the official custodian [1] to surrender it to him. The subsequent history of this relic may be briefly told. Giraldus Cambrensis [2] says it was brought from Armagh to Dublin by William FitzAdelm in 1180, perhaps for greater security, and also on account of the prestige which the possession of it conferred on the government. It was frequently used after the Conquest, as an object of special sanctity, for the administration of oaths. For instance, in March 1529, Sir Gerald MacShayne, knight, is sworn "on the Holy Masse Booke, and the great relic of Erlonde, called Baculum Christi, in presence of the King's deputy, chancellor, treasurer, and justice." [3] It was held in high veneration down to the Reformation, when it was publicly burnt in 1538 as an instrument of superstition.

After his installation as Coarb, Malachi, having proceeded on a visitation to Munster, Niall, with the aid of his friends, again took possession of the primacy. Hence it appears that S. Bernard was inaccurate in stating that on his departure he "ever after remained silent." It was evident that the struggle for the primacy was not over, and Malachi, on his return, finding the difficulties that lay in his path, determined to resign the office; but before doing so, he appointed as his successor Gilla mac Liag or Gelasius, who was acceptable to the clergy and people. He retired to Down himself, and subsequently pro-

[1] Annals of the Four Masters, A.D. 1135. The Warden of the Bachall, Flann O'Sinaigh, died the same year, which may have afforded Malachi his opportunity.

[2] Book of Obits, pp. viii.-xviii. [3] Ibid., p. xv.

ceeded to Rome to request that Palls might be granted by the Pope to the Archbishops of Armagh and Cashel. On his way to Rome he stayed at Clairvaux, where he made S. Bernard's acquaintance, a circumstance to which we owe the Life here referred to. He was well received by Pope Innocent II., who appointed him his legate on the resignation of Gille. He also confirmed the erection of the new See of Cashel, but declined to grant the Palls. It was too solemn a matter, he said, and it would be necessary to assemble a council and appoint a deputation to present the request. Returning by Clairvaux, he left four of his companions there to receive instruction in the rules of the Cistercian Order, that they might establish it in Ireland. Occupying now the position of legate, and free from the anxieties connected with his contest for the primacy, he was in a position to devote all his energies to the advancement of the Papal cause. An opportunity of doing so presented itself in the case of the appointment to the bishopric of Cork. For the various interests concerned being unable to agree, he induced them to place the matter in his hands, and he then nominated a prelate supposed to be Gilla Aedh O'Mugain.[1] On another occasion we find him engaged in a controversy with an ecclesiastic at Lismore, from which we learn incidentally that there were some in Ireland who did not hold the view of the Eucharist then prevalent in Rome. This divine is said to have held that in the Eucharist there was "only a sacrament, and not the substance of a sacrament"—that is, only a sanctifying of the elements, and not a corporeal reality. He defended his view with much ability, and declared that he was overborne by

---

[1] Founder of Gill Abbey, near Cork, where now the Queen's College stands.

the authority of Malachi, though not worsted in argument. S. Bernard describes how a divine judgment overtook him, and he was compelled to confess the truth, but we may suspect that the story of the miracle was introduced to compensate for the weakness of Malachi's arguments.

The improvement of church architecture also received his attention, and he endeavoured to introduce the style then prevalent on the Continent. The innovation was unpopular, and while laying the foundations of the Abbey Church of Bangor, one of the inhabitants remonstrated with him, saying, "What has come over you, good man, that you should undertake to introduce such a novelty into our country? we are Irishmen, not foreigners."[1] It seemed to the natives to be planned on too ambitious a scale. Hitherto the largest church in Ireland, except perhaps that of Armagh, was only sixty feet in length, the absence of the diocesan system rendering it unnecessary to have a cathedral, which, as the mother-church of the diocese, should exceed the others in size and architecture. In compliance with the Pope's suggestion he summoned a council at Inispatrick in 1148 to consider the application for the Palls. It was attended by fifteen bishops and two hundred priests, and a resolution was passed requesting that the favour should be sought for. Provided with this, Malachi set out for Clairvaux to see Pope Eugenius III., but found he had left before his arrival, and being taken ill himself, he died there in 1148, in the fifty-fourth year of his age,[2] having done more than any previous occupant of the Primatial Chair to bring the Church

---

[1] *Galli*, literally Gauls; but the Irish form of the word, *Gaill*, was used simply as meaning "foreigners." It was applied to the Danes, and afterwards to the English.

[2] Lanigan, iv. 133.

into line with Rome. He was canonised by Clement III. in 1190, being the first of those that lived and laboured in Ireland who was indebted to Papal authority for that honour, as distinguished from the long roll of saints canonised by the Irish Church in the preceding ages.

As the old Irish Church government was thus giving place gradually to the diocesan system, so the monasteries began to be occupied by foreign orders. A few years before Malachi's death the Cistercian Rule which he introduced had acquired considerable influence, and in 1142 the Abbey of Mellifont was founded for monks of that order. It is said to have derived its name, " sweet water," from the legend that a well sprang up there to supply water for the baptism of S. Buite of Monasterboice.[1] It was the policy of the Roman party to build on the old foundations, and thus to smooth over, as far as possible, the transition from the old system to the new. A few years later Bective was founded, and Boyle in Roscommon, Monasteranena in Limerick, and Baltinglas, all for the Cistercian Order. Mellifont was presided over as first abbot by Christian O'Conairche, one of those who were sent to Clairvaux by Malachi to study the Cistercian Rule. He was afterwards removed to Lismore as bishop, and received the appointment of Papal legate.

Gelasius, who succeeded Malachi as Primate, is termed son of the poet, his father having been bard to the Huí Birnn.[2] He had been previously Erenach or hereditary warden of Derry and Coarb of Columcillé, and as Derry had always been closely associated with Armagh, his appointment was received

[1] S. Buite, "Dictionary of National Biography."
[2] Harleian MS., No. 1802. Revue Celtique, tom. viii. p. 369.

with favour. He entered on his office in 1137, and the Annals at 1145 specially notice his building a large limekiln, in order, as it would seem, that building with stone and mortar might be facilitated at Armagh. Three years after Malachi's death Cardinal Paparo arrived in Ireland, bringing with him the Palls applied for. He stayed a week with Gelasius, when no doubt measures were concerted for this summoning of the Synod held at Kells,[1] A.D. 1152. The principal object of this "general council of the Church of Ireland,"[2] as it is termed, was to establish four archbishoprics, viz., those of Armagh, Dublin, Cashel, and Tuam. According to the Four Masters it was presided over by the Coarb of S. Patrick and the Cardinal, though Keating has Christian Bishop of Lismore and Legate instead of the former. Twenty-two bishops and five bishops elect, according to Keating, attended, and three thousand other ecclesiastics. The Sees appointed by it were thirty-four, exclusive of the four archbishoprics. From this it appears that the decree of Rathbreasil, limiting them to twenty-four, was not carried out. Amongst the enactments were those against simony and usury, as well as against marriage[3] and concubinage among the clergy, and the charging of fees for unction and baptism. The Cardinal, "by his apostolic authority," ordered the payment of tithes, from which it may be presumed that the Synod did not entertain the matter. The Sees of Waterford and Lismore, which were jointly created at Rathbreasil, were now disconnected, as well as

---

[1] In the county of Meath. The "Four Masters" have Drogheda erroneously.
[2] These are Keating's words (*comairle choitchion eaglaise eirinn*), probably the first instance of the expression "Church of Ireland."
[3] Moore's "History of Ireland," vol. ii. p. 91. Lanigan, according to his custom, omits this.

those of Dublin and Glendalough; the attempt to unite the modern Danish bishoprics with the ancient foundations having proved at that time impracticable.[1] The institution of the two new archbishoprics of Dublin and Tuam was unpopular with the Northern clergy, though it was carried out in disregard of their opposition. Whether the other enactments were obeyed does not appear, but the order of the Cardinal as to the payment of tithes remained almost a dead letter[2], and while Ireland maintained her independence very little was heard of them. The completion of the Church of Mellifont gave an opportunity of displaying the ceremonial of the Roman Church to the Irish princes and people, of which Gelasius and the Papal legate took advantage. Four kings and seventeen bishops assembled there, and the Church was consecrated with a highly impressive ceremonial, great liberality being displayed by the laity. One king presented as an offering 140 cows and sixty ounces of gold, another the same amount of gold, and Dervorgill gave a third offering of sixty ounces with a golden chalice.[3]

Gelasius next proceeded to establish uniformity of Church teaching, for hitherto there had been four great ecclesiastical schools—those of Armagh, Cashel, Downpatrick, and Lismore. So highly was the latter esteemed that many incumbents of churches in distant parts of Ireland were chosen from it.[4] To prevent the diversity of teaching arising from so many different centres, he now assembled a Synod at Clane in the county of Kildare, in which it was enacted that

---

[1] On the scenes of violence between the bishops of Waterford and Lismore, see King, "Primacy," p. 90.
[2] Lanigan, iv. 146.
[3] Keating, p. 264.
[4] Codex Salmanticensis, p. 650.

no one should hold the office of lector who had not been trained at Armagh, or in other words, indoctrinated with the new ideas then introduced there. It is remarkable that the Four Masters make no reference to what other writers describe as the great object of the Cardinal's visit and of the Synod of Kells, the establishment of the four archbishoprics, and the conferring of the Palls. Nor do they mention the latter in their account of the Synod of Inispatrick, at which it was resolved that they should be applied for. The same silence is observed by them about the Synod of Rathbreasil, and about Gille of Limerick, whose name they do not mention, although no one played a more important part than he as first Papal legate. These omissions are evidently intentional, and show that the changes in progress were unpopular. For this reason, as well as from the absence of a central authority, the decisions of those Synods seem to have had but little effect; and it was evident that the new system of Church organisation, and of the maintenance of the clergy, was yet far from being completely established in Ireland.

CHAPTER XIV.

THE ANGLO-NORMANS AND ADRIAN'S BULL.

THE history of the Church of Ireland is marked off into definite periods by certain historical events which permanently affected its welfare. One of these was the inroads of the Northmen. We have now reached another stage in the march of events, when the Anglo-Norman conquest, as it is termed, took place. The energetic and powerful race, already masters of a great part of France, and recently conquerors of England, were not likely to stay their advance when Ireland, with its weak and unsettled government, lay so temptingly near.

The usurpation of the monarchy by Brian had broken through the old constitutional rule under which the King of Ireland was elected from the descendants of Niall of the nine hostages, a rule which had lasted for five centuries. Thenceforth it was open to any provincial king to aspire to supreme power, and the country was convulsed by the incessant struggles for supremacy between the O'Neills, O'Connors, O'Briens, and the Leinster kings. No one, however, succeeded in attaining complete authority, or, as it was expressed in native fashion, no one became king "without opposition."[1] There was a like confusion in the Church,

---

[1] *Cen fresabhra.* Diarmaid Mac Mael-na-m-bo may possibly be an exception ("Book of Rights," Preface, p. xiv.). The rule was, if the candidate had the command of the North of Ireland, *Leth Cuinn*, and one province of the South, he might become king "without opposition." But if he belonged to *Leth Mogha*, the South, he must have not only the

for the old system was not superseded, while the new had been merely introduced. The Synod of Rathbreasil might pass enactments giving over the Church lands to the bishops for their maintenance free from tributes, chief rents, and other public contributions.[1] But this was merely a clerical synod, and it had no power to bind the chieftains and compel them to forego their rights : or the legate might order the payment of tithes by his apostolical authority, but there was no executive power to enforce them. The resistance of the chieftains to such interference with their rights[2] thus added another element of confusion and weakness.

But the Anglo-Norman invasion put an end to the struggles for the monarchy, and gave the final blow to the independence of the Irish Church. The immediate cause, or rather pretext, was the application of Dermod MacMurrough, King of Leinster, to Henry II. for assistance against his enemies. This prince was noted for his cruelty and baseness, even in that age. Of giant stature and bulk, fierce of aspect, his voice hoarse from shouting his war-cry in battle, his hand was against every one, and every one's hand against him.[3] He had been trained in cruelty by his father, who caused seventeen of his subordinate chieftains to be put to death or deprived of their sight. One of Dermod's many crimes was the carrying off of Dervorgill, wife of Ternan O'Ruark, Prince of Brefne, in the county of Cavan ; but as this occurred sixteen years before the invasion, it could not have been the cause of his expulsion and flight to England, as sometimes supposed, though an important item in the long

whole of it, but also Meath and the province of Ulster or Connaught, if not both. Otherwise he would be only king *co fresabhra*, " with opposition."
[1] Reeves' " Antiq. Down," &c., p. 162. Keating.
[2] Giraldus Cambrensis.   [3] Ibid.

indictment against him. Evil as was his life, he was the founder of many religious houses. In 1146 he established the convent of S. Mary de Hogges,[1] near the site of the present Church of S. Andrew's in Dublin, for nuns of the Augustinian Order, according to the Aroasian rule. In this he had the co-operation of Gregory, Archbishop of Dublin, and Malachy, the Primate. Five years after, he subjected to it two other foundations, one at Kilclehin, in the county of Kilkenny, and the other at Ahade, in the county of Carlow. In the same year, 1151, he founded the Abbey of Baltinglas for Cistercian monks, and in 1160 or 1161 another for Augustinian canons at Ferns, his own residence. His last foundation was the Priory of All Saints, at Hoggin Green, the site and revenues of which were afterwards made over to Trinity College. This was established about 1166 for Aroasian canons, and endowed by him with lands in Fingal. It is important to observe that Dermod had thus shown his interest in the party of change by founding institutions in close connection with the Roman Church.

This man, whose life exhibited a union of vice and cruelty, with the sort of piety which consists in making gifts to the Church, was at length expelled from his kingdom in 1167 by the combined forces of Roderick O'Conor, King of Ireland, and O'Ruark, of Brefne. A ruined and desperate man, he fled to England to lay his case before Henry II., but finding the king in France, he followed him thither, and offered to become his vassal and place his kingdom under his dominion if he would aid him to recover it. Henry, having his own troubles to occupy him, was unable to afford him any direct assistance, but granted him letters patent authorising any of his subjects, English, Norman,

[1] Hogges may be a corruption of the Irish *og*, virgin.

Welsh, or Scots, to help him in the attainment of his
object. Armed with this document Dermod returned
to England, and succeeded in engaging Richard de
Clare, Earl of Strigul, near Chepstow, better known
as Strongbow, and subsequently Robert Fitzstephen
and Maurice Fitzgerald, valiant Norman knights, to
whom the prospect of carving out a kingdom for themselves was highly attractive. His engagement with
Richard de Clare was that in the following spring
he should come to Dermod's assistance, receiving as
remuneration the right of succession to the kingdom
of Leinster, and the hand of his daughter Eva. Meanwhile Dermod returned to Ireland, and making his
way secretly[1] to the monastery he had founded at
Ferns, he lay concealed there during the winter, the
monks letting no hint escape of his presence.

About May 1, 1170, Fitzstephen landed at Wexford, and the following day Maurice de Prendergast,
and, accompanied by Dermod at the head of six hundred men, advanced against the town. Unsuccessful
in his first attack, Fitzstephen burnt his ships, and
next day ordering divine service to be performed in
the camp with all solemnity, he led them again to the
assault. The inhabitants, awed by the resolution of
the allies, and influenced by the urgent advice of the
bishops, consented to treat with the besiegers, and a
deputation with two bishops at its head came forth,
and terms were arranged. The city was surrendered
and immediately granted to Fitzstephen and Fitzgerald, as promised. The Danes of Wexford, like those
of the other maritime cities, seem to have been in
communion with the Church of England, and this
could not have been without influence on the action
of the bishops in advising the inhabitants to open their

[1] "Like a ghost," as an Irish poem expresses it.

gates to invaders belonging to the same Church. In
the following year Maurice Fitzgerald and Raymond
le Gros arrived, and afterwards Earl Richard himself.
Thus was begun the Anglo-Norman invasion, and it
soon became evident that those formidable warriors
were a real danger to the independence of Ireland.
The general alarm found expression in the resolution
of a synod of the clergy assembled at Armagh, which
met to consider to what cause this judgment was to
be attributed. The conclusion unanimously arrived at
was that the trade carried on in English slaves had
drawn down on Ireland this divine judgment, and it
was publicly ordered that all should be set free. The
Irish were unable to see that it was their political
and religious disorganisation and general lawlessness
that rendered the adventurers so formidable, and the
grave conclusion at which they arrived showed a
strange blindness to the course of events.

Henry, having seen reason to believe that the
Anglo-Norman knights meant to establish independent principalities for themselves, determined to go
over to Ireland in person. In pursuance of this
intention he assembled an army of five hundred
knights and four thousand men-at-arms, and set sail
for Ireland, landing at Waterford on October 18, 1171.
His professed design was not to conquer but to take
possession of a country granted to him by the Pope.
The chieftains whose territories adjoined Waterford,
and afterwards all the others, with the exception of
the kings of the northern part of Ulster, who held
aloof, made their submission, agreeing to hold their
territories from him and to do him homage. By
these agreements an endless source of confusion was
introduced, for they were feudal tenures of a character
entirely unknown to Irish law. Those who made

their submission could only do so for themselves, and had no power to deal with the territories belonging to the clan. Thus while such instruments had one meaning for the Anglo-Norman authorities they had quite a different one for the chiefs, and hence they became subsequently a fertile source of misunderstanding and social trouble. The submission of the kings has been attributed to fear, inspired by the large army which accompanied Henry; but this could not have influenced those who were remote from the scene, nor were the Irish so spiritless as to offer no opposition whatever to his march if they regarded him as an enemy. If they were not in sufficient force to meet his army in the field, they could have harassed and impeded his march through the woods and defiles, and caused him serious losses. But it is clear he was received as a friend, as Alexander III. declares in his letter to the kings and princes of Ireland.[1] The way being thus prepared for him, he made a royal progress with his army and a splendid court from Waterford to Dublin, receiving on his way the submission of kings and chieftains. Arrived in Dublin he entertained the Irish chiefs with lavish hospitality in a temporary building erected in native fashion of wattled work, plastered over, and fitted up with all the elegance possible at the time. The display of wealth and magnificence made by the king on this occasion excited the astonishment and admiration of the Irish princes.

Such was the conquest of Ireland. No blood was shed, no blow was struck. The king was received as a friend come to compose their feuds, to revive religion, and to bring in a new golden age of prosperity; for the ostensible ground of his coming was the Bull of

[1] See p. 249.

Adrian IV., granting the country to him, and authorising him to take possession of it. This document had been obtained as long before as 1155, according to Roger de Wendover, through the agency of Henry's chaplain, John of Salisbury. No opportunity of making use of it occurred until now. Hence it appears that King Dermod's appeal was merely the pretext for his interference. As this Bull had an immense and deeply injurious influence on the subsequent history of the Church and country, it is given here at length :

"Adrian the bishop, the servant of the servants of God, to his most dearly beloved son in Christ, the illustrious King of England, sendeth greeting with the apostolic benediction. Your Majesty laudably and profitably considers how you may best promote your glory on earth, and lay up for yourself an eternal reward in heaven, when, as becomes a Catholic prince you labour to extend the borders of the Church, to teach the truths of the Christian faith to a rude and unlettered people, and to root out the weeds of wickedness from the field of the Lord. For this purpose you crave the advice and assistance of the Apostolic See, and in so doing we are persuaded that the higher are your aims and the more discreet your proceedings, the greater under God will be your success. For those who begin with zeal for the faith and love for religion may always have the best hopes of bringing their undertakings to a prosperous end. It is beyond all doubt, as your highness acknowledgeth, that Ireland and all the other islands on which the light of the Gospel of Christ has dawned, and which have received the knowledge of the Christian faith, do of right belong and appertain to S. Peter and the Holy Roman Church. Wherefore we are the more desirous to sow in them the acceptable seed of God's word, because we know that it will be strictly required of us hereafter. You have signified to us, our well-beloved son in Christ, that you propose to enter the island of Ireland in order to reduce the people to obedience unto laws, and to root out from among them the weeds of sin ; and that you are willing to yield and pay yearly from every house the pension of one penny to S. Peter, and to keep and preserve the rights of the churches in that land whole and inviolate. We therefore regarding your pious and laudable design with due favour, and graciously assenting to your petition, do hereby declare our will and pleasure that for the purpose of enlarging the borders of the Church, setting bounds to the progress of wickedness, reforming evil manners, planting virtue, and increasing the Christian religion, you do enter that island, and execute therein whatsoever shall be for God's honour and the welfare of the same. And further, we do also strictly charge and require that the people of that land shall accept you with all honour, and reverence you as their lord, saving only the rights of the churches, which we will have inviolably preserved, and reserving to S. Peter and the Holy Roman Church the yearly pension of one penny from each house. If, therefore, you bring your purpose to good effect, let it be your study to improve the habits of that people, and take such orders by yourself or by others whom you shall think fitting for their lives, manners, and conversation, that the Church there may be adorned by them, the Christian faith planted and increased, and all that concerns the honour of God and the salvation of souls be ordered by you in like manner, so that you may receive at God's hands the blessed reward of everlasting life, and may obtain on earth a glorious name in ages to come."[1]

This Bull was confirmed by Adrian's successor, Alexander III., in a brief which has been published by Archbishop Ussher.[2] From this and other documents it appears that the Pope had received a very bad account of the Irish and their "horrible sins and unclean and evil life." Giraldus Cambrensis, however, does not confirm this, though no friend to Ireland. All he says to their disadvantage is that they were ignorant as to the faith, did not pay tithes nor observe the Roman table of affinity in their marriages. He also vindicates the character of the clergy, praising them for their piety and continence, and the regularity of their performance of the services of the psalms, hours, lessons, and prayers, in which and

---

[1] From Richey, "Short History of the Irish People," Dublin, 1887, pp. 157-159, with some amendments.
[2] Ussher, Works, iv. 546.

other clerical duties their whole time was occupied, though he does not conceal the fact that after the excessive fasts which continued almost every day until dusk they indulged rather too much in wine and other liquors.[1]

The grant to Henry by Adrian and his successor is a cause of much concern to some writers, and attempts have been made to represent the Bull as a forgery. But it is attested by overwhelming contemporary evidence, and it was consistently acted on by later Popes. "Never," says Dr. Lanigan, "did there exist a more real or authentic document."[2] It is not disputed at the present day by any writer of authority, though Dr. Bellesheim advances a few very weak arguments against it—one of these being that Pope Adrian refused to permit the invasion of Spain,[3] but that, of course, depended on circumstances. The grant of Ireland and the gold ring[4] sent to Henry as a token of investiture, were quite in accordance with Papal practice. When William the Conqueror projected the invasion of England, Hildebrand, then Archdeacon and afterwards Pope, insisted on helping William, because whether William was right or wrong, his scheme at any rate opened a great opportunity for increasing the power of the Pope in England. Hence he made Pope Alexander II. approve of the undertaking, and when William was going to set out the Pope sent him a hair of S. Peter in a ring and a consecrated banner.[5] The ring was "a token of

[1] Giraldus, Bohn, p. 141.
[2] Eccl. Hist., iv. 167, note 20. Ussher, iv. 548. Destruction of Cyprus, Irish Archæol. Soc., p. 242. Besides Ussher and Lanigan, Bossuet, Fleury, and recently Döllinger, hold it to be genuine. So the *Lebar Brecc*, p. 102, "Peter's successor sold the tribute and due of Ireland to the Saxons." [3] Geschichte, p. 373.
[4] Giraldus, Conquest of Ireland, Book ii. chap. 6.
[5] Old English History, E. A. Freeman, D.C.L., 3rd ed., pp. 301-2.

the divine and papal investiture of the land to be conquered," and one of the objects in view was "to effect the restoration of S. Peter's penny.[1] But the grants now referred to are trivial compared to that of Martin V., who conceded to the crown of Portugal all the lands it might discover from Cape Bogador to the Indies, and the Catholic sovereigns (Ferdinand and Isabella), in a treaty concluded in 1479 with the Portuguese monarch, engaged themselves to respect the territorial rights thus acquired. Another Bull was issued May 2, 1495, ceding the same rights to the Spanish sovereigns, under the like conditions of planting and propagating the Catholic faith.[2]

Hence it appears that the transaction with regard to Ireland was but a minor exercise of Papal authority. Honorius III., in his epistle to the Legate, A.D. 1221, accepts it as a fact. He recites how "it was stated before him that a certain custom existed in Ireland from the time at which the English entering Ireland by the mandate of the apostolic See subjugated it to the obedience of the Roman Church."[3] He treats the grant as a matter of course, which in fact it was.

In pursuance of his engagement to promote religion, Henry summoned a council, which met at Cashel, A.D. 1172. It was presided over by the Papal legate, Christian, Bishop of Lismore, and attended by three archbishops, Donatus of Cashel, Laurence of Dublin, and Cadhla or Catholicus of Tuam, their suffragans, fellow-bishops, and other ecclesiastics, and two commissioners of the king; but the primate and the Northern bishops held aloof. The age and infirmities

---

[1] Lappenberg, "England under the Anglo-Saxon Kings," translated by Thorpe. London, 1845, vol. ii. p. 238.
[2] "Life and Voyages of Christopher Columbus," by Washington Irving, vol. i. pp. 278-281.
[3] Theiner, "Vetera Monumenta Hib." Letter xlvi.

of Gelasius are given as an excuse for his non-attendance by Giraldus, but erroneously, for he was at the time carrying out a "complete visitation of the province of Connaught."[1] The assertion of the same author that he afterwards came to Dublin and gave his assent is entirely unsupported by evidence, and we may take it that the attitude of the northern clergy on this occasion was the same as at an earlier period, when they adhered to their national customs and resisted the Roman innovations. Canons were passed at the Synod relating to marriage within the prohibited degrees, which the Irish were in the habit of contracting, and the rules laid down in the Canon law[2] were introduced. Baptism was ordered to be administered at the consecrated fonts in the baptisteries of the churches; tithes of beasts, corn, and other produce to be paid; all the lands and possessions of the Church to be entirely free from all exactions of secular men; no provisions or lodgings should be demanded on ecclesiastical territories; in the case of a homicide no part of the Eric or fine should be exacted from any ecclesiastic; every Christian should make a will;[3] burial to take place with masses, vigils, &c.; lastly, divine service was to be henceforth celebrated in every part of Ireland, according to the forms and usages of the Church of England. "For it is right and just that as by divine providence Ireland has received her lord and king from England, she should also submit to a reformation from the same source."[4]

[1] Annals of the Four Masters, vol. iii. p. 7; *lán chuairt*, *i.e.*, a full circuit.
[2] The canon law was in collision with the native laws, which encouraged marriages of those who were near akin. "Ancient Laws," iv.; Introduction, cxvi.
[3] This also was opposed to the laws of Ireland, which provided for the disposal of property.
[4] Giraldus Cambrensis, "Conquest of Ireland," Book i. chap. xxxiv.

The last of the canons of the Synod swept away at a stroke all the ancient rituals of the Irish Church, from the time of S. Patrick onwards, and substituted one in use in the Church of England. There were several "uses" or forms of service at that time in England, but the one intended here is stated in another authority[1] to have been the use, custom, rite and ceremony called the "Use of Sarum" (Salisbury), which was that most in favour at the time.

From this canon we may judge how little success could have attended Gille's efforts to supersede the old liturgies. In spite of all his exertions he had been unable to wean the people from them, and it remained for this Synod to take the first effectual step in the matter.

Much consideration was shown by the Synod for the immunities and comforts of the clergy, for Henry's policy was to attach them to him by every means, and thus to secure their co-operation. The proceedings were ratified by the king, and copies were sent to Rome, with a letter drawn up in the Synod, describing the enormities of the Irish, and enclosing a copy of the submission of the bishops. It was on receiving this that Alexander III. issued the Bull of Confirmation already referred to, and at the same time he addressed three letters,[2] one to the king, the others to the clergy and princes. He congratulates Henry on "triumphing wonderfully and gloriously over a kingdom which the Roman conquerors of the world did not attempt to invade, as he heard." He considers Henry without doubt was "divinely moved to exert his power against this wild and uncultivated race." He entreats him to

---

[1] Dowling's "Annals edited by Butler," Archæolog. Soc., p. 12.
[2] For these letters see Rymer's "Fœdera," Clark & Holbrooke, vol. i. part i. p. 49.

extend the power of the Church, and tells him he ought "to confer rights on it where it has none."[1] He is carefully to conserve the rights of S. Peter to the Pope, and even if he has none there,[2] Henry is to appoint and assign such rights in the same Church.

To the princes he speaks a different language. They have not been conquered. They have submitted of their free will, and have sworn allegiance to him.[3] To the prelates, again, he speaks of the king as a conqueror, and tells them how the king, touched by divine inspiration, collecting his strength, subdued that wild and ignorant people. They are to help the king with all their might to hold and keep that land,[4] and all who oppose him are to be smitten with ecclesiastical censures. "One seeks in vain in Adrian's Bull for any command to the Irish to submit to the English rule," Dr. Bellesheim says,[5] but Alexander III. certainly understood its meaning, and this letter is his interpretation of it.

Soon after the conclusion of the Synod, Henry returned to England, having accomplished the purpose of his expedition. He was publicly acknowledged by the Irish princes as their liege lord, and also by the authorities of the Church. The Bull of Confirmation was read at a Synod of bishops convened for the purpose at Waterford, and with it the original Bull of Adrian, and so the matter was concluded in due form. The Synod of Cashel differed essentially from any of those previously held in Ireland. The

---

[1] "Ubi nullum jus habet id debes sibe conferre." Ibid.
[2] "Si etiam ibi non habet." Ibid.
[3] "Vos voluntate libera subdidistis," vol. i. part i. p. 49.
[4] "Memorato regi . . . ad manutenendam et conservandam terram illam . . . diligentes et viriliter assistatis." "Siquis regum principum vel aliorum hominum . . . cum censura ecclesiastica percellatis." Ibid.
[5] Geschichte, p. 371. It is clear that they were ordered to receive Henry as their Lord, and to reverence him.

Synods of Rathbreasil and Kells had for their object the reorganisation of the Church as an Irish institution on the diocesan system. They represented the growing feeling in Ireland that the old system has been hopelessly shattered by the Danish troubles, and had outlived the state of society in which it grew up. Hence the desire for the more orderly method of diocesan church government, but obedience to their decisions rested on opinion only, and they had no efficient support from the secular power. At the Synod of Cashel the summons came from a foreign king in alliance with a foreign bishop, and the Synod proceeded to Anglicise the Irish Church, taking no notice of ancient laws, customs, or traditions; to give the power of appointment to ecclesiastical offices to the king and the Pope, and instead of the voluntary obedience of the old Irish Church, its decrees were to be enforced by foreign arms. The previous Synods were efforts at reform due to the inherent energy of the Irish Church; this was revolution brought about by an external agency. Yet it was acceptable to the bishops, as it conferred substantial advantages on them in point of rank as well as endowments. In the Irish system, the bishop ranked third[1] in order in the monastery; now he was to be first, and might rival the dignity and state of those Anglo-Norman prelates who held so high a place in the Church of England. It is not easy to understand the general belief in the beneficence of Henry's mission unless we regard it as due to the influence of the Church. A contemporary writer describes the feeling as generally prevalent in Ireland. "The princes," he says, "were induced to submit by the hope of peace and improvement in the kingdom, and the prelates by the hope

---

[1] The order was Coarb, Lector, Bishop.

of amendment in the religious condition of the people through the intervention of the Pope.[1] To the same effect is Keating's account of the matter. But Henry soon after his return entered on a course of policy entirely different from that which he had pursued when in Ireland. The very kingdom of Connaught, of which he had recognised Roderick as king, he now granted to William FitzAdelm in 1179. The largest territory in the south, that of Cork, was granted to Miles de Cogan and Robert Fitzstephen, and so with others. The adventurers proceeded to acquire these territories by conquest, making war upon the former owners to the best of their ability, and when it suited their convenience. The native Irish were not recognised as having any legal rights under feudal law. They were regarded as alien and hostile, with the exception of the families known as "the five[2] bloods." They were not allowed to sue in the king's courts, and were beyond the protection of the king's peace. If we turn now to the Church, we find the rulers, as already seen at the Synod of Cashel, in alliance with the English government. But a difference soon began to exhibit itself between the Anglo-Norman clergy and those who ministered to the Irish-speaking population. They became divided into two factions though belonging to the same Church, and in the main accepting the same doctrines. The only difference in religious matters was that the Irish retained as many of their ancient ecclesiastical usages as they could in the parts remote from English authority. The state of things is thus described in Friar Clynn's Annals.[3] "There was discord almost

---

[1] Ralph de Diceto, King, "Church History," ii. 513.
[2] They were O'Neill, O'Melaghlen, O'Connor, O'Brien, and Mac-Murrough, who claimed to be the royal races of the five kingdoms.
[3] A.D. 1325.

universally among the poor religious of Ireland, some of them upholding and cherishing the part of their own nation, blood, and tongue; others of them canvassing for the office of prelates and superiors." The decrees of the Synod of Cashel, it thus appears, were not generally obeyed.[1] The inferior clergy took no part in it, nor was the Irish lay element represented on it. The "men of Ireland" who held so important a place in the management of the native Church[2] were not consulted, and had not assented to it. The Irish were soon undeceived as to the results to be hoped for from Henry's patronage, and amongst the earliest to show his sense of disappointment was Laurence O'Toole, Archbishop of Dublin. This remarkable man, who was Abbot of Glendalough at the age of twenty-five, was the son of the chief of a large territory[3] in the county of Kildare. Elected to the See of Dublin in 1162, his activity in promoting religious observances was incessant. He altered the constitution of Christ Church Cathedral, converting the clergy into canons regular, according to the system of Aroasia. In his personal austerities he rivalled the early saints, and often like them retired to a cave, choosing one at Glendalough, rendered memorable by traditions of S. Kevin. He was at first a warm supporter of Henry, took part in the Synod of Cashel, and was subsequently one of the commissioners of King Roderick at the council of Windsor; but eventually he incurred Henry's displeasure by "asserting some privileges at the Lateran Council against the king's dignity and honour, led, as is reported, by zeal for his nation."[4] It was at this

---

[1] Lanigan, iv. 217.
[2] Annals of the Four Masters, A.D. 1105, 1106.
[3] Hy Muireadhaig, "Annals of the Four Masters," 1180, note.
[4] Giraldus Cambrensis, "Conquest of Ireland," Book ii. chap. xxiii.

council, or soon after, he was appointed Legate by the Pope, but Henry refused to permit him to return to Ireland. He was taken ill at Abbeville and died, A.D. 1180, at the castle of Eu in Normandy, lamenting the condition of Ireland, and saying in the Irish language: "Ah, foolish and senseless people, what are you now to do? Who will cure your misfortunes? Who will heal you?"[1] He was canonised by Pope Honorius III. in 1226.

Numerous monasteries were founded about this period for monks of the foreign orders lately introduced into Ireland. Amongst these were Jerpoint, in the county of Kilkenny, for Cistercian monks, by Donald O'Brien, Prince of Ossory; the Cistercian Abbey of Chore,[2] at Midleton, county of Cork, which was supplied with monks from the monastery of Maigheo; another Cistercian house, De Castro Dei, was at Fermoy. The monastery of S. Maur,[3] of the same order, in the county of Cork, was founded by Dermod Mac Cormac M'Carthy, King of Desmond, and received its members from Baltinglas. Inis Courcey, near Downpatrick, founded by De Courcey, was supplied with monks from Furness, in Lancashire. The Black Priory of S. Andrew de Stokes for Benedictines was founded in the Ardes, in the county of Down. A few years after, between 1182 and 1186, were founded Holy Cross, in Tipperary, by Donald O'Brien, King of North Munster; and Dunbrody, in Wexford, for Cistercians, by Henry de Monte Marisco. Hugh de Lacy erected two for Augustinian canons; one at Duleek, which he made a cell to the Priory of Lanthony, near Gloucester, and the other at Colp, at the mouth of the Boyne, which he made a cell to Lanthony, in Monmouthshire.

---

[1] Lanigan, Eccl. Hist., iv. 244.   [2] De Choro Benedicti.
[3] De fonte vivo.

John De Courcey removed the secular canons from Down Cathedral in 1183, and substituted for them Benedictines from S. Werburgh's in Chester, changing the dedication from the Holy Trinity to S. Patrick, in order to ingratiate himself with the Irish by an affected regard for their patron saint. In the same year he founded Neddrum,[1] making it a cell to the Abbey of S. Bega of Coupland, in Cumberland; also the Priory of John the Baptist in Down for Cruciferi, a branch of the Augustinian canons.

Some time before these events Cardinal Vivian had arrived in Ireland as the Pope's legate, and finding De Courcey and Dunlevy, King of Down, at war, endeavoured to persuade the former to withdraw his forces on condition that Dunlevy paid tribute to King Henry. This would have been carrying out the original theory of the conquest, but it was the last thing De Courcey wished. On finding this the Cardinal went in anger to Dunlevy, and advised him to take up arms and defend his territory. Urged by so high an authority he did so, but was defeated, and both the Cardinal and the Bishop of Down were made prisoners. De Courcey, however, instead of treating Vivian harshly, set him free, and also at his request released the bishop. Vivian soon discovered that to join the Irish was unprofitable, and he quickly changed sides, and became a warm supporter of De Courcey. On leaving Down he proceeded to Dublin, where he held a synod of bishops and abbots about 1177, in which, setting forth Henry's right to the sovereignty of Ireland by virtue of the Pope's authority,[2] he

---

[1] Oendruim, now Mahee Island, in Tullynakill Parish, Strangford Lough.

[2] Lanigan, iv. 233. Those who question the authenticity of Adrian's Bull must consider Vivian and all the Papal authorities parties to the fraud. This council was held five years after the Synod of Cashel.

threatened excommunication to all who refused to obey him.

The action of Vivian and De Courcey in a subsequent transaction illustrates the methods of the Anglo-Normans in availing themselves of the attachment of the Irish to the memory of their saints, and especially of S. Patrick. Though master of Downpatrick, De Courcey felt he held it by a precarious tenure, and he resolved to enlist the religious feelings of the Irish on his side. In pursuance of this policy it was contrived that Malachy, Bishop of Down, should have a vision, and he accordingly affirmed that he saw S. Patrick thrust his hand up from his supposed burial-place in the cathedral of Down. Having thus made known where he was interred, the ground was opened, and his body, with those of SS. Brigit and Columba, were duly found,[1] and De Courcey immediately made arrangements for their translation to a more honourable part of the cathedral. Cardinal Vivian came over specially for the ceremony in 1185, and it was carried out with much pomp, fifteen bishops, besides deans, abbots, priors, and others being present on the occasion. It was at this time that the stanza already referred to was set forth.[2] It is a strange fact, as Dr. O'Donovan observes, that the body of S. Patrick, the Apostle of Ireland, was said to have been pointed out by an angel at Glastonbury the year before.

Another circumstance worthy of notice is that this history of the discovery at Downpatrick is not mentioned by any Irish authority. It is the exclusive property of the Anglo-Normans, and the Irish, though they must have heard of it, evidently did not believe

---

[1] On the history of this transaction see "Annals of the Four Masters," vol. iii. pp. 456-458, note *f*.
[2] Chapter III. p. 48.

it. The silence of the native authorities in this, as in so many other instances, is clearly intentional.

The impressive ceremonial of the translation, and the publication of the whole story in the interest of De Courcey, caused the Irish Primate, Nicholas mac Maelisa, a violent opponent of the invaders, to make a rival discovery. So in A.D. 1293 he also had a vision, and discovered the remains of the three, not at Down, but at Saul. This is recorded in the "Annals of the Four Masters," who add they were "taken up by him (the Primate), and great virtues and miracles were afterwards wrought by means of them; and after having been honourably covered, they were deposited in a shrine." Thus deception begot deception, and the Irish Primate was forced, as it were, by circumstances, to follow the evil example of the Cardinal and the Norman adventurer.

CHAPTER XV.

THE RELATIONS OF THE ANGLO-NORMAN AND NATIVE CLERGY.

IF we were to confine ourselves to a consideration of the proceedings of those ecclesiastics who were busily engaged in the politics of the day, we should obtain an imperfect and misleading view of the period. All were not politicians or self-seekers, however generally those titles were applicable. Some there were who took a genuine interest in the welfare of the people, and endeavoured to elevate and improve them. An instance of a prelate of this class was David MacKelly, Bishop of Cloyne, afterwards translated to Cashel, who planned and carried out what may be regarded as a missionary settlement in the county of Cork. He saw the connection between religion and industry, and with a view to setting an example of the latter, he determined to establish a village, and invite artizans from England to occupy it as settlers. For this purpose he made use of the estate of Kilmaclenine,[1] about four miles north-west of Mallow. It belonged to the See of Cloyne, and being of small extent, containing only 609 acres, it was convenient for the purpose. Here, then, between the years 1228 and 1237, during which he occupied the See of Cloyne, he "measured and perambulated certain lands which he bestowed on his beloved sons, the burgesses of Kylmaclenyn," as re-

---
[1] "On some ancient remains at Kilmaclenine." A paper read before the Royal Irish Academy by Rev. T. Olden. Proceedings, Second Series, vol. ii.

corded in the Pipe Roll[1] of Cloyne. In the rental of the village made by three of the burgesses with the Provost, all sworn and elected by the whole community, the names of twenty-nine tenants are given, with the rent paid by each, and the quantity of land he held. Then there were forty-eight joint tenants who had no land; these seem to have been of the labouring class, and probably serfs. The settlement was governed by the "law of Bristol," a modified form of Magna Charta. Some of the settlers were farmers; but though nothing is said in the Roll of the occupation of the rest, there is good reason to believe they were tanners. In Smith's "History of Cork" it is mentioned that there is a deposit of yellow ochre at Kilmaclenine, "used by the glovers and skinners of the neighbourhood," and as the chief export trade of Ireland in early times was in hides, the occupants of the village would have no difficulty in carrying on the trade. The bishop provided for the spiritual needs of his village by the erection of a church, the walls of which are still standing, and by the appointment of a vicar. No doubt the services carried on there would be instructive to those who were as yet unacquainted with the ritual of Sarum, which the Synod of Cashel had ordered to be observed, and which the settlers, as a matter of course, would bring with them from England. The native occupants of the land are termed "S. Colman's men," by which is meant that they were attached to the soil, and the property of their feudal lord, who in this case was the bishop; they were, in fact, hewers of wood and drawers of water to the settlers.

The project was successful for a time, and the vil-

[1] The Pipa Colmani, or Pipe Roll of Cloyne, was known to Sir James Ware, but disappeared. It was found about the middle of the present century in the Registry of Cloyne, and published by Dr. Caulfield (Corcagiæ, 1859).

lage appears to have been flourishing in 1364, when Bishop Swaffham began the Pipe Roll, and entered all previous documents in it. But it shared the fate of many similar enterprises in Ireland, for in the year 1380 a member of the O'Brien family, termed by Spenser " Maurice of the Ferns, or wild waste places," who had been receiving an allowance from Government, finding his pay in arrear, " brake forth like a tempest," and sweeping through Connaught and Munster, " brake down," Spenser tells us, "all the holds and fortresses of the English," and " clean wyped out " all the towns in the north of the county of Cork. The village of wooden houses was reduced to ashes, the colony disappeared, and nothing remains but the ruined church and the wall or fortification still crowning the summit of a lofty rock hard by. This is termed the " Mote " by the people, but in the Pipe Roll it is the " castrum," where the bishop took up his residence when in the neighbourhood. This indicates its twofold use—by the settlers for their "folkmote," and by the bishop as his castle, where he dwelt secure from the Irish enemy.

The history of the manor and Burgage of Kilmaclenine further illustrates the contests frequently arising between the Anglo-Norman nobles and the Church as to the lands of the Church. One of the Barry family, who in later times occupied the mediæval castle of Kilmaclenine, claimed rights over the bishop's estate on the ground that he was lord of Kilmaclenine. The bishop summoned a jury of his burgesses, to whom he submitted the question, and they found in the bishop's favour. "They say by the sacrament that the Lord Bishop of Cloyne is chief lord of Kilmaclenine, and that there is no other lord there." Barry's reply to this is not recorded, but that he did not accept their verdict as decisive appears from the inscription on his tombstone, found some years ago at a depth of several feet in Mallow Churchyard, and now preserved in the porch of the Church, which, translated, reads: "Here lies James, son of William de Barré, Lord of Kilmaclenine in temporals."

The ill-feeling between the settlers and the native inhabitants which sometimes resulted in such deeds of violence as the destruction of this settlement, is seen also dividing the Church itself, and exhibiting itself among ecclesiastics ministering at the same altars. The monasteries founded by the Anglo-Normans sympathised with the conquering race, and aided them in carrying out their designs. Furnished, for the most part, with monks from England, they formed so many garrisons planted among the Irish, from whom they differed not only in habits and language, but also in political views. The two races felt it mutually inconvenient to live in the same community, and it came to be the practice for monasteries of English foundation to refuse to admit Irish monks, and for Irish monasteries to adopt a similar rule with regard to the English. The Irish felt it as a grievance also that many of those foundations from which they were now driven out to make way for strangers had been established by their own ancestors.

The new Orders generally availed themselves of the veneration felt for some historic site of the old Irish Church, and reared their new buildings on the same spot. They knew not and did not care anything about the saint to whom the place owed its sanctity, for, as we have seen, he was not a saint of their Church. S. Mary's Nunnery at Termon-Fechin, in the county of Louth, occupied the site of the Termonn or Sanctuary of S. Fechin, a celebrated saint of the seventh century. Neddrum, founded by

John de Courcey, was on the site of S. Mochaoi's Monastery, an institution of the fifth century, and the monasteries for Augustinian canons erected by De Lacey at Duleek, in the county of Meath, were on the site of S. Cianan's Church, a saint believed to be coeval with S. Patrick. Thus it was sought to attract the reverence for the old locality to the new Order, which had no connection with it. The removal of the Irish monks from those historic sites showed that the line of division which separated the Anglo-Norman from the Irish layman ran through the Church as well. So strong was the feeling that, according to an Irish account, the English monks would audaciously affirm that "if it were to happen to them to kill an Irishman, they would not for this reason refrain from the celebration of mass even for a single day."[1] Amongst those specified as putting this in practice were the Cistercian monks of Granard in the diocese of Ardagh, and those of Inch in the county of Down, who, "making their appearance publicly in arms, invaded and slaughtered the Irish people, and yet celebrated their masses notwithstanding."

It was not long after the Conquest that the Irish had further reason to lament the Bull of Adrian, for, in addition to the payment of tithes, which were now compulsory wherever the English power extended, there were new exactions hitherto unknown in Ireland. These were the taxes imposed by the Popes. As early as 1229 a tax was levied by Gregory IX. to enable him to carry on his war with the Emperor Frederick. In 1240 an emissary arrived from the same Pope with a demand, under pain of excommunication, of the twentieth of the whole land, besides donations and

---

[1] The complaint of the Irish to Pope John XXII. King, "Church History of Ireland," vol. iii. p. 1130.

private gratuities, for the same war. In 1251 there was a levy of "Saladin's tenths,"[1] as they were termed, for the carrying on of the war for the recovery of the holy sepulchre from the infidels. Another levy was made in 1270 to enable the Pope to carry on his war with the King of Arragon. In 1288 Edward I. obtained from the Pope a grant of the six years' tenths which had been collected, and also the tenths which were to accrue in the following six years. In order to ascertain the amount payable by each of the clergy, a taxation of ecclesiastical property was drawn up in 1291, which is known as that of Nicholas IV. In 1302 an assessment for three years was made to enable Boniface VIII. to carry on his war with the King of Arragon, and in order to ensure its being duly levied, he granted the king half the annual proceeds. In 1306 the king procured from Clement V. a grant of two years' tenths, which was afterwards extended to four, and then to seven years. Those repeated exactions were not acquiesced in without considerable murmurs, for the Church was in a very impoverished state.

On the occasion of the grant made by Nicholas IV. in 1288 to Edward I., the king addressed a letter to the archbishops, requesting them to convene their suffragans and clergy, and to levy the tax. To this the Archbishops of Tuam and Cashel, and the Bishop of Kildare, severally replied that they and their clergy were so reduced by war, rebellion, and depredation as to be in extreme poverty. How true this was appears from the Roll of the Taxation of Dublin, A.D. 1294. There are thirty-seven entries in it, fourteen of which refer to the inability of the ecclesiastic taxed to pay ; either on account[2] of war, or

---

[1] That is, the tenth part of the annual income of the clergy.
[2] *Propter guerram.*

because the lands were waste, or on account of extreme poverty.¹ So oppressive was the tax felt to be that a meeting ² of prelates took place at Trim in September 1291, in which was drawn up a document entitled "The Confederation of the Lord Primate and the three other Archbishops of Ireland, and of their suffragans, deans, clergy, and chapters." The object of it was to defend their privileges, jurisdictions, liberties, and customs from undue impediment, annoyance, encroachment, oppression, or grievance from person or persons invested with any lay jurisdiction whatsoever. They engage also to confirm and carry out in all dioceses any sentence of excommunication or interdict passed in one, and finally bind themselves under penalties to abide by the terms of the agreement. The tax originally imposed for the rescue of the Holy Land was subsequently, as it appears, devoted to the Pope's use, and by him made over in whole or part to the king. The change in its destination is expressed on the occasion of the grant of 1302, when it is termed "Papal tenths." In endeavouring to meet the tax of 1229 "the clergy sent after their money Irish curses (Hanmer tells us), for they were driven at the worst hand to sell unto the merciless merchants their cows, hackneys, caddows (blankets), and aqua vitæ to make present payment, and were driven to that extremity to pawn and sell their cups, chalices, copes, altar-cloths, and vestments.³

In pursuance of the policy of the Anglo-Norman clergy in availing themselves of the veneration of the Irish for their native saints, we find the name of S. Patrick attached to a place in Lough Derg, in the county of Donegal, which soon became famous. This was S. Patrick's Purgatory, which was celebrated

¹ Reeves, "Eccl. Antiq.," Introd., pp. vi.-xii.
² Harris' "Ware," vol. i. p. 70.   ³ Hanmer's "Chronicle," p. 380.

all over Europe as a place of pilgrimage in the middle ages. The first account of it is from an English source. It was published by Henry of Saltrey, a monk of Huntingdonshire, in 1152, who heard it from Gilbert, Abbot of Louth, in Lincolnshire, who professed to have received it from Owen, an Irish knight. Sir Owen had served in the wars of King Stephen, and having obtained licence to visit his native country, was struck with remorse for his many sins. He applied to a bishop for a suitable penance, but the bishop having imposed too light a punishment, as he thought, he expressed a wish to enter S. Patrick's Purgatory. The course followed on such occasions is described by him. The bishop, pointing out the great peril of the venture, refused permission; but the applicant persevering, he gave him letters of licence addressed to the Prior of the Purgatory. The Prior then earnestly dissuaded him, many persons, it was understood, having perished in the Purgatory. If he still continued steadfast he was taken into the church, where he passed fifteen days in prayer and fasting. On the fifteenth morning, having confessed and received the Sacrament, he was led in procession to the door of the Purgatory. Here the Prior made a last solemn attempt to dissuade him from entering, but if he still persisted, he was suffered to go in. The Prior then locked the door, and it was not opened again until the following morning. If the pilgrim was found when the door was opened he was received with great joy, and led in procession to the church, where he prayed and fasted for another fifteen days before he returned home. But if he was not found when the door was opened it was understood that he had perished in the Purgatory. The door was closed, and the name of the unfortunate man was never mentioned after.

The story suited the temper of the age, and quickly obtained immense circulation. Distinguished visitors flocked from all parts of Europe to undergo the treatment which in one night would cancel the sins of a lifetime,[1] for it was a Purgatory in the present life, and had no reference to the state after death.

There was, however, another Purgatory of much earlier date, and also connected with S. Patrick, to which, according to Dr. Lanigan,[2] this at Lough Derg was meant as a rival. Jocelyn describes it in his life of S. Patrick, written in 1185. "Numbers are in the habit of fasting and praying on the summit of the mountain Croagh Patrick,[3] with the idea that it will save them from hell, S. Patrick having obtained this privilege by his merits and prayers. Some say they suffered terrible things during the night, and were thus purged from their sins, and therefore they call it S. Patrick's Purgatory."[4] This was a native legend founded on the old tradition that S. Patrick spent forty days and forty nights on the mountain, as described in the "Book of Armagh" and the "Tripartite" life. In the latter it is said "he went to the Rick on Saturday in Shrovetide, and refused to leave it at the request of an angel until God granted him his petitions." "He abode there without drink, without food, from Shrove Saturday to Easter Saturday, after the manner of Moses, the son of Amram."[5] The dialogue between him and the angel is given in detail in the "Tripartite" life, and "in the end all his requests were granted."[6] From this legend grew the habit of going on pilgrimage to the mountain. "Why then

---

[1] Lanigan, vol. i. p. 369, note 152.   [2] Ibid., p. 370.
[3] *Cruach Patraic*, S. Patrick's Rick (or Reek, as popularly pronounced), is five miles from Westport, Co. Mayo. It is still visited by pilgrims. See "Annals of the Four Masters," A.D. 1351, note.
[4] Lanigan, p. 370, *n.* 155.   [5] Trip., vol. i. p. 115.   [6] Ibid., pp. 113-121.

should not the Anglo-Norman clergy, the Canons Regular of St. Augustine, have another Purgatory at Lough Derg?" asks Dr. Lanigan. They evidently saw no reason why they should not get up one on their own account, and so they contrived that the name and fame of S. Patrick should be transferred to the new Purgatory, and connected in the popular mind with the lately-introduced Canons Regular. It was a very gross imposture, and such representations were made on the subject to the Pope that he authorised its destruction. The fact and the reason are thus given by Dr. O'Donovan[1] from the "Annals of Ulster": "The cave of S. Patrick's Purgatory in Lough Derg was destroyed about the Festival of S. Patrick this year by the guardian of Donegal and by the representative[2] of the bishop in the Deanery of Lough Erne, by authority of the Pope, the people in general having understood from the 'History of the Knight'[3] and other old books that this was not the Purgatory which S. Patrick obtained from God, though the people in general were visiting it." It might have been thought that this was the end of it; but such superstitions, deliberately fostered by those in authority, are not easily eradicated. The Purgatory was revived, and we find the Lords Justices, who governed Ireland before the appointment of Wentworth as Lord Lieutenant in 1633, again ordering its suppression. Still later, Henrietta Maria, Queen of Charles I., at the instance of some persons unknown, wrote to Lord Wentworth begging him to allow the people to visit it, and that it may not be abolished. In reply he points out, with many protestations of his anxious

[1] Annals of the Four Masters, A.D. 1497, vol. iv. p. 1238.
[2] Cathal Maguire.
[3] The story of Sir Owen, Owen Miles, or the Knight, is found in many forms, Latin, French, and English, in prose and poetry, and excited great interest.

desire to please Her Majesty, that it would be impolitic and dangerous to suffer it to continue.[1]

Turning from the remoter districts to the metropolis, we find the prelates who held office there statesmen and secular rulers as well as ecclesiastics. Down to the period of the Synod of Cashel, the prelates were either Danes or Irishmen; but after the supremacy of the English Crown was acknowledged, we find an Anglo-Norman archbishop. This was John Comyn, a monk of Evesham, who was elected by the king's influence without much opposition by the clergy of Dublin, and ordained and consecrated by Pope Lucius III. at Velletri in 1184. The diocese of Dublin originally consisted of the city only, the jurisdiction of the bishop being included within the walls. But at the Synod of Kells it was provided that the better part of the diocese of Glendalough should be assigned for a diocese to it, and the remainder on the death of the Bishop of Glendalough. Cardinal Paparo, who presided at the Synod, would have had this carried out at once, " had he not been obstructed by the insolence of the Irish, who were then powerful in that part of the country." Henry, on being made acquainted with the decision of Kells, confirmed it by a grant, and John, when Lord of Ireland, did the same, but without effect. The subject was further dealt with in a Synod held in Dublin in 1192, and presided over by Matthew O'h-Enni, Archbishop of Cashel and Apostolic Legate, when the grants alluded to were confirmed to Archbishop Comyn. Nevertheless, the union did not become an accomplished fact until 1214; and even then it was little more than nominal until 1497. Such were the difficulties in

---

[1] Stafford's Letters, vol. ii. pp. 221, 222. She calls it, *une devotion que le peuple de ce pays a toujours eu.* She evidently believed it to have been founded by S. Patrick.

carrying out the diocesan system even long after the
Anglo-Norman Conquest. The Irish clans, who maintained their independence in the mountain country,
would not admit the rights of Anglo-Norman bishops
or kings. And yet, in an abstract point of view, it would
have been highly desirable that they should acquiesce
in the arrangement. For the system to which they
clung so tenaciously, though hallowed by the memory
of their famous saint, Kevin, had lost its vitality, and
was incapable of having new life infused into it. Yet
to assent to the transfer of the extensive and valuable
estates of their monastery in order to augment the dignity of the stranger, was to forfeit their independence,
and to allow the validity of the grants of the English
kings. Influenced by these feelings, they held out against
the change until nearly three centuries had elapsed.

Archbishop Comyn, though not destined to administer the See of Glendalough, signalised his occupation
of Dublin by some useful works. One of these was
the foundation of S. Patrick's, which he erected on the
site of an ancient church, for, as before observed,
Dublin and the neighbourhood were provided with
churches before the Danes became Christians. He
made the new foundation a collegiate church, and it
was subsequently erected into a cathedral. Christ
Church had already been founded in Danish times, and
also became a cathedral, and thus it comes to pass
that Dublin enjoys the distinction of possessing two
cathedrals. The foundation of this cathedral under
Anglo-Norman auspices emphasised the change in the
Church system which had now taken place. In the
early Church there was no place for cathedrals. All
churches were small, and though often highly decorated
and of beautiful design and workmanship, offered no
opportunity of conducting such solemn and impressive

services as the cathedral admits of. While thus adding dignity to the See of Dublin, he had taken care, when at Rome on the occasion of his consecration, to obtain a Bull from the Pope restraining the powers anciently exercised in Dublin by the Archbishops of Armagh. This Bull, which he brought with him, forbade "any archbishop or bishop to hold meetings in the diocese of Dublin, or to treat of ecclesiastical causes and affairs of said diocese without the consent of the Archbishop of Dublin." This limited the authority allowed by the early Church to the Primate, in the days of its independence, and still in force until Archbishop Comyn's time. In 1186 he held a Synod in Christ Church Cathedral, and before the regular proceedings began sermons were delivered on three days before the Assembly, the first being by the Archbishop. On the second day Albin Molloy, Abbot of Baltinglas, preached, and was very outspoken as to the characters and conduct of the English and Welsh clergy who had come over to Ireland, whose vicious example, he said, had corrupted the Irish clergy. On the third day Gerald de Barré (Cambrensis) spoke, and while finding fault with much in Ireland, gives a very favourable account of the Irish clergy, especially with regard to their chastity.[1] Proceeding to business, they passed several canons. The first prohibits priests from celebrating mass on a wooden[2] altar, according to the Irish usage. It directed that stone altars should be used, or, if this was impossible, a square of polished stone must be let into the altar broad enough to contain five crosses,

---

[1] Hence, perhaps, we may understand that the 140 clergymen sent to Rome for incontinence by S. Laurence O'Toole were really only guilty of marrying.
[2] When S. Brigit was receiving the veil she laid hold of "the leg of the altar," which thenceforward became incombustible. Oengus, p. xlviii.

and to bear the foot of the largest chalice. All vestments and coverings of the church were to be fine and white. The eleventh canon prohibited burial in any churchyard, "unless it can be shown by authentic writing or undeniable evidence that it was consecrated by a bishop." This was directed against the reverence felt for the burial-grounds of famous saints of the early Church, to which, as already mentioned, extraordinary privileges were supposed to belong. It was hoped to wean the people from their attachment to their memory by means of this canon. It was, however, in the highest degree unlikely that the required evidence, documentary or otherwise, could be produced after so many centuries had passed since the saints in question flourished. But such enactments were wholly disregarded by the native Irish, who still retained their independence. The nineteenth canon provided that tithes should be paid out of provisions, hay, the young of animals, flax, wool, gardens, orchards, and out of all things that grow or renew yearly, under pain of anathema after the third monition. The demands of the Anglo-Norman clergy grew with their power. The Synod of Cashel had ordered that the tithes of animals, corn, and "other produce" should be paid, but the expression was elastic, and the Synod of Dublin now stretched its meaning to the utmost extent, holding it, in short, to warrant them in including everything taxable. This view of their rights subsequently brought them into frequent collision with the citizens of Dublin.

In the beginning of the thirteenth century we find a state of things in Waterford similar to that in Dublin with reference to Glendalough. The Synod of Rathbreasil,[1] as well as that of Kells, had ordered

---

[1] King's "Primacy," p. 90.

the union of Waterford and Lismore, the former being a city of Danish origin, the other a celebrated Irish foundation of high importance in the early Church. That it should now occupy a subordinate position, and surrender its rights and possessions, did not suit the views of the authorities at Lismore, who could look back on a long and famous history centuries before Dane or Norman set foot in Ireland. David, an Anglo-Norman, and kinsman of the Lord-Justice of Ireland of that day, was consecrated Bishop of Waterford, A.D. 1204. Thenceforward there was a constant strife between him and the Bishop of Lismore about the possessions of the latter See. David, relying on the support of the government, seized on them, and a lawsuit followed, which was carried on before the Pope's delegates, the Bishops of Killaloe and Cork, and the Archdeacon of Cashel. It was of long continuance, but before it reached a conclusion, Bishop David was murdered in 1209 by a chieftain named O'Faelan, whose territory was situated in the Deïsies, a district belonging to Lismore. The "Annals of Inisfallen," in recording the event, simply say, "The English bishop was slain."

The next Bishop of Waterford, Robert, consecrated in 1210, pursued a similar course to his predecessors. He seized on the property of Lismore, and again the Pope's delegates, the Bishops of Norwich, Clonfert, and Enachdune, heard the case, and gave their decision in favour of the Bishop of Lismore, ordering the restitution of the estates taken from him, and condemning the Bishop of Waterford in costs. The latter then resorted to actual violence, he and his followers attacking the Bishop of Lismore as he came out of church, tearing off his episcopal robes, and finally immuring him in a dungeon. The delegates having cited the Bishop of Waterford to make satisfaction for these wrongs, he appeared, threatened them with the King of England's vengeance, and contumaciously departed. In 1221 he had another suit with the Bishop of Lismore, who this time was an Englishman, also named Robert. In his argument he appealed to the decision of Cardinal Paparo in the Synod of Kells, ordering the union of the Sees; he admitted that, during the government of the Irish, they had for some time been divided. But the decision was against him. Such were some of the struggles carried on by the native authorities to preserve what remained of their ancient church system and endowments.

At the beginning of the fourteenth century the authority of the English sovereigns was generally acquiesced in throughout Ireland, but it was not based on a solid foundation. The settlers were in occupation of the level and fertile lands, and the Irish clans whom they displaced occupied the remote and mountainous districts, where the great forests afforded them protection, and rendered their conquest a matter of immense difficulty. Here they maintained a rude independence, ready to take advantage of any opportunity of regaining their former possessions. In 1315 occurred an event which formed a turning-point in the history of the country, and had far-reaching results,—this was the invasion of Edward Bruce. On this occasion Donald O'Neill, King of Ulster, and claimant to the throne of Ireland, with "the princes and nobles and the Irish people in general," sent forward a complaint to the Pope[1] of the proceedings of the English in Ireland, in which they inform him that they had invited Edward Bruce, and made over the kingdom to him by letters patent, constituting

[1] John XXII.

him king by unanimous consent. They state that for want of "a proper supreme authority," judgment, justice, and equity had failed in the land, but Bruce was ready to make "to the Irish Church a full restitution of those possessions and privileges of which she had been damnably despoiled." They ask the Pope to sanction their proceedings with Bruce, and to prohibit the King of England from further molesting him.

Amongst other statements which form the ground of their appeal in this important document, they remind the Pope of the grant of Ireland made by Adrian IV., who, as an Englishman, was prejudiced in favour of his own country. "We hold it," they say, "for an undoubted truth that in consequence of the false suggestion of King Henry, and the grant founded thereon, more than 50,000 persons of the two nations, from the time when the grant was made to the present date, have perished by the sword, independently of those who have been worn out by famine or destroyed in dungeons." This document, with a copy of Pope Adrian's Bull, was sent by the Pope to Edward II., with a request that he would redress the grievances complained of. But in the meantime he issued a Bull to the Irish archbishops, ordering them to excommunicate all those who aided Bruce in any way.[1] He naturally took the side of the English Government, in pursuance of the original compact with Henry II.

During the progress of this war, which continued three years and a half, immense destruction of life and property took place. Edward Bruce and his brother passed through the whole land of Ulster, where he landed, almost to Limerick ; burning, slay-

---

[1] Scotichronicon of J. Fordun, at A.D. 1318.

ing, plundering, sacking towns, castles, and even churches.[1] He was defeated and slain at Dundalk, but after inflicting such serious losses on the English colonists that their power was thoroughly shaken. "Many generations passed before the devastating effects of the Scottish invasion, passing thus like a stream of lava through the country, were done away." "The animosity between the English and Irish was embittered, the sense of the greatness of the English power was diminished, the authority of law and order was impaired, the castle and the farmhouse were alike ruined."[2]

Thus we find, one hundred and fifty years after the Conquest, the power of the colonists reduced, that of the Irish tribes correspondingly increased, and the Pope in direct antagonism to them, excommunicating with bell, book, and candle the invader, who came at their request.

[1] Clynn's Annals.
[2] Rev. W. Butler, Introduction to Clynn's Annals.

CHAPTER XVI.

THE STATUTE OF KILKENNY.

AFTER the invasion of Edward Bruce matters became worse than ever. The English sovereigns, occupied with wars in France or Scotland, and at home with domestic troubles, amongst which the contests between the houses of York and Lancaster occupied the chief place, had neither time nor means to assert their authority in Ireland. So far from making any effort to do so, they were constantly drawing supplies of men from it to recruit their armies. The power of the central authority in Ireland therefore grew weaker; the lords, whether Irish or English, grew more independent and irresponsible, and consequently more arbitrary and tyrannical; and private feuds, resulting in open violence, increased in number. Then the Irish clans, descending from the mountain districts into which they had been driven, began to repossess themselves of territory in the lowlands.

During the whole period of the occupation of Ireland the native Irish showed a singular power of assimilating the settlers to themselves, and absorbing them into their own mass, which gave infinite trouble to the Government. In the case of the great lords, one of the motives for the adoption of native usages was no doubt the independence of restraint and the absolute authority which, as chieftains surrounded by a band of devoted followers, they enjoyed. But, apart from this, allowance must also be made for the sympathetic and emotional nature of the Irish, which has always exercised an attractive influence on the undemonstrative English. Intermingled with the natives, they of necessity became acquainted with their language, habits, and laws; and their children, growing up amidst these surroundings, gradually became undistinguishable from the natives around.

It was evident that the weakness of the Government had reached its lowest point when the De Burgos, in 1333, adopted the Irish language, exchanged the feudal for the Brehon law, and dividing the lordship of Connaught between them, took the names of MacWilliam *Uachtar*, or the Upper, and MacWilliam *Iochtar*, or the Lower, titles now represented by the Marquisate of Clanricarde and the Earldom of Mayo. In presence of the royal garrison at Athlone, they stripped off their Norman dress and arms and assumed the saffron robes of Celtic chieftains. In 1341 the Earl of Desmond and the chief nobles informed the king that the Irish enemy had retaken more than a third of their lands, and that the settlers were reduced to extreme poverty in consequence. Even in the neighbourhood of Dublin the Viceroy was scarcely able to maintain his ground, and had to enter into negotiations with the border septs, such as the O'Tooles, whose chief he hired to protect the English borders about Tallaght and in parts of Wicklow. Discouraged by the aspect of affairs, the settlers began to quit Ireland, and the king was obliged to issue a proclamation forbidding their departure. At length, in 1366, the Government were compelled to recognise the fact that the Celtic population and the degenerate Anglo-Normans paid no attention to their orders, and, in fact, acted as if wholly independent. It became evident that the only course open to them was to adopt a defensive attitude, and to confine their efforts to the maintenance of English law and custom in the districts which were still loyal, and to treat their opponents as foreigners. This was the policy of the statute of Kilkenny, passed in 1366. It has been regarded by some as "a declaration of war" against the Irish race generally; but this appears to be a mistake, as it related only to the English Pale, and its provisions were not applicable to the Irish districts. The Pale [1] was not a definite territory, it merely meant the district in which the king's writ ran, and in which the Irish Parliament actually exercised authority. Accordingly it fluctuated from time to time in extent as the power of the native Irish increased or diminished. The preamble states that the statute was passed because of the "forsaking of the English language, manners, laws, and usages" by the English of the land, and the making of divers marriages and alliances between themselves and the Irish enemies. It ordered that no alliance by marriage, gossipred, fostering of children, or in any other manner, was to be henceforth made between the English and Irish. Every Englishman was to use the English language, and every Irishman living amongst the English. So must beneficed persons of holy Church living among the English. The common law was to be used, the Brehon law being strictly forbidden. The Irish were not to pasture their cattle on lands belonging to the English without leave; but if they should do so, the cattle were to be safely kept for them, and handed over, on their making reasonable satisfaction. No

---

[1] It was termed by the Irish *Galldacht*, "the foreign (or English) district." See "Annals of the Four Masters," 1432, vol. iv. p. 892. This was the word used by the Highlanders also with reference to the lowlands of Scotland. The term Pale came into general use about the close of the fifteenth century. Bagwell, vol. i. p. 123.

Irishman could be inducted into a living or received into a monastery among the English. The concluding section of the statute contains the names of three archbishops and five bishops, who pledged themselves to denounce the spiritual sentence of excommunication against all violators of the Act. They were—Thomas Mynot, Archbishop of Dublin; Thomas O'Carrol, of Cashel; John O'Grada, of Tuam; Thomas le Reve, of Lismore and Waterford; Thomas O'Cormacan, of Killaloe; William, of Ossory;[1] John Young, of Leighlin; and John de Swaffham, of Cloyne. These prelates all owed their promotion to Papal provisions, and some of them were consecrated at Avignon, where the Papal Court was then held. It is evident, therefore, that the Roman Catholic Church is as fully responsible as England for the great political mistake of erecting a wall of partition between the races, and especially for the clause excluding Irish monks from the monasteries of the Pale. But the law, severe as it was in theory, was never carried out thoroughly, though many acts were passed from time to time re-enacting it in whole or part. The result of this policy is seen in the description given by Richard II. in the following reign of the condition of the country. "In our land of Ireland there are three kinds of people—wild Irish, our enemies; Irish rebels; and obedient English." Those termed Irish rebels were the descendants of the first conquerors, who were Irish in language and manners, but not openly aggressive, though disaffected to the Government. With the "wild Irish," or natives, on the other hand, there was open war. So weak was the Government now that at the beginning of the fifteenth century the Pale consisted only of portions of the four shires of Dublin, Meath, Kildare, and Louth.

[1] Or perhaps ' of Emly." King, Ch. Hist. iii. 1141.

The English inhabitants, finding themselves without an efficient government, and enjoying no security for life and property, began to return to England in large numbers. With them appear also to have gone many native Irish, who took advantage of the movement. In consequence of this an act was passed in the English parliament ordering any Irishman or Irish mendicant clerics to be sent back to Ireland. Finally, as a last effort to check the incursions of the Irish, the parliament held at Drogheda in 1494 fell back on the expedient adopted by the Romans in Britain to restrain the inroads of the Picts and Scots of an earlier period. Every "inhabitant earth tiller and occupier" in the county of Dublin was directed to take part in the making of a double ditch six feet high from Louth to "the mountain in Kildare," as a barrier against them.

In such a condition of society it is evident religion must have suffered grievously. A state paper of the reign of Henry VIII. thus describes the shortcomings of the Church: "Some sayeth that the prelates of the Church and clergy is much cause of all the misorder of the land: for there is no archbishop, ne bishop, abbot, ne prior, parson, ne vicar, ne any other person of the Church, high or low, great or small, English or Irish, that useth to preach the word of God, saving the poor friars beggars: and where the word of God do cease there can be no grace, and without the special (grace) of God, the land may never be reformed: and by teaching and preaching of prelates of the Church, and by prayer or orison of devout persons in the same, God always useth to grant His abundant grace; ergo the Church not using the premises is much cause of all the said misorder in the land."[1] The Franciscan friars appear

[1] Calendar of State Papers, Tempore Henry VIII., vol. ii. p. 11.

to have kept religion alive in a kind of way, but the writer of the foregoing account did not regard them as capable of supplying the preaching the Word of God which he desired, or elevating the population from their debased and ignorant condition. The lowest classes were in a state of the deepest ignorance, and the Church, which ought to have laboured for their welfare, was divided against itself. The principal clergy in districts where the authority of government was acknowledged were educated in England, and naturally were in sympathy with English ideas. It reads like modern history to find a clergyman in the thirteenth century appointed to a benefice in the county of Cork, which he was to hold until a scion of the great family to whom the lands belonged "returned from school in England." On his arrival the temporary occupant resigned, and the youthful successor was inducted by the Bishop of Cloyne.[1]

What the "Irish enemy" was in religion or morals was little known or regarded. And yet it is of considerable interest to inquire, in view of their recovery of so many of their former territories on the decay of the English power. They were eminently tenacious of their ancient national customs. The Brehon law was still in force among them, and every territory had its Brehon, who acted as judge or assessor in the decision of the causes of that country, and "maintained their controversies against their neighbours." This implied the existence of schools, in which the necessary legal training for the office could be had. From time immemorial such schools had been in existence, the income by which they were maintained being derived from endowments in land, and the profession of teachers being hereditary in certain families.

[1] Pipa Colmani, p. 25.

Campion describing them says, "The professors speak Latin like a vulgar language learned in their common schools of leachcraft and law, whereat they begin children and hold on sixteen or twenty years, conning by rote the aphorisms of Hypocrates and the Civil Institutions (*i.e.*, the Pandects of Justinian), and a few other parings of these two faculties." Whatever these schools might have been in better days, there is little doubt that in the fifteenth century the education given in them must have been little more than nominal. Irish writers have devoted their attention chiefly to the incidents of the warfare perpetually going on between the Irish clans. When a historian is dealing with wars carried on between great kingdoms, and under the command of famous leaders, the importance of the issues at stake keeps up the interest of the reader. But it has been felt of recent years that the history of a country is not told when its wars and the stirring events of the battlefield are detailed. The reader desires to know something of the social condition of the people, and how the changes which alter the face of society have come about. The Irish annalists, following the prevalent custom, give us copious details of the native warfare; but these trivial conflicts, accompanied by circumstances sometimes of shocking barbarity, are not only tiresome to read, but leave the impression that they constitute all that is worth telling of Irish history. Yet this would be an erroneous conclusion, for in the lowest condition of Irish society there survived the tradition of better things, and a literary class existed which endeavoured after a fashion to emulate the scholars of an earlier time. During the fifteenth century twenty-four writers who used the Irish language are enumerated by O'Reilly, some of whom were poets, others annalists and historians. Augustin Magraidin, who flourished in 1405, continued the Annals of Tigernach, which terminated in 1088, the year of his death. In 1418 Giolla Isa MacFirbis took the chief part in the compilation of the "Book of Lecan," now one of the chief treasures of the Royal Irish Academy.[1] He was also the author of a poem which gives the synchronisms of the Roman emperors with the monarchs of Ireland from Augustus Cæsar to the Emperor Theodosius.[2] One of his assistants was Adam O'Cuirnin, who wrote "The Book of Conquests or Invasions, and the Synchronisms of the Assyrian, Persian, and Grecian Kings with the Monarchs of Ireland."

In the humble position of their race and country at this period the native writers were fond of dwelling on the past, and proudly classed their sovereigns with those of the great nations of antiquity. The "Book of Lecan" is a manuscript of considerable importance. It was the source from which O'Flaherty drew the materials for his work on Irish Chronology,[3] and Keating for his "History of Ireland."[4] It contains extracts from documents no longer in existence relating to Irish history, a translation into Irish[5] of Nennius' "History of the Britons," the "Book of Rights,"[6] and an immense quantity of traditional matter relating to the early races who occupied Ireland. This manuscript was carried off to France by James II., who gave it to the Irish College in Paris; but it was recovered in 1787 by the Chevalier O'Reilly, who induced the head of the seminary to allow it to be

---

[1] Classed II. 2, 16.   [2] O'Reilly, "Irish Writers," p. cxiv.
[3] The "Ogygia," published in 1665.
[4] *Forus Feasa air eirinn.* Keating flourished in the middle of the seventeenth century.
[5] Edited by Dr. Todd and Hon. A. Herbert for the Irish Archæological Society, Dublin, 1848.
[6] Edited by Dr. O'Donovan for the Celtic Society, Dublin, 1847.

handed over to the Royal Irish Academy. In 1420 flourished O'Heerin, author of a topographical poem,[1] which gives an account of the principal families of *Leth Mogha*, or the southern division of Ireland. Eight years afterwards was transcribed a manuscript of five hundred pages, which gives a summary of the medical knowledge of the day, concluding with a translation of Aristotle's treatise on the nature of matter.[2] At the close of the fifteenth century Charles Maguire compiled the "Annals of Ulster,"[3] one of the most valuable of the records relating to Irish history, and now in course of publication by the Royal Irish Academy. The author is described by the Four Masters A.D. 1498 "as Canon Chorister in Armagh, and in the bishopric of Clogher, Parson of Iniskeen, Deacon of Lough Erne, and coadjutor of the Bishop of Clogher: the repertory of the wisdom and science of his own country, and a fruitful branch of the Canon," *i.e.*, the Bible. This reference to the Bible is worthy of notice, for amidst the ignorance and superstition of this distracted time it appears that the ancient reverence for the Scriptures had not quite died out. The panegyric on them from the "Lebar Brecc," compiled in the fourteenth century, has already been referred to.[4]

The chieftains encouraged such learning as still existed amongst the literary class, which was never entirely extinct, and the Four Masters[5] particularly commend Margaret, the wife of O'Conor Faly, for her generosity to them; and Dr. O'Donovan gives from the "Annals of Duald Mac Firbis"[6] the following interesting account of two feasts or entertainments given

---

[1] Edited by Dr. O'Donovan for the Archæological Society, Dublin, 1862.
[2] O'Reilly, "Irish Writers," cxxx.
[3] Also termed the "Annals of Senat." Maguire's name was Cathalog-Macmanus, but it was Anglicised as above.
[4] *Supra*, p. 209, 210.   [5] A.D. 1451.   [6] Ibid., note *t*.

to the *literati* of Ireland by her. At the first, which took place at Killeigh, in the King's County, "there gathered the number of 2700 persons, as it was recorded in a roll for that purpose, and that account was made thus: The chief kindred of each family of the learned Irish was written in the Roll by O'Connor's chief judge, and his adherents and kinsmen, so that the aforesaid number of 2700 was listed in that Roll with the arts of poetry, music, and antiquity. Every one as he was paid was written in that Roll for fear of mistake, and was set down to eat afterwards. The hostess, Margaret, was on the garrots (in the gallery?) of the great church of Da Sinchell,[1] clad in cloth of gold, her dearest friends about her, her clergy and judges too. Her husband, Calvagh O'Conor himself, on horseback by the church's outward side, to the end that all things might be done orderly and each one served successively. And first of all she gave two chalices of gold as offerings that day on the altar to God Almighty, and she also caused to nurse or foster two young orphans." A second feast was given by her on the festival of the Assumption in harvest, which, the author adds, was "nothing inferior to the first day." The relation of these O'Conors to the Government was one of open hostility, and Calvagh's son, a few years before, had taken the Lord Justice prisoner, and kept him in custody until he was ransomed by the English of Dublin.

Although the ancient saints were to a large extent superseded in the English Pale by those of the Roman Church, they retained all their influence in the Irish districts, and their Termonns were still places of safety, though occasionally violated in those lawless times. The Termonn of S. Daveog, at the

[1] The two Sinchells, Sean-Sinchell and Sinchell-og. It is now the Church of Killeigh in the Barony of Geshill, King's County.

remote region of Lough Derg, in Donegal, was a sacred place when Con O'Donnell arrived there in 1496 in pursuit of two of his enemies. He was met by the Coarb or Warden, who warned him and his followers not to violate his protection, or the protection of the place, by attacking the fugitives. In spite of this warning they entered the Termonn and captured their enemies, but had subsequently to surrender them. The Termoners are described in an ancient authority as "the tenants of Church lands, and for the most part scholars, and able to speak Latin, and anciently the chief tenants were the determiners of all civil questions and controversies among their neighbours."

In all parts of Ireland education of the clergy was at a very low ebb, owing to the want of schools for such as were unable to resort to England. Nor was it very much better there, for in the middle of the fourteenth century, Richard FitzRalph, Archbishop of Armagh, wishing to promote education among them, sent three or four priests of his diocese to Oxford to study divinity, but even there it was hardly obtainable, for they were unable to find a Bible to purchase, and had to return in consequence.

In Dublin it was sought to impart some religious instruction to the general population by means of miracle plays, like the Ober Ammergau performance. One of these took place in 1506, "when the awful occurrences of our Saviour's passion were set forth in a play in the Hoggin Green, since called College Green," and again in 1528. Some such entertainment took place in S. Patrick's Cathedral in 1509, where an allowance is required of " three shillings and one penny, paid to Thomas Mayowe, playing with seven candles, on the feast of the Lord's Nativity and the Purification this year ; and of four shillings and seven-pence paid to those who played with the great and little angel and the dragon on the feast of Pentecost." These performances were not confined to scriptural subjects, for legends of the saints were also represented. The same method was adopted by Bishop Bale of Ossory, an earnest opponent of the Church of Rome, in the reign of Edward VI. He had a tragedy of God's promises in the old law acted at Kilkenny, and a comedy of John the Baptist's preachings, of Christ's baptizing, and of his temptation in the wilderness. It seems to have been almost the only way of bringing scriptural truths to the knowledge of an illiterate people in those days, in default of preaching by the clergy.

Several efforts were made to remedy the want of instruction for the clergy. In 1310 John Lech, Archbishop of Dublin, formed a plan of a university for scholars, but he died before he could accomplish it. In 1320 a scheme was again undertaken by his successor, Alexander Bicknor, and Edward III. founded a divinity lecture in it, but there was no endowment, and it eventually died out. Once more, in 1465, in a parliament convened at Drogheda by Thomas, Earl of Desmond, an act was passed for founding a university in that town which was to possess privileges similar to those of the University of Oxford, but it also came to nothing. Apart from education, the condition of the clergy was exceedingly low. This was mainly due to two causes—the constant wars, and the abstraction of the incomes of their benefices by the monasteries. Thus impoverished, their churches also were neglected and out of repair, while the frequent wars completed their ruin. Even the most famous sites, illustrious by the great divines and missionaries who were educated there, were allowed to fall into utter decay. Clonmacnois, well known at the court of Charlemagne in the eighth century, is thus reported on by a Papal Commissary in 1515. "The town of Clonmacnois is situated in the island of Ireland and province of Tuam, placed among woods towards the west, and consisting of scarcely twelve cabins, built of wicker-work and mud, close to which, on the left hand, flows a river styled, in the language of the inhabitants, the Sinin (Shannon). On the right, towards the east, is a cathedral church, almost ruined, unroofed, with one altar only, covered with straw, having a small sacristy, with one set of vestments only, and a brass crucifix. Here mass is seldom celebrated. In it there is the body of an Irish saint, of whose name the witness is ignorant, and to whom the church is dedicated."[1] In this melancholy description who would recognise the once famous establishment of S. Kieran? The ecclesiastic who makes the report is unable to give the Pope any information about one of the most celebrated of Irish saints. He had never even heard his name. He seems to be giving an account of some unknown country, and it is quite evident that those who were now in authority in the Irish Church had no knowledge of its ancient history, and were, in fact, strangers in a strange land.

The ruinous state of Clonmacnois was mainly caused by the warfare which was the normal condition of the country in Church as well as State. The Annals frequently record the outrages committed on ecclesiastics, or by them. In 1500 Barrymore was killed by his cousin, the Archdeacon of Cloyne, who was himself hanged by Thomas Barry. In 1505 Donald Kane, Abbot of Macosquin, was hanged by Donald O'Kane, who was himself hanged subsequently.

[1] Theiner, p. 578. *Civitas* is the usual term in Irish Church Latin a monastery comprising a group of buildings.

In 1506 John Burke was killed in the monastery of Tubberpatrick. Such are the entries in those years in the "Annals of the Four Masters." The possession of the revenues of the parishes by the monasteries further lowered the status of the clergy. Holding a large number of advowsons, and being the perpetual rector, the monastery employed a stipendiary curate to perform divine service in those parishes. It was the interest of the abbey to have the parochial service performed at the lowest rate, and the interest of the vicar, thus badly paid, to do as little as he could. The monasteries might have been useful, or at least might have become a refuge for those tired of the prevalent disorder, but divided as they were into English and Irish, they took an active part in the contests going on around them. The English did not spare the Irish houses, and the Irish were as ready to ravage the estates of the English monks. What must have been the state of religion when the following could occur:—" So outrageous were the Leinster Irish that in one church they burned eighty innocent souls, asking no more but the life of their priest, then at masse, whom they, notwithstanding, sticked with their javelins, spurned the blessed sacrament, and wasted all with fire ; neither feared they the Pope's interdiction, nor any censures ecclesiastical denounced against them." [1]

While the Lord Deputy was " taming the Irish," the clergy of Dublin, twice every week, in solemn procession, prayed for his success.[2] Finally, when Stephen Scroope, with other captains and men of war, encountered the Irish and " manfully put them to flight, slaying their leader and eight hundred men," it was averred by many that the sun stood still for a space that day till the Englishmen had ridden six

---

[1] Campion, vol. i. p. 129. Dublin, 1809.   [2] Ibid., p. 145.

miles, which was much to be wondered at.[1] But, though members of the same Church, the Celtic Irish were not even at this period fully in accord with the discipline of the English Church. The marriage of the clergy was still practised, even by those holding prominent positions. Cathal Maguire, who, as we have seen,[2] was one of the most eminent ecclesiastics of the fifteenth century, was a married man with a family, and does not seem to have been interfered with by the authorities; and there are numerous references in the Annals during this century to the sons of clergymen. The Celtic population still married within the degrees prohibited by the Canon law, following their ancient custom. Unable to bring them to conformity, the Pope had no resource but to confer on the bishops the power of granting dispensations, and thus a seeming conformity to the new system was obtained. "Never," says Campion afterwards, "did I see so many dispensations." So it was with their native customs generally, and the two sections of the Church stood apart, somewhat as those religious bodies in America, who, though belonging to the same communion, are yet divided in North and South by the question of colour. It needed some external pressure to force them into real union, and this was one of the results of the Reformation. All who opposed it, however differing in sentiment and practice, were driven to take their places in the same camp. The unreformed Anglo-Irish and Celtic Irish became fused together, or rather the latter absorbed the former, as often before. And so, once again, Ireland was to present the spectacle of two religious bodies with different views—one putting their trust in the Papal system, the other seeing no hope for Ireland but in the restoration of primitive truth by means of the Reformation.

[1] "Henry of Marlborough," p. 21.   [2] Supra, p. 283.

CHAPTER XVII.

THE REFORMATION.

THE distracted condition of Ireland at the commencement of the sixteenth century, and the continued decay of education and learning resulting from it, as well as the difference of language, rendered the mass of the people less accessible than those of England to the movement of thought which resulted in the Reformation. Still the metropolis and the chief towns must have sympathised to a considerable degree with it. The inhabitants, especially the mercantile classes, were largely connected with England by ties of kinship, and there was constant communication with Bristol and other seaports. By various channels the ideas then stirring the minds of men in England would reach those who spoke the same language and looked to England as the country of their origin. Indications are not wanting that at the close of the fifteenth century there was a movement of the kind in Ireland, and that "some of the feelings which afterwards found vent at the Reformation had begun to show themselves in Dublin."[1] Two documents preserved in the White Book of Christ Church Cathedral give a glimpse of the condition of things in the metropolis at this period. The first is an exemplification of an act made in 1493 in a Parliament held in Dublin before Walter

[1] "The Book of Obits of Christ Church," by Rev. I. H. Todd. Irish Archæological Society, Dublin, MDCCCXLIV., p. xxiii.

Fitzsymon, Archbishop of Dublin, Deputy of Jasper, Duke of Bedford, Lord-Lieutenant. This act relates to the protection of pilgrims visiting the relics and other sacred objects in Christ Church, from which a large revenue was derived by the Prior and community. The pilgrims were molested by persons who probably, as in England, objected to such observances. In the act it is recited that "now of late certain persons maliciously disposed have let and interrupted certain pilgrymes which were cummyng in pilgrymage unto the said blessed Trinite to do their devotion, contrary to all good natural disposicion, in contempt of our modire the Church, and to the great hurt and prejudice of the said prior and convent . . . any person trowbling such pilgrim is ordered to pay xx pounds of lawful money to the Prior and his successors."[1] Another document of the same purport is a protection granted to the pilgrims by the mayor and citizens of Dublin about three years later[2] than the former. By this it is ordered at the instance of the Prior that pilgrims coming on pilgrimage to the Blessed Trinity, to the holy rode (crucifix), the staff of Jesus, or any other image or relic within the said place, should not be vexed, troubled, or arrested, coming or going during the Pilgrimage.

A little before, in 1495, another act[3] declared that "the acts against Lollards and heretics are authorised by the present Parliament."

It thus appears that Ireland shared to some extent in the general feeling of the time in religious matters, at least as far as the inhabitants of the towns and the English-speaking portion of the population were concerned. There are also instances as early as the

[1] 9 Henry VII. From the White Book of Christ Church, fol. 34 *b*.
[2] 12 Henry VII. Ibid., fol. 56 *b*.
[3] 10 Henry VII, cap. 31. King, "Primer," ii. 743.

fourteenth century of charges of heresy brought against men of Irish race, which shows that the opinions against which those acts of Parliament were directed had reached them. One of the O'Tooles,[1] the tribe who occupied a mountainous district in the county of Wicklow, was condemned on several charges of heresy, and burned to death on Hoggin Green, near Dublin in 1326, or 1327, and two of the tribe of Clan Coilen, or the Macnamaras, were convicted of heresy in 1353, and burnt by order of the Bishop of Waterford. But the masses, in the lowest condition as to education and degraded by perpetual civil wars could not be expected to enter into the questions now engaging the attention of thinking men throughout Europe.

If we distinguish the Papacy as a system of Church government from the tenets of the Roman Catholic Church, there is little reason to think that the clergy were dissatisfied with the latter. Deficient in education, and reduced to poverty by the constant warfare, they seem to have been little superior to those among whom they ministered. Archbishop Browne, writing in 1535, gives a description of them, which applies also to the preceding century: "As for their secular clergy, they be in a manner as ignorant as the people, being not able to say mass or pronounce the words, they not knowing what they themselves say in the Romish tongue." Charges of immorality were freely made against them, and appear to have been well founded.[2] With men such as these the Reform movement had no point of contact; they were outside the sphere of its influence. The higher clergy, while taking apparently no interest in the changes of doc-

---

[1] Mant, vol. i. pp. 30, 31.
[2] See Hardiman's "History of Galway," and the statute of Elizabeth quoted in Mant, vol. i. pp. 34, 35.

trine then in progress, had experience of the extortions and abuses of the Papal system, which must have seriously affected their attachment to it. The latter part of the fifteenth century supplies us with an instance of the manner in which so important a person as the Primate of Ireland was treated by the Pope and the officials of the Roman Court. In the year 1474 John Foxals, an English Franciscan friar, was appointed to the See of Armagh and consecrated, but being unable to pay the fees, he obtained a loan from the Florentine merchants who attended the court of Rome, of eleven hundred golden florins, which he paid for the apostolic letters, ordering the delivery of the pallium and for the furtherance of his promotion. Dying soon after he left this debt undischarged, and three years later the legal question arose as to the person responsible for it, and it was decided by the Pope that his successor should pay the amount. In 1477 Edmund Connesburgh was appointed and consecrated, and, in accordance with the Pope's decision, was required to pay half the amount before-mentioned within eighteen months, and the remainder eighteen months after. Meanwhile the apostolic letters were impounded and lodged with the merchants as their security. He also was found to be unable to pay, and Octavian, the Pope's nuncio in Ireland, obtained a rescript from the Pope granting him plenary powers in jurisdiction both as regards the diocese and province, thus practically superseding Connesburgh, who had been unable to obtain possession of his cathedral owing to the official documents being in the hands of the merchants. The Dean and Chapter would not venture to admit him, nor would they deliver him his archiepiscopal cross, neither was he authorised to wear his pallium, the emblem of his rank. Eventually he found he had no alternative but to resign the See in favour of Octavian, covenanting only for the retention of his archiepiscopal dignity and a pension of twenty marks a year. In this case there was the same conflict between the royal and the Papal authority which was so constantly occurring in England. The Crown was unable to put its nominee into actual possession, though giving him the title and benefit of the temporalities; the Pope, on the other hand, was unable to confer the office or the revenues, though investing his favourite with absolute jurisdiction. Three years after the compromise, Connesburgh died an exile in England, and Octavian, who, notwithstanding the powers conferred on him, was only a priest, was now consecrated. He had covenanted to defray Connesburgh's debt to the Italian merchants, but when securely seated on his archiepiscopal throne he refused, and in the end, by petitioning the Pope and giving a lamentable description of his See, he succeeded in evading the payment altogether, and the Italian merchants lost their money.[1]

Those who suffered like Edmund Connesburgh, and we may be sure there were many, had no redress, for the Pope was not restrained as in England he was to some extent by public opinion, and the King's support was of little value. Under such circumstances they were not likely to make sacrifices for the maintenance of the Papal authority, however attached they may have been to the doctrines of the Church of Rome, and, as we shall see afterwards, they were ready enough to take the oath of allegiance. The great nobles, whether of English or Irish descent, were not indebted to the Pope for any favour; on the

---

[1] "Octavianus del Palacio," by Bishop Reeves, Royal Historical and Archæological Society of Ireland. Fourth series, vol. iii.

contrary, whenever they, especially the latter, endeavoured to cast off the yoke of England, they experienced his determined opposition, and as in the case of the supporters of Edward Bruce, the terrors of the Church were always ready to be launched against them. It was, therefore, natural that they should be ready to reject the Pope's authority.

Henry VIII. succeeded to the throne in 1509. His supremacy had been recognised by the clergy and authorised by the Parliament of England, and he desired that it should be admitted also in Ireland in the same way. It was important that such a proposal should be made by one of high position and character, and the See of Dublin being then vacant, he took advantage of the opportunity to appoint George Browne, an eminent divine who was favourable to his views. Browne had been a monk of the Dominican Order, which so long contended against the doctrine of the immaculate conception of the Virgin Mary. He had risen to be Provincial of the Order, and was distinguished for his piety and goodness. "He was to the poor merciful and compassionate, pitying the state and condition of the souls of the people, and while he was Provincial of the Augustinian Order in England, he advised the people to make their application for aid to Christ alone," and not to the Virgin Mary and other saints, for which doctrine he was much taken notice of.[1] The concurrence of the authorities of S. Patrick's and Christ Church having been obtained to his appointment, the King's mandate was issued for his consecration, which accordingly took place in London on March 19, 1535, Archbishop Cranmer, Fisher, Bishop of Rochester, and Shaxton, Bishop of Salisbury, being the officiating prelates.

[1] Ware's Bishops, 152, 349.

When he entered on his office as archbishop, he and some other persons of eminence were commissioned by the King to confer with the nobility and gentry, and to procure their support for his ecclesiastical policy, but their efforts were unsuccessful. The principal opponent of the King's supremacy was Archbishop Cromer of Armagh, whose character as well as position rendered him highly influential. Henry, he said, had no right to reject the Pope's authority, for "the Pope's predecessors had given the kingdom to the King's ancestors."[1]

Archbishop Browne advised that a parliament should be called, and the subject brought before them in due form. The Lords and Commons of Ireland were therefore summoned, and Parliament began to sit in Dublin in May 1536. The Upper House was composed of the Lords temporal and spiritual, the latter being the bishops and the superiors of twenty-four religious houses. The House of Commons was returned by the counties, then twelve in number, and by the cities and boroughs situated in them. With Parliament were usually summoned to the Lower House two proctors from each diocese, whose position and rights were not clearly defined. When the subject of the King's supremacy came before Parliament, it was found that the proctors were determined to oppose it. Parliament was therefore prorogued until the 20th of July, and in the meantime, the legal authorities having been consulted, gave their opinion that the proctors were merely assessors and had no votes, and accordingly an act was passed to that effect. This matter having been disposed of, several bills were introduced, one enacting that "the King, his heirs and successors, should be

[1] Ball, p. 18.

supreme head on earth of the Church of Ireland," and investing him with power to visit and reform. Another act took away appeals to Rome in spiritual causes and referred them to the Crown. A further act was directed against the authority of the Bishop of Rome, and imposed an oath of supremacy on all ecclesiastical and lay officers. These bills encountered much opposition from the spiritual peers, but were eventually passed, chiefly owing to the speech of Archbishop Browne, who, affirming his own conscientious acceptance of the principle of the supremacy, declared that he who should oppose it was no true subject of the King. He also argued that the Popes had always acknowledged sovereigns to be supreme over their dominions, quoting as an instance the case of Pope Eleutherius and the British king, Lucius. It is something like poetical justice to find this story, which is known to be a forgery[1] of the fifth century, intended to support Roman claims in Britain, used on this occasion to overthrow them in Ireland.

The Parliament was essentially English, for no native Irish layman could sit in it; and it is highly probable that those proctors who belonged to dioceses outside the Pale were in a large number of cases native clergymen, who would naturally be decided opponents of anything the King proposed, and that this was the special ground for desiring their removal from Parliament. Several other acts were passed in the same Parliament; that for first-fruits, which ordered that all persons holding any ecclesiastical preferment should pay to the king the profits for one year; that the first-fruits of abbeys, priories, and hospitals should be vested in him; an act for the assurance of pensions to the

[1] Haddan and Stubbs, Councils, vol. i. pp. 25, 26. It is still firmly believed in Wales.

abbots of suppressed monasteries; also one for the annual payment of the twentieth part of all spiritual promotions to the King for ever. Lastly, Peter's pence and all payments to the Bishop of Rome were prohibited, as well as the procuring of dispensations, licences, and faculties from him. The Parliament wound up its proceedings by ordering the suppression of thirteen religious houses, and closed its sittings on December 20, 1537.

Here, it will be observed, there is no mention of convocation, and the clergy were taxed, not as in England, by their own Order, but by Parliament. Ireland did not at this time possess a convocation, nor was one summoned until the reign of James I. Soon after the rising of Parliament, the Pope took active measures to counteract the King's plans, for in April 1538 a letter was written to O'Neill by the Bishop of Metz, in the name of the Pope and Cardinals, urging him to suppress heresy. On this occasion the familiar device was employed of bringing forward a pretended prophecy of S. Laserian or Molaise, erroneously said to be Bishop of Cashel, but really Abbot of Leighlin in the seventh century. He was affirmed to have said that "the mother Church of Rome falleth when in Ireland the Catholic faith is overcome."[1]

In further pursuance of his policy it seemed to Henry desirable that the title of Lord of Ireland borne by him and his predecessors should now be exchanged for that of King. The former designation was connected in the popular mind with the donation of Pope Adrian, the belief being that the regal estate of Ireland consisted in the Bishop of Rome, under whom the kings of England ruled as Lords.[2] To

---

[1] Mant, i. 140.   [2] State Papers, ii. 480.

remove this erroneous impression, an act was passed in 1542, providing that the King, his heirs and successors, Kings of England, should be always Kings of Ireland.[1]

While these changes in the laws were going forward, Archbishop Browne was diligent in seeking the spiritual welfare of the people by preaching; but finding, as he says in a letter to Cromwell in April 1538, that "the relics and images of both his cathedrals took off the common people from the true worship,"[2] he besought that an express order might be sent from government for their removal, and the canons rebuked for their lukewarmness in the matter. In consequence, probably, of this remonstrance, several of those objects of veneration were taken away and destroyed. Amongst these was the famous Bachall, or Staff of Jesus, which was publicly burned.[3] The antiquary will regret the loss of this venerable memorial of the early Church, but in revolutionary times such feelings meet with slender sympathy. The "Annals of the Four Masters" thus refer to these proceedings. "They (the King and council) burned the celebrated image of Mary which was at Trim, which used to perform wonders and miracles; which used to heal the blind, the deaf, and the lame, and the sufferers from all diseases; and the Staff of Jesus, which was in Dublin performing miracles from the time of Patrick down to that time, and which was in the hand of Christ, while He was among men."[4] Meanwhile a letter from the Council of Ireland in 1538 assured the Lord Privy Seal that they were diligent in setting forth the Word of God, abolishing the Bishop of Rome's usurped authority

---

[1] Ball, 25.   [2] Mant, i.
[3] In 1538, according to one authority, "Book of Obits," p. xvi., but this does not seem quite certain. See p. xviii., note *w*.
[4] Annals of the Four Masters, A.D. 1537.

and extinguishing idolatry. In the same year the
Archbishop, taking advantage of a circuit of assize,
accompanied the judges to the counties of Carlow,
Wexford, Waterford, and Tipperary, and in all those
towns preached to large congregations. At Kilkenny he preached on New Year's Day, at Wexford
he preached "on the Epiphany Day, having great
audience." At Waterford, again, he preached on
Sunday, having a "very great audience." At his
sermon at Clonmel all the bishops of Munster attended
by his command. An incident of great importance
occurred at Clonmel, two archbishops and eight
bishops, after the archbishop had preached, in open
audience took the oath mentioned in the Acts of Parliament, both touching the King's succession and primacy
before the King's chancellor, and divers others there
present did the like. It is evident that these men must
have drawn a distinction between the Papal system
and the Roman Catholic religion, just as Bonner and
others had done in England, and entertained no real
objection to renouncing the former. A letter from
Clonmel of January 15, 1539, asks that thanks may
be given to him for his pains and diligence in setting
forth the Word of God on that occasion. An interesting feature in the Archbishop's plans is detailed in
a letter written about a week later. "I intend," he
says, "to travel the country as far as any English is
to be understanded, and whereas I may not be understanded, I have provided a suffragan named Doctor
Nangle, Bishop of Clonfert, who is not only well-
learned but also a right honest man, and undoubtedly
will set forth as well the Word of God as our prince's
cause in the Irish tongue to the discharge and trust
of my conscience."[1] This seemed to afford a promise

[1] Mant, i. 153.

of a reversal of the policy so long pursued in Ireland of proscribing the language of the people. It was a bold policy on the part of the Archbishop, for the laws were still on the Statute Book forbidding the use of the language within the Pale; nevertheless, he disregarded them, deeming it his duty to consider the spiritual welfare of the people rather than to comply with the law. But the traditions of government were too inveterate to be overcome by his zeal, and we hear no more of his employing an Irish preacher.

In the course of the Archbishop's tour he published the King's injunctions as well as his translation of the Pater Noster, Ave Maria, the Articles of Faith, and the Ten Commandments in English. There was at this time little actual change of doctrine either in England or Ireland, and the form of beads (or prayers) which he put forth to be addressed by all the clergy to the people directing them what they should pray for, dwells chiefly on the King's supremacy, and the duty of repudiating "the unlawful jurisdiction usurped by the Bishop of Rome." The conclusion of the document, however, indicates the change which was approaching. "Let us," the Archbishop says, "put all our confidence and trust in our Saviour Jesus Christ, which is gentle and loving, and requireth nothing of us when we have offended Him but that we should repent and forsake our sins, and believe steadfastly that He is Christ, the Son of the living God, and that He died for our sins and so forth, as it is contained in the Creed, and that through Him and by Him, and by none other, we shall have remission of our sins according to His promise made to us in many and divers places of Scripture."[1]

[1] Mant, i. 146.

The letter of the Bishop of Metz to O'Neill produced the desired effect, and that chieftain immediately took up arms against the King. Negotiations had been going on between him, the King of Scotland, and the Pope, and in the spring of 1539 a plan was drawn up for a campaign in Ireland in combination with projected movements on the Continent. The Emperor Francis was to invade England, the King of the Scots was to cross over to Ulster, and to march on Dublin with the united forces of the North; the Geraldines were to rise in the Pale; O'Neill to proclaim himself king at Tara. One is reminded here of the complaint of Donald O'Neill and the nobles of Ireland in the year 1318, when they trace the bloodshed and cruelty through which Ireland had then passed to the Papal interference. The clergy now threw themselves into the struggle. "The friars and priests of all the Irishry did preach daily that every man ought, for the salvation of his soul, to fight and make war against the King's Majesty and his true subjects; and if any of them did die in the struggle, his soul that should so be dead should go to heaven as the souls of S. Peter and S. Paul, which suffered death and martyrdom for God's sake." But the scheme came to nothing. O'Neill and the Ulster chiefs were the only ones who moved, and he, preferring plunder to martyrdom for the faith, drove off the cattle and movables of the Pale, and retreated towards Ulster. He had arrived at Bellahoe, on the borders of Meath and Monaghan, when he was overtaken and defeated with great slaughter by Lord Leonard Grey with the forces of the English colony. This battle broke for years the power of the Ulster chieftains.[1] The victory of the Royal forces produced a marked effect on the Irish

[1] Richey, pp. 311, 312.

THE REFORMATION.

and Anglo-Irish lords. O'Neill's true feeling on the subject of the Papal system, as distinguished from the Roman Catholic religion, was shown when he solemnly renounced the Pope's authority, an example followed by that of most of the Irish chieftains. Not only the other Northern chieftains, but those of Connaught, Meath, and Munster, of both races, executed indentures of submission, and acknowledged the King's supremacy. The great Earl of Desmond, whose privilege it was never to enter a walled town, now waived his right, and made his submission. The renunciation of the Pope's supremacy was made a necessary article in those submissions. None of the chieftains seem to have had any hesitation on the subject. The instruments remaining are so numerous as to forbid our considering the arrangement less than universal.[1] In O'Neill's case the words are: "I entirely renounce obedience to the Roman Pontiff and his usurped authority, and recognise the King to be supreme head of the Church of England and Ireland under Christ, and I will compel all living under my rule to do the same."

In the year 1540 there is a list of twenty-seven indentures of submission, and in 1542 another list, in which we find O'Donnell, O'Neill, M'Mahon, O'Connor, O'Brien, O'Moore, Maguire, M'Donnell, O'Byrne, O'Rourke, the De Barries, &c.[2] It is worthy of notice that before January 1541, the date of the earliest of these submissions, they must have had full notice that the Pope denounced submission to the King, and called upon all true Catholics to support the Holy See.[3] But the antagonism between patriotism and religion, which had characterised the whole period between the Norman Conquest and the Reformation,

---

[1] Richey, p. 363.   [2] Ibid., p. 333.   [3] Ibid., p. 364.

had rendered the gentry, whether of native or English origin, lukewarm in their attachment to the Papal system, and even to religion. The Papacy imposed on them by the Synod of Cashel, in which they were not represented, was associated in their minds with the invaders, whose cruelty and treachery the Annals of the period sufficiently prove. Hence the acceptance of the King's supremacy met with little objection on their part.

Ireland was now, outwardly at least, loyal to the King, no lord or chieftain venturing to dispute his authority. But in the measures for the advancement of religion the fatal error was committed of neglecting the language of the people. Henry pursued the traditional policy of the Irish Government, which was to Anglicise the people, disregarding or proscribing their language, laws, and customs. This policy was formally sanctioned by the Parliament in 1536,[1] which repeated all the most objectionable provisions of the statute of Kilkenny, and applied them to the whole country. The position of the inhabitants of the Pale was in many respects analogous to that of the inhabitants of the Lowlands of Scotland, and both were known by the same name to the natives, as we have seen. It was unfortunate that a course was pursued in Ireland unlike that adopted in Scotland. "Indifferent to the condition, the wants, and the wishes of the broad mass of the population, the Tudor sovereigns merely sought how to force the Irish into compliance with English manners, English habits, dress, and customs, and when this proved impossible nothing remained except to retreat or ride roughshod over all obstacles to good government and improvement."[2] In conse-

---

[1] See the Act of 28 Henry VIII., cap. 15.
[2] Mr. Brewer, "Carew Papers," vol. ii. p. 25.

quence of this policy neither the Form of Beads nor any other document connected with religion, much less the Bible itself, was translated into the Irish language. Instead of this, the better feelings of the native Irish were enlisted against a policy which aimed at suppressing all national sentiment, and which, when identified with the Reformation, was calculated to render it unpopular. The people who spoke the Irish language—that is, the descendants of the original settlers and the Celtic natives—were hitherto separated by differences of race and traditional prejudices, but they were now supplied with a common grievance, which became a bond of union. The keen-sighted Archbishop of Dublin discerned the result. "It is observed," he says, "that ever since his highness's ancestors had this nation in possession the old natives have been craving foreign powers to assist and rule them. And now both English race and Irish begin to oppose your Lordship's orders, and do lay aside their national old quarrels."[1] His words were verified when after a time the idea originated of a party opposed to the government, whose rallying cry should be religion. The dissolution of the monasteries had an indirect effect in promoting this cry, for they were responsible for the performance of divine service in the parishes of which they held the rectorial tithes. But when the possessions of the monastery were granted to laymen, the tithes passed with them, and no provision remained for the maintenance of divine service. An act, it is true, was passed in 1542 to erect and incorporate a vicarage in such parishes, but it was quite inadequate. In this state of spiritual destitution, the people came more than ever under the influence of the Franciscan monks, who,

[1] Archbishop Browne to Cromwell, Mant, i. 130.

amidst all the changes which took place held their ground. As begging friars they needed neither houses nor revenues to carry on the work, and as they were more intimately connected with the Pope, who was the only bishop they acknowledged, than the secular clergy, they were infinitely more zealous in maintaining his supremacy.

Turning now to the metropolis, Christ Church, which was originally a priory with canons, had been altered to a cathedral with a Dean and Chapter in 1539; but three years later the Lord Deputy proposed a further change, and advised that it should be reserved as a house for the residence and entertainment of the Council, and the revenues used to establish a free school. "Whereof there is great lack in this land, having never a one within the same."[1] But the property turning out on inquiry to be much less than was supposed, the mayor and commons of the city, fearing their city would be "totally defaced and disparaged," earnestly remonstrated, and the scheme was abandoned.

On the death of Archbishop Cromer, March 16, 1543, he was succeeded by George Dowdall, a native of the county of Louth, who received his appointment from the King, but did not succeed in obtaining a provision from the Pope, who nominated Waucop in his place. Waucop was unable to obtain possession of the See; nevertheless, he attended the sessions of the Council of Trent from 1545 to 1547, and attached his signature to the proceedings as Primate of Ireland. He was the father of the modern titular hierarchy, and enjoys the unenviable distinction of having been the first to introduce the Jesuits into Ireland.

Dowdall, the actual Primate, attempted to canonize

[1] Mant, i. 174.

Fitzralph, the most famous of his predecessors at Armagh, and in a Synod held in Drogheda on June 20, 1545, he ordered that Fitzralph's festival should be celebrated with nine lessons yearly, on the 27th of June; but the Pope refused to confirm the proceedings, and nothing more was heard of it. This proposal appears to indicate the position Dowdall had taken up, for Fitzralph was a reformer before the Reformation. He was appointed Primate of Ireland in 1347 by the Pope, and was eminent as a learned and eloquent preacher; but he is chiefly remarkable for the stand he made against the mendicant orders, whom he denounced as "a kind of creature unknown to the Church for twelve hundred years after Christ." At their instance he was cited before the Pope, and during the three years which the trial lasted he defended his position. The Pope is said to have decided in favour of the friars, but before the contest had concluded Fitzralph died. Dowdall would also apparently have desired a reformation without change of doctrine.

Henry has been censured for his arbitrary proceedings in interfering with the faith of the people, and particularly for the appointment of Archbishop Browne, whose action with regard to the images and relics in the churches under his jurisdiction has been stigmatised as an insult to their feelings. But Browne must be judged by the standard of his own age, and the circumstances in which he was placed. His high character and abilities were well known when he was appointed to the See of Dublin, and he was sincere in his advocacy of the Reformation. The removal of the images was due, in the first instance, to instructions from the Government,[1] in pursuance of a policy then in force in England. He undoubtedly approved

---

[1] Mant i. 125.

of and encouraged it, regarding them as maintained by the Prior and clergy on account of the gain derived from the pilgrims who visited them. Henry had not adopted the reformed doctrines—he had only cast off the Papal supremacy; and though much more was involved in that, he had not gone any further. It was to carry out his views on this point chiefly that Browne was sent to Ireland, and if he often made it the subject of his preaching, it was because it was the corner-stone of the Roman system.

Henry's assumption of the supremacy was only carrying out to its logical conclusion the legislation of an earlier date, for in the reign of Edward III. and subsequent kings, Parliament had from time to time passed laws restraining and limiting the authority of the Pope. Henry swept it away altogether by declaring himself supreme head of the Church of England, and now of Ireland. The Pope, however, on his part, was not idle, for Archbishop Browne, writing to Cromwell in 1538, informs him there has come to the Primate and his clergy a private [1] commission from the Bishop of Rome prohibiting his gracious highness's people here in this nation to own his royal supremacy, and joining a curse to all them and theirs who shall not, within forty days, confess to their confessors after the publishing of it to them, that they have done amiss in so doing. Henry's action is not unlike that of Henry II. three hundred and sixty years before. That monarch, supported by a powerful army, summoned the Synod of Cashel, at which his agents were present, and canons were enacted ordering divine service to be conducted in accordance with the forms and usages of the Church of England. This involved the whole Papal system, and the Pope from

[1] Mant., vol. i. p. 138.

that date appointed or confirmed the appointment of every bishop; he taxed the clergy, collected Peter's pence, excommunicated rebels against the King, and enjoyed the full authority expressed by the words Papal supremacy. This authority was now withdrawn by another English king. The parallel may be carried farther, for both in the Synod of Cashel and the parliament of Henry, the Archbishop of Armagh and his suffragans were absent, and in neither case were the proceedings much regarded by the population, being opposed to the popular feeling. It may be added that the reasons assigned by the two assemblies for the changes are substantially the same; in the former, that as Ireland received her king from England, she should also submit to a reformation from the same source;[1] in the latter, "that like as the King's majesty justly and rightfully is, and ought to be, supreme head of the Church of England . . . so, in like manner of wise, for as much as this land of Ireland is depending and belonging rightfully to the Imperial Crown of England," for this reason the Act of Supremacy[2] declares "the King, his heirs and successors, kings of the realm of England, and lords of this land of Ireland, shall be accepted, taken, and reported the only supreme head on earth of the whole Church of Ireland, called *Hibernica ecclesia*."

In each case it was a revolution descending from the higher to the lower class, which it reached only by slow degrees; but in that of Henry VIII., in particular, it was the first step in a series of changes which, though at long intervals, have since taken place, and completely reversed the ecclesiastical legislation of the Synod of Cashel.

[1] Giraldus Cambrensis, p. 234 (Bohn).
[2] 28 Henry VIII., cap. 5, Ireland, A.D. 1537, and Preamble to the same. Ball, pp. 21, 22.

CHAPTER XVIII.

EDWARD VI. TO JAMES I. (1547–1603).

THE accession of Edward VI. had no immediate effect on the cause of the Reformation in Ireland. The preaching of Archbishop Browne and others had become less diligent, owing, no doubt, to the discouragements they met with; and the Lord Deputy, Sir Anthony S. Leger, even stated in 1549 that there had been but one sermon made in the country for three years, and that by Staples, Bishop of Meath. In that year the first prayer-book of Edward VI. had been ratified by Parliament and Convocation, and began to be used in all parish churches in England. But it was not until two years later that it was introduced into Ireland by an order from the King, addressed to the Lord Deputy in February 6, 1551. On its receipt he called together an assembly of the bishops and clergy to inform them of his Majesty's order, and of the opinions of the bishops and clergy of England on the subject. He was at once opposed by the Primate, Archbishop Dowdall, whose chief argument against the English service was that if it was established then should "every illiterate fellow read mass." "No," said the Viceroy, "your grace is mistaken, for we have too many illiterate priests among us already who neither can pronounce the Latin, nor know what it means no more than the common people that hear them; but when the people hear the liturgy in English, they and the priest will then understand what they pray for." The Primate's only reply was, " Beware the clergy's curse." " I fear no strange curse," replied S. Leger, "so long as I have the blessing of that Church which I believe to be the true one." " Can there be a truer Church," replied the Archbishop, "than the Church of S. Peter, the Mother Church of Rome?" " I thought," replied the Deputy, "we had all been of the Church of Christ; for He calls all true believers in Him His Church, and Himself the Head thereof." The Archbishop again asked, "And is not S. Peter's Church the Church of Christ?" The dialogue closed with the Deputy's reply, " S. Peter was a member of Christ's Church, but the Church was not S. Peter's, neither was S. Peter but Christ the Head thereof."[1] Notwithstanding the Primate's opposition, Archbishop Browne accepted the order, and many of the other bishops adhered to him, amongst whom were Staples, Bishop of Meath, Lancaster of Kildare, Travers of Leighlin, and Casey of Limerick; but whether any others took the same course is not known. Soon after, the Lord Deputy issued a proclamation pursuant to the King's order, and divine service was performed according to the English liturgy on Easter Day, 1551, in the presence of the Viceroy, the Archbishop, the mayor, and bailiffs of the city. The Archbishop preached, taking for his text Psalm cxix. 18: "Open Thou mine eyes, that I may see the wondrous things of Thy law."

Shortly after, Sir Anthony S. Leger was recalled to England, and Sir James Crofts arrived to take his place as Lord Deputy. S. Leger belonged to a class which such times as he lived in tended to produce. At one time unwilling to take part in the Reforma-

[1] Mant, i. 196.

tion, attending mass, and kneeling before the "Idol of Trim."[1] Then going on circuit with Archbishop Browne who was preaching the Reformed doctrines, and when he received Edward VI.'s order, proclaiming the English liturgy, and being present at the first performance of it. Recalled to England, he is next reappointed on the accession of Mary to restore the mass, which he does with the same diligence, and once more is recalled on the charge of ridiculing the mass. The sudden alternations of doctrine following the changes of government tended to unsettle men's faith, and disposed them to those extreme inconsistencies which in calmer times would be wholly inexcusable. Sir James Crofts, before coming to Ireland, received instructions, one of which deserves special notice. He was to propagate the worship of God in the English tongue, to which was added the important qualification that the service was to be translated into Irish in those places which needed it. This addition is an evidence of the good faith of those in England who were endeavouring to promote the Reformation. They knew that the majority of the Irish people were only acquainted with their own language, and if the principle of the Reformation was that the service should be in a language understanded of the people, it was absolutely inconsistent with it to have the liturgy in English only. "It would have been well," says Bishop Mant, "had this purpose been as promptly and vigorously executed as it was happily and prudently projected." But the traditions and practice of the Irish government for four centuries were against it, and unfortunately rendered abortive this and other efforts of the kind."

It was in 1551, the year of the arrival of Sir James

---

[1] A miraculous image of the Virgin Mary.

Crofts, that the first book printed in Dublin issued from the press. This was "The Book of Common Prayer, after the use of the Church of England." It was the first book of Edward VI., with a local title-page, and a prayer for the Lord-Lieutenant, to be said between the two last collects of the Litany. A copy of this book, the only one known to exist, is preserved in the library of Trinity College, Dublin. The new Deputy was earnest in promoting the Reformation, and one of his first steps was to communicate with the Primate, inviting him to a conference with the other bishops, and as a token of respect sending the letter by his principal suffragan, the Bishop of Meath. Dowdall accepted the invitation, though expressing his doubts that it would lead to any result, and accordingly he met the Lord Deputy, with the Bishops of Meath and Kildare, at S. Mary's Abbey. In the discussion which ensued he was treated with the highest respect by the Viceroy and the suffragan bishops, but at the same time his objections were fully answered. In the course of the discussion, which was intended to promote unity, he said: "The way to be in unity is not to alter the mass." The Bishop of Meath replied: "There is no Church on the face of the earth hath altered the mass more often than the Church of Rome, which hath been the reason that causeth the rationaller sort of men to desire the liturgy to be established in a known tongue, that they may know what additions have been made, and what they pray for." Subsequently the Bishop observed that two prayers referred to as being S. Ambrose's were not in his works, "which hath caused a wise and learned man lately to write that those two prayers were forged, and not to be really S. Ambrose's." The Archbishop replied, "What writer dares write or say so?" The Bishop replied, "Erasmus, a man who may well be compared to either of us, or the standers by. Nay, my lord, no disparagement if I say so to yourself; for he was a wise and judicious man, otherwise I would not have been so bold as to parallel your Lordship with him."[1]

In consequence of Dowdall's opposition, and to reward Archbishop Browne's zeal, the Primacy was removed from Armagh and attached to the See of Dublin, thus deciding for a time an old dispute as to precedence which had existed between Armagh and Dublin. It broke out again, however, and was not finally closed until the reign of Charles I., since which the Archbishop of Armagh enjoys the title of Primate of all Ireland.[2] It is uncertain whether the Primate withdrew from his See in anger on this account, or whether he was actually deprived of his office, but he left the country and remained abroad. His See was then treated as vacant, and application was made by Cecil to Cranmer to recommend worthy persons to fill it, and the bishopric of Ossory, then vacant, "so that, by the influence of very wise and very learned men and good preachers, the Gospel might be better propagated in that dark region." Cranmer recommended four, adding the name of a fifth, though he doubted whether he could be persuaded to accept it.[3] All four having, however, declined to go to Ireland, it was offered to the fifth, Henry Goodacre, "a wise and well learned man," who accepted the post, and at the same time the See of Ossory was filled by the appointment of Bale, who had been imprisoned in the reign of Henry for preaching against

[1] Harleian MSS. C., vol. v.
[2] For part of this controversy see Ussher, Works, vol. i., Appendix vi., pp. cxxx.-cxlii.
[3] Strype, "Eccl. Biography," vol. i. p. 112.

the invocation of saints and the worship of images, and had afterwards escaped to Germany. At the consecration of these prelates it was proposed to use the old Pontifical according to which bishops had hitherto been consecrated. But Bale absolutely refused, and eventually an English service was used, and the ceremony took place on February 2, 1553. This has been supposed to be the Ordinal attached to the Act of Parliament which authorised the Second Book of Edward VI.,[1] but as that book was only used for the first time in England on November 1, 1552, and had not yet been authorised in Ireland, this is highly improbable. It is more likely that the service used was that for the consecration of bishops and priests added[2] to the First Book by Act of Parliament on January 31, 1550.

Bale, immediately on his consecration, proceeded to his See, and, taking up his residence in Kilkenny, began to preach with great earnestness, exhorting the people to repentance for sin, and requiring them to give credit to the Gospel of salvation. "In this work helpers found I none," he says, "among my prebendaries and clergy, but adversaries a great number." His preaching, nevertheless, seems to have been acceptable to the people, but his episcopate was of short continuance, as the King died in July 1553, six months after his appointment, and Queen Mary ascended the throne.

On a review of the proceedings from the appointment of Browne in 1535 to the death of Edward, it appears that little more had been done to promote the Reformation than the abolition of the Papal supremacy and the introduction of the English liturgy. The work of preaching the Reformed doctrines was confined

---

[1] Mant, vol. i. p. 219.
[2] Froude, "History of England," vol. v. p. 20.

to one or two bishops, none of their clergy being
mentioned as taking part in it; and their sermons,
with the single exception of Bishop Nagle's, were
addressed to English-speaking people. It was evident that the mass of the people, who were only acquainted with Irish, were not reached at all by the
measures adopted. They had their native clergy and
the "friars beggars," and, by no means least, their
poets, whose compositions of a religious character
were highly valued. Fifteen of them lived between
1520-1560, and the themes of their poems are either
the fame of the native chieftains, who are exhorted to
emulate the deeds of their ancestors of the heroic age,
or else religious subjects, chiefly the praise of the Virgin
Mary.[1] As the Reformation advanced the poetry
assumes a more controversial tone, as in Owen O'Duffey
and the poem of Fergal Og in 1600, who treats of "the
people of Scotland renouncing the religion of their
forefathers, and denying the real Presence of our
Lord Jesus Christ in the Eucharist."[2] If the poet is
more influential than the law-maker, according to a
well-known adage, these men must have exercised a
powerful influence in confirming the people in the
Roman Catholic faith, and opposing the Reformation.

Irish poetry of this age is unreal, and even morbid
in the extravagance of its devotional language, especially towards the Virgin Mary, in strange contrast to
the attitude of the native Church towards her in early
times. She had changed places with S. Brigit as
regards this way of speaking, and her dignity, like
Brigit's, was exaggerated out of opposition—in the
present instance—to the Reformers.[3]

Queen Mary having been proclaimed in Ireland on

[1] Angus O'Daly, A.D. 1570, has left eight on this subject. O'Reilly,
"Irish Writers," p. cxxxix.
[2] Ibid., p. clix.   [3] Supra, p. 47.

July 20, 1553, Archbishop Dowdall was immediately recalled and restored to the Primacy, which once again became "of all Ireland," the previous patent transferring the title to Dublin being cancelled. Dowdall had never been recognised by the Pope, but this seems to have made little difference with Mary. Next year a commission was issued to Walsh and Leverous, afterwards Bishops of Meath and Kildare respectively, to re-establish the Roman Catholic religion. In pursuance of this commission five bishops were deprived—Staples of Meath, Archbishop Browne, Lancaster of Kildare, Travers of Leighlin, and Casey of Limerick. Bale of Ossory had already left the country. The general charge against them was that of being married men, though in the case of Browne there was the special accusation of conspiracy against the Pope.

The tradition [1] that Browne was reconciled to the Church of Rome is not supported by sufficient evidence. He, Staples, Lancaster, and Travers are supposed to have died soon after their deprivation. Bishop Bale, after many perils, arrived at Basle, where he remained five years, not venturing to England until Elizabeth was on the throne. He was one of the seven bishops named in the warrant for the consecration of Parker to the Archbishopric of Canterbury. The Sees of the deprived bishops were filled up with prelates whose views agreed with Mary's, some of them being appointed by herself, others apparently by the Pope. To the See of Dublin, Hugh Curwen was elected by the Dean and Chapter of Christ Church, in accordance with the Queen's licence. He was Doctor of Laws, Dean of Hereford, and Archdeacon of Oxford. His consecration took place in S. Paul's Cathedral, London,

---

[1] Mentioned in a tract in fifth vol. "Harleian Miscellany."

on September 8, 1555, and being appointed Lord Chancellor of Ireland, he proceeded there without delay. He had formerly been chaplain to Henry VIII., and in his sermons advocated the royal supremacy and defended the King's marriage with Anne Boleyn, but at the same time he held Roman doctrine generally, especially on the corporal presence.

The spirit of Mary's policy with regard to the Reformation is seen in the Instructions brought to Ireland by Lord Fitzwalter, who succeeded as Lord Deputy on the recall of Sir Anthony S. Leger. He and his Council were required by their example, and in all possible ways, to advance the honour of God and the Catholic faith; to set forth the dignity of the Pope and the Apostolic See; and to be ready to aid with the secular power the spiritual authorities in punishing and repressing all heretics and Lollards, and their damnable sects, opinions, and errors.[1] In accordance with these Instructions, Acts were passed in the Parliament which assembled on June 1, 1556, those being the earliest Irish Acts passed against the doctrines of the Reformed Church. One of them revived the three statutes passed respectively in the reigns of Richard II., Henry IV., and Henry V., concerning the arresting and apprehension of erroneous and heretical preachers, and concerning repression of heresies and punishing of heretics, and concerning the suppression of heresy and Lollardy. If any one who was convicted under these statutes refused to abjure, or having abjured, relapsed, he was to be delivered to the secular arm and burnt. This was the fate to which all sincere supporters of the Reformation were now exposed, whenever the authorities chose to put those laws into execution against them. Mary had thus taken measures to suppress

[1] Mant, i. 243.

the open profession of attachment to the Reformation, but to say that "with the bishops the Reformed Church disappeared"[1] is to make the same mistake as the prophet when he said, "I only remain a prophet of the Lord," while there were seven thousand unknown to him who had not bowed the knee to Baal. The very fact of the revival of those obsolete laws being deemed necessary is a proof that there were many in sympathy with the Reformed doctrines, however unpopular they might be with the monks and clergy, whose interests were seriously affected by them. The story has often been told of the Queen having issued a commission to punish those in Ireland who dissented from her views, and appointed a Dr. Cole to carry it out. On his way to Ireland he stopped at Chester, and boasted that he had a commission which should lash the heretics of Ireland. The woman of the house, who had a brother in Dublin "of the Protestant religion," managed to steal the commission from the box, and to substitute a pack of cards. On his arrival he appeared before the Lord Deputy and Privy Council, but opening his box, to his consternation found his commission had disappeared, and instead was the pack of cards with the knave of clubs uppermost.[2]

It might have been supposed that the accession of a Roman Catholic sovereign would lead to a new policy in Church and State, but with regard to the former there was in many respects no change. Mary neither surrendered any power or title which her father had possessed, nor did she restore any of the confiscated property. In the letter from the English

[1] Richey, "A Short History of the Irish People," p. 423, 2nd Ed. Dublin, 1887.
[2] Robert Ware's Life of Archbishop Browne, quoted in Ball, Appendix K.

Privy Council announcing her accession she is described as "Queen of England, France, and Ireland, Defender of the Faith, and on earth Supreme Head of the Churches of England and Ireland."[1] In this capacity she appointed new bishops; she reinstated Dowdall, who had been appointed by Henry VIII., and had never been confirmed by the Holy See; she refused to allow the Pope to appoint by proviso. "With all her respect for the Pope as the spiritual head of her Church, with all her desire of securing his approbation, with all her attachment to the old religion, it is quite clear that she never intended to abate or diminish that authority in ecclesiastical matters which her father and her brother had exercised before her. As their supremacy had been employed in maintaining the rites, ceremonies, and liberties of the Church conformably to their own interpretation of them and that of the nation at their time, so hers is governed by similar considerations but with different results."[2] The Crown retained possession of the estates of the monasteries, and continued to make grants of them down to the end of the reign, in pursuance of the rights confirmed by an Act passed for the purpose.[3]

If religion had been the cause of division, then on the restoration of the Roman Catholic faith the English and Irish inhabitants should have become a united body. Yet the bishops were quite ready to use their spiritual powers against the "wild Irish," and except the temporary establishment of the Latin service there was little change. The people were not united into a common Church; the feeling between the two sections of the population remained as before; and the Church

---

[1] Carew MSS., vol. iii. p. xxii.   [2] Morrin, vol. i. p. 304.
[3] 3rd and 4th Philip and Mary, cap. 8.

as reorganised showed but little vitality. It is evident from the events of this reign that religious differences had originally no connection with the action of the native Irish or of the English government. A Roman Catholic sovereign had to enforce order as a Protestant sovereign had, and villages were sacked and burnt, and Irish tribes hunted down and shot as rebels, by her government without the least compunction; and her Lord Deputy even burned the cathedral of Armagh and three churches, on one of his expeditions, a sacrilege never committed under Henry or Edward. Her government was, in fact, more severe to the natives than that of any of her predecessors, for she entered on a policy of confiscation of Irish territory and planting it with settlers. The O'Connors and O'Moores, who occupied the present King and Queen's Counties, had given much trouble; but the Earl of Sussex having reduced them to obedience, Mary's government confiscated the entire territory, two Acts of Parliament being passed for the purpose.[1] Their lands were granted to English settlers. All tribe rights, native laws, language, and manners were to disappear, and the districts were to form the first English settlement or plantation. The territory thus taken from the Irish was formed into two counties, the chief town of one being named Maryborough, from the Queen, the other Philipstown, from her husband, and the settlers were to build a church in every town within three years. But the country not having been completely conquered, the settlers had to fight for the lands granted to them. The warfare which ensued resembled that waged by the early settlers in America with the native tribes. No mercy was shown, no act of treachery was considered dishonourable, no personal tortures and indig-

[1] 3rd and 4th Philip and Mary, caps. 1, 2.

x

nities were spared to the captives. The struggle went on into Elizabeth's reign, until the native tribes, reduced in numbers and utterly savage, sank to the level of banditti and ultimately disappeared. Evidently if the Irish people expected much from a Roman Catholic sovereign they must have been grievously disappointed. Mary died on November 17, 1558.

In treating of the measures taken to promote the Reformation in Ireland during the reign of her successor, Queen Elizabeth, and the state of religion there, it is necessary to bear in mind her position as regards European politics. During the greater part of her reign her deposition was generally expected abroad. Excommunicated by the Pope and her subjects absolved from their allegiance, exposed to the hostility of the two great powers of France and Spain, and having at the same time to deal with formidable rebellions in Ireland, it seemed scarcely possible that she could hold her own. The promotion of the Reformation was thus, in some measure, subordinate to the maintenance of her authority amid the perils by which she was surrounded. The English service had ceased to be used during the reign of Mary; but on the arrival of the new Viceroy, the Earl of Sussex, the Litany was sung in English, and was followed by the Te Deum and a flourish of trumpets, in joyful recognition of the restoration of the former state of things. The statesmen of that day present us with remarkable instances of indifference in religious matters. Sir Anthony S. Leger's readiness to take either side has been mentioned, and we have the Earl of Sussex, who carried out Mary's orders for the restoration of the Roman Catholic faith, now appointed by Elizabeth to re-establish the Reformed Liturgy. It is characteristic of the age that another great official,

Paulet, Marquis of Winchester, and Lord Treasurer of England during four reigns, being asked by a friend how he held his place during so many changes, replied, " I was made of the pliable willow, not of the stubborn oak."[1] Sussex received orders "to set up the worship of God as it is in England, and to make such statutes next parliament as were lately made in England, *mutatis mutandis.*" For this purpose a parliament was summoned in January 1560, and during its session, which continued a month, several Acts were passed. One restored to the Crown the ancient jurisdiction over the State, ecclesiastical and spiritual, and abrogated all foreign power repugnant to the same.[2] The three statutes for the punishment of heresy were repealed. The oath of supremacy was made obligatory on all ecclesiastical persons, officers, and ministers, and forfeiture of office and promotion during life was enacted as the penalty for refusal. The oath differed from that of Henry, for, instead of Supreme Head, the Queen is styled " Supreme Governor," " of this realm, and of all other her highness's dominions and countries in all spiritual or ecclesiastical things or causes, as well as temporal." Her motive is mentioned by Jewell, who, writing to Bullinger, says she is unwilling to be addressed in speaking or writing as Head of the Church of England, saying that this honour is due to Christ alone, and cannot belong to any human being whatever. Another Act sanctioned the Second Book of Edward VI., which, in a slightly altered form, had been passed by the English Parliament of the previous year.[3]

In England the Thirty-nine Articles were adopted a few years later, but they were not introduced into the Church of Ireland until the time of Charles I.

[1] "Ortus sum ex salice non ex quercu." [2] Eliz., ch. i. [3] 2 Eliz., ch. ii.

Instead of them, in Ireland a short collection of Articles, eleven in number, was prescribed to be read by parsons, vicars, and curates on first entering into their cures, and also on two days in each year afterwards. This was published in 1566 by the authority of the Deputy, and the archbishops and bishops. The Act authorising the Book of Common Prayer contained a clause that "it could not be had in the Irish language, as well for the difficulty to get it printed, as that few in the whole realm can read the Irish letters." Therefore Parliament petitions the Queen to allow the service to be used in Latin, where English is not understood. "But in what way," asks Bishop Mant, "was the Latin version to be provided? Was it by public authority? Of that there are no traces of information, nor does it appear at all probable." Yet there certainly was such a translation in use, however authorised,[1] for in the account of the visit of the Earl of Cumberland and his party to Dingle in the county of Kerry in 1589, the writer says of the Church service there, "They have the same form of Common Prayer word for word, in Latin, that we have here in England."[2] Hence it appears that Elizabeth's[3] ecclesiastical legislation was in force even in the remotest town in the South-west.

Another Act of this Parliament restored the first-fruits and twentieths of ecclesiastical benefices to the Crown, repealing the Act of Mary. The former were the revenues for one year of ecclesiastical benefices; the twentieths were one shilling in the pound, paid annually, out of all ecclesiastical benefices.

This Parliament was composed of three archbishops (the primacy being vacant), eighteen bishops, twenty-

---

[1] Proctor, "Hist. Book of Com. Prayer," pp. 75, 76. Macmillan, 1870.
[2] "Hakluyt's Voyages," vol. i. part ii. pp. 165, 166. London, 1599.
[3] If this clause really was hers, but see Leland, "History of Ireland," vol. ii. p. 225.

three peers, and the representatives of twenty-nine cities and boroughs.¹ Twelve of these bishops had been appointed by Mary, and the Upper House might easily have rejected the Queen's policy if they had chosen. The next step was the removal from Christ Church of all "reliques and images," the effacing of all pictures from the walls, and the substitution of texts of Scripture. A large Bible was placed in the middle of the choir of each cathedral, where a great number resorted to read or hear them read. From this it appears that there must have been at this time a considerable desire on the part of the intelligent members of the community to study the Scriptures, as in England and elsewhere. An additional proof of this is afforded by the sale of seven thousand of them in Dublin by one bookseller in the course of two years, when the book was first printed and brought over into Ireland, in the year 1559— a large number, when regard is had to the probable population of the country and to the small proportion of those who were capable of reading.²

Archbishop Dowdall having died about the time of Elizabeth's accession, the See remained vacant until 1563, when Adam Loftus was consecrated as his successor by Archbishop Curwen. Curwen having been appointed by Mary, was consecrated according to the Roman Pontifical, and now transmitted the succession to Loftus, as Archbishop Browne had done through Goodacre. On the passing of the Act of Uniformity, Leverous, Bishop of Kildare, and Walsh, Bishop of Meath, refused to take the oath of supremacy, and were accordingly deprived, and Alexander Craike and Hugh Brady appointed respectively to their Sees.

There has been much discussion recently as to the

¹ Richey, p. 496. ² Ware's Annals.

position of the bishops of other dioceses who were not deprived. It has been always believed that they accepted the Reformations so far at least as to assist in the ordination of bishops when required, but Mr. Froude denies this. "I am thoroughly convinced," he says, "that with the exception of the Archbishop of Dublin (Curwen) not one of Queen Mary's bishops, nor any one of the clergy, went over to the Reformation." Assuming this to be true, the inference has been drawn that Curwen was unable to get any bishops to assist him, and was therefore obliged to act alone in the consecration of Loftus. And it further results that Curwen's orders being English, the bishops so consecrated would not have had the Irish succession. This does not seem of much consequence, as the Churches have been so closely connected; but it is important to vindicate the regularity of Loftus's consecration, and to show that it was performed in accordance with ecclesiastical order. No doubt with regard to it was expressed at the time, when there were so many vigilant opponents of the Reformation ready to point out any shortcomings, and Archbishop Bramhall, writing a hundred years later with reference to the first consecration of bishops under Elizabeth in England, says if there were any want of English bishops, Irish bishops could have been had recourse to. "If it had been needful, they might have had seven more out of Ireland, archbishops and bishops. For such a work as a consecration Ireland never wanted store of ordainers: nor ever yet did any man assert the want of a competent number of consecrators to an Irish Protestant bishop. They who concurred freely in the consecration of Protestant bishops at home, would not have denied their concurrence in England, if they had been commanded."[1] From his day to the present no doubt has ever been expressed as to the action of the bishops referred to, and those who would now reverse the verdict of three centuries will be expected to bring forward convincing arguments, but this is by no means the case. Mr. Froude seems to have misunderstood the question with regard to the Marian prelates, which is not whether they accepted the reformed doctrines, but whether they complied with the law, by taking the oath of supremacy, and in other respects recognising the Queen's authority. This was what she required, and she was not concerned with their private opinions. There is abundant evidence that many did comply. Thus, Maurice O'Fihelly, termed by the "Four Masters" "a professor of divinity of the highest ecclesiastical renown,"[2] took the oath of allegiance and of abjuration of all foreign jurisdiction in 1559, and acted as the Queen's Commissioner.[3] What difficulty is there in supposing he would have joined in the consecration of Loftus?

Again, Bishop le Baron of Cashel, Archbishop Bodkin of Tuam, Bishop Devereux of Ferns, Walsh of Waterford, and Lacy of Limerick, also accepted commissions from the Queen, and this implied the taking of the oath of supremacy. To this it is replied, that the Queen's power did not extend beyond the pale, and that she was unable to enforce the oath. The patent rolls, however, prove that this assertion is quite unfounded, for more than forty of them within the Queen's reign relate to bishoprics, appointing and translating to them, or permitting other benefices to be held with them. "Unless,"

[1] Anglo-Catholic Library, vol. ii. p. 52.
[2] Annals of the Four Masters, A.D. 1513. He was known by his contemporaries as *flos mun.ii*—"the flower of the world."
[3] Ball, Appendix O., p. 325.

says Mr. Brewer, "Elizabeth's deputies and council were so negligent and ignorant as never to complain, and never to betray, the emptiness and vanity of the Queen's commands as well as the impossibility of complying with them, we must admit that from the first year of her reign, and all through to the close of it, she exercised her jurisdiction far beyond the limits of the English pale."[1] This is in accordance with the language of Bishop Rothe of Ossory, an eminent Roman Catholic writer. "Whoever," he says, "refused to take the oath fell at once from his rank and prelacy, and ceased to be a member of the Episcopal body."[2] Another argument against the conformity of the bishops is derived from certain records at Rome, in which the names of five of them are said to be entered as "of happy memory" (*bonæ memoriæ*), which implies that they were not regarded at Rome as having conformed. It only proves, however, that they contrived to hold their Sees and keep on terms both with the Queen and the Roman authorities. This is quite possible and does not conflict with what has been stated. At the same time, we know very little of the records referred to, nor when the alleged entries were made, nor by what authority.[3]

[1] Ball, *ut supra*.   [2] Ibid.
[3] A friend who was in Rome in 1889 made inquiry for those documents vaguely described by Cardinal Moran as "Vatican MSS.," but found that they were not at the Vatican nor the Archivio, but he was given to understand that some papers of the kind were in private hands. Even if he had found them, there were no references by which he could identify the particular documents required. None of the officials consulted were aware of any such entries as Cardinal Moran mentions. Knowing that transcripts of many Roman MSS. have been made for the English Record Office, I asked another friend to inquire at Chancery Lane in December 1891. He was kind enough to do so, and reported to me that there are one hundred volumes of such transcripts, but after a search of several hours he had to give up the attempt to discover the records referred to. The Cardinal with regard to his mode of reference reminds one of the Irish gentleman in one of Thackeray's stories who, when asked for his address, pointed to London and said, "I live *there*."

There is no reason whatever to doubt that the consecration of Loftus in 1563 was duly performed, and by the proper number of bishops. The scrupulous care of the Queen in these matters is evident from the Act [1] which she caused to be passed three years before, which ordered that the canonical number of bishops should attend, that the Queen's collation should be signified to the prelates who were to officiate at the consecration, and obedience was required under the penalties of the Statute of Premunire. No one appears to have incurred those formidable penalties, nor were the bishops so rigid in their principles as to run the risk. Certainly as far as the discipline of the Church was concerned they were not, for Devereux, Bishop of Ferns, had two sons, and, we must presume, was a married man. James Fitzmaurice, Bishop of Ardfert and Aghadoe, "a vessel full of wisdom," as the "Four Masters" describe him, also had a family,[2] and the same remark applies to him.

Three years after the Queen's accession the Pope appointed Donat O'Teige to Armagh as the titular primate, and his proceedings are highly significant of the line the rival episcopate were henceforth to take in Ireland. We find him in alliance with Shane O'Neill, the Queen's enemy, at Armagh in 1561, and the first thing we hear of him is that having said mass with the friars, he, accompanied by them, "went thrice about Shane's men saying certain prayers, and willed them to go forward, for God was on their side; whereupon Shane and all his men made a solemn vow, and took their oaths never to turn their faces from the Church till they had burned it, and all the English churches, and so with a great shout set

---

[1] Second Elizabeth, chap. iv., secs. 2, 3. 5.
[2] Annals of the Four Masters, vol. v. p. 1787.

forward, and assaulted the churchyard, where divers of them quickly left their bodies."[1] Here we have revived the old pagan practice of Desiul, or going right-hand wise round any object.[2] "It had found its way into the Irish Church in early times, but was not introduced from Rome. Now, however, Bishop O'Teige adopts it in order to ingratiate himself with the Irish chief and his followers. Thus many a superstition which would have died out under more favourable conditions was fostered and encouraged thenceforward by the new prelates for the sake of popularity. In another point of view this bishop's action was singular, for he presents the spectacle of one claiming to be primate, and yet urging on the soldiery to burn the cathedral of his See.

The condition of the Church at this period was pitiable. The chief county as regards population and importance was Meath, and Sir Henry Sidney states that in 1556, out of 224 parish churches, 105 were impropriate, no parson or vicar resident upon any of them, and only a very simple and sorry curate for the most part appointed to serve them. The means of supporting the clergy were few, they had no houses, and so dilapidated were the churches that the very walls were down in some places. From the state of the premier county that of the remote districts may be inferred. "So profane and heathenish," he says, "are some parts of this country become as it hath been preached publicly before me that the sacrament of baptism is not used among them, and truly I believe it." The remedy he suggests for those distant parts is that ministers should be chosen "who can speak Irish, for which search would be

---

[1] Bagwell's "Irish under the Tudors," vol. ii. p. 356, London, 1885.
[2] *Supra*, p. 67.

made first and speedily in your own universities, and any found there well affected in religion and well conditioned beside, they would be sent hither animated by your majesty; yea, though it were somewhat to your highness's charge, and on the peril of my life you shall find it returned with gain before three years be expired."[1] If the English universities did not afford a supply, he advises that the Regent of Scotland should be written to. "Whereas I learn there are many of the Reformed Church that are of this language that he would prefer to your highness so many as shall seem good to you to demand of honest, zealous, and learned men, and that could speak this language. Thus," he adds, "thousands would be gained to Christ that now are lost or left at the worst." Five years later, 1565, the Report of the Privy Council exhibits a state of things which afforded little hope for religion. The pale was overrun with thieves and robbers, and plundered by a lawless soldiery. In Leinster six native tribes harassed the land, and the county of Kilkenny was almost desolate. In Munster the Earls of Desmond and Ormond were at war. Tipperary and Kerry were nearly ruined. Ormond and Thomond were overrun. Connaught was wasted by the Earl of Clanricarde and MacWilliam Outer, and Ulster was in open rebellion under Shane O'Neill. The report concludes, "As for religion there was but small appearance of it. The churches uncovered, and the clergy scattered, and scarce the being of a God known to those ignorant and barbarous people."[2] One of the remedies proposed was the establishment of free schools, the master to be an Englishman or of English

---

[1] Mant, i. 299, 300. Sir H. Sidney's Letters, i. 112.
[2] Cox, "History of Ireland," i. 319.

birth of this realm, and the English language to be taught. It was the old policy of Anglicising the Irish, which had never succeeded.

In 1570 Pope Pius V. issued his Bull excommunicating Elizabeth and deposing her, a proceeding to which according to Mr. Richey, may be traced the subsequent misfortunes of the Roman Catholics of England and Ireland. From that time to the end of her reign the national party began more and more to put forward the religious side of the quarrel, and to connect themselves with the Roman Catholic party on the Continent. Meanwhile a movement was taking place which, if followed up, would have had important results. John Kearney, treasurer of S. Patrick's, who had been educated at Cambridge, and Nicholas Walsh, chancellor of the cathedral, got an order made that the Church services should be printed in the Irish language, and a church set apart in the chief town of every diocese where they were to be read and a sermon preached to the common people.[1] The Queen was warmly interested in the design, and provided at her own expense a printing-press and Irish type, "in hope that God in His mercy would raise up some to translate the New Testament" into their mother tongue.[2] She even set about learning the language herself, and there is in existence a small elegantly written volume prepared for her by Lord Delvin, containing the Irish alphabet, with instructions for reading the language. "Proceed, therefore, proceed, most gracious sovereign, in your holy intent," Lord Delvin says; and he tells the Queen that "in this generous act she will excel all

---

[1] Ware's Annals, A.D. 1571.
[2] The dedication of the Irish New Testament.

her ancestors."[1] The first book printed with the type provided by the Queen for the instruction of the native Irish was a catechism and primer, the title of which was: "*Alphabetum et ratio legendi Hibernicum et Catechismus in eadem lingua.* John a Kearnagh, 1571, 8vo." Two years after, Walsh began to work at a translation of the New Testament, assisted by Kearney, and continued after his appointment to the See of Ossory in 1577, and until his death in 1585, when he was assassinated in his own house by a profligate whom he had summoned before him. A little before Nehemiah Donellan, also a graduate of Cambridge, had joined them. He was subsequently appointed Archbishop of Tuam, and in a Privy Seal dated May 24, 1575, it is mentioned that "he had taken great pains in translating and putting to the press the Communion Book and New Testament in the Irish language, which Queen Elizabeth greatly approved of." The work was taken up by William Daniel or O'Donell, who was well qualified for the undertaking, and proceeded with it at the request of the Lord Deputy and Privy Council, being assisted by Murtogh O'Cionga or King. Shortly after the accession of James in March 1603 this New Testament was published with a dedication to the King, in which Daniel mentions that he "tied himself to the original Greek." The Irish, therefore, is an independent translation, and as the English Authorised Version was not published until A.D. 1611, it appears that the Irish version preceded it by eight years. The expense of the publication was defrayed by the province of Connaught and Sir William Ussher, Clerk of the Council. Daniel also translated the Book of

[1] Account of Facsimiles of National Manuscripts of Ireland, pp. 187-189. She seems to have been the only English sovereign who ever attempted to learn the language.

Common Prayer into Irish, except the Psalms, and this he published at his own expense in quarto, A.D. 1608, the year previous to his appointment to the Archbishoprick of Tuam. He was one of the first three scholars of Trinity College who were nominated by the Charter, and one of the earliest elected fellows, and either the first or second who received the degree of D.D. The course thus adopted for the promotion of the Reformation was in accordance with the views of the most enlightened statesmen of England. The use of the Irish language was recommended in the instructions of Edward VI., Sir Henry Sidney strongly advised it, and Queen Elizabeth encouraged it. Sir Francis Bacon desired that means should be used "for the recovery of the hearts of the people," by taking care amongst other things to have "versions of Bibles, and catechisms, and other books of instructions made in the Irish language."[1] But whatever was effected was by private individuals, and mainly at their own expense. The Irish government gave no assistance. It is, therefore, not surprising that from the date of the publication of Kearney's work thirty years were suffered to elapse before another in the Irish language appeared. Thus the advice of the most eminent English statesmen, and the efforts of the Queen herself, were neutralised by the apathy, if not actual hostility, of the Irish government, whose policy was still as of old to discourage the language. It is characteristic of the spirit which prevailed in the Irish government departments that the very Irish types which the Queen had provided were sold to the Jesuits by the King's printer. They were carried off to the Continent, and made use of in printing books to oppose the Reformation.

[1] Mant, i. 329.

Encouraged by the excommunication of the Queen and her deposition by the Pope, several adventurers sought aid abroad to invade Ireland. One of these, Stukeley, was supplied by the Pope with seven or eight hundred men, banditti[1] who had been in jail, but were released on condition of serving against the Queen. Stukeley sailed with this force, but being induced to join the King of Portugal in an expedition to Morocco, he was killed with the greater part of his followers. The remainder made their way to Ireland, and, accompanied by James Fitzmaurice,[2] who had also been a suitor to the Pope for aid, landed at Fort del Ore, which was situated on an island in Smerwick Harbour. In the following year[3] another body of troops arrived, termed "a Papal army," and fortified themselves in the island; but they were besieged by the Lord Deputy Gray, and having been compelled to surrender, were all put to the sword. The Queen was greatly displeased at this severity, and in fact the warfare was carried on in a barbarous fashion on both sides. Shortly before, Sir John of Desmond had murdered the chief marshal of Munster, Arthur Carter, Henry Davels, Judge Meade, and others, in their beds in the town of Tralee, having bribed a servant to leave the door unbarred. O'Sullevan termed this "a worthy deed," and Saunders, the Papal legate, lauded it as "a sweet sacrifice to God."[4] Such was the spirit on both sides at this time. The Irish believed that these expeditions were intended for their benefit, but Camden,[5] mentioning that they were fitted out at the joint expense of the Pope and the King of Spain, says the real object was to create a diversion,

---

[1] Philip O'Sullevan, "Historia Catholica," tom. ii. lib. iv. cap. xv. p. 94.
[2] Annals of the Four Masters, v. p. 1714. [3] Ibid., pp. 1739-40.
[4] Ibid., 1715, note 4. [5] Ibid., 1742, note.

and, by obliging the Queen to keep her troops in Ireland, to lessen her power of assisting the Netherlands in their struggle with Philip.

In 1599 an order was issued in conformity with the standing instructions to the Irish government, directing Roman Catholics to attend Divine service every Sunday in compliance with the provisions of the Act of Uniformity, the penalty for disobedience being twelve pence.[1] A stimulus to the carrying out of this Act was supplied by the defeat of the Spaniards at Kinsale in 1601, but the English ministers discouraged the employment of authority in this matter, and Lord Mountjoy, the Deputy, was of the same mind. He had already advised that "a more restrained hand should be held therein." He indicates the policy of the Queen, when he says in the conclusion of his letter, that "we may be advised how we do punish in their bodies or goods any such only for religion as do profess to be faithful subjects to her Majesty, and against whom the contrary cannot be proved."[2] The immediate consequence of the withdrawal of the legal compulsion was that Roman Catholics who had attended the Church services stayed away, and the outward conformity of many ceased.

The defective state of education had some time before forced itself on the attention of those in authority, and led to an instruction being sent to the Lord Deputy in 1584 to consider how a college may be erected, and S. Patrick's Church and the revenue thereof appropriated thereunto. But the project was opposed by Archbishop Loftus, who instead entered into negotiations with the mayor, aldermen, and commons for the decayed monastery

[1] The High Commission Court for trying such offences was established in 1593, according to Bishop Mant, but Dr. Elrington considers this a misprint for 1563. Life of Ussher, Works, vol. i. p. 42, note a.
[2] Leland, ii. 382.

of All Hallows, which had been given to them by Henry VIII. The result was the erection there of "the College of the Holy and undivided Trinity, founded by the most serene Queen Elizabeth." The first stone was laid on March 1592, and thus came into existence this famous university, illustrious for the great men it has produced and the services it has rendered to religion and learning. The college was opened on January 9, 1593, and one of the first scholars admitted was the celebrated Ussher, whose learning has been described by a foreign writer as "almost miraculous." At the age of nineteen he engaged in a polemical discussion with a very learned Jesuit, Henry Fitz Symonds, then a prisoner in the castle of Dublin, who expressed a wish for some one to argue with, being, as he said, "like a bear tied to a stake and wanting some one to bait him."

The difficulty of extending the Reformation in Ireland was now very greatly increased by the Pope's appointment of bishops to the Sees already filled by Elizabeth, at the same time that he engaged the Irish lords to unite with him in opposition to the Queen. The old hostility which had been exhibited to English rule since the Anglo-Norman Conquest by the native Irish, and at a later period by the Anglo-Irish lords also, had no mode hitherto of exhibiting itself except in isolated acts of outrage and defiance of the law. Now it was provided with one in the defence of the Roman Catholic cause, which also served to unite the members of both races, and, moreover, it was strengthened by the support of the Continental powers in alliance with Rome. Hence the difficulty of winning over the people to the Church was much enhanced. At the same time, owing to the establishment of a firm government and the influx of settlers from England, the English-speaking people began to form a body of Churchmen, whose influence would have been felt throughout the country if only peace and order could have been permanently restored. This, however, was not to be in her reign; but amidst all her difficulties she exhibited an anxious desire for the spiritual welfare of the people, and she probably effected as much as was possible in the circumstances in which she was placed.

CHAPTER XIX.

JAMES I. TO CHARLES II. (1603-1649).

THE extension of the benefits of English law to all the population of Ireland, which took place in the reign of James I., marks an epoch in the history of the country. Hitherto there had been two populations in Ireland, each possessing its own laws, now all were to be one. Had this course been taken at an earlier period of the Reformation it might have facilitated its reception, but now the old division was prevented from healing by the policy of the Roman Catholic Church, supported by foreign powers, and carried on by agents trained abroad. In the reign of Elizabeth this had begun to take place. Natives who had gone abroad to Rheims, Douay, Louvain, and other foreign universities, and foreigners with them, crossed the sea from Italy or Spain into Ireland, there to maintain the authority of the Church of Rome.[1] And now, in order to add emphasis to the situation, the Universities of Salamanca and Valladolid had been consulted on the question "whether an Irish Roman Catholic may obey or assist his Protestant king."[2] To this they replied that since the Earl of Tyrone undertook the war for religion by the Pope's approbation, it was as meritorious to aid him against the heretics as to fight against the Turks, and it was a mortal sin to assist the English. Thus the breach was widened, and religion

[1] Mant, vol. i. p. 324.   [2] Cox's "History," vol. ii. p. 3.

and patriotism were enlisted in the cause of division. Meanwhile the Church of Ireland was proceeding with a work which appeared well calculated to win over the native Irish. It has been mentioned that the earliest instance of the publication of a work in the Irish language was by one of the clergy in 1571. This was followed in 1603 by the Irish New Testament, and in 1608 the Book of Common Prayer appeared in the Irish language. Archbishop Daniel, in his epistle dedicatory to the Lord Deputy, Sir Arthur Chichester, prefixed to this translation, says: "It pleased your Lordship to impose upon myself the burden of translating the Book of Common Prayer into the mother tongue." In executing the commands laid on him he had in view the traditional habits and modes of speech of the general population, and accordingly he is careful to use their familiar names for the festivals of the Church. Thus the Circumcision is Little Christmas Day; Epiphany, Twelfth Day; the Sunday before Easter, Yew Sunday, that tree being the recognised substitute for the palm; S. Philip and S. James' Day, Beltine, the old name for the heathen festival held on the same day; similarly All Saints' Day is termed Samain's Day, another heathen festival celebrated on November 1. It was no doubt with the same object in view that the Book of Common Prayer in the English language, printed in Dublin in 1637, gives S. Patrick a place in the Calendar,[1] though by what authority this was done does not appear. All the publications in the Irish language now referred to were of a private character, and no information is attainable as to the number of copies of each printed, but there can be little doubt that under the circumstances it must have been entirely inadequate.

[1] Proceedings of Royal Irish Academy, August 1891. Minutes, p. 82.

While the Lord Deputy was thus encouraging the use of the Irish language for the spiritual welfare of the people, the political measures he found it necessary, as head of the government, to adopt were calculated to frustrate his object.[1] At the same time, the Pope, by a bull of December 7, 1605, declared it as safe to sacrifice to idols as to be present at the Common Prayer, and he encouraged the Irish by promising them the aid of a great force of Romans, Germans, and Spanish by next harvest, and great store of arms to resist their governors. But while thus animating the Irish to resist the secular power, more effectual measures were employed to counteract the efforts for the spread of the Reformed doctrines by means of the Irish language. The Roman Catholic authorities had hitherto entirely neglected to take any steps to have the language printed, but now they found it necessary to do so in order to counteract the circulation of the New Testament and the Book of Common Prayer. They already had two colleges on the Continent before the foundation of Trinity College. These were that of Salamanca, founded in 1582, and Alcala, 1590; and before the close of the seventeenth century nineteen others were established with the assistance of foreign authorities, ecclesiastical and lay.[2] From these as centres Irish catechisms and books of devotion began to pour into Ireland. The first work printed in Irish and in the Irish character on the Continent seems to have been a Catechism of Christian doctrine by Bonaventure O'Hussey, published at Louvain in 1608, five years after the New Testament appeared. The numerous works of this class were

[1] Mant, vol. i. p. 349.
[2] These were at Lisbon, Douai, Antwerp, Tournay, Lille, Louvain (two), Rome (four), Prague, Toulouse, Bordeaux, Poitiers, Nantes, Boulay, and Paris.

generally reprinted more than once, and the circulation of them was very large. There were even many on sale in Ireland in the middle of the present century, which were generally admirably printed, and in some cases furnished with illustrations.[1] Thus the progress of the Reformation now experienced a difficulty much greater than the mere difference of race could have caused, for the doctrines of the Roman Catholic faith were instilled into the minds of the Irish-speaking population with a diligence and care never before exhibited. The two prominent leaders of the Irish, the Earls of Tyrone and Tyrconnell, having fled the country, were attainted in 1608, and their estates being forfeited to the Crown, it was determined to plant them with settlers. Amongst these, besides the people introduced by the London Companies, were many Scotch, who being Presbyterians had their own ministers. In this manner Presbyterian congregations were formed, the earliest of which was at Broad Island, in the county of Antrim, in 1611. Thus a new body of Protestants, differing in discipline from the Church, was introduced into Ireland, a circumstance which could not but have had a tendency to weaken the position of the Church.

The first Convocation, properly so called, of the Irish Church was held in 1613–1615, for the assembly called in the reign of Edward VI. by Sir Anthony St. Leger, consisting of the archbishops and bishops with others of the clergy of Ireland, was not one. Nor when Elizabeth signified her pleasure to Lord Sussex, the Lord-Lieutenant, for a "general meeting of the

---

[1] "The Paradise of the Soul"—*Parrthas an Anma*—by Anthony Gernon, a Franciscan friar, printed at Louvain in 1645, is a book 4½ inches by 3, and containing 432 pages. It is divided into ten sections, and is profusely illustrated. It was evidently intended for intelligent readers, being supplied with references to the Bulls of the different Popes.

clergy and the establishment of the Protestant religion," is there any mention of Convocation. That which was now summoned was framed on the model of the English Convocation, but its proceedings exhibited a want of familiarity with the forms usual in such assemblies. On their meeting the clergy set about framing Articles of religion which should state the doctrines of the Church of Ireland. The Articles thus drawn up, 104 in number, were in general agreement with the Lambeth Articles, which appear to have been in accordance with the views of many of the Irish clergy at that period. Bishop Mant says: "In a notice prefixed, it is stated that they comprehended almost word for word the nine Articles agreed on at Lambeth on the 20th of November 1595." But he was misled by a late edition or copy of them which has the notice referred to, for in the original edition, published in Dublin in 1615, there is no allusion to the Lambeth Articles, no notice prefixed, and no index in the margin.[1] In the Articles as drawn up the doctrine of reprobation was stated thus under the third head, section 12: "By the same eternal counsel God hath predestinated some unto life and reprobated some unto death; of both which there is a certain number known only to God which can neither be increased nor diminished."[2] This was to determine with great precision a question about which good men have always differed. They also dealt with subjects which had hitherto never been introduced into Articles of Faith.[3] For this reason it was unfortunate that they should have been passed. But it

---

[1] Life of Ussher, Works, vol. i. p. 44, note *f*.
[2] Ibid., Appendix iv. p. xxxv.
[3] They treated of the primæval state of man, of the fall of the angels, the state of the soul after death, and pronounced the Pope to be the Man of Sin.

was within the competence of Convocation to draw up such Articles, nor if there was a general agreement between them and the English Articles is there any reason for supposing they would have placed any impediment in the way of the union of the Churches. These Articles, however, as we shall see, did not become the permanent standard of the Church.

About this time a Royal Commission visited and reported on the condition of several of the northern dioceses, which they found to be ill supplied with churches as well as incomes for the clergy. The Bishop of Derry made a complaint that the Vicar-General appointed by the Pope had placed priests in every parish who, though they were "rude, ignorant, and vicious fellows," yet carried the natives after them generally.[1] A rival Church had been set up, and the result of the conflict of jurisdiction was serious injury to religion and morality, an instance of which is given in the Report. The Vicar-General had four officials who, "amongst many other abominations that they practise, do for small rewards divorce married couples, and set them at liberty to marry others; insomuch that there is scarce any of years but he hath more wives living, and few women which have not plurality of husbands." A similar complaint was made by Lord Wentworth, writing to Archbishop Laud in 1634. He proposed a High Commission to annul all foreign jurisdiction, which, he says, "daily grows more insolent than other; to punish the abominable polygamies, incests, and adulteries, which both in respect of the exercise of a foreign jurisdiction and for the fore-mentioned reasons are here too frequent."[2] How little true interest in religion or morality, or the welfare of the Irish people, can the "foreign authority" really

[1] Mant, vol. i. p. 403.   [2] Strafford's Letters, vol. i. pp. 187, 188.

have felt which brought about this state of things!
A grievance laid before the Commissioners by the
Bishop of Raphoe deserves special notice. "Whereas,"
he said, "in the said diocese there are divers Irish
scholars who have conformed themselves in religion,
and are curates in divers parishes under British
ministers, and yet are fined as the rest of the multitude of the natives, for that they have their residence
upon undertaker's[1] lands, which should be planted
with British tenants." In consequence of this they
pray that they may be relieved of such fines, seeing
they serve the Church and endeavour by all means the
conversion of their country people.[2] Here the law is
found as before in conflict with the measures required
for the promotion of religion, and the long-standing
policy of the Government causes a clergyman to be
fined for preaching the Gospel in a language understanded of the people. How thoughtlessly is the
Church sometimes blamed for its neglect of the native
population! The laws by which the undertakers
referred to were bound are reported as constantly
evaded by them in their most important provisions,
and no penalty seems to have been enforced; but
notice is immediately taken when the Church is the
offender, notwithstanding the excellence of the object
in view.

Ussher, at the time Bishop of Meath, was active
in preaching and lecturing on the doctrines of the
Church of Rome, but he found the people warmly
attached to what they believed to be the religion of
their forefathers. Of the true history of their
Church, its early doctrine and independence of Rome,
they knew absolutely nothing. Impressed with this

---

[1] Those who on receiving lands "undertook" to place on them British tenants.   [2] Mant, vol. i. p. 406.

fact, he composed his learned treatise "On the religion anciently professed by the Irish and British," a work in which he vindicates the position of the early Church with his usual learning.

The religious dissensions which were a source of trouble in England at the time of the accession of Charles I. were reflected in Ireland, but in a fainter form, and their relative position was different. The controversy between those whose opinions were known as Puritan, and the party who held higher views on Church questions, was little heard of in Ireland. It was dwarfed in Ireland by the prominence of the Roman Catholic controversy, which engrossed the whole attention of those engaged in the promotion of religion. This differed essentially from the former in not being a matter simply between two parties in the same kingdom, both acknowledging the sovereign's authority and submitting to the laws. A letter addressed to the Lord Deputy in the year before that just quoted, by Bedell, Bishop of Kilmore, states the position in very plain language. "In this kingdom of his majesty, the Pope hath another kingdom far greater in number, and constantly guided and directed by the orders of the new congregations 'De Propaganda Fide,' lately erected at Rome, and by the means of the Pope's Nuncios residing at Brussels and Paris. The Pope hath here a clergy, if I may guess by my own diocese, double in number to us, the hands whereof are by corporal oath bound to him to maintain him and his regalities ' *contra omnem hominem*,' and to execute his mandates to their utmost forces." The contest was like one of those historic sieges in which the occupants of the fortress, having the country open to their rear, receive constant re-

[1] Mant, vol. i. p. 448.

inforcements and supplies, and can thus continue the conflict for an indefinite period. The Church of Ireland was engaged in an effort to reclaim Irishmen, whom it regarded as in error, and in doing so it had to contend with the whole papal influence directed from abroad, with foreign missionaries poured into the country, many of them fanatics, and with the moral, and sometimes material power of France and Spain wielded in the interest of the Papacy, while native superstitions were deliberately fostered for the same end.

About this period we meet with one of the most pleasing characters which the history of the Irish Church brings to our notice. Among the many self-seeking and worthless men who found their way into its high places at that time, Bishop Bedell is conspicuous for his single-minded devotion to his sacred office, as well as for the line which he, almost alone, took with regard to the native population. A fellow and graduate of Cambridge, like most of those who were prominent in the Irish Church, he became chaplain to Sir Henry Wotton, Ambassador to Venice, and during his stay of eight years in that city he made the acquaintance of Paul Sarpi, the historian of the Council of Trent. They became fast friends, and while Bedell acquired a thorough knowledge of Italian from Sarpi, he repaid it by instructing his teacher in English. On his return to England he was offered the Provostship of Trinity College, Dublin, although personally unknown to the fellows. The modesty and simplicity of his character appears in his reply to Archbishop Ussher's letter: "I am married, and have three children; therefore, if the place requires a single man, the business is at an end. I have no want, I thank my God, of anything necessary for this life.... I have often heard that changing seldom brings better, especially to those who are well. And I see well that my wife, though resolving, as she ought, to be contented with whatever God shall appoint, had rather continue with her friends in her native country than put herself into hazard of the seas and a foreign land, with many casualties of travel, which she, perhaps, out of fear, apprehends more than there is cause ; yet . . . I consider the end wherefore I came into the world, and the business of a subject of our Lord Jesus Christ, of a minister of the Gospel, of a good patriot, and of an honest man. If I may be of any better use to my country or to God's Church, or of any better service to our common Master, I must close mine eyes against all private respects ; and if God call me I must answer ' Here I am.' "[1]

In 1629 he became Bishop of Kilmore and Ardagh, where he experienced the usual difficulties, the recital of which in Irish history becomes monotonous. A cathedral in ruins, the See house in the same condition, the revenues wasted, the clergy poor and illiterate, requisitions for the support of the military pressing heavily—all these things presented a dismal prospect in contrast with his quiet English living. To afford an example to the non-resident clergy of his diocese, he resigned Ardagh, one of his bishoprics. There were only seven or eight clergy capable of assisting him, and these being Englishmen, were unable to perform the service in the language of the people, nor could they converse with them. This was a matter which engaged his earnest attention, and he succeeded in getting the Church service performed in the cathedral in the Irish language. He then drew up an elementary catechism, which he had printed in English and Irish, and circulated among the people, who gladly re-

[1] "The Native Irish," p. 35, by C. Anderson, London, 1846.

ceived it. The New Testament and the Book of Common Prayer having been already translated, he resolved that the Old Testament should also be made available for the people, and at sixty years of age he sat down to study the Irish language for this purpose. It was an extraordinary display of energy and zeal, but he was a linguist of considerable ability, noted at Cambridge for his acquirements in Greek, Latin, and Hebrew, and it is not long before we find him composing a grammar of the Irish language, and displaying no small knowledge of it. Engaging two clergymen to assist him, named King and Sheridan, he lost no time in beginning his work. His knowledge of Hebrew, already considerable, had been further improved by his studies with the Rabbi Leo of Venice, and he was thus peculiarly qualified for the undertaking. As the translation progressed, he was careful to compare it with the English, the Septuagint, and the Italian of Diodati. It was in the fifth year of his episcopate that he first experienced the difficulties which always impeded undertakings associated with the Irish language. In the Convocation of 1634, when the use of the language in Divine service, and the circulation of the Scriptures was under discussion, Bramhall, Bishop of Derry, strenuously opposed it. His arguments were founded on political considerations, on maxims of state policy hitherto in force, and especially on the statute of Henry VIII.[1] Bedell set aside all these reasons as irrelevant, and declared he regarded only the good of the people's souls. He was seconded by Archbishop Ussher, and in the end two canons were passed which authorise the use of the language in Divine service. The 86th, on parish clerks to be chosen by the minister, contains the

[1] 28th Henry VIII., cap. 15.

following: "And where the minister is an Englishman and many Irish in the parish, such a one as shall be able to read those parts of the service which shall be appointed to be read in Irish (if it may be)." And the 94th to the same purport: "And where all or the most part of the people are Irish, they (the churchwardens) shall provide also the said books in the Irish tongue as soon as they may be had."

The opposition he experienced on this occasion was only the beginning of troubles. It was asserted that his assistant, King, was incompetent[1] to the undertaking. Archbishop Law, who became Chancellor of Trinity College in 1633, and Strafford, the Lord-Lieutenant, were induced to join in the opposition. Ussher had recommended King and Bedell provided him with a living, but now a charge of a frivolous nature was brought against him. It was heard in his absence; he was deprived of his living, fined £100 and imprisoned, and his parish bestowed on his accuser. Bedell recounts the whole transaction in an indignant letter to the Lord-Lieutenant, whom he refers to Archbishop Ussher, the Bishop of Meath, Sir James Ware, and other competent authorities for the character and abilities of King. "My Lord," he adds, "if I understand what is right, divine or human, there be wrongs

[1] The translation made under such difficulties is naturally unequal. Bedell's work was chiefly that of revision, and there is evidence that he "tied himself to the original." Thus in Isaiah iii. 22, for the Authorised "crisping pins" he has "purses" (*sparain*), which is the translation preferred by Lowth, and corresponds with the "satchels" of the Revised Version. Those who superintended the New Testament also consulted the original, and frequently prefer the marginal readings, as in Romans vii. 15; 2 Cor. xiii. 4; Ephes. i. 12. Sometimes readings not found in the margin, but now appearing in the Revised Version, occur, as in Hebrews iii. 1, where "our confession" (*ar n-admháia*) takes the place of "our profession" of the Authorised. It is a marvellous work considering the difficulties under which it was effected.

upon wrongs." But it was all in vain; the difficulties in the way of the undertaking were inherent in the position of the Government, and it was impossible for any individual to stem the tide. Bedell, however, was a man of indomitable perseverance, and if Government would not help he would do all himself. So he resolved to print the translation not only at his own expense but in his own house. How the project fared we shall see shortly. In the meantime, returning from this digression, we find the Presbyterian system was gathering strength in the North owing to the influx of Scotch settlers. The Bishops of Down and Raphoe appear to have made an attempt to admit some Presbyterian clergy on condition of their accepting Episcopal ordination. One of these was Robert Blair, who was invited from Scotland by Lord Claneboy to the parish of Bangor, in the county of Down, but declined the offer, as he would not use the English Liturgy, and objected to the bishops' sole ordination. His patron, however, was confident of procuring him a "free entry," which Blair describes as being effected by "the bishop at the ordination coming in among the other clergy in no other relation than a presbyter." But in the Royal Visitation Book of the Diocese of Down and Connor he is described as admitted to the orders of deacon and priest in 1623, and he must be assumed to have been duly ordained. A similar case is that of John Liviestone, admitted in 1630 by the Bishop of Raphoe. The fact would appear to be that in the dearth of good preachers the bishops seem to have attempted a compromise in order to retain the services of these men. Blair appears to have been an eloquent preacher, as we find him invited by Bishop Echlin to preach at the Primate's Triennial Visitation, and again before the Lords Justices at the assizes. But like all attempts to bridge over difficulties where strong feelings exist on both sides, it broke down, and Bishop Echlin had to suspend Blair and Liviestone, with two others, in 1632. They appealed to Ussher and to the Lord-Lieutenant, but in vain.

In 1635 Convocation was summoned with Parliament, and on their assembling passed some useful measures regarding Church property, proceeding next to spiritual matters. The principal object Strafford had in view in calling them together was to establish complete agreement in doctrine and discipline with the Church of England, by having the English Articles and Canons passed. He relied on Ussher to carry the proposal, but found to his surprise that the Lower House had appointed a committee, who had proceeded to examine and select from the English Canons, and in the Fifth, as drawn up by them, the Irish Articles were to be "allowed and received under pain of excommunication." In great indignation he at once sent for the chairman of the committee, the Dean of Limerick, ordering him to bring the draft, and having read it, told him he was like Ananias, and commanded him on his allegiance to make no report until he heard from him. Next morning he had a meeting with the Primate, four other bishops, the Prolocutor, and committee, and addressing them in stern language told them they were Brownists.[1] He intimated to the Prolocutor that nothing was to be said about the Irish Articles, and the question as to the receiving those of the Church of England was to be merely "content or non-content," and he requested Archbishop Ussher to draw up a canon to that effect. What followed is thus described by Strafford in a letter to Laud. "The Primate accord-

[1] Robert Brown was the founder of the Independents.

ingly framed a canon, which I not well approving drew up one myself, more after the words of the canon in England, which I held best for me to keep as close as I could [to], and then sent it to my Lord. His Grace came instantly, and told me he feared the canon would not pass in such form as I had made it, but he was hopeful as he had drawn it, it might. . . . I told his Lordship I was resolved to put it to them in those very words, and was most confident there were not six in the House that would refuse them."[1] The canon having been passed according to order in the Upper House, Strafford sent it to the Prolocutor enclosed in a letter, and on that afternoon it was "unanimously voted by the clergy, excepting one man." Strafford thus succeeded in browbeating Convocation. His chief difficulty was with the Lower House, as the bishops, having been appointed by the Government, were more disposed to yield to his wishes. He says "there were some hot spirits who moved that they should petition him for a free Synod,"[2] but they were intimidated by his imperious tone. Ussher had yielded a reluctant assent to the shelving of the Irish Articles, but when Bramhall next proposed that the English Canons of 1604 should be received and adopted by the Church of Ireland, this was too much for him. He said it would be a betrayal of the privileges of a National Church; that some discrepancy ought to appear, so that the Church of Ireland might declare its independence of the Church of England, and also express her opinion that rites and ceremonies need not be the same in all churches which are independent of each other, but that different canons might coexist with the same faith and com-

---

[1] Elrington's Life of Ussher (Works), vol. i. p. 172.
[2] Ibid., p. 171, note *t*.

munion.[1] His arguments were successful, and a body of canons was drawn up, founded on those of the Church of England but not identical with them, and were duly passed. The arrangement was different from that of the English Book, and the number was reduced from 141 to 100. Strafford, in writing to Laud, is scornful about the anxiety shown by Ussher for the independence of the Irish Church. "The Primate," he says, "is hugely against it" (*i.e.*, the reception of the English Canons). "The business is merely a point of honour, lest Ireland should become subject to the Church of England, as the province of York is to that of Canterbury. Needs forsooth we must be a Church to ourselves. . . . This crochet put the good man (Ussher) into such an agony as you cannot believe so learned a man should be troubled withal."[2]

Ussher's position is vindicated by the instance of the Church in the United States of America at the present day, which, though not verbally identical in Articles, Canons, and Liturgy with the Church of England, is in full communion with her. The whole circumstances show that the Irish Church still retained the spirit of independence which had always distinguished it in early times.

A question subsequently arose as to the effect of the First Canon on the Irish Articles, which are neither affirmed nor denied by it. It has been held that they were repealed by it; but it seems, Dr. Elrington says, to be a mere question of words. The Primate, in a letter to Dr. Ward, says: "The Articles of religion agreed upon in our former Synod, anno 1615, we let stand, as they did before. But for the manifesting of our agreement with the Church of Eng-

---

[1] Elrington's. Life of Ussher (Works), vol. i. p. 178.
[2] Ibid., note *a*.

land we have received and approved your Articles also, concluded in the year 1652, as you may see in the first of our Canons." His view appears to have been that they contained the same doctrine as the English, though more fully set forth, and that the latter were only received in the sense of, and as they might be expounded by, those of the Church of Ireland. Acting on this view, he required candidates for Orders to sign both the Irish and English Articles, a practice in which he was followed by some other bishops.[1] This continued until the rebellion of 1641, after which the Irish Articles are no more heard of.

Troubles were now thickening round the Church in the North of Ireland, the Presbyterian party, encouraged by the successes of the Scotch against Charles, assuming a more independent attitude. "All the Puritans in my diocese," writes Bishop Leslie of Down, "are confident that the arms raised against the King in Scotland will procure them a liberty to set up their own discipline among themselves."[2] The solemn league and covenant was introduced, and many proprietors of estates had taken it. To check this movement an oath was framed promising all due submission and obedience to the King, and engaging not to bear arms or do any rebellious act contrary to his commands, and renouncing and abjuring all oaths and covenants contrary to what was therein sworn, professed, and promised. This, by a proclamation of May 21, 1639, was required to be taken by all persons of the Scottish nation of sixteen years of age and upwards, inhabiting or having any estate in the kingdom of Ireland.[3] Strafford's departure from Ireland in 1640 gave further encouragement to the Presby-

---
[1] Elrington's Life of Ussher (Works), vol. i. p. 176.
[2] Mant, vol. i. p. 528.   [3] Killen, vol. ii. p. 27.

terians, and a petition was drawn up against the bishops, who were termed in it "children of Ishmael and Esau." It was presented to the Long Parliament by Sir John Clotworthy, but with what result is not known. Bramhall, the ablest of the bishops next to the Primate, was impeached before the Irish Parliament; and it is significant of the course events were taking that the charges were brought against him by Sir Brian O'Neill, a Roman Catholic, supported by Protestant Nonconformists. The Bishop was eventually restored to liberty; but "these," says Archbishop Vesey, "were but flashes: the fiery matter at last burst forth into such thunder-claps that the foundation of the whole kingdom reeled."[1] This was the rebellion which broke out on October 3, 1641, when a dreadful massacre of the English and Protestant inhabitants took place in the counties of Ulster, which had been planted with English settlers. The number killed has been variously stated; the latest estimate, founded on the depositions preserved in the library of Trinity College, Dublin, is that 25,000 lost their lives in the first three or four years, not including those slain in battle.[2]

Dean Swift held the English Parliament largely responsible for the rebellion, for "the leaders," he said, "would not have dared to stir a finger, but that they knew that Parliament would prevent the King from sending supplies."[3] The chief cause of this fearful outbreak was the plantation of Ulster, and the consequent dispossessing of the native inhabitants. Feelings of intense bitterness were excited among them by seeing strangers occupying the lands from

[1] Mant, vol. i. p. 553.
[2] Miss Hickson's "Ireland in the Seventeenth Century," Ball, Appendix x., p. 337.
[3] Swift's Works, vol. ix. p. 179.

which they were forcibly removed. The Roman
Catholic clergy sympathised with this feeling, and
availed[1] themselves of it in the hope of gaining advantages for their Church. It is easy to see how
much it must have added to the violence of the insurgents when the stimulus of religious animosity was
united with the feeling of personal wrong. The immediate result of the rebellion was the total overthrow
of the Church in the North of Ireland. The bishops
fled, some to Dublin, others to England, and two were
taken prisoners—Bedell of Kilmore, and Webb of
Limerick. Extraordinary respect was shown to Bedell
amidst these scenes of horror. He was the only
Englishman in the county of Cavan permitted to
remain in his own house from October 23 to December 18. Here many fled to him for shelter, filling
not only his house, but his church and churchyard.
On December 18 he was arrested and confined in
Lough Oughter Castle,[2] where he was detained until
the 7th of January, when he and his family were exchanged for other prisoners just one month before his
death. His funeral was largely attended by the insurgents, who regarded him as "the last of the English," while a Roman Catholic priest uttered the pious
wish that "his soul might be with Bedell's." This
exceptional treatment at such a time was certainly due
chiefly to his sympathy with the native Irish, as shown
in his efforts to win them through their own language,
as well as to his Christian character. Nor must it
be forgotten that he was indebted to Dr. Swiney,
Roman Catholic Bishop of Kilmore, who offered to

---

[1] It was "organised" by them, according to Pope Urban VIII.
See the "Memoirs of Rinnuccini in Killen," vol. ii. p. 58, note 1.
[2] More exactly Cloch-locha-uachtair. The stone (castle) of Lough
Oughter, not far from Kilmore, county of Cavan. See "Annals of the
Four Masters," A.D. 1369.

take up his residence with him for his protection. Archbishop Ussher had left Ireland the year before the rebellion, and never returned. Everything he possessed was very soon destroyed or carried away, except his library, which remained in his house at Drogheda, and was only saved by the strength of the place. The insurgents intended, he heard, "to burn him, using his own books as fuel." While the rebellion was in progress the Roman Catholic bishops held an assembly at Kilkenny, at which they pronounced the war just and lawful. Provincial councils of clergy and laity were appointed, and it was arranged that a General Assembly should meet at Kilkenny. Sanguine hopes were entertained by them of obtaining possession of all the churches and livings with the assistance of the Pope, the Emperor, and the King of France, to whom a deputation was to be sent.[1] About the same time a gathering of a different character met at Westminster, whose object was to "bring the government of the Church into nearer agreement with the Church of Scotland and other reformed Churches abroad." The great learning of Ussher pointed him out as one who should take part in such a discussion, and he was named as a member, but refusing to act his name was struck out. The open hostility of the Government to the Church was now manifested in the prohibition of the public use of the Book of Common Prayer. The first instance of this was an order issued on the surrender of Dublin to the Parliamentary Commissioners in 1647, when the Directory was required to be observed in all churches and chapels within the city. The clergy declined to conduct divine service otherwise than according to the Prayer Book, assigning eight reasons for their inability to comply, one of which

[1] Mant, vol. i. p. 573.

was "that the Reformed Church is a free national Church, and not subordinate or depending upon the Convocation of any other Church; and should they receive or admit of any other form without the authority of this Church, they should be guilty of betraying the liberty of the free national Church of Ireland."[1] The Liturgy was read for the last time before the Restoration in S. Patrick's Cathedral on November 1, 1649. The suppression of the Church service was subsequently extended to the whole country. This continued during the Commonwealth, and Cromwell adopted a method of his own for supplying the ministrations of religion, for in 1651 the Commissioners of Parliament were required to provide salaries out of the public revenue for "all such persons of pious life and conversation as they shall find qualified with gifts for the preaching of the Gospel." Four years after, one hundred and fifty ministers, with incomes varying from £300 to £20 a year, were distributed over Ireland, the greater part being Methodists or Baptists. But the experiment was unsuccessful, as might have been anticipated, for "some of the Baptists promulgated the dreams of a distempered fancy as divine communications. Some were fifth monarchy men, and some objected to singing psalms in public worship. Some of them were unlettered mechanics, and some inferior officers of the army. Such a motley company of preachers, venting such a variety of doctrines, were ill fitted for the religious instruction of the population."[2]

[1] Mant, vol. i. p. 589.
[2] Killen, vol. ii. pp. 123, 124.

CHAPTER XX.

CHARLES II. TO GEORGE I. (1660-1714).

WHEN Charles II. succeeded to the throne in 1660, the laws by which the Liturgy had been established, not having been repealed during the Commonwealth, were still in force, and it became his first duty to fill up the bishoprics which had been allowed to remain vacant. Bramhall, one of the ablest of the prelates, was advanced to the Primacy, a post for which his great abilities fitted him, and Jeremy Taylor became Bishop of Down and Connor. To supply the vacant Archbishoprics of Dublin and Tuam and ten other Sees, it became necessary to consecrate twelve bishops. It was a great event in the history of the Church when the ceremony took place on January 27, 1661, in S. Patrick's Cathedral, in presence of the authorities of the City and University, and the General Convention with their Speaker, "the whole proceedings being conducted without any confusion or the least clamour heard, save many prayers and blessings from the people, although the throng was great, and the windows throughout the whole passage of the procession to and fro from the Cathedral filled with spectators."[1] The sermon was preached by Taylor, and his splendid eloquence was listened to with admiration by the vast throng who filled the Cathedral. The Episcopate was soon after raised to its full number by the appointment of Thomas Price, who

[1] Archbishop King to Mr. Annesley, June 10, 1719.

was consecrated Bishop of Kildare on March 6, 1661, thus making up the twenty-one prelates, namely, four archbishops and seventeen bishops, who constituted the hierarchy of the Church.

The bishops of the North, in taking the oversight of their dioceses after the great political and religious changes of the previous eleven or twelve years, found their task a very difficult one. The Roman Catholics were little accessible to any efforts to reclaim them, embittered as they were by the memory of the vengeance which Cromwell exacted from them for the massacre of 1641. The Presbyterian ministers, on the other hand, were in actual possession of many of the Church livings, holding them with the sanction of the authorities during the Commonwealth, and, so far as it appears, legally in occupation. In pursuance of his duty to the Roman Catholics, Jeremy Taylor published his " Dissuasive from Popery," a work of great learning and research. But his efforts on their behalf were attended with little success. " They are taught," he says, " to make that their excuse for not coming to our churches to hear our advice, or converse with us in religious intercourses, because they understand us not."[1] The chief difficulty, however, is referred to only incidentally in his preface. " The Church of Rome is here amongst us a faction and State party and design to recover their own laws and barbarous manner of living, a device to enable them to dwell alone, and to be '*populus unius labii*'—a people of one language, and unmingled with others."[2] The chief strength of the Church of Rome since the Reformation has lain in her alliance[3] with national feelings

---

[1] Mant, vol. i. p. 614.   [2] Ibid., p. 619.
[3] Froude mentions the boast of a cardinal that "Irish nationality is the Catholic religion." " English in Ireland," vol. ii. p. 300.

and traditions, fostered by an entire perversion of the early history of the Irish Church. On such a state of mind, in which imagination and feeling were predominant, mere reasoning could have little effect, and Taylor's work, though valuable as a storehouse of arguments, was ineffectual for his immediate purpose.

In dealing with the Presbyterian ministers, two courses were open to him. He might, it has been said, have allowed them to remain in occupation, and provided that hereafter they should be succeeded by duly ordained members of the Church ; or he might have demanded that they should submit to reordination at his hands. Bramhall had succeeded in persuading a few—seven or eight in all—to accept ordination from him, his arguments being purely legal, not theological—the most convincing probably being, that otherwise they could not recover their tithes. Taylor does not seem to have argued the matter, as he declared thirty-six churches vacant at his first visitation, and sent "people of his own " to supply the places of the ministers who were deprived for nonconformity. It must have been an unpleasant course to him to remove these ministers, but he seems to have felt it to be his duty to insist on their conformity, and the fact of their having subscribed the solemn league and covenant with its engagement against prelacy, made it difficult for him to take any other course. And even had he seen his way to permit them to remain they could only have held office for a few years, as an Act was passed by the Irish Parliament, four years after, by which it was provided "that from the 29th of September 1667 no person who is now incumbent and in possession of any benefice, and who is not already in holy orders by episcopal ordination, or shall not before the said 29th of September be ordained priest or deacon according to said form of episcopal ordination, shall hold said ecclesiastical benefice, but shall be utterly disabled, and, *ipso facto*, deprived of the same."[1]

Still it was for many reasons to be regretted that in some way the services of these men could not have been retained in connection with the Church, especially if it is true that there were "not a hundred episcopally ordained clergy in Ireland,"[2] and therefore no means existed of adequately supplying their places. One is not surprised, therefore, to find the Earl of Clarendon writing thus to the Archbishop of Canterbury : " The state of the Church at this time is very miserable . . . very few of the clergy reside on their cures, but employ pitiful curates, which necessitates the people to look after a Romish priest or a Nonconformist minister, and there are plenty of both. I find it an ordinary thing for a minister to have five or six cures of souls, and to get them supplied by those who will do it cheapest. . . ."[3]

Mr. Froude connects the emigration from the North with the attitude of the Church to the Presbyterians. "Then commenced," he says, "the fatal emigration of Nonconformist Protestants from Ireland to New England, which, enduring for more than a century, drained Ireland of its soundest Protestant blood, and assisted in raising up beyond the Atlantic the power and the spirit which by and by paid England home."[4] To judge of those proceedings by our ideas at the present day would be distinctly unfair. The bishops were undoubtedly in a difficult position, and probably neither party would have entered into the views of the present day on the subject of tolera-

---

[1] 17 & 18 Charles II., 1665.
[2] Froude, "English in Ireland," vol. i. p. 172.
[3] Ibid., p. 175. [4] Ibid., p. 173.

tion. Bramhall's death took place in 1663, and his funeral sermon was preached by Taylor. He was undoubtedly a man of ability, but he was one of those who followed the policy of Anglicising the people, and he had no sympathy with those who were endeavouring to introduce the Gospel to them by means of their own language.

In the year 1662 the Revised Book of Common Prayer was printed in London, and on the ninth of May in that year the Act of Uniformity, with the Manuscript Book attached, received the Royal assent. The Irish Convocation of 1662 adopted this Liturgy, but it was nearly four years before the formalities were completed, giving it the sanction of law in Ireland. The bill was only read a first time in the House of Commons on May 18, 1866, and received the Royal assent on June 18 that year.[1] This great delay seems to be connected with the "transmiss" of 1663, to which a manuscript copy of the Book of Common Prayer was attached, for this had to be set aside and another substituted for it. The second transmiss, instead of a manuscript, had the book as printed in London in 1662 attached to it. This book is the nearest approach in existence to the genuine text of the Irish Book of Common Prayer. Before the Forms of Prayer to be Used at Sea, and the Occasional Services, was a Royal warrant ordering the use of the service for October 23, the anniversary of the breaking out of the rebellion of 1641; for November 5, January 30, and May 29. The ornaments rubric, which was absent through accident, not design, from the draught manuscript, agrees with the English precedent except one word. It has "the" Church of England instead of "this"

[1] The 17th Charles II., 1665. Mant, vol. i. p. 645.

Church of England. Subsequent copies printed in Dublin do not always observe this distinction. In the year 1710 a translation of the book into German was made, and published in Dublin in German and English for the Palatines who had come from Germany, and were planted in the South in 1709. A French translation was also made and published in 1715.

The state of the Church at this time may be gathered from Bishop Williams' account of the diocese of Ossory, which he regarded as applicable to the Church generally. "If you walk through Ireland as I rode from Carlingford to Dublin, and from Dublin to Kilkenny, and in my visitation thrice over the diocese of Ossory, I believe that throughout all your travel you shall find it as I found it in all the ways that I went, scarce one church standing and sufficiently repaired for seven that are ruined, and have only walls without ornaments, and most of them without roofs, without doors, and without windows."[1] Parishes were grouped to form a "living," and the average value of such livings in his diocese was £43, 14s. "Do you think," the Bishop asks, "that this value is sufficient to maintain an able ministry, to supply all these churches and parishes as they ought to be?" He accounts for the insufficiency of the incomes of the clergy by the "ecclesiastical livings of the country having been given to the King's nobility and lay gentry." "They do yield little or nothing," he says, "for the service of God in those churches, neither dare the poor vicars and curates, according to the Bishop's appointment, ask them anything for the serving of those churches."[2]

Nothing had been done with regard to the publica-

[1] Mant, vol. i. p. 663.   [2] Ibid., p. 664.

tion of the Scriptures in the Irish language since the rebellion of 1641,[1] but now the matter was taken up again by the Hon. Robert Boyle, one of the most eminent men of his day. In 1680 he published the Church Catechism in Irish, and next year the New Testament, followed in 1685 by the Old Testament, which had lain in manuscript since Bedell's death. To these publications Wake, afterwards Archbishop of Canterbury, contributed liberally. Great pains were taken with the work, the translation being first revised and corrected by Mr. Kirk, a Scotch clergyman, then sent to the Provost of Trinity College, Narcissus Marsh, who was afterwards Primate. He procured the assistance of the most competent Irish scholars, and himself superintended the revision. Thus Bedell's design, after a long interval, was at length carried into effect. One cannot help contrasting with this the policy pursued with regard to the Celtic dialect spoken in Wales. An Act of Parliament[2] was passed in the reign of Elizabeth, in which it was covenanted that the Bible and the Book of Common Prayer should be translated into Welsh under the supervision of the four Welsh bishops and the Bishop of Hereford. The translation of the Bible was completed and published in 1588, nearly one hundred years before it was published in Irish. There can be little doubt that Elizabeth contemplated doing the same for Ireland, but the Irish government representing the policy of the Anglo-Norman Conquest rendered it impossible. No similar Act was passed by the Irish Parliament. The types she provided were made away with, and whatever was done

[1] A catechism in Irish with Scripture proofs was published during the Commonwealth in 1652.
[2] 5th Elizabeth, cap. 28.

was chiefly at the private expense of individuals, and was wholly inadequate to the needs of the country. The political effect of giving the Bible in their own language to Celtic populations is touched on in the preface to Bishop Carsuel's Gaelic translation of the Confession of Faith, Forms of Prayer, &c., used in the Reformed Church of Scotland, printed in 1567. After expressing "the great distress and want the Gaels of Alba (Scotland) and Erin labour under as contrasted with other peoples in not having the Holy Bible printed in Gaelic," he condemns those who are "more desirous and more accustomed to compose, maintain, and cultivate idle, turbulent, lying, worldly stories concerning the Tuatha dé Danaans, the sons of Milesius, the heroes of the Red Branch, and Finn Mac Cool and others, rather than to write, teach, and maintain the faithful word of God, and the perfect ways of truth."[1] He desires to turn their thoughts to the Bible from those legends, the common property of both countries, which helped powerfully to keep up a separate nationality and prevent a fusion of races. The Bible had been the usual reading-book of the early Irish, and it has since become that of the Scotch people, throwing their ancient legends into the shade. Had the Irish people been provided at the same time with the Bible in their own language, it is not improbable that it might have also in their case superseded the tales of the past which formed their only literature up to a comparatively recent period.

The short reign of James II. was fruitful in trouble to the Irish Church. No sooner was Lord Tyrconnell appointed Lord Deputy than fifteen hundred Protestant families left Ireland. It was seen that the King, whose zeal for his new faith every one was aware of,

[1] O'Donovan's Irish Grammar, Dublin, 1845, pp. 455, 456.

would stop at nothing to force it on the country. The four bishoprics which fell vacant after his accession were not filled up, but their revenues were collected by the Crown, and paid by the King's order to the Roman Catholic bishops. Then a dispensation was offered to those of the clergy who would become Roman Catholics, permitting them to retain their benefices, but the effect of this was only to induce two persons to abandon their faith. One of these was a vicar-choral of S. Patrick's, who was deprived by the Dean and Chapter, but appealed from the sentence to the King in his Court of Chancery. The King then ordered his restoration, but the Cathedral authorities successfully resisted this violation of the law. Many of the bishops had to take refuge in England, and throughout the country there was a general apprehension of a massacre like that of 1641.

In 1689 James took refuge in Ireland, and one of his first proceedings was to call a Parliament, at the instance, it is supposed, of those whose estates had been forfeited in the rebellion. An Act of Settlement was passed by which all Protestants who were in possession of lands which formerly belonged to Roman Catholics, whether they bought or inherited them, were to give them up.[1] Then an Act of Attainder proscribed 2445 persons of all ranks who possessed landed property. The churches were seized, the clergy ill-treated, and finally Colonel Luttrell, Governor of Dublin, issued an order on June 18, 1690, forbidding more than five Protestants to meet and converse together on pain of death, or such other punishment as should be thought fit, by court-martial. The King next attempted to force a Roman Catholic Fellow on Trinity College, and when the authorities resisted

[1] Mant, vol. i. p. 708.

they were forcibly expelled. The Provost and several of the Fellows escaped to England, and two Roman Catholic priests were put in possession, one as Provost and the other as librarian. But these intolerant proceedings were brought to an end by the Battle of the Boyne, and the Church once more emerged from the dark clouds which enveloped it.

The first act of the new sovereigns, William and Mary, was the filling up of the bishoprics which had been intentionally left vacant by James. Among those appointed on this occasion the most eminent were Narcissus Marsh, promoted from Leighlin and Ferns to the Archbishopric of Cashel, and William King, Dean of S. Patrick's, who became Bishop of Derry on the death of Rev. George Walker, who had been designed for the bishopric by King William. Walker, who was Rector of Donoughmore, a parish a few miles from Londonderry, had distinguished himself in the famous siege of that town, having raised a regiment for the defence of the Protestant cause, and had shown such energy and ability that he was appointed governor of the town, and was the chief instrument in maintaining the defence against the army of James. William's intention of appointing him to Derry was frustrated by his military ardour, which led him to join in the Battle of the Boyne, where he was killed. An influx of Highlanders into the diocese took place soon after King's appointment, and as they understood only Gaelic, they petitioned him for a clergyman who could minister to them in their own language. He complied, and a congregation of 400 or 500 was formed. On a former occasion people from the Western Isles who could not speak English migrated to Carrickfergus, and at their first arrival they attended church, but being unable to understand the English service, became

Roman Catholics, because the priest preached in Irish.

After the accession of William and Mary eight bishops and four hundred of the clergy in England refused to take the oath of allegiance, as James II. was still alive. From this they were called Nonjurors. In Ireland only one bishop adopted this course, Sheridan, Bishop of Kilmore and Ardagh, who was deprived in consequence and reduced to poverty, but was supported by the contributions of the bishops. Amongst the clergy of lower rank, one of the most eminent of the Nonjurors was the celebrated Charles Leslie, Chancellor of Connor, whose works are still held in esteem, especially his "Short and Easy Method with a Deist." Another nonjuror was Henry Dodwell, a layman and Camden Professor of History in the University of Oxford, previously a Fellow of Trinity College, Dublin. He was a man of great learning, but held extreme and peculiar views on Church questions. One of the earliest acts of William was to abolish the statute for the burning of heretics, which, though previously removed from the statute-book by Queen Elizabeth, had been re-enacted by Mary. He also had acts passed suppressing profane swearing, regulating the days to be observed as holy days, and enforcing the observance of Sunday. A useful law for the erection of glebe houses was also passed. During his reign Michael Boyle occupied the See of Armagh, and was also Lord Chancellor, the last ecclesiastic who filled the office in Ireland. Great abuses flourished in the Church at this time. Boyle, when Bishop of Cork, thought it consistent with his duty to hold six parochial benefices with his bishopric, and did not resign them until compelled. A more flagrant instance was Bishop Hackett of Down. Appointed in 1672, he was for the most part absent from his diocese for twenty years; but at length a Royal Commission was issued in 1693, addressed to three Irish bishops, and he was deprived, one of the charges against him being simony. Episcopal appointments were made chiefly for political reasons, and as living in Ireland was not pleasant, the bishops avoided residence as much as they could, holding perhaps other appointments in England.

An instructive instance of the way in which the Church was impeded in her work by the Irish authorities is that of the parishes of Templemore and Kilcrohane, which lie along the opposite shores of the arm of the sea known as the Kenmare River, for a distance of twenty miles. The incumbents having died in the years 1673 and 1676, a faculty was granted to a clergyman named Palmer to hold both. He appointed curates and the work was done, and in 1689 the Protestant colonies settled in that remote district were flourishing. "Now," says Mr. Froude, "comes the downward progress." Tralee is forty miles from Kenmare, the Killarney Mountains lying between; Kilmakilloge is twenty miles beyond Kenmare. Dr. Richards, Dean of Tralee, though overburdened with preferments, set his mind on obtaining these parishes, and secured a presentation by his influence at the Castle, and also an order to the Bishop of Limerick to institute him. The Bishop remonstrated by a letter to the Secretary, October 9, 1702, and stated that the Dean had imposed on the Lord Justices by telling them the livings were contiguous to his Deanery. But remonstrances of bishops and resolutions of Parliament weighed little, it seems, against the carelessness or corruption with which the Irish government trifled away the interests of Protestantism. The Lords Justices, in reply to the Bishop's earnest remonstrance, sent him word that Dean Richards must be instituted notwithstanding. The Bishop could only leave on record his ineffectual protest, adding that the Dean would with these have at least fourteen parishes. "The Irish Church Establishment has been reproached for its missionary failures. What chance had an institution so conditioned? With what spirit could the better kind of clergy go about their work with the poison breath of the Castle blighting their endeavours?" The Dean had his promotion, and the last English service was held in the church of Kilmakilloge. The church itself lies a roofless ruin littered with skulls.[1]

To prevent the holding of pluralities the Irish Parliament had passed an Act[2] disabling clergymen from holding livings in England and Ireland at the same time. But the Parliament of England assumed a right to suspend it, for which there was no precedent. "I suppose," said Bishop King, "all our preferments, civil and ecclesiastical, will hereafter be filled from England." During the administration of Wentworth, 1625-1641, an Act had been passed imposing prohibitory duties on the woollen trade of Ireland, a proceeding due to the commercial jealousy of the English. This was fatal to the trade, and the English settlers by whom it was carried on, deprived of their employment, left the country. At this time the growth of the linen manufacture in the North led to an influx of Scotch people who were engaged in it, and by this means the Presbyterian congregations were increased. Weakened as the Church was by those causes, she experienced a further and most serious hindrance from the penal laws. Those barbarous laws were

[1] Froude, "English in Ireland," vol. i. pp. 274-276.
[2] 17 and 18 Charles II., cap. 10.

partly due to the reaction against the Roman Catholic domination under James II., and still more to indignation at the revocation of the Edict of Nantes in 1689, and the persecution of the Waldenses in the years 1655, 1686, and 1696. The refugees who made their escape from France and found a home in England and Ireland, brought with them a deadly hatred of the religious system to which they owed all their troubles, and diffused it throughout both countries. Parliament gave expression to the general sentiment of pity and horror at such cruelty by visiting the adherents of the Roman Catholic religion with penalties of the most minute and vexatious character. It was supposed that by these laws the Church was strengthened, and the policy of that day was to raise such barriers round it. But the spirit of exasperation which they produced rendered quite hopeless the prospect of the Church effecting any good among the people. A few Roman Catholics, especially of the upper class, were induced to conform, but they carried no weight, and were of little advantage to the Church. One of the statutes passed at this time was the Test Act, by which it was provided that all who held any office of trust under the Crown were required to receive the sacrament of the Lord's Supper according to the usage of the Established Church. This Act, primarily intended to be applied to Roman Catholics, also affected Presbyterians, and several justices of the peace were obliged in consequence of it to retire from the magisterial bench, and some officers in the army forfeited their commissions. It was a degradation of the most sacred rite of the Christian religion thus to convert it into a mere form, for its spiritual efficacy never entered into the consideration of those who partook of it, and provided they accepted it as a test, it mattered little how careless or irreverent they were. The Act is an evidence of the low state of religion; it was an age of unbelief. "The faith of religion," says Bishop King, writing in 1697, "is very weak amongst all, and the sense of it almost lost; and the matter is laid deeper than most men are aware of. 'Tis come to a formed conspiracy, and agents and emissaries are employed to cry down the credit of religion in general, and instil profane maxims and principles into youth." The position of the Church was very difficult. "'Tis hard for us to know what to do in these circumstances," he says. "If we appear openly and resolutely for our faith we are twitted with the story of the Ephesine craftsmen; if we are silent and retire, these good men, if they get their bishoprics and their case, they are as indifferent as to religion as their neighbours." About forty years later, Bishop Butler, in the advertisement to his "Analogy," writes: "It is come, I know not how, to be taken for granted by many persons that Christianity is not so much as a subject of inquiry, but that it is now at length discovered to be fictitious. And accordingly they treat it as if in the present age this were an agreed point among all people of discernment." The correlative of infidelity is generally superstition, one extreme seems to generate the other. It is in accordance with this law that we now find S. Patrick's Purgatory again flourishing. It had been destroyed twice, but was restored, and became as popular as ever. Such vast numbers assembled there as to constitute a political danger, and it became necessary to pass an Act[1] to prohibit pilgrimages to it. The suppression of it had the effect of increasing its popularity; it was regarded as a per-

[1] 2 Anne, cap. 6, clause 26.

secution of the Roman Catholics. "They esteem it meritorious," a writer says in 1727, "to adhere obstinately to a practice prohibited by heretics, and if any punishment be inflicted on them for it, they believe they suffer for righteousness' sake."[1]

The example of the bishops in holding many benefices and not residing in their dioceses affected their clergy, whose object it was to hold several livings, appoint curates, and reside themselves in Dublin or London. Archbishop King, referring to the state of the province of Armagh in 1714, in which there were eight bishoprics, including the Primacy, says, "There has been but one bishop resident at a time in that province for several years. There are now two in it. I can't count the Bishop of Derry resident, or any other that only goes there to settle his rents or make a visitation."

In 1703 Convocation[2] was summoned after an interval of thirty-seven years, and the Lower House sent a resolution to the Upper, asking them to take into consideration the appointment of preachers in the Irish tongue in every diocese.[3] This course had been adopted by some individuals with success, amongst them by Rev. Nicholas Brown of the diocese of Clogher, and Rev. Walter Atkins, Treasurer of Cloyne, whose ministrations were highly acceptable to the people. In 1709 Convocation again took up the subject, encouraged by Dr. Hall, Provost of Trinity College, at whose instance an Irish professor was appointed. Many of the students attended his lectures, and made considerable progress in the language. A further proposal was made by the Hon. Francis

[1] "A Description of S. Patrick's Purgatory in Lough Derg," by Rev. Mr. Hewson, Rector of S. Andrew's, Dublin.
[2] It met along with Parliament also in 1705, 1709, 1711, and 1713.
[3] Mant, vol. ii. p. 165.

Annesley that the work should be done at the public charge, and a petition was presented to the Lord-Lieutenant on the subject. In this he mentions that there were no printed books of religion in the Irish language (except a very few Bibles and Common Prayer Books), and only one set of Irish characters in Britain. The petition states the object to be "that the whole nation may be made both Protestant and English." But the project of Mr. Annesley, like those of the Lower House of Convocation, came to nothing. The Government and the bishops were apathetic or hostile. In a letter of Archbishop King to Mr. Annesley, November 13, 1712, he says, "If the bishops of Ireland had heartily and unanimously come into the work, and the Government had given it countenance, certain methods might, in my opinion, have been taken."[1] But writing again in 1724, after the experience of many years, "It is plain to me," he says, "by the methods that have been taken since the Reformation, and which are yet pursued by both the civil and ecclesiastical powers, that there never was nor is any design that all should be Protestants."

Amongst the difficulties inherited by the Church from pre-Reformation times, one of the most serious was the loss of income caused originally by the granting of tithes to the monasteries. On the dissolution of the monasteries those tithes were granted away with the other property belonging to them, and thus came into lay hands, or, as it was termed, became "impropriate." Thus, in the diocese of Ferns, the Archbishop says there were one hundred and thirty-one parishes, of which seventy-one were impropriate, twenty-eight belonged to bishops and dignitaries, and

[1] Mant, vol. ii. p. 230.

only thirty-two to the parochial clergy. Those were always the poorest parishes, as the monks never troubled themselves with any but the best.[1] It was impossible under such circumstances that the work of the diocese could be efficiently done. A further difficulty was the class of men who were sent to Ireland. "They thought in England," Archbishop King says, "that anything would pass on us. . . . I have sent back half a dozen worthless clergymen recommended to my provisions."

At this time the Society for Promoting Christian Knowledge opened a subscription for the purpose of supplying Irish books, and printed an edition of 6000 copies each of the Book of Common Prayer and the Church Catechism, which were distributed partly in Ireland and in the Highlands of Scotland. The Rev. John Richardson, Rector of Belturbet, who has given an account[2] of the various attempts of the kind, took an active part in these undertakings, and superintended the publication of the books for the Christian Knowledge Society. The Irish Convocation met for the last time before disestablishment in 1711, when five canons were passed, which are annexed to the canons of 1634, with Queen Anne's approbation prefixed, though there is some uncertainty as to when it was given. An important concession of the Government at this time was the granting of the firstfruits and twentieths to the Church, which was due to the exertions of Dean Swift. The twentieths, that is, one shilling in the pound, paid annually out of all ecclesiastical benefices, were entirely remitted, and the firstfruits, or the profits of one year of every

---

[1] Mant, vol. ii. p. 206.
[2] "A History of the Attempts to Convert the Popish Natives of Ireland to the Established Religion," by Rev. John Richardson, 1712.

ecclesiastical preferment, were made payable to a Board, by which they were to be applied for ever towards purchasing glebes, building houses, and buying in impropriations for the clergy. The letters patent of Queen Anne by which the grant was made were confirmed by an Act [1] of Parliament in the reign of George I., and by another [2] Act the Board of Trustees was incorporated, and the firstfruits vested in them and their successors. But the measures of the Government on the whole appear not to have been productive of advantage to the Church. "It had lost," Archbishop King says, "more hearts and ground for the last four years of the Queen's reign than since King James came to Ireland." He explains himself in another letter of April 15, 1715. "I never observed the countenance of a Government to add much to the security of the Church. I will maintain that under King William, when we did not reckon ourselves great favourites, we had advanced our congregations more every four years than we did under the four years of the late management here, in which, I fear, we lost ground; the diligence, piety, humility, and prudent management of the clergy, when they had nothing else to trust to, proving much stronger motives to gain the people than the favour of the Government, which put the clergy on other methods and made them odious to their people."

On the subject of the consecration of churches Archbishop King experienced some difficulty. It was ordered in the 43rd canon that, "As often as churches are newly-built where formerly they were not, or churchyards appointed for burial, they shall be dedicated or consecrated," but no authorised

[1] 2 George I., cap. 15.   [2] 10 George I., cap. 7.

form for doing so was provided. In a letter to the Bishop of Carlisle, written in 1715, he says, "I have consecrated or restored near forty churches, and some in a crowd of dissenters, and yet so managed the matter that they seemed very well satisfied with what was done; and in truth great care ought to be taken to make the form unexceptionable. We have a form in Ireland, but without any authority, and I altered it to my own mind, which I reckoned myself, as a bishop, empowered to do, because the canon requiring bishops to consecrate churches, but prescribing no form, leaves the form to their discretion."[1] The form which the Archbishop adapted is believed by Bishop Reeves to have been that originally drawn up by Cosin, Bishop of Durham, for the Convocation of Canterbury, and presented by him on the 20th of June 1661, though never formally passed. Meanwhile the Irish bishops, glad to obtain a compilation which proceeded from so able a hand, were prepared, with the Prayer Book, to receive a collateral formula of great merit, though wanting the ratification of synodical assent. This appeared in the Quarto Prayer Book of 1666 under the title, "A Form of Consecration or Dedication of Churches and Chappels, &c., Dublin, printed by John Crook, printer to the King's Most Excellent Majesty, 1666," and bears on the back of the title-page the imprimatur of the Primate and the Archbishop of Dublin, who was also Lord Chancellor. But though approved by those high authorities, it had not the full ecclesiastical sanction required to warrant the statement which appeared on the title-page of some copies, that it was "according to the use of the Church of Ireland." In the Convocation

[1] Mant, vol. ii. p. 207.

of 1709 it was "ordered that whereas there is not in the Church of Ireland any settled and approved form of dedicating churches to the service of God, that it be referred to a committee to prepare materials for a form," &c. It appears to have been in pursuance of this minute that the Archbishop in 1719 put forth an "Office to be used in the consecration of a church new built, and restoration of a church rebuilt, in the Diocese of Dublin." This was approved by the Synod of Dublin. Another form with which he was unacquainted was prepared and approved by both Houses of the English Convocation in 1712, and signed by Archbishop Tenison. This was superseded by another, drawn up in 1715, which was substantially the same, but this was never ratified by Convocation. Thus it came to pass that neither the Church of England nor that of Ireland while an Established Church, possessed a duly authorised office. Now, however, the Church of Ireland possesses a suitable "Form for the Consecration of a Church," and another for the "Consecration of a Churchyard or other Burial-ground," enjoying full ecclesiastical sanction, and published under the authority of the General Synod of the Church of Ireland.

CHAPTER XXI.

GEORGE I. TO DISESTABLISHMENT (1714-1870).

ON Queen Anne's death "the House of Hanover was established on the throne, and the political supremacy of the bishops of the Church of Ireland was at an end for ever."[1] The prevailing indifference to religion affected them as well as other classes, and they exhibited in general little sense of the obligations they undertook as chief pastors of their dioceses. Pooley was eleven years (1702-1712) Bishop of Raphoe, and during that time he hardly resided eighteen months. Kilmore and Ardagh were sixteen or seventeen years without a bishop, the occupants of the See living chiefly in Dublin or England. Some of them impoverished their Sees, like Bishop Wetenhall, who cut down and sold woods valued at £10,000.[2] The clergy were few in number, owing to the poverty of the parishes, ten of which in the diocese of Killaloe were held by one man,[3] who could not possibly have done the duty efficiently. It was the more unlikely that he would if he happened to be one of those termed by Archbishop King "cast clergymen," whom they would not promote in England but who were esteemed good enough for Ireland.

In 1715 we find another of those abortive attempts to make use of the Irish language, Archbishop King

---

[1] Froude's "English in Ireland," vol. i. p. 400.
[2] Archbishop King to the Archbishop of Canterbury, Mant, vol. ii. p. 286.   [3] Ibid., p 288.

having provided that forty-five divinity students should be instructed in it, that they might minister in a language understanded of the people, "which," he says, "I take to be the doctrine of our Church."

About 1718 a large emigration took place from the North of Ireland which tended to weaken the Church and to increase the number of Roman Catholics there. "Hundreds of families about that period departed from the northern parts of the kingdom for the West Indies, Cape Breton, and other countries of North America, for the purpose of seeking more eligible settlements in those remote regions." Amongst the reasons assigned for this movement the chief was the raising of the rents of the land by the landlords to such an extent that the farmers were unable to live, and the preference given to Roman Catholic tenants, who, from their habits of living, were enabled to give or to promise larger rents.[1] "The landlords," Mr. Froude says, "in stupid selfishness were expelling their Protestant tenantry because Roman Catholics promised them a larger rent."[2] In the two years which followed the Antrim evictions, 30,000 Protestants are estimated to have left Ulster, and as these were the most industrious and intelligent part of the population—not only farmers, but artificers, weavers, and others connected with the linen trade—the loss not only to the cause of religion, but to the prosperity of the country, was very serious.

The injury done to the Church by impropriations has been noticed more than once, but it is difficult to understand how the Earl of Thomond can have got possession not only of the whole tithes of the parish of Holmpatrick,[3] both rectorial and vicarial, but also

---

[1] Mant, vol. ii. p. 230. [2] "English in Ireland," vol. ii. p. 135.
[3] Archbishop King to the Earl of Thomond, March 5, 1719.

the fees described as "altarages, offerings, and oblations." There was a considerable congregation of Protestants who were thus deprived of the ministrations of a clergyman, while their church was allowed to remain in ruins. One is reminded of the prophet's question, "Will a man rob God? Yet ye have robbed Me. But ye say, Wherein have we robbed Thee? In tithes and offerings."[1] The efficiency of the Church was second in the eyes of the Government of that day to the necessity of maintaining the English interest. The appointments, especially to the Primacy, were purely political, from the Revolution onward.

Archbishop Boulter was sent over from England in 1742 that he might support the English interest, and though he conferred many benefits on the Church, he was chiefly employed in the business of the State. At this time there were the usual two parties even in the Episcopate, the Irish and the English—the former being men of English origin but born in Ireland, the latter those immediately promoted from England; the very same difference which in Anglo-Norman times is found between the descendants of the invaders and the new arrivals from England, and which had always perplexed Government.[2] Archbishop King had been very ill, and in anticipation of his death Primate Boulter wrote to the Duke of Newcastle: "All that I shall say now is that I think His Majesty's service absolutely requires that whenever he drops the place be filled with an Englishman." Dean Swift looked on it as a great misfortune "to have bishops perpetually from England." "They drew after them," he says, "colonies of sons, nephews, cousins, and old college companions, to whom they bestow the best

---

[1] Malachi iii. 8.
[2] Leland, "History of Ireland," vol. ii. pp. 299, 300.

preferments in their gift." The consequence is expressed in a letter of Archbishop King. "'Tis a grief to me to consider that I have above forty curates in my diocese, most of them worthy men, and some that have served near twenty years, and I am not able to give or procure them a vicarage." Those who favoured the appointment of Irishmen were termed by Archbishop Boulter "the Dublin faction."

In 1730 was founded the Incorporated Society for Promoting Irish Protestant Schools. The petition to the King for a charter for it was signed by the Lord Chancellor, the Archbishops of Dublin, Cashel, and Tuam, six earls, five viscounts, and other eminent persons. The pupils were to be instructed in religion and taught husbandry, housewifery, and trades or manufactures, or such like manual occupations as the said society shall think proper.[1] "Ingenuity," Mr. Froude says, "could have devised no better gift to impoverished Ireland than a school of this kind in every barony. For care and honesty might have made the intentions of the founders into act. But there was only neglect and jobbery. The masters and mistresses plundered the funds, starved the children, and made the industrial system an excuse for using the pupils as slaves to fill their own pockets."[2] When Wesley visited the Charter School of Ballinrobe he was informed there were fourteen or fifteen boys and nineteen girls, for whose maintenance the master was allowed a penny farthing a day. As far as he could learn they were taught nothing.[3]

In 1729 took place the death of Archbishop King, whose letters throw so much light on the history of the Church during his episcopate. He was a man of

[1] Mant, vol. ii. p. 514. [2] "English in Ireland," vol. ii. p. 492.
[3] Steven's "Enquiry," p. 126.

remarkable ability, "and may be justly reckoned," Dean Swift says, "among the greatest and most learned prelates of this age."[1] His work on the Origin of Evil, and his "Discourse on Predestination" are of such importance that they are still always referred to when the topics they treat of come under consideration. The latter was republished by the late Archbishop Whately, with comments, as a model treatise on that difficult subject. So much were the Archbishop's thoughts engrossed by the external circumstances of the Church that very little appears in his letters "on the religious, moral, theological, or literary characters of those who are put forward for supplying vacancies in the Episcopate, and their recommendations rest in a prominent degree on political and secular considerations."[2] A contemporary of King's was Peter Browne, Bishop of Cork, who was not only a metaphysician of eminence, but also a mathematician, a theologian, and a highly effective preacher. But the most interesting character of the age was Berkeley, Bishop of Cloyne. He had been a Fellow of Trinity College, Dublin, whence he was promoted to the Deanery of Derry. This preferment he proposed to resign, though the richest Deanery in Ireland, in order to set out for Bermuda, and establish a college there for the civilisation of the savage tribes of America. But his project failed, not being supported by the Home Government. The greatness and originality of his metaphysical genius is universally acknowledged. His "Theory of Vision" was followed by his work on the Principles of Human Knowledge, in which he maintained the theory for which he is especially famous, that all the external world exists only in mind. That nothing is

[1] Mant, vol. ii. p. 498.
[2] Ibid., p. 44.

real[1] but spirit—the Divine Spirit, and the finite spirits created by the Divine. These speculations have exercised a considerable influence on the course of modern thought in Europe, and continue to excite deep interest at the present day. In his views on Irish affairs he has been contrasted[2] with Swift. The latter only considered the Anglo-Irish, and took little interest in the natives. Berkeley, on the other hand, in his "Querist,"[3] regards the entire nation as the object of a statesman's care. In many of the ideas he puts forward in that work he was far in advance of his age. He is described by Swift as perfectly indifferent to money, titles, and power, and another writer ascribes to him every virtue under heaven. Swift and Berkeley offer a contrast, also, in their views of the best way of bringing religion to bear on the native Irish. "I am deceived," the former says, "if anything hath more contributed to prevent the Irish from being tamed than the encouragement of their language, which might easily be abolished, and become a dead one in half an age, with little expense and less trouble."[4] Again, he says: "It would be a noble achievement to abolish the Irish language in this kingdom, so far, at least, as to oblige all the natives to speak only English on every occasion of business. Yet I am wholly deceived if this might not be effectually done in less than half an age, and at a very trifling expense; for such I look upon a tax to be, of only six thousand pounds a year to accomplish so great a work."[5] Berkeley, on the other hand, asks, "Whether there

---

[1] It is sometimes asserted that Berkeley denied the existence of matter; but it was the popular theory of substance, not matter, that he questioned.
[2] Ball, p. 187.
[3] "Tracts on Ireland," Thom, Dublin, 1861.
[4] Swift's Works, vol. vii. p. 360 (Scott's edition).
[5] Ibid., p. 393.

be any instance of a people being converted in a Christian sense, otherwise than by preaching to them and instructing them in their own language."[1]

The religious character of the population generally is little referred to at this period, but from the glimpse we have of the condition of the upper classes it must have been extremely low. Clubs or societies[2] existed for the encouragement of profanity. The Rev. Philip Skelton, who was Rector of Templecarn, on the borders of Fermanagh and Donegal, describes the people as sunk in profound ignorance. It was hardly to be supposed that they were born and bred in a Christian country, yet many of them were nominally Protestants. They scarcely knew more of the Gospel than the Indians of America, so that he considered himself a missionary sent to convert them to Christianity. Nor was this state of things confined to the lower class, for, officiating one day at a gentleman's house in his parish, he, according to his custom, asked questions of those present on religion. One of them, a person of quality, told him there were two Gods, another that there were three.

It was about this time that Williams, the first of Wesley's preachers, came to Ireland. Meeting with some success in Dublin, he wrote to Wesley, who determined to come over himself, and arriving in Dublin in 1747, preached in S. Mary's Church. A preaching-house was afterwards established in Marlborough Street, where he preached on Sunday evenings. In the following year he came over with two preachers, and this time he addressed audiences wherever he could collect them—in the open air, in the

---

[1] "The Querist," No. 260.
[2] In the life of Rev. Philip Skelton, A.D. 1750, a club is mentioned of which several noblemen were members, called the Hell Fire Club.

street, in the market-place, and by the road-side. Societies were formed in Munster, Leinster, and Connaught, and afterwards in Ulster. Wesley made it a rule always to attend Divine service in the parish church on Sunday mornings, wherever he was. At Newcastle a Scotchman went away because he and his preachers "were Church of England men." "We are so," said Wesley, "though we condemn none who have been brought up in another way." The system subsequently changed its character, as is well known, and now claims the title of the Wesleyan Church. The time had now arrived when the theory that the Church was to be protected from dissenters and Roman Catholics by means of penal laws was giving way to other views. It was the belief of good men up to the beginning of the eighteenth century that these laws were essential to the existence of religion. When the Toleration Act became law in 1719, by which Presbyterians and others were relieved from the penalties of the Act of Uniformity, and allowed to administer the Lord's Supper without incurring a fine of £100, Archbishop King was greatly alarmed. "I cannot see," he said, "how our Church can stand here if God do not, by a peculiar and unforeseen providence, support it."[1] A short time after he writes again: "To be allowed to profess what religion one pleases is a fair step, in my opinion, to bring people to confess none."[2] But political events, the loyalty of the Presbyterian body to the House of Hanover, and the position of their Church in Scotland, tended to modify the views of statesmen in their favour. The revocation of the Edict of Nantes had also led to the immigration of large numbers of Huguenots, who

---

[1] Letter to Archbishop Wake, November 10, 1719. Mant, vol. ii. p. 337. [2] Ibid., p. 340.

settled in the country under the protection of a special Act of Parliament "for the encouragement of Protestant strangers to settle in the kingdom of Ireland."[1] The Act provided that they were to have and enjoy the free exercise of their religion, and have liberty of meeting together publicly for the worship of God, and of hearing Divine service, and performing other religious duties in their own several rites used in their own countries. This Act was manifestly inconsistent with the theory hitherto maintained by the rulers of the Church, and caused some difficulty, an instance of which, in the case of the French Protestant refugees living at Portarlington, the following letter brings before us. It is from William Moreton, Bishop of Kildare,[2] and addressed to the colony. "Dearly beloved in the Lord. Intending, by the blessing of God, according to my duty, to consecrate two churches in Portarlington for the more duly celebrating Divine service, I think fit not only to give you notice of it, but likewise to send you the form of consecration which I intend to make use of translated[3] into your language, that you may not be strangers and pilgrims here still, but that you may be thoroughly acquainted with all our proceedings, the want of which acquaintance has done both you and us more prejudice than we can well imagine. For whereas you have hitherto thought fit to heap to yourselves teachers utterly against the Apostolical injunction, and particularly condemned by S. Paul (2 Tim. iv. 3), and of great disadvantage at this time to our common Christianity, I take this opportunity to let you know that I am your *Pastor* and *Patron* too

[1] 4th William and Mary, cap. 2, A.D. 1692.
[2] 1682-1705.
[3] A copy of this translation is in the library of Evelyn Philip Shirley of Lough Fea.

—the one by Divine and ecclesiastical appointment, and the other by human authority and the laws of the land. And, by the help of God, I will perform both these offices with all the tenderness and care I can : with no design to lord it over you, but with all possible meekness, and condescension, and kindness, too, I will make it my business to bring you by degrees to such compliance, as you shall have no reason to complain of." The Bishop, who was evidently kind and thoughtful, then mentions that he had offered to compensate their present teacher, M. Daillon, if he superseded him by a new establishment, but he found him too tenacious of his consistorial rights to part with them on any terms. He goes on to say, "Notwithstanding all the privileges allowed you by a late Act of Parliament, you know you are within my diocese, and consequently within my pastoral care." He will make it his constant endeavour, by all gentle and easy means, to bring them all to conformity with "this innocent and harmless, as well as orthodox Church." It is evident that when a foreign community, with their own mode of worship, were authorised by law to settle in the diocese of Kildare with their pastors and Church polity, it would be difficult to maintain the restrictions on Presbyterian worship of a like kind among natives of Ireland. Acts imposing disabilities on Roman Catholics had continued to be passed during the reign of George II., yet the laws against them were mildly administered, and towards the end of his reign they began to be treated with indulgence. After the failure of the Pretender in 1745, there was no longer danger from that quarter, and twelve years later they were for the first time since the Revolution admitted to enlist as soldiers. About the same time was drawn up a

GEORGE I. TO DISESTABLISHMENT. 391

Declaration by the Roman Catholic body, in which they disclaimed the objectionable tenets imputed to them. They declared, amongst other things, that it is not an article of the Catholic faith, "neither are we thereby required to believe or profess that the Pope is infallible."[1] This document, after being transmitted to Rome, was republished in 1792 as an authentic exposition of the views of the Irish Roman Catholic body. Not only was the spirit of the age in favour of relaxing penal enactments respecting religion, but the foreign alliances of the Government with Roman Catholic Powers tended in the same direction. When a bill of this character was before Parliament, Archbishop King writes : "The foreign ministers cannot with any reason or decency make any application to his Majesty against this bill."[2] The growth of this feeling led to the withdrawal of nearly all the disabilities under which Roman Catholics laboured before the close of the eighteenth century. A further step was the endowment of Maynooth College in 1795, a sum of £40,000 being granted by Parliament for the erection of buildings, and £800 a year in each succeeding session for the maintenance and education of two hundred students. The necessity for it was represented to be the danger lest students, educated abroad as heretofore, might imbibe the revolutionary spirit then prevalent. The contagion, nevertheless, reached Ireland, and in 1798 the rebellion broke out, encouraged by promises of support from France. It was quickly suppressed, and two years after, the Act of Union was carried in the Irish Parliament, though against much opposition. The experiment of a separate and independent legislature had been tried for

[1] Plowden's "Historical Review," Appendix lxxxviii.
[2] 1 George II., cap. 20.

eighteen years, and it was plain that two parliaments with co-ordinate authority could not work harmoniously in these islands.

From the 1st of January 1801 the kingdoms of Great Britain and Ireland were to be for ever united into one kingdom, by the name of the United Kingdom of Great Britain and Ireland. By the Fifth Article of Union it was enacted that "the Churches of England and Ireland, as now by law established, be united into one Protestant Episcopal Church, to be called the United Church of England and Ireland; and that the doctrine, worship, discipline, and government of said United Church shall be and shall remain in full force for ever, as the same are now by law established for the Church of England." On this Bishop Mant observes: "The Church of Ireland, and with it the Church of England, each ceased to have an independent separate national existence, and the two were thenceforth united into one Protestant Episcopal Church." One prelate of the Irish bench, Bishop O'Beirne, thought the statute did not go far enough, and was of opinion that there should be only one Church for the two countries, with the Archbishop of Canterbury as Primate. He appears, however, to have stood alone in that view, and he showed entire ignorance of the history of his Church when he quoted as a precedent the subjection of the bishops of the Danish cities of Dublin, Waterford, and Limerick to Canterbury, prelates who never belonged to the Church of Ireland.

The Church of Ireland as a Church was not committed to the union with the Church of England, for no Synod or Convocation was summoned to consider the matter, and it rested entirely on the authority of the Parliaments of the two kingdoms. It is, perhaps, uncertain whether the Irish Convocation, if summoned, would have assented to the arrangement, as thereby it would have parted with its right to have its own independent formularies, and would have been bound thenceforth to the same "doctrine, worship, discipline, and government" as the Church of England. It was possibly for this reason that the clause in the original draft relating to the summoning of Convocation was omitted from the bill. The Act accordingly makes no mention of Convocation.

About this time the Evangelical movement began to make itself felt in Ireland. One of the earliest of the clergy connected with it was the Rev. B. W. Matthias, who occupied the newly-erected chapel in Dublin termed the Bethesda, in 1805, and continued to act as chaplain there for thirty years. He was extremely popular; but, owing to his high Calvinistic opinions, he was not in favour with the ecclesiastical authorities. In other parts of Ireland the movement had zealous and active adherents as in Donegal,[1] Down,[2] and Cork.[3] In Kilkenny, Rev. Peter Roe, who was ordained by the Bishop of Cork at twenty years of age, occupied for many years an extremely prominent position in the movement. The bishops of the day, being older men, were not easily receptive of new ideas; and being chiefly appointed for political reasons, had little sympathy with the clergy referred to. Further legislative changes were in progress at this time, and in 1829 the last remaining disability was removed from Roman Catholics, and they were admitted to the Imperial Parliament. Soon after followed an agitation against tithes, which pressed heavily on the smaller farmers, and as it appeared there was no prospect of its subsiding, an Act was passed in 1832 directing the com-

---

[1] Rev. Joseph Stopford. [2] Rev. T. Tighe.
     [3] Rev. John Quarry.

position of the tithes for an equivalent in money. This was followed in 1834 by the Church Temporalities Act, amended by another in the following year.[1] By this Act the number of archbishoprics was reduced to two, and the bishoprics to ten. The revenues of the suppressed bishoprics and of sinecures to be suspended, to which was to be added a tax on all benefices over £300 a year in value, formed a fund out of which the expense of building and repairing churches and providing requisites for Divine service were to be defrayed, a Board of Commissioners being appointed to administer it. The Tithe Composition Act not producing the desired result, another was passed in 1838, by which the commuted tithe was altered to a tithe rent charge, payable by the landlord instead of the tenant. Twenty-five per cent. was taken off the composition by this law; but, though nominally smaller, the income, being fully paid, was of more value than the composition, which it was difficult to recover.

In 1854 "minister's money," a tax for the maintenance of the clergy in towns, was abolished, and an equivalent made payable by the Board of Commissioners. These successive changes indicated in what direction the current was setting, but for a time nothing further was done in the way of ecclesiastical changes.

In the following year the national system of education was established. It was advocated with much earnestness by Archbishop Whately, who was believed, but erroneously, to have been concerned in its establishment. It appeared to him that it was possible to give a united secular and separate religious education

---

[1] 3 & 4 William IV., cap. 37, A.D. 1833; and 4 & 5 William IV., cap. 90, A.D. 1834.

to children belonging to different persuasions. The greater part of the Irish clergy were violently opposed to the system, as seeming to do dishonour to the Bible; and in consequence of this feeling the Church Education Society was established, one of the rules of which was that the Scriptures must be read every day during school hours. The objections formerly entertained by so many excellent men to the system are now generally felt to be unfounded. It is seen that the Bible may be read every day in a national school on the condition that the hour is fixed, and that all who object to being present may withdraw at the time; and the clergy of the present day generally place their schools under the Board, to the great advantage of the children.

In the first half of the nineteenth century more than 500 new churches were erected, 172 schoolhouses were licensed for Divine service, and the clergy had increased by 919. For the maintenance of schools voluntary contributions to the amount of £1,049,000 were given. There were in 1868 thirty-five Protestant orphan societies, and more than 400,000 had been contributed to the support of 10,000 orphans. Additional evidence of the activity of the Church at this time is the contribution of £188,000 to the Church Missionary Society and that for the Propagation of the Gospel, and £126,593 to the Society for Promoting Christianity among the Jews. The Irish Society, established in 1818, has for its object the promoting the scriptural education and religious instruction of Irish Roman Catholics, chiefly through the medium of their own language. The numbers who used the language were very large at this time, the Commissioners of Education in their first report, 1825, having estimated those who spoke it exclusively, at half a million, and those who used it in preference to English as at least a million more. After the lapse of fifty years there were still, according to the census of 1881, 949,932 who could speak Irish, and 64,167 who spoke nothing else. Had such a society existed two centuries before, when Louvain and Douay were flooding the country with Irish catechisms and books of devotion, events might have taken a different course in Ireland.[1]

The time was now drawing near, long anticipated by thoughtful members of the Church, when the exigencies of party politics would bring to the front the question of the Disestablishment and disendowment of the Church—a measure sought for by English and Scotch nonconformists, as well as the Roman Catholic population. The Acts before referred to had prepared the way, and on March 6, 1869, a bill was introduced in the Imperial Parliament "to put an end to the Established Church of Ireland, and to make provision in respect of the Temporalities thereof, and in respect of the Royal College of Maynooth." It passed both Houses, and received the Royal assent in July of that year. By this Act the Church of Ireland was at once stripped of everything she possessed in the shape of property, lands, tithes, churches, and houses; her constitution was dissolved, and she was left naked to her enemies. It was unparalleled in its character. "I don't know," Mr. Gladstone said, "in what country so great a

[1] Some statistics as to the condition of the various Celtic dialects are given in the "Revue Celtique" for 1879-1880 (après le travail de M. Ravensteen). It gives the estimated number in Ireland, the Isle of Man, Wales, and Scotland who spoke only Celtic as 456,733, and those who spoke both Celtic and English as 1,729,160. In the French Departments of Côtes du Nord, Finistère, Morbihan, and Loire Inferieure, 768,200 spoke only Celtic (Breton), 524,000 Breton and French. Total for Europe understanding only Celtic dialects, 1,224,735; speaking Celtic and French or English, 2,353,158; grand total of Celtic speakers, 3,315,893.

transition has been proposed to the ministers of a religious communion which has enjoyed for many ages the preferred position of an Established Church." Happily the Church never was in a better position to bear this heavy trial, for before it came the appointments to the Episcopal bench had ceased to be governed by purely political considerations. Merit had come to be recognised in these and other appointments in the Church, and the Government had done its duty in placing in authority men of the highest character and ability, in whom all members of the Church placed confidence. During the debates on the bill the clergy received the fullest recognition as a body of men against whom no default of duty could be alleged. Nothing could have been more important when the Church had to brace herself for the great effort she was now called on to make. No time was lost in preparing for the task. The two archbishops summoned their Synods by mandates addressed to their suffragan bishops, and the assembly thus convened formed itself into a Convocation. The first resolution, which was passed unanimously, declared that "they were now called on not to originate a constitution for a new communion, but to repair a sudden breach in one of the most ancient Churches in Christendom." Another resolution was that "under the present circumstances of the Church of Ireland the co-operation of the faithful laity had become more than ever desirable." It was agreed that a General Synod should be summoned, to be composed not only of bishops and clergy, but of laity also. Shortly after a meeting of eminent laymen was held, and by them a request was addressed to the archbishops that they would convene a representative assembly under the name of a "lay conference," in order to make arrangements for lay representation. Representatives of all the parishes in Ireland, duly elected to the number of 417, attended in Dublin in October 1869. It was then arranged that a Convention of bishops, clergy, and laity should be held. On February 15, 1870, the Convention met in S. Patrick's Cathedral, and continued to sit until April 2, and afterwards in autumn, and completed the formation of the Constitution and a code of laws.

In the Preamble and Declaration prefixed to the statutes the Convention placed on record the faith of the Church, and its continuity of belief, in the following words: "The Church of Ireland doth as heretofore accept and believe all the Canonical Scriptures of the Old and New Testament as given by inspiration of God, and as containing all things necessary to salvation, and doth continue to profess the faith of Christ as professed by the primitive Church. It will continue to administer the doctrine and sacraments and discipline of Christ as the Lord hath commanded, and will maintain inviolate the three orders of bishops, priests, and deacons: as a reformed and Protestant Church it reaffirms its constant witness against all these innovations in doctrine and worship whereby the primitive faith hath been from time to time defaced or overlaid, and which at the Reformation this Church did disown and reject. The Convention further declared that the Church approves of the Book of Articles of Religion, commonly called the Thirty-nine Articles, which had been accepted by the bishops and clergy of Ireland in the Synod holden in Dublin in 1634; and also the Book of Common Prayer, and the form and manner of ordaining bishops, priests, and deacons which had been approved in the Synod holden in Dublin in 1662, and hitherto in use in this Church.

It will maintain communion with the sister Church of England, and with all other Christian Churches agreeing in the principle of this Declaration." Such is the account of the position of the Church of Ireland put forth on the eve of Disestablishment.

In the Constitution then framed the parish is the unit, and the registered vestrymen, each of whom signs a declaration that he is a member of the Church, elect two representatives to the Diocesan Synod, who must be communicants. The Diocesan Synod then elects representatives, clerical and lay, to the General Synod every third year. It also elects a Diocesan Council of clergy and laity, of which the bishop is president. If a bishop is to be appointed, he is elected by the Synod; but appointments to parishes are made by a Board consisting of three diocesan and three parochial nominators elected by the registered vestrymen, the bishop being chairman and having a casting vote.

No modification or alteration can be made in the Articles, doctrines, rites, rubrics, or in the formularies of the Church, unless by a bill, and a bill for such a purpose must be founded upon a resolution passed by the Synod, and no such bill or resolution shall be deemed to be passed except by majorities of not less than two-thirds of each Order of the House of Representatives present and voting. Such resolution must then be communicated to every Diocesan Synod at its meeting next after the session of the General Synod, and one year must elapse after this communication before a bill founded on it can be introduced into the Synod. This careful arrangement secures the Church against hasty changes, and allows ample time for the examination of any proposal which may be made.

It was inevitable when the Church obtained power to act that some members would desire to have their views expressed with more distinctness than they seemed to be in the formularies of the Church. Several resolutions were proposed in the General Synod with this view, but the feeling of the Church was against any change which would narrow the liberty of interpretation hitherto enjoyed by the clergy. Heated as the discussions sometimes were on the subjects of Baptism and the Holy Communion, they left no injurious result. The preface to the revised edition of the Book of Common Prayer thus refers to the latter: "Some of our brethren were at first earnest that we should remove from the Prayer Book certain expressions which they thought might seem to lend some pretext for the teaching of doctrine concerning the presence of Christ in that Sacrament repugnant to that set forth in the Articles of Religion." The Synod, however, made no change, except the addition of one question to the Church Catechism, with an answer taken out of the twenty-eighth Article. It goes on, "And with regard to the error of those who taught that Christ has given Himself, His Body and Blood, in this Sacrament to be reserved, lifted up, carried about, and worshipped under the veils of bread and wine," it simply refers to the canons in which are prohibited "such acts and gestures as might be grounded on it or lead thereto." In the formularies relating to Baptism, no substantial change has been made, though efforts were made to alter some expressions.

In the Office for the Visitation of the Sick the special absolution, as being "a form unknown to the Church in ancient times, and causing offence to many," has been replaced by that appointed in the Office of the Holy Communion. No change has been made in the

Form of Ordination of Priests, and with reference to the Athanasian Creed the only alteration is that the rubric directing its use on certain days has been removed, "but in so doing this Church has not withdrawn its witness, as expressed in the Articles of Religion, and here again renewed to the truth of the Articles of the Christian faith therein contained." The Table of Lessons, as revised, follows generally the new Table of the Church of England, except that no lessons are taken out of the Apocrypha, and that the whole Revelation of S. John is included.

Such were the slight changes,[1] in no way affecting doctrine, which were introduced by this new assembly gathered together for the first time, and with the consciousness of power to which they were unused. The result was due to the religious feeling and the high principle and conscientiousness of the members. In the course of the debates they learned to look at subjects from different points of view. Thus by degrees prejudices abated, reasonable views prevailed, and in the end the Book came forth unscathed. If any one regrets that those debates took place they should remember that the Book of Common Prayer, as it stands now, has thereby become that of the Church of Ireland, approved and acknowledged in every line and phrase by her General Synod.

In the Act of Disestablishment the life interests of the clergy were preserved, and they were invited to

[1] Letters and articles occasionally appear in English clerical newspapers in which strong language is used as to the changes said to have been made in the Irish Book of Common Prayer. There have been no changes whatever made in doctrine, and the actual alterations, chiefly omissions, are very slight. The feeling which inspires those articles appears to be a belief that the Church of Ireland is to be regarded as a branch of the Church of England, and therefore not entitled to differ from it in any way. It is the attitude of Strafford to the Convocation of 1635, see *supra*, pages 352-354. The writers may be recommended to study the Thirty-Fourth Article of Religion on the subject of the authority of national Churches.

commute their annuities, a bonus of twelve per cent. being granted on condition of three-fourths of a diocese doing so. It was provided that the capitalised value of their incomes might be paid over to a body which was incorporated by charter on October 19, 1870, and termed the Representative Church Body. The sums so paid over were charged with the payment to the commuting clergy of their annuities for life. The bishops and clergy, with a few exceptions, commuted for the benefit of the Church, thus surrendering their annuities for what might seem a precarious security. But it was not so, because the admirable management of the funds, and the contributions of the members of the Church, have made them perfectly safe. These are now matters of history.

It is the twenty-second year since the Act came into operation, and we may look back on the past and inquire how the Church stands with reference to it. At the Synod of Cashel in 1172 the Church was conformed to the Church of England, then in communion with Rome. "Ever since the Synod of Cashel," Archbishop King writes, "great care has been taken to keep up an exact conformity between the two Churches [of England and Ireland]. As soon as the Acts against provisions from Rome were enacted in England, care was taken to have them likewise enacted in Ireland. As soon as the Reformation was introduced in England, the Pope's power was abolished here, and the King's supremacy established."[1] It was enacted at Cashel that "All divine offices of Holy Church should from thenceforth be handled in all parts of Ireland, according as the Church of England did observe them."[2] Tithes were then made compulsory, and the Pope or the English sovereign for the first time appointed to all bishoprics and dignities, while Papal

---

[1] Mant, vol. ii. p. 388. [2] Ussher, vol. iv. p. 275.

taxations made the subjection of the Church a felt reality. The reversal of this legislation began at the Reformation, and first the Papal supremacy was abolished. Then the Reformed Liturgy superseded that introduced at Cashel; and now the Act of Disestablishment completed the work, and swept away with the tithes the last remnant of that legislation. Whatever opinions may be entertained of the Act which so many look on as unjust and sacrilegious, it has, at any rate, restored the Church of Ireland to her original freedom. She now has again her own Liturgy, as before the Anglo-Norman Conquest; for her, tithes have ceased; and she is maintained, as in her early days, by the voluntary contributions of her members. She is governed by her own synods of clergy and laity, and, as of old, the "Men of Ireland" take their part in them. Now, as before the Synod of Kells, she has two archbishops—one for the North and the other for the South, and she knows no earthly authority in spiritual matters beyond the shores of Ireland. The ancient sites of churches, and the Church lands granted to her by pious donors before Dane or Norman set foot in Ireland, are hers by universal admission, taken away for a time, indeed, but restored to her as the rightful owner with the full consent of all parties in the legislature, and she has resumed her ancient title of the Church of Ireland.

Disestablishment was a heavy blow; many thought it a fatal one, and believed the Church had fallen, never to rise again. It is no matter of surprise that such an impression should have prevailed, for, associated as she has been since the twelfth century with English misgovernment, and used by English statesmen too often for political ends, she seemed to be but a creature of the State, which must inevitably perish when stricken down by the hand of power.[1] Those evil days have passed away, and Government now seeks to promote the welfare of the people by means of just laws impartially administered. But, prejudiced against the Church by the history of the past, the Irish masses were unable to discern her true character and her rightful claims to their allegiance. And when Disestablishment came it was with them somewhat as with the people of Melita, of whom we read in the Acts of the Apostles that, when a viper came out of the heat and fastened on S. Paul's hand, they said among themselves, "No doubt this man is a murderer, whom, though he hath escaped the sea, vengeance suffereth not to live." And so "they looked when he should have swollen and fallen down dead suddenly." Perhaps in the providence of God the sequel of the story may also, in some sort, have its application in the future history of the Church of Ireland, for the sacred writer goes on to say, "After they had looked a great while and saw no harm come to him, they changed their minds, and said he was a god."[2] So it may be that the Irish people will in due time come to recognise the divine mission of the Church of Ireland and her historic claims, and to understand that by her the pure Word of God is preached, and the sacraments duly administered, according to Christ's ordinance.

---

[1] It is strange to find one in Cardinal Cullen's position entertaining the vulgar belief that the members of the Church were influenced only by money considerations in their religion. He affixed his *imprimatur* to an article in the "Irish Ecclesiastical Record" (June 1868, p. 460), in which it is affirmed that "Protestantism has no other hold on its followers than the mere temporal endowments. The great motive is money. Remove this inducement and they will become the followers of Rome." In curious contrast to this unfortunate prediction is the fact that at the close of 1890 the contributions of members of the Church to its maintenance had reached the amount of £3,899,352, 10s. 7d.

[2] Acts xxviii. 1-6.

APPENDIX.

A.—S. PATRICK.

FEW saints have been the subject of more biographies than S. Patrick. In the time of Gibbon there were sixty-six in existence, and ever since others are constantly appearing. The most important collection is that of Colgan in his "Trias Thaumaturga," or Wonder-working Triad (*i.e.*, Patrick, Brigit, and Colum Cillé). It contains seven Lives, edited with learning; but Colgan's materials were defective, as he had no opportunity of consulting the two earliest and most valuable documents, the Confession and the Life by Muirchu in the Book of Armagh. The former was not published until 1656, nine years after the appearance of his work, and the latter not until a year or two since. Dr. Lanigan had the further advantage of being acquainted with the Confession, but not with the Book of Armagh. Dr. Todd had, in addition, the Book of Armagh, which had been deposited in the Library of Trinity College six years before his work appeared. But unfortunately the most important document in it, the Life by Muirchu, was imperfect owing to the loss of the first page of the manuscript which contained the beginning of it, and the contents of the missing sections could only be guessed at from a table of contents supposed to refer to them. So matters remained until a few years ago, when the Bollandist fathers discovered a manuscript in the Royal Library of Brussels containing a Life of S. Patrick, which on examination proved to be the same as that of Muirchu, and as it was complete, the loss of the leaf of the Book of Armagh was thus supplied. It differs from the Life in the Book of Armagh in a few readings, and it is, therefore, not a transcript of it; it is also in some respects a better copy, as it supplies some omissions which are due to the carelessness of the scribe of Armagh. It has been published with accuracy and learning under the competent editorship of the Rev. Edmund Hogan, S.J.[1] The recovery of the lost chapter of this Life is the most important event connected with the history of S. Patrick which has occurred in recent times, from the new light it throws on the narrative of Muirchu, and its publication renders desirable a re-examination of the whole subject. The following observations are offered as a contribution to that end, with the object of clearing up some of the confusion which exists about the identity of S. Patrick.

For convenience, the view generally held of the facts of S. Patrick's history is here given after Dr. Petrie,[2] as gathered from the Lebar Brecc.

He was born in 372.

Was brought captive to Ireland in his sixteenth year, A.D. 388, and after four or seven years' slavery was liberated in 392 or 395.

On the death of Palladius in 432 he was sent to Ireland as archbishop, having been first, according to some authorities, consecrated by Pope Celestine, or, as others state, by Bishop Amathorex or Amator in Gaul. He arrived in Ireland in 432, and after preaching there for sixty years died in 492 or 493, at the age of about one hundred and twenty years.

The tract in the Lebar Brecc from which these particulars are gathered is assigned to the year 1100 by Dr. Petrie, though Sir S. Ferguson thinks it may be as early as 1095. This latter date, however, being still at least six hundred years after the death of S. Patrick, it is desirable to consult the earlier authorities, and inquire how far the tract is borne out by them. The first is the "Chronicle of Prosper of Aquitaine," in which at the year 431 we find the entry, "Ad Scotos in Christum credentes ordinatus a Papa

---

[1] Analecta Bollandiana. Bruxellis, 1882.
[2] History and Antiquities of Tara Hill, p. 93. Transactions of the Royal Irish Academy, vol. xviii.

APPENDIX. 407

Celestino Palladius primus episcopus mittitur."[1] This is the authority for the mission of Palladius. In the same century we have in the epistles of S. Patrick and the poem of Secundinus evidence of S. Patrick's mission to Ireland, which is not alluded to by Prosper. From the fifth until we reach the ninth century there is no further mention of Palladius, but in each of the intervening centuries S. Patrick is referred to by native and foreign authorities.[2] When we arrive at the ninth century Palladius is found again, in the Book of Armagh (A.D. 807), and now associated with him for the first time, S. Patrick. The following is the passage from the collections of Tirechan: "Palladius episcopus primo mittitur qui Patricius alio nomine appellabatur qui martirium passus est apud Scottos ut tradunt sancti antiqui. Deinde Patricius secundus ab angelo Dei Victor nomine et a Celestino Papa mittitur cui Hibernia tota credidit, qui cum pene totum baptizavit."[3]

We have here the statement that Celestine not only sent Palladius, but that in the following year on his failure he sent Patrick.

I. On this it is to be observed that the assertion of S. Patrick's mission from Celestine is made now for the first time by a writer who lived more than 200 years after the event, Tirechan's date being probably 650, and whose work is only known to us in a manuscript dating at least 150 years later still.

II. The absence of any mention of such a mission of S. Patrick from the Chronicle of Prosper has to be accounted for. He was the panegyrist of Celestine, and if he recorded the mission of Palladius which failed would surely have mentioned that which succeeded.

III. Palladius' mission is mentioned by Bede in his "Ecclesiastical History," but he is silent as to any other missionary having been sent after him by Celestine. This, as Dr. Petrie[4] observes, is fatal to the story of S. Patrick's mission from him. Bede died A.D. 735.

---

[1] Tripartite, vol. ii. p. 493.
[2] Ibid., Introduction, pp. cxxix-cxxx.
[3] Hogan, "Analecta Bollandiana," p. 89.   [4] Tara Hill, p. 106.

IV. There was no time between the sending of Palladius and the death of Celestine for such a mission, as Palladius is said to have been consecrated A.D. 431, and Celestine died in July 432. A mode of evading this difficulty is to antedate the mission of Palladius, who is said accordingly by some to have come in 429, although this is a direct contradiction of Prosper,[1] and by modern writers of the sixteenth and nineteenth centuries, such as Keating and Bishop Greith.[2] Again, if S. Patrick's mission can be brought down somewhat later, the same end will be attained, therefore it is said by some that he came not during Celestine's occupation but in that of Xistus, his successor. In either case, the passage in Tirechan, as well as all the Annals, are contradicted, for, as Archbishop Ussher observes, there is some uncertainty as to the date of his death, but none as to that of his mission.

V. According to this account S. Patrick was the second missionary, "Patricius secundus," as Tirechan terms him. But this is to contradict the early Martyrologies.

1. The old Roman (Paris, 1745), which at March 17 has "Sancti Patritii episcopi qui *primus* apud Scotos predicavit."

2. That of Rhabanus, 855: "In Scotia natalis Patricii episcopi qui in Hibernia insula *primum* prædicavit nomen Domini Jesu Christi."

3. That of Ado of Vienne, 858: "Qui *primus* ibidem Christum evangelizavit."

4. That of Usuard, 875: "Natalis Sancti Patricii episcopi et confessoris qui *primus* ibidem Christum evangelizavit."

5. That of Notker, 894: "Nativitas Sancti Patricii episcopi natione Britanni qui in Hibernia insula Scotis *primum* evangelizavit nomen Domini nostri Jesu Christi."[3]

VI. S. Patrick in his Confession makes no mention of the Pope, or of any predecessor in the mission. He says

---

[1] Who says he came in the consulship of Bassus and Antiochus, *i.e.* A.D. 431.
[2] Geschichte, p. 79.
[3] For these facts see Haddan and Stubbs, vol. i. p. 29-32.

the Irish were heathen when he came, and that before his death they had become the Lord's people. If, therefore, we accept the statement that he succeeded Palladius, we have "the spectacle of a conscientious missionary following in the track of an authorised predecessor, and arrogating to himself all the credit of what had been accomplished by Palladius, if not by Palladius and others."[1]

Reviewing the foregoing considerations, it seems impossible to accept Tirechan's account of the relations between the two missionaries. The passage quoted from him is the only one in the Book of Armagh, or any work of that age, which asserts the mission of S. Patrick from Celestine. It has all the appearance of an interpolation, from the manner in which it is introduced, and there was ample opportunity for its insertion, as more than one hundred and fifty years elapsed between Tirechan's death and the transcribing of the Book of Armagh. If there is any weight in the arguments just advanced, it must be an interpolation. But whether it is or not, there is abundant reason for holding that S. Patrick could not have succeeded Palladius.

The alternative, then, is that he must have preceded him, and we have therefore now to inquire whether there is evidence to support this view.

1. In the first place the Martyrologies, as we have seen, are in accord with it.

2. Prosper's words on this hypothesis may be taken in their natural sense. The Irish were "believers in Christ" when Palladius was sent. So Fordun[2] understood the words of the Chronicle. This argument acquires force by contrast with the efforts made to explain the words on the usual theory. They have been held to mean that there were "many scattered individuals, and probably some isolated congregations"[3] in Ireland when he came. But this is not an adequate interpretation of Prosper's distinct statement. Again, it is said that Nennius has instead of "in Christum credentes," the words "in Christum conver-

[1] Ferguson, "The Patrician Documents," p. 131.
[2] Hist. Brit., p. 161.
[3] Todd, pp. 189, 284.

tendos," and Muirchu " ad insulam convertendam." Bishop
Greith relies on this as a solution of the difficulty. But
one may ask what right an author of the ninth century,
much less one later still, has to alter the language of one of
the fifth century. These changes only serve to show at
how early a date the difficulty was felt.

3. The word *primus*, altered by Tirechan to *primo*,
by another to *primum*, may be understood to mean
"Primate."[1] Prosper intended to say that Palladius was
sent to those Christian believers as Augustine afterwards to
Britain. With this agrees his other statement that Celestine
"made the barbarous island Christian," which, as Dr. Todd
said, may mean that "by a formal nomination of a bishop
for them they were recognised as Christians." [2]

4. The chronological tract from the Lebar Brecc assumes
S. Patrick to have preceded Palladius, in the following passage : " Ten years from Augustine's death till Palladius was
sent by Pope Celestine with a gospel with him to Patrick
to preach to the Irish." [3]

5. The placing of Palladius first, and the double Roman
mission in Tirechan, involve the following conclusions
according to the Lives :—

(1.) That both landed at the same harbour in the county
of Wicklow within a year of each other.

(2.) They were opposed by the same chief.

(3.) Brought the same relics of the Apostles from Rome,
although, according to Muirchu, S. Patrick never proceeded
further than Gaul.

(4.) Both were unsuccessful in their mission, and both left
Ireland to return to Rome.[4]

This parallel need only be stated for its improbability to
be seen.

The considerations here offered tend to show that the
positions usually assigned to S. Patrick and Palladius should
be reversed. The latter is an entirely unimportant person
in Irish history, as he did nothing, or next to nothing, in
Ireland. "God hindered him," as Muirchu informs us,

---

[1] Ussher, Works, vi. 355.   [2] Todd, p. 309.
[3] Tripartite, vol. ii. p. 555.   [4] Petrie, " Tara Hill," pp. 117, 118.

quoting John iii. 27, "for neither did those fierce and savage men receive his doctrine readily, nor did he wish to spend time in a land not his own, but he returned to him that sent him."[1] Tirechan, an authority as early, gives a different account, and says he suffered martyrdom among the Scots (Irish). Later writers, as usual, go more into detail, and ascribe the foundation of three churches in the county of Wicklow to him. They also give their names, and the names of the disciples he left there. Dr. Todd[2] shows that these particulars are untrustworthy; but even if we accept them as authentic they amount to little. The fourth Life in Colgan limits his stay to "three days," and, on the whole, he is a shadowy personage, who flits across the stage and disappears, leaving no trace[3] of his visit to Ireland. The suspicion, indeed, crosses the mind that he never came at all. The sole authority of his mission is Prosper, whose statements with regard to Pope Celestine are not always consistent with other authorities.[4] "It would be difficult," Mr. Warren says, "to find any other sentence penned by any other ecclesiastical historian which has caused so much confusion." It is singular that there should be no mention of Palladius anywhere else before the ninth century, while S. Patrick is noticed, as we have seen, by foreign and native authorities in every century after his arrival. One would suppose that the missionary of Pope Celestine, with his foreign connections, would have been more likely to attract the attention of his contemporaries, but for 350 years after his alleged mission no one seems to have known anything of him. It is a suspicious circumstance, also, that the story of the conversion of Britain by missionaries sent by Pope Eleutherius is a Roman invention of this century. There are, therefore, grounds for some hesitation in accepting the mission of Palladius as authentic.

[1] Hogan, p. 25.   [2] Todd, pp. 292, 293.
[3] An ingenious attempt to connect Palladius with Ireland is made by the author of the second Life. He says Palladius' writing-tablets were called Pallere, which he wishes to interpret *Pall-ad-ere*, "the burthen of Palladius;" but the word is *polaire*, and it is derived from the Latin *pugillares*, and has nothing to do with Palladius.
[4] Rev. F. E. Warren, "Liturgy and Ritual," pp. 30-32.

The Life of S. Patrick by Muirchu in its complete state, as published by Rev. E. Hogan, is of great importance in this inquiry. From it we gather that he had before him the Confession and also a mass of current tradition, the flotsam and jetsam of two centuries, altogether divergent from, and inconsistent with, the Confession. The problem he had to solve was to steer his way through the different views,[1] and to combine his discordant materials so as to give a single consistent narrative.[2] The diversity of views, he says, made this extremely difficult,[3] and he deprecates criticism.

His method of proceeding was very simple. It was to follow the Confession a certain way, and then tack on the legendary matter. The result is that the latter part of the Life is quite inconsistent with the former. The Confession, with some embellishments and additions, is followed up to the time when S. Patrick returned to his parents on his escape from slavery. The author then sums up the rest with the words, "And he saw many visions,"[4] and then passes on to the legendary matter, beginning with an account of his setting out for Rome, his stay with German, &c. The inconsistency of this with the Confession, from which the former part is derived, will immediately appear when a few passages are placed in parallel columns.

CONFESSION.	MUIRCHU.
When at *home* he *dreams* that he hears children calling him.	He actually hears them when at Auxerre.—Hogan, p. 25.
He *dreams* that a *man* named Victor visits him.	An angel, Victor, often visits him. Hogan, p. 52.
	The angel comes every Saturday.—P. 55.
	Ascends to heaven visibly.—Ibid.
He complains of want of education, and opportunity of acquiring it.	He was forty or thirty years studying with German.
Has no miracles.	Abounds in them.
He tended cattle (*pecora*).	He tended swine (*sues*).

But the value of this memoir arises from the fact that it

---

[1] "Diversas opiniones et plurimorum plurimas suspiciones."—Hogan, p. 17.
[2] "Unum certumque historiæ tramitem."—Ibid.
[3] Difficillimum narrationis opus.—Ibid. [4] Ibid., p. 23.

identifies the Patrick of the Confession with the legendary Patrick, and the author seems to be unconscious of the inconsistencies of his story. Uncritical himself, and writing for uncritical readers, his biography is clumsily put together. Anachronisms give him little concern, and he tells us that S. Patrick stayed forty or thirty years with S. German, and was ordained priest by him, afterwards receiving episcopal consecration from Amator. He does not appear to have known that Amator was dead[1] before German became Bishop of Auxerre.

In the following century appeared a Life of S. Patrick by Probus,[2] which, as Rev. E. Hogan points out, is a revised edition[3] of Muirchu's memoir, but with the Roman mission added, which he derived from Tirechan. The inconsistency between the two parts of Muirchu being palpable, and only one Patrick being then recognised, Probus endeavours to harmonise them by inventing a double mission for him. "S. Patrick," he says, "came to Ireland at first without a commission from Rome." Here we have the authentic Patrick of the Confession. He goes on: "After labouring for thirty years without success, he proceeded to Rome, obtained the Pope's sanction, came back, and converted Ireland." This represents the second part of Muirchu, the S. Patrick of legend, with his Roman connection. Probus' mode of meeting the difficulty, however, is inconsistent with the Confession, for, according to S. Patrick's own account,[4] he never left the country after he began his mission.

This Life, taken with that of Muirchu, clearly shows that the S. Patrick of the Confession and the S. Patrick of legend are one and the same person, seen at one time, in the dry light of his own autobiography, as a simple Christian missionary, and at another looming a gigantic

[1] He died in 418, and was succeeded by German. Ussher, v. 436.
[2] Identified by Colgan with Caeineachair, Lector of Slane, who was burnt by the Danes in the Round Tower there. "Annals of the Four Masters," 948.
[3] "Vita quæ Probi nomine inscribitur ita insistit vestigiis Muirchu (nisi quod de missione Romana Patricii quædam hausit ex Tirechano) ut manifesta habenda sit illius magis Latina et elegantior recensio."— Hogan, Præfatio, p. 15.
[4] Tripartite, vol. ii. p. 361, line 6; p. 370, line 18.

thaumaturge through a haze of legend and fraudulent invention. To the latter belongs the Roman mission, which has been connected by Professor Zimmer with the efforts of Adamnan to introduce the New Easter, as it was termed, into the North of Ireland. Adamnan had accepted the Roman system, and was present at Synods in the North, where he was influential in promoting the change. Part of his policy may have been to represent S. Patrick as having come from Rome: "The connection of Ireland through him with Rome was contrived not without design."[1]

The discrepancies and difficulties which Muirchu and Probus tried to harmonise began afterwards to be treated in a different manner. It came to be held that the double[2] aspect under which he appeared represented two different persons—an earlier, or original, and a later Patrick; and the earlier began to be known to Irish writers as Sen Patrick, or Patrick the Elder, the other as Patrick the Apostle, *i.e.*, of Celestine. The term *sen*, translated by Ussher "old," which is its literal meaning, signifies "elder," when used to distinguish two saints of the same name. It refers to the period[3] in which the person is supposed to have flourished, and not to his age. Sen Patrick, then, is "the former Patrick," and we have now to inquire how he appears in Irish literature when separated from his legendary double.

In the Calendar of Œngus (tenth century) he is noticed at August 24 :—

"Sen Patrick, champion of battle,
Lovable tutor[4] of our sage."

In the "Chronicon Scotorum," at A.D. 457 :—

"Dormitatio sancti senis Patricii episcopi,"—*i.e.*, of the Church of Glastonbury.

In the "Annals of the Four Masters," A.D. 451 :—

"Sen Patrick breathed out his spirit."

---

[1] Keltische Studien, vol. ii. p. 183.
[2] Muirchu's Patrick might say with Faust :—
"Zwei seelen wohnen, ach ! in meiner brust
Die eine will sich von der andern trennen."
[3] Petrie, "Tara Hill," p. 94.   [4] *Oide*.

In the "Hymn of Fiacc":—

"When Patrick went to the other Patrick,
Together they ascended to the Son of Mary."

"The other" is explained by the "Scholiast" (eleventh century) to be Sen Patrick.

The Four Masters [1] quote a poem relating to S. Patrick's household, a copy of which is found in the Book of Lecan, but they omit the following:—

"Sen Patrick, famous,[2] hostful,
Head of his wise elders."[3]
"Secundinus et senex Patricius in pace dormierunt."[4]

It is evident that no theory of S. Patrick's history is satisfactory which does not take these entries into account and explain who this person was.

Ussher,[5] comparing the list of S. Patrick's successors in the ancient Munster authorities with the Annals of Ulster, found that Sen Patrick occupied the same place in one that S. Patrick did in the other, and is thus identified with him:—

ANNALS OF MUNSTER.	ANNALS OF ULSTER.
Patraic.	...
Sechnall.	...
Sen Patrick.	Patrick.
Benén.	Benén.

"Not only here, but elsewhere more than once," he continues, "Sen Patrick has been confused (?) with our great S. Patrick."[6] Dr. Lanigan, referring to this, says there is no confusion, as "they ought not to be distinguished," for though the authors of the Annals, or at least some of them, distinguished Sen Patrick from the great S. Patrick, but as contemporary with him, yet in reality they were one and the same. ... There is not mentioned in any of the Lives of S. Patrick any such person as distinct from him.[7]

[1] Vol. i. p. 135.
[2] *Sochla*, translated by Ussher *mitis*, gentle; but see Windisch Wörterbuch, s. v.
[3] Ussher, vol. vi. p. 458.
[4] Book of Lecan in Petrie, "Tara Hill," p. 87.
[5] Ussher, vol. vi. p. 437.   [6] Ibid., p. 438.
[7] Lanigan, "Eccles. History," vol. i. pp. 324, 325.

S. Bernard, writing in the twelfth century, and deriving his information from Irish sources, says S. Patrick's remains lie at Armagh, "where in life he presided and in death he rests."[1] But the Lebar Brecc[2] informs us that the relics there were those of Sen Patrick. Mr. Hennessy, the editor of the Annals of Ulster, says at A.D. 457: "So far the Apostle [of Celestine] does not appear at all in official connection with Armagh."[3]

The date of Sen Patrick's death is given in the Annals of Ulster as 457 or 461; but Muirchu and Tirechan concur in assigning the death of S. Patrick to 458 or 461, and Giraldus also has the former date for that event.[4] With these early authorities agree Baronius, Petavius, and the Bollandists.[5] Thus the two are again identified.

The poem of Secundinus, S. Patrick's contemporary, written during his lifetime, is said in the Book of Leinster to be in praise of "Patrick of Macha"[6] (Armagh). The title of the hymn in the Antiphonary of Bangor is "Hymnus Patricii magister (*sic*) Scotorum;" but the word "magister" is the Latin equivalent of the Irish *oide*, "tutor," by which, as already mentioned, Sen Patrick is described in the Calendar of Œngus. This panegyric, which is entirely in harmony with the Confession, is therefore a description of Sen Patrick.

The fanciful parallel with Moses, which led to the fixing of 493[7] as the date of the death of the Apostle of Ireland, belonged originally to Sen Patrick. In the Homily of the Lebar Brecc four points of resemblance between S. Patrick and Moses are mentioned:—

> He was a leader of the people.
> He fasted forty days.
> He lived to the age of 120.
> His grave is unknown.[8]

Now the Annals of Ulster have the birth of Sen Patrick at 341, and his death at 461, which gives him a life of 120 years. The parallel was afterwards transferred to the

---

[1] Ussher, vol. vi. p. 420. [2] Tripartite, vol. ii. p. 505.
[3] Vol. i. p. 17, note. [4] Tara Hill, p. 112. [5] Todd, p. 495.
[6] Facsimile, p. 361, "*molad Patraic Macha.*"
[7] Tripartite, Introduction, p. cxliii., note 3.
[8] Ibid., vol. ii. p. 475.

legendary Patrick, his mission being assigned to 432, and his death to 493.

The legend of the Bachall Isa or Staff of Jesus, so highly reverenced in Ireland, belongs to Sen Patrick, and is connected with the parallel to Moses. When Patrick was at Hermon "The Lord spake unto him in that place, as He had spoken to Moses on Mount Sinai, and told him to go and preach to the Gael, and He gave him therein the staff of Jesus."[1] The bachall or crozier was the emblem of ecclesiastical authority, and the idea intended to be conveyed undoubtedly was that he had his commission direct from the Lord. He is represented as refusing to go except on that condition: "He said he would not go until the Lord should speak unto himself."[2] Accordingly, it is said of Sen Patrick in the Hymn of Secundinus:—

> "The Lord chose him to teach the barbarous clans,
> To fish for men with the nets of doctrine,
> To draw believers from the world unto grace,
> That they might follow the Lord to the heavenly seat."[3]

He is thus identified[4] with the author of the Confession, who so often dwells on his divine call. "Christ the Lord," he says, "commanded me to come and be with them the remainder of my life."[5] While these allusions to him as an elder Patrick are occasionally met with in early literature, the legendary view of him was constantly acquiring more and more popularity. The advocates of the new opinions were zealous in propagating it, and the marvels and prodigies with which it was accompanied fell in with the popular taste, and commended it to general acceptance in an illiterate age.

There was little, on the contrary, in the Confession and the other contemporary documents to suit the period. They therefore gradually dropped out of sight,[6] while Sen Patrick himself retired into the distance, and was seldom heard of. In later times he was wholly forgotten. He remained, however, as a kind of skeleton in the closet to

---

[1] Trip., vol. ii. p. 475. This staff was in all probability the actual one used by S. Patrick.
[2] Ibid., p. 446, line 16.
[3] Ibid., p. 386, lines 13-16.
[4] Tara Hill, p. 116.
[5] Trip., vol. ii., p. 370, lines 17, 18.
[6] Todd, p. 387.

embarrass all who, like Dr. Todd and others, formed theories about the conversion of Ireland which did not assign him the first place. The "Chronicon Scotorum" makes him over to the monks of Glastonbury. Ussher adds him to his two other S. Patricks, and Dr. Todd mentions him and promised[1] to treat of him, but he found it expedient to avoid the subject. He was, no doubt, much perplexed by his presence, as his theory left no place for him, which was a fatal blot on it.

The identification of Sen Patrick with the Apostle is objected to by Dr. Petrie,[2] who believed him to be a Saint of Glastonbury. He considers it a serious thing to reject the various accounts of his burial at Glastonbury, and the notices of him in the charters of Baldred Ina and Eldred. But all the Glastonbury legends on this subject are post-Norman and of no authority, and the charters referred to are forgeries.[3]

From the conclusions here attempted to be established, it will follow that the dates referred to in the summary from the Lebar Brecc are untenable. The year 432 was fixed on for S. Patrick's mission, because, being the year of Celestine's death, it was the latest period at which Patrick could have received a commission from him. If he was sixty when he came, and if he laboured for sixty years, he would have reached the hundred and twenty years required for his likeness to Moses, and the inference would follow that he was born in 372, and died in 492 or 493. But as Dr. Todd says, "The story of his mission in 432 is the story of his mission by Pope Celestine, and with that story must fall to the ground."[4]

In the uncertainty which thus exists, the dates given by Mr. Whitley Stokes[5] have been followed, and, accordingly, in Chapter II. his birth is stated at about 373, his mission at 397, and his death at 463. The date of his birth here given is that accepted by Ussher and Colgan, but it should be mentioned that the earliest authority for it is Florence

[1] Todd, p. 307.   [2] Tara Hill, p. 95.
[3] Haddan and Stubbs, vol. i. 24, vol. iii. p. 307.
[4] Todd, p. 393.   [5] Tripartite, Introduction.

of Worcester, who lived in the twelfth century. It cannot, therefore, be regarded as certain; but, assuming it to be true, a better date for his mission would be the alternative one of Nennius mentioned in the note, *i.e.*, 405.[1] This would allow of his being thirty years of age when he was consecrated bishop before coming to Ireland. On the other hand, assuming 397 to be the true date of his mission, his birth should be assigned to an earlier period for the same reason. One of the dates deduced by Ussher from Probus is 361. The year assigned to his death, 463, is nearly the same as that accepted by Dr. Lanigan, viz., 465. It is worthy of notice that his mission at 405, and death at 465, would exactly allow the sixty years he is traditionally believed to have laboured in Ireland. These dates and calculations seem to be the least improbable of those proposed.

His burial is said by Probus to have taken place at Downpatrick, the evidence for which is, that when it was attempted to open his tomb, fire burst forth on the workmen.[2] But the monks of Glastonbury, who claimed to have the bodies of Patrick, Brigit, and Benignus, say a similar miracle occurred there, and his remains were reputed to have been dug up at the same time in both places.[3]

Not to prolong these remarks, it is evident that the transfer of the popular regard to the legendary S. Patrick was a gradual process, which was facilitated by two circumstances—the uncertainty of the traditions about him in the seventh century, and the Danish troubles which had already begun before the Book of Armagh was written. Little more than twenty years after that time, Armagh was plundered by the Danes three times in one month, and again in 840 890, 893, 919, 931, 941. During the long night of heathen oppression which settled down on Ireland, when churches were ruined and men of learning driven away, there could have been no one to criticise this account of S. Patrick, and when the Danish inroads ceased, the story was too firmly established to be overthrown.

[1] Page 23, note 3.
[2] Tripartite, vol. ii. p. 298.
[3] Ussher, vi. 455, 456.

B.—THE CELTIC DOGS.

Arrian, in his treatise on hunting,[1] written in the second century, describes the Celtic hunting dogs (αἱ κύνες κελτικαί). Before they became known in the East, it was necessary to use nets for catching hares, as there were no dogs swift enough to run them down. "The most highly bred of these Celtic dogs are a wonderful sight," he says, "as to eyes, body, hair, and colour. If variegated the colours are bright, or if of one colour it shines, and altogether the sight is delightful to a hunting man."[2]

When these dogs were exported to the East, a great demand sprang up for them. They were common to Gaul, Britain, and Ireland; but the earliest source appears to have been Gaul, as may be judged from the name by which they were known.[3] They were exhibited in the circus at Rome, and greatly admired for their strength and swiftness. When their value became known the Welsh princes established a monopoly in them, and it may be inferred from the Book of Rights that it was the same in Ireland. For amongst the gifts appointed to be bestowed by the King of Ireland on his provincial kings, and by them on their lesser princes, these dogs are frequently mentioned. Thus at p. 75, "Seven hounds for the purpose of the chase" are given by the King of Cashel to one of his princes. To another he gives "seven hounds to chase down stags." At p. 77 he gives "six beautiful hounds all white."[4]

Reserved as they were for the use of princes and nobles, the attendants would be experienced in their breeding and management. It is, therefore, highly probable that Patrick, as the slave of Miliuc, King of North Dalaradia, to whom, according to his Lives, he was sold by his captors, may have been employed not only in tending cattle, but also

[1] Κυνηγετικός, C. Abicht, Lipsiæ, 1854. [2] Ibid., vol. ii. p. 60.
[3] *Vertragus*, from Gaulish *tra*, to run, with an intensitive prefix. Zeuss, Gram.-Celt, 2nd ed., p. 4. So Martial:—

"Non sibi sed Domino venatur,
Vertragus acer."

[4] The Book of Rights, edited by Dr. O'Donovan, Celtic Society, Dublin, 1847.

in looking after these valuable dogs. So highly were they esteemed for their noble qualities that no prefix to the name of a warrior was more esteemed than *Cu*, a hunting dog, and so we have Cuchulainn, Curoi mac Daire, and others famed in legend; and even ecclesiastics were proud of it, such as Cu-Ciarain, Prior of Clonmacnois, and Cu-caech, who was Abbot of Cloyne.

As late as the seventeenth century, Archbishop Ussher sent a brace of wolf-dogs as a most valuable present to Cardinal Richelieu.

More on the subject will be found in Bell's "British Quadrupeds," p. 241; Scrope's "Art of Deer-Stalking," p. 342; and Thompson's "Natural History of Ireland," vol. iv. p. 33. According to Scrope, the Irish wolf-dog, Irish greyhound, Highland deerhound, and Scotch greyhound are all the same.

C.—On the Word "Canóin" (Greek κανών).

A good deal of uncertainty appears to be felt as to the exact meaning of this word in Irish literature. Colgan regarded it as a plural and translated it "canons," and his authority caused his view to be accepted until recently. It is now known to be a noun in the singular number, but its true meaning seems to be still a matter of conjecture. Dr. Todd in one place treats it as signifying "a collection of sacred books,"[1] and elsewhere as "a code of laws."[2] And now the Rev. Edmund Hogan, in his learned edition of the Brussels manuscript already mentioned, again follows Colgan, and translates it as a plural.[3]

It is, therefore, desirable to state the usage regarding it, and to give some instances. The full expression is, *Canóin petarlaice ocus nui-fhiadnaisse*—" The Canon of the Old and New Testament." But the word *Canóin* was generally used alone in the sense of "Scripture" by the early Irish, and

---

[1] Book of Hymns, part i. p. 49.   [2] Ibid., part ii., p. 250.
[3] Analecta Bollandiana. Bruxellis, 1882. Præfatio, p. 8, "canones."

with the meanings of: (1) The Bible; (2) either the Old or New Testament; (3) one of the Books of the Bible; or (4) a single text.

Iar bfoghuim immorro Canóne petarlaice ocus nui-fhiadnaisse do Brenainn—"When Brendan had learnt the Canon of the Old and New Testament."—Lives of Saints from the Book of Lismore, p. 103.

Légais (Patraic) Canóin la German—"He (Patrick) read the Canon with German."—The Hymn of Fiacc, Tripartite, ii. 406.

Mairg brisses cath can chori ar marcachaib Canóni—"Woe to him that wages unjust war with the horsemen (or knights) of the Canon" (*i.e.*, the Clergy).—Book of Leinster, 149, *b.* 33.

Do fir in berlai buain .'. na Canóni náimi—"To the man of the lasting speech (the everlasting word)." *i.e.*, the holy Canon.—Lebar na h-Uidre. Tripartite, ii. 566.

A Tairchell duind no-t-aircfider lind . . . cid do Chanóin—"O Tairchell (or Molling), we will rob you in spite of your Canon, *i.e.* Bible."—Betha Mollinc., Bibliotheque Royale, Bruxelles, folio, 45 *b.*

Mar innisit trachtaireda na Canóni nóimi—"As commentators on the holy Canon relate."—Revue Celtique, vol. iv. p. 252.

Craobh cnuasaigh na Canóine—"A fruitful branch of the Canon" (said of a Bishop of Derry).—Annals of the Four Masters, vol. iii. p. 9.

Torrces an Canóin—"He interpolates the Canon."—Book of Hymns, vol. ii. p. 250.

Ní dén dna ciall uaim pein isin Canóini acht amail no gebh isna leobhruib diadhuibh—"I will put no sense of my own into the Canon, but such as I shall find in the divine books."—Ibid.

In berla mbán mbiaid . . Canóin—"The white language of beatitude, *i.e.*, the Canon, viz., the New Testament."—Senchus Mor, vol. i. p. 16, *note.*

Do fir in bherla báin .|. ina Canóine—"The man of the white language, *i.e.*, the Gospel."—Ibid., p. 18.

Canóin Patraic—"S. Patrick's New Testament." "The

name by which the Irish designated S. Patrick's copy of the Gospels[1] [New Testament], now known as the Book of Armagh." Dr. O'Donovan, "Annals of the Four Masters," vol. i. p. 134, *note*.

For Canóin fatha ro fothaiged—"On a Canon of the Prophet it was founded," *i.e.*, on a text. Goidelica, 2nd ed., p. 94. The text referred to is Nahum i. 15.

In Chanóin Chomdeta chanait clerig—"The Scripture of the Lord which the clergy chant."—Book of Leinster, p. 302, *b*. 40.

Debe Canóne—"Difference of reading," *i.e.*, in a passage of Scripture.—Revue Celtique, vol. i. p. 64.

From this selection of passages the meaning of the word in Old and Middle Irish usage will be evident. But an apparent exception to this is the appellation of Fothad, a Lector of Armagh, who is termed "Fothad na Canóine," a title which has been supposed to refer to a decision given by him exempting the clergy from military service, and here assumed to be termed a Canon. Dr. Todd accepted this, and refers to O'Curry[2] and O'Donovan[3] as his authorities. But the latter eminent scholar does not call the decision a Canon, in fact, he could hardly do so, because in the very passage referred to he gives Colgan's interpretation of the name as "Fothadius cognomento de canonibus," Colgan, as already mentioned, having believed the word to be a plural. Dr. Lanigan followed Colgan, and accounted for the name by assuming that he obtained it "from his knowledge of the Canons." This view is now abandoned, and the question arises whether that referred to by Dr. Todd can be accepted. The only authority for it is O'Curry, and he gives no proof. Fothad's decision is termed *breith*, a judgment, *sententia*, as Colgan has it, but nowhere is it called a Canon.

He wrote two poems, one called the "Poem of the Complaint"—*cetul na cosaite*, and the other the "Poem of the canon"—*cetul na canóine;* but these were different from

---

[1] Dr. O'Donovan seems to have been misled by S. Bernard, who terms the Book of Armagh, "librum *evangeliorum* qui fuit beati Patricii." It really contains the whole New Testament.
[2] Lectures, pp. 363, 364.
[3] Annals of the Four Masters, vol. i. p. 408, note *e*.

the judgment. Fothad, according to Dr. Lanigan, was "a most holy lecturer and writer," and there can be no doubt from the foregoing facts that it was from his special knowledge of the Scriptures he received the appellation of "Fothad of the Canon." The following fragment of a poem of his is in accordance with this view. It is founded on Isaiah xi. 2, 3.

> "Wisdom, understanding, counsel,
> Knowledge, strength, severe devotion,
> Fear of God in this world,
> Are God's seven gifts to us."[1]

D.—LOUGH EIRKÉ.

I take this opportunity of correcting an error in my article on S. Finn Barr of Cork, in the "Dictionary of National Biography," as to the situation of his famous school of Lough Eirké. Colgan having stated that it was "in the south and maritime part of Munster," it has been looked for in the county of Cork, one conjecture identifying with Lough Mahon the expanse of the river Lee below the city of Cork. Dr. Lanigan again thought it was the part of the city called "the Marsh;" but the favourite view, which I followed, was that Gougane Barra, at the source of the Lee, was the spot, yet there is no reason to believe that the name of Eirké was ever known in any of those places. A further examination of the Irish Life of S. Finn Barr, however, has convinced me that all the opinions referred to are erroneous, and that Colgan was merely guessing in his vague account of its position. This Life states that S. Barré, or Finn Barr, after his education in Leinster, continued to labour for some time in Kilkenny and the Queen's County, and founded twelve churches before going to Cork. It was during this period he established the school in question, which is described as "at Lough Eirce in Eadargabhail." The last name, which occurs frequently in Ireland, is Anglicised Addergoole, or Adrigole; but the only one which answers the conditions required is that in the south of the Queen's

[1] Proceedings of the Royal Irish Academy, vol. v. p. 45.

County adjoining Kilkenny. It is situated, as the name implies (*eadar*), between the fork (*gabhal*), formed by the junction of two rivers, which here are the Gaul and the Erkina, tributaries to the Nore. Between them, near the monastery of Aghmacart, on the bank of the Gaul, is a ruin known as the College, near which is a depression, now a marsh, which was evidently once a lake. There is every reason to believe that this is the spot, especially as adjoining it, in the county of Kilkenny, is the parish of Eirké. The writers of the three Latin Lives, published by Dr. Caulfield, though concurring with the Irish Life as to his labours in Leinster, suppress all mention of this school, probably for fear of lessening the importance of that at Cork, which has in a great measure eclipsed the earlier one. The cave or grotto at Gougane Barra, called in the Irish Life *Cuas Barra*, was a hermitage, and there never could have been a school at the place.

E.—Parallel Saints.

The following enumeration of native and foreign saints is taken from the Book of Leinster (facsimile), p. 370 *c, d*. The heading is, "*Hic incipiunt sancti qui erant bini unius moris*"—" Here begin the pairs of saints who were of one manner of life."

John the Baptist.	Bishop Ibar.
Peter, Apostle.	Patricius.
Paul, Apostle.	Finnian of Clonard.
Andrew, Apostle.	Colum Cillé.
John, Apostle.	Ciaran of Clonmacnois.
Philip, Apostle.	Cainnech.
Bartholomew, Apostle.	Brendan, senior.
Thomas, Apostle.	Brendan of Clonfert.
Matthew, Apostle.	Colman of Terryglas.
James, Apostle.	Comgall of Bangor.
Simon, Apostle.	Molaisse of Devenish Island.
Tatheus (Thaddeus), Apostle.	Sinchell, jun.
Matthias, Apostle.	Ruadan of Lothra.
Maria.	Brigita.
Martin.	Bishop Erc of Slane.
Paul the Hermit.	Coemgen (Kevin) of Glendalough.
Anthony the Monk.	Lonngarad.
Ambrose, hymn writer.	Mac-ind-eicis.

Job of the Patience.
Jerome the Wise.
Clement, Pope.
Gregory of the Morals.
Cyprian of Carthage.
Laurence the Deacon.
Beda, sage and monk.
Hilary, bishop and sage.
Cornelius, Pope.
Silvester, Pope.
Boniface, Pope.
Paucomius, monk.
Pastor, monk.
Benedict, head of the monks of all Europe.
Augustine, bishop of the English.

Munnu, son of Tulchan.
Manchan of Liath.
Kieran of Saigir.
Cummin the Tall.
Mochuda of Lismore.
Deacon Nessain.
Buite, son of Bronach.
Bishop Sechnall.
Moedoc of Ferns.
Bishop Adamnan.
Molaisse of Lethglin.
Gerald, monk.
Cammine, monk (of Inis Caltra).
Fintan of Clonenagh, head of the monks of all Ireland.
Barré, Bishop of Munster and Connaught.

There is a similar list prefixed to the Martyrology of Tamlaght, in the Royal Library of Brussels, which gives thirteen apostles—Paul and Matthias being included. The present list has only twelve—one, James, being omitted. In the Brussels manuscript he appears as James, Apostle = Finnian of Moville.

F.—A Hymn in Two Languages.

The following is a specimen of Irish sacred poetry by Maelisu O'Brolchain (1086) from the Lebar Brecc (fourteenth century).[1] Each verse has four lines—two consisting of a Latin line repeated, and two of an Irish line repeated. In the following translation the English of each is given instead of the repetition of the line:—

"My God, my God, to Thee I flee,
Deus meus adjuva me.
O give Thy love, I humbly pray,
Tuc dam do shere a maic mo dé.

Into my heart, though still unfit,
In meum cor ut sanum sit.
Pour Thou Thy love that I may live,
Tuc a ri rán do grad co gribb.

---

[1] "Calendar of Oengus," p. clxxxv. Inadvertently said at p. 96, note 2, to be anonymous.

Lord, grant me what I ask of Thee,
Domine da quod peto a te.
O give, Thou Sun of brilliant ray,
Tuc, Tuc co dian a grian glan glé.

This thing I ever seeking am,
Hanc spero rem et quæro quam.
That Thy love may my heart enthral,
Do shere dam sund do shere dam tall.

O give it as Thy pleasure is,
Tuum amorem sicut vis.
With power, O grant my earnest wish,
Tuc dam co trén atber doris.

I seek, demand, entreat of Thee,
Quæro, postulo, peto a te.
That I with Thee in heaven may be,
Mo beith a nim a maic dil dé.

O Lord, my God, I cry to Thee,
Domine, Domine, exaudi me.
Fill Thou my soul with love alway,
M'animm rop lán dot grad a dé.

Deus, Deus, adjuva me,
My God, my God, to Thee I flee."

G.—LITURGICAL TERMS.

On some vernacular ecclesiastical terms in early use in Ireland, afterwards for the most part superseded by others imported from abroad.

Soscél, the Gospel, a translation of εὐάγγελλιον, and compounded in a similar way. From *so*, good, and *scél*, story or tidings. Still in use.

Congbáil, a monastery, a translation of συναγωγή, and signifying in the Senchus Mor "an assembly" (vol. i. p. 151), and then, like the Greek word, the building in which it took place. It survives in local names, as Nohoval or Noughaval, *i.e.*, *Nua-chongbail*, translated by Colgan "Nova habitatio." Modern term, *Mainister* (Monasterium).

Eclas (*eaglais*), a church, from ἐκκλησία. It is found in local names, as Aglish and Eglish. Modern term, *Tempoll* (templum).

Mullach, a paten. Loan word, *Teisc* (discus).

Nemed (Gaulish, *nemeton*), signifies in Old Irish a chapel. It was originally a heathen term. Modern word, *Sepéal* (Capella).

Culebadh, an ecclesiastical fan, the native equivalent of the Greek ῥιπίδιον and the Latin *flabellum*, but both word and article are obsolete in Ireland. That the fan was in use formerly appears from the representations in the Book of Kells.

Cruimther, a priest, from Welsh *Premter*, by the regular interchange of *p* and *c*. *Premter* is for *Prebiter*, a low Latin form of Presbyter. Calendar of Œngus, Index. Modern term, *sagart* (sacerd-os).

Sruith, an elder, corresponding with the Greek πρισ-βύτερος, and used occasionally in that sense. Lives from the Book of Lismore, p. cxvi.

Timthirid, a deacon, a translation of διακόνος. Calendar of Œngus, pp. lxxii., lxxiii. More usual term, *Deochain*. This is not given as certain, but it is founded on the following incident. A child of noble birth is brought to the monastery of Kildare for baptism. The *Timthirid* baptizes it, Brigit herself holding the child at the font. The presumption is that he was an ecclesiastic. In the Würzburgh Glosses, Paul and Barnabas are called by this name (1 Cor. iii. 4), and Διακόνια is rendered by *Timthirect* at Romans xii. 7; 1 Cor. xvi. 15; 2 Cor. viii. 4; Col. iv. 7.

Duirtech, a prayer-house or oratory, corresponding with οἶκος προσευχῆς, or προσευχή, Acts xvi. 13-16 (Revised Version). Whitley Stokes, " On the Linguistic Value of the Irish Annals," Philological Society, 1890, pp. 7, 13.

Oiffrend, the Mass, from the Latin *offerendum*. Now *Aifrion*.

Sacarbaic, the sacrifice, from *sacrificium*.

Both these terms seem to be derived from Malachi i. 2 (Vulgate), " In omni loco *sacrificatur* et *offertur* nomini meo oblatio munda."

The word *Missa*, the Mass, has never found its way into the Irish language. It is part of the phrase "*missa est*," used in dismissing assemblies, secular or otherwise, and perhaps had not been restricted to religious congregations at the time of the conversion of Ireland, or the Irish might have thought the words of Scripture more appropriate to apply to the most sacred rite of the Christian Church.

H.—A Poem on Rome by John Scotus.

This poem by John Scotus Erigena (ninth century), is prefixed to his translation of the pseudo-Dionysius the Areopagite. Migne's "Patrologia," tom. 121, 122, sec. 9 (868–872). Proem, pp. xxii., xxiii.

> "Nobilibus quondam fueras constructa patronis
> Subdita nunc servis heu ! male Roma ruis.
> Deseruere tui tanto te tempore reges
> Cessit et ad Græcos nomen honosque tuus.
> Constantinopolis florens nova Roma vocatur
> Moribus et muribus Roma vetusta cadis.
> Transiit imperium mansitque superbia tecum
> Cultus avaritiæ te nimium superat.
> Vulgus ab extremis distractum partibus orbis
> Servorum servi nunc tibi sunt domini
> In te nobilium rectorum nemo remansit
> Ingenuique tui rura pelasga colunt.
> Truncasti viros crudeli vulnere sanctos
> Vendere nunc horum mortua membra soles.
> Iam ni te meritum Petri Paulique foveret
> Tempore jam longa Roma misella fores."

(Translation.)

> "Built up by noble deeds in ancient days,
> Now ruled by slaves, O Rome, thy fame decays.
> Long since thy kings have left thy ruined walls ;
> Thy name, once precious, to the Greek now falls.
> New Rome, Constantinople, holds thy power ;
> And, ancient Rome, thou seest thy final hour.
> Empire is gone from thee, but pride yet stays,
> And basest avarice shames thy closing days.
> A people from the earth's most distant lands,
> A servile race, impose on thee commands.
> Thy noble sons are gone, what greater ill !
> And free-born Romans Grecian fields now till.
> Once thou to cruel death the saints didst hale,
> Their lifeless bones thou now dost keep on sale.
> But that saints Paul and Peter sleep with thee,[1]
> Surely most pitiful thy state would be."

---

[1] *Supra*, p. 96.

THE FULL TITLES OF SOME AUTHORITIES QUOTED.

Adamnan.—"Adamnan's Vita Columbæ." Edited by Bishop REEVES. Irish Archæological and Celtic Society, 1887.
Ancient Laws.—"The Ancient Laws of Ireland." Brehon Law Series.
Annals of the Kingdom of Ireland by the Four Masters.—Edited by JOHN O'DONOVAN, LL.D. Five volumes. Dublin, 1848-1851.
Antiphonary of Bangor.—Notice of, by Bishop REEVES. Ulster Journal of Archæology, 1853, pp. 168-179.
Ball.—"The Reformed Church of Ireland," 1573-1886. By the Right Hon. J. T. BALL. Dublin, 1886.
Bellesheim.—"Geschichte der Katholischen Kirche in Irland." By A. Bellesheim. Mainz, 1890. Three vols.
Book of Ballymote.—A Collection of Pieces in Irish (fourteenth century). Royal Irish Academy.
Book of Hymns.—"The Book of Hymns of the Ancient Church of Ireland." I. II. TODD, D.D. Archæological and Celtic Society. Part I., 1855; Part II., 1869.
The Book of Rights.—Edited by Dr. O'DONOVAN. Celtic Society, Dublin, 1847.
Book of Leinster.—A Collection of Pieces in Irish (twelfth century). Royal Irish Academy, 1880.
Brandan.—"Sanct Brandan Herausgegeben von Carl Schröder." Erlangen, 1871.
Chronicon Scotorum.—Edited by W. M. HENNESSEY. Roll's Series. London, 1866.
Codex Salmanticensis.—London, 1888.
Cogadh Gaedhel re Gallaib.—"The Wars of the Irish with the Foreigners." I. H. TODD, D.D. Roll's Series, 1867.
Cogitosi.—"Vita Brigidæ." Trias Thaumaturga, pp. 518-526.
Colgan—"Trias Thaumaturga." Louvain, 1647.
—— "Acta Sanctorum Hiberniæ." Louvain, 1645.
Dictionary of National Biography.—Articles quoted:—

Buite	Colman Ela	Dunan
Brendan of Clonfert	Conn na m-bocht	Dungal
Brigit	Conn of 100 battles	Enda
Caillin	Condlaed	Fechin
Cellach	Deicola	Fergil
Ciaran of Saigir	Disibod [Lugair	Fiacre
Colchu	Dubhthach maccu	Finn Barr

Finnian of Clonard
Finnchu
Fintan (Munnu)
Flannan
Forannan
Fursa
Gelasius
Gerald
Gille
Gobban
Grellan
Kevin (Coemghen)
Molling (Dairchell)

Dungal.—"Bibliotheca Patrum," tom. xiv. p. 196.
Duchesne.—"Origines du Culte Chretien." By l'Abbé DUCHESNE. Paris, 1889.
Goidelica.—"Old and Early Middle Irish Glosses." WHITLEY STOKES, D.C.L. 2nd edition. London, 1872.
Grammatica Celtica.—J. C. ZEUSS. 2nd edition. Berlin, 1871.
Greith.—"Geschichte der Altirischen Kirche." Breisgau, 1867.
H. and S.—"Councils and Ecclesiastical Documents Relating to Great Britain and Ireland." By A. W. HADDAN and Bishop STUBBS. Oxford, 1881.
Hogan.—"Vita S. Patricii (Analecta Bollandiana) ex Libro Armachano." Edited by Rev. E. HOGAN, S.J. Bruxellis, 1882.
Killen.—"The Ecclesiastical History of Ireland." W. D. KILLEN, D.D. London, 1875. Two vols.
King.—"A Primer of the History of the Holy Catholic Church in Ireland." Rev. R. KING. 3rd edition. 1845.
King.—"A Memoir Introductory to the Early History of the Primacy of Armagh." By the same. 2nd edition. Armagh, 1854.
Lanigan.—"An Ecclesiastical History of Ireland." By Rev. J. LANIGAN, D.D. Dublin, 1829.
Lebar na h-Uidhre.—A Collection of Pieces in Irish (about A.D. 1100). Royal Irish Academy.
Lebar Brecc.—A Collection of Pieces in Irish and Latin (fourteenth century).
Lismore.—"Lives of Saints from the Book of Lismore." WHITLEY STOKES, D.C.L., in the Anecdota Oxoniensia. Oxford, 1890.
Mant.—"A History of the Church of Ireland from the Reformation to the Revolution." By Bishop MANT. London, 1840.
Montalembert.—"Les Moines d'Occident." Paris, 1860-1877.
Œngus.—"On the Calendar of Œngus Cele Dé." By WHITLEY STOKES, D.C.L. MS. Series. Royal Irish Academy, 1871.
Ozanam.—"La Civilisation Chretienne chez les Francs." Paris, 1849.
Reeves.—"The Ecclesiastical Antiquities of Down, Connor, and Dromore." By Bishop REEVES. Dublin, 1847.
Richey.—"A Short History of the Irish People." By A. I. RICHEY. Edited by R. R. KANE. Dublin, 1887.
Round Towers.—"The Ecclesiastical Architecture of Ireland anterior to the Anglo-Norman Invasion." By G. PETRIE. Transactions of the Royal Irish Academy, vol. xx.
Stowe Missal.—"On the Stowe Missal." By Rev. B. M'CARTHY, D.D. Transactions of the Royal Irish Academy, 1886.

Theiner.—"Vetera Monumenta Hibernorum et Scotorum." AUGUSTINUS THEINER. Rome, 1864.

Todd, Rev. J. H.—"Life of S. Patrick." Dublin, 1864.

Tripartite.—"The Tripartite Life of S. Patrick, with other Documents relating to that Saint." Edited by WHITLEY STOKES, D.C.L. Roll's Series. Two vols. 1887.

Warren.—"The Liturgy and Ritual of the Celtic Church." By F. E. WARREN, D.D. Oxford, 1881.

Wasserschleben.—Irische Kanonensammlung, Zweite Auflage. Leipzic, 1885.

Würzburgh Glosses.—Selections from, by Rev. T. OLDEN. S.P.C.K., 1890.

Zimmer.—"Keltische Studien." Von HEINRICH ZIMMER. Berlin, 1881.

—— "Brendan's Meerfahrt." Zeitschrift für Deutsches Alterthum, Herausgegeben von Elias Steinmeyer. HEINRICH ZIMMER. Berlin, 1889.

INDEX.

ADAMNAN . . 59, 77, 104, 119	Bachall Isa, the . . . 208, 230
Adrian's Bull 243	,, burnt 299
Aelfrick's homilies 176	Badb, goddess 4
Aidan, King 77	Baithin 78
Aidan, S. 79, 121, 139	Bale, Bishop 286, 315
Ailbe, S. 24, 37	Ballaghmoon, battle of . 178
Ailclyde 15, 29	Ballymote, Book of . . . 80, 202
Albin Molloy 269	Baltinglas 233, 239
Albinus 157	Bangors, three . 97, 111, 226, 232
Alcuin 155, 157, 211	Baptism in milk 141
Alexander, Pope 113, 242, 248, 249	Bardsey 97
Amator 23	Baronius 95
Anicetus, Pope 93	Barré, S., or Finn Barr . 27, 34
Anker Houses 199	Basilica 150
Annals of Lough Cé . . 113, 215	Beads, form of . . . 232, 305
Anselm 194	Bede 55
Antiphonary of Bangor 62, 97, 139	Bedell, Bishop . . . 346-350
Ardagh Chalice 140	Bells 208
Ardpatrick 226	,, S. Patrick's 207
Arles 19	Bellahoe, battle of . . 302
Armagh, Diocese of . . 228	Bellesheim 104, 245, 249
,, court of 120	Beltine 6
,, synod of 241	Benedict, S. 107
,, school of 235	Benedictine monasteries . . 253
,, cathedral burnt . . 321	Berach, S. 6
,, stone church of . . 225	Berengarius 176
,, jurisdiction of . . . 193	Berikert 85
,, Book of 72, 121	Berkeley, Bishop 385
,, canon of 152	Bernard, S. . 62, 73, 112, 113, 220,
Articles, Irish 343, 352	224-229
,, eleven 324	Bible, Irish, the . . . 350
Ascetics 71, 72	,, the, in Dublin . . . 325
Athos, Mount 132	Bishops, groups of . . . 33
Augustine, S. 102	,, of tribes 124
,, of Canterbury . 80, 144	,, twelve consecrated . 260
	,, before S. Patrick . . 24
BABYLON 97	Blathmac, King 69

433 2 E

INDEX.

Bloods, the five 251
Board of Firstfruits 378
Bobbio 94
Boniface IV., Pope 95
„ Archbishop . . . 101
Book of Rights . . 17, 178, 193
Boruma, the 189
Boulter, Archbishop . . . 383
Boyle, Archbishop 370
„ abbey of 233
Bramhall, Archbishop . . . 349
Bregenz 94
Breifne 65
Brendan, S. 65, 203
Brewer, Mr. 327
Brian, King . 177, 187-190, 221
Brigit, goddess 4
„ S. 38 48, 75
„ baptism of 141
British Church 9
Brittany 43
Browne, Archbishop . . 292, 307
„ Bishop 385
Broccan's hymn 40
Bruce, Edward 272
Brunehaut 94
Buidhe Chonnail. See Yellow Plague.
Buite, S. 233
Burnet, Bishop 144
Butler, Bishop 374

CAILLIN, S. 65, 208
Calpornius 14
Campion 289
Canair, S. 67
Canon, the Roman . . . 214
Canons, English (1604) . . 353
„ of 1634 377
Canonisation, Irish . . . 34
Carrickfergus 370
Carsuel, Bishop 367
Cashel, Convention at . . 212
„ Archbishopric of . . 221
„ Synod of . . . 246, 402
Catechumens 142
Cathachs 66, 67
Cathal Maguire 289
„ Crobderg 113
Cedd, Bishop 81

Celestine, Pope 11, 14
Cellach (Kellach) 114
Celsus, Archbishop . 215, 221, 229
Celtic in Europe 390
Cenn Cruaich 4
Centuriators of Magdeburgh . 130
Charlemagne . . 155, 156, 211
Children, deserted . . 125, 150
Christ Church . . . 193, 268, 306
Church, British 127
Church of Ireland independent 359
Church of Ireland, three divisions of 128
Church of Rome and Nationality 361
Church, service in Irish . . 348
Church Temporalities Act . 394
Churches, consecration of . 378
„ the Western . . 93
Cistercian Rule 233
Claudius of Turin 317
Churchyards, privileged . . 270
Clairvaux 231
Clane, Synod of 235
Clement III., Pope . . . 233
Clement, teacher . . 109, 157
Clergy from England . . 377
Clerical transportation . . 151
Clocháns 200
Cloictheach, bell-house . . 180
Clonard 516
Clonmacnois 123
Clontarf, battle of . . 190, 202
Cluain Comarda 169
Clynn's Annals 251
Coarbs 111, 116
„ lay 227
Colchu 155, 211
Cole, Dr. 319
Colman, S., of Lindisfarne 80, 121
Colman Ela, S. 114
Colman ua Cluasaig, S. . 68, 69
Colmans, many 70
Colours, ecclesiastical . . 209
Columba, S. . . 65, 75-78, 121
Columbanus, S. . . 91-99, 137
„ his Monosticha . 138
„ Commentary . . 97
Comgall, S. . . . 34, 92, 137

INDEX. 435

	PAGE
Communion in both kinds	209
Commutation	402
Comyn, Archbishop	267
Conall, Lord of Dalriada	77
Condlaed, Bishop	42
Confession, Auricular	209, 225
Conn's Half (*Leth Chuinn*)	118
Conn of the poor	123
Connesburgh, Edmund	293
Connor mac Nessa	9
Connor, Diocese of	226
Consecration, joint	140
,, by one bishop	143
Constantinople, First Council	94
Constantius	20
Convention, the	398
Convocation first	342
,, others	352, 375, 377, 397
Cork, ancient Diocese of	217
Cormac mac Airt	9
Cormac mac Carthy	225, 228
Cormac mac Cuillenan	117
,, his glossary	178
Cormac's chapel	178, 199
Coronation chair, the	78
Coroticus	12, 129, 141
Council of Arles	54
,, Tours	55
,, Rouen	55
Covenant, the	355
Cranmer, Archbishop	176
Crofts, Sir J.	311, 313, 314
Cromer, Archbishop	306
Cromwell, the Lord	299
,, his preachers	359
Crowns, Episcopal	44, 108
Cucuimne	146
Culebadh, the	140, 204
Cumal	127
Cumin the Tall	125
Cummian	117, 144, 153
Curwen, Archbishop	317, 325
DAL CAIS	187, 196
Dalaradia	228
Dalriada	76
Danes	167
,, Christian	193
Danish oppression	169, 184

	PAGE
Daniel, Archbishop	334, 319
Daughters of saints	122
De Clare, Richard (Strongbow)	240
Declaration (Roman Catholic)	391
De Courcey	48, 254
Deer's Cry, The	29
Deicola	91, 99
Dermod, King of Ireland	69
,, Duke	195
,, mac Murrough	238
Derry	76, 119
,, siege of	369
Dervorgill	235, 238
Desert, a	18
Desiul, the	67
,, revived	330
Destiny, the Stone of	77
Dicuil's geography	157
Diocese, monastic	116
Dionysius the Areopagite	174
Directory, the	358
Disestablishment Act	396
Disibod	105
Dodwell, Henry	370
Domnach airgid, the	28
Donald, Bishop	195
Donnan, S., of Egg	79
Dowdall, Archbishop	306, 310, 317
Downpatrick	48, 255
Drogheda, Parliament of	279, 286
Druids	3, 9, 39, 201
Drumceatt, Convention of	78
Dubh-da-crich	106
Dubdalethe III.	196
Dublinia	193
Dublin, Synod of,	269
Duffack, poet	28, 38
Duleek	261
Dungal	83, 172
Dunlaing	41
Dunlevy	254
Dunan, Bishop	191, 194
Dunraven, Lord	200
Durrow	76
EASTER	80-87, 93, 117
Eastern Church	83
,, usages	132
Echlin, Bishop	352
Egyptian monks	134

INDEX.

	PAGE
Elizabeth, Queen	322
,, studies Irish	332
Elysium, Irish	7
Emigration from the North	363, 367, 382
Epiphany	133
Erdathe	3
Eric of Auxerre	20, 172
Erigena, John Scotus	83, 84, 174
Eugenius III., Pope	232
FEASTS, literary	283
Fechin, S.	70
Felim, King-bishop	170
,, Prince	111
Ferdomnach, Bishop	195
Fergna, King	65
Ferguson, Sir S.	13, 25, 30, 131
Fergusson, Mr.	132, 201
Fiacc, Bishop	28, 101
Fiadh mac Aenghusa	215
Finan, S.	79
Finn Barr, S.	34
Finnchu, S.	119, 133, 208, 200
Fintan (Munnu), S.	74, 206
Firbolgs	3
Fire, sacred, Brigit's	45
,, at Saigir	45
Fire-houses	46
Firstfruits	113, 377
Firstlings	73
FitzAdelm	230, 251
Fitzgerald, Maurice	240
Fitzmaurice, Bishop	329
Fitzralph, Archbishop	285, 307
Fitzsymon, Archbishop	291
Fitzstephen, Robert	240
Fitzwalter, Lord	318
Flann Febla of Armagh	119
Forannán of Wassor	185
,, Coarb of Armagh	169
Fort del' Ore	335
Foxals, John	293
Friars, begging	306
Froude, Mr.	326, 371, 384
Fulda	197
Fursa, S.	87-90, 293
GALL, S.	96
Gentiles, Black. *See* Danes.	

	PAGE
Gentiles, Fair	167
Gerald, S.	34, 69, 85
German, S.	19
Gilla Aedh O'Mugain	231
Gilla mac Liag	230, 233, 247
Gillé, Bishop	195, 212, 228
Giraldus Cambrensis	54, 118, 119, 204, 244, 269
Glastonbury	255
Gobán Saer	5
Goodacre, Archbishop	314, 315
Gothric, King	194
Gottescalk	176
Greek	98, 148
Gregory IX., Pope	122
Gregory, Archbishop	222, 239
Greith, Bishop	19, 53, 144
HACKETT, Bishop	370
Hallam, Mr.	174
Head of cities	153
Henry of Marlborough	289
Henry II.	239, 241, 250, 298
Heptateuch, the	26
Heretics, Irish	339
,, ,, burnt	292
Hermits, Egyptian	72
Hiberio	3
Hilda, Abbess	81
Hildegardis, Abbess	107
Honorius III., Pope	145, 246
Hubritan	85
Hy or Iona	76, 77
Hymns, Book of	68, 82, 202
IBAR, Bishop	24
Idunan, Bishop	195
Inclusus, an	198
Inisbofin	84
Inismurray	46
Inispatrick	232, 383
Innocent II., Pope	231
Irish book, first	333
,, Bibles and Prayer-books	376
,, New Testament	340
,, language	334, 382
,, Roman Catholic books	341
,, speakers	399
,, Liturgy	345
,, type	334, 365

INDEX.

Ita, S.	133
Itinerating clergy	124
Iveragh	228
JERUSALEM, prerogative of	96
KELLACH, Life of	74
Kells, Synod of	113, 234
Kevin, S.	72
Kieran of Saigir	45
,, Clonmacnois	74
Kilkenny, Assembly at	358
Kilmaclenine	257
Kilmakilloge	372
King, Archbishop	369-391
,, Irish scholar	349
LAEGAIRE, King	29
Laichtin, S.	127
Lanfranc, Archbishop	192, 194, 210, 212
Lanigan's Eccles. History	12-16, 23-27, 85, 102, 245
Laserian, S.	298
Lateran Council	253
Laurence, Archbishop	81, 92
Laud, Archbishop	344
Law of a Saint, the	126
Law schools	281
Lech, Archbishop	286
Legate, first Papal	196
Leo, Emperor	182
Lerins	19
Leslie, Charles	370
Letha (Brittany)	43
Lex Innocentium	38
Linen manufacture	372
Lindisfarne	79
Lismore	56, 225
Litany in English	322
Liturgy interdicted	359
,, restored	360
,, Irish	213
,, Roman	213
Liturgies, ancient Irish	213
Livestone	351
Lochlann	157
Loftus, Archbishop	325
Loire, the	18, 94
Lollards	291, 318
Lord's Day	114
Lough Cé, Annals of	113
Lough Derg	265, 267
Lough Irche (Eirke)	34
Lucius, King	297
Luirech or Lorica	210
Lure (Luthra)	95, 100
Luttrell, Colonel	368
Luxeuil	93, 99
MABILLON	93, 103
Mac Carthenn	28
Mac Carthy, Cormac	223, 225
Mac Donnell, Murtough	227
Mac Kelly, Bishop	257
Mac Maelisa, Nicholas	255
Maelbrigid of Armagh	227
Maelsuthain O'Carroll	135
Magh Léné, Synod of	117
Maguire Cathal	289
Mahon, King	187
Maine, Sir H.	70, 73
Malachi O'Morgair	112, 223-233
Malachi, King	190
,, of Down	255
Malchus, Bishop	195-225
Marcus, Bishop	20
Marianus Scotus	197
Marriage laws	225
,, of clergy	121, 289
Marsh, Narcissus	369
Martin, Bishop	19, 52
Martin V., Pope	246
Martyrs	54
Mary of the Gael	47
Mary de Hogges	239
Massacre of 1641	356
Maynooth College	391
Mel, plain of	7
Mellefont	233, 235
Mentz	197
Metz, Bishop of	298, 302
Minna, the, of Armagh	229
Miracle-plays	285
Missal, the Stowe	139, 211
Mochaemog	208
Mochta, S.	32
Molaisse, S.	5
Molling, S.	5, 139, 140
Molua mac Ocha	125

INDEX.

	PAGE
Molua of Clonfert	139
Moluog	79
Monasteranena	233
Monastery, double	44
Monogram, the, IHS.	135
Montalembert, M. De	28, 77, 123
Moran, Cardinal	328
Mount Tabor	133
Muirchu maccu Machtheni	19
Murtough, King	195, 212
NANTES	18
,, Edict of	373, 388
Niall, Coarb	230
Niall, son of Hugh	228
Nonjurors	370
O'BRIEN, Connor, King	223
O'Connor, Roderick	239
O'Curry, Professor	123, 197
Octavian, Cardinal	293, 294
O'Dunan, Bishop	212
O'Fihelly, Bishop	327
O'h-Enni, Donald	213
O'Neill, Shane	329
O'Toole, S. Laurence	252
,, burnt	292
O'Mulholland	207
Orders, concealing	103
O'Hussey, Bonaventure	341
Orders, the Three	121
Origen	83, 161
O'Rourke, Ternan	238
Oswy, King	79
Ota, responses of	169
O'Teige, Donat	329
Ozanam	54, 217
PALLS, the	231
Palladius	10, 14
Paparo, Cardinal	113, 143, 234
Papal bishops	337
,, clergy	346
,, grants	245, 246
,, taxes	261
Parliament of 1530	296, 304
,, 1560	324
Parrthas an Anma	342
Patrick, S.	12-16, 23
,, burial-place, Armagh	416

	PAGE
Patrick, S., burial-place, supposed—	
Down	416
Saul	256
Glastonbury	255, 419
Unknown, like Moses'	416
Patrick, S., Canon of	27
,, Ordo or Liturgy of	313
,, fasts like Moses	220
,, his champion	28
,, his crozier	30
,, his bell	30
Patrick's Cathedral	268
Patrick, Bishop	194
Paul the Hermit	107
Pedilavium, the	141
Pelagius	161
Penal laws	318, 372
Pepin, King	101
Perfect ones	142
Peter's Pence	298
Petrie, Dr.	10, 12, 181
Petroleum	165
Photius, Patriarch	175
Pilgrim, i.e., Irishman	99
Pilgrim fathers, early	85
Plague, yellow	68, 75
Plato	162
Polycarp	93, 131
Portarlington	389
Prayer-book in Irish	333
,, in French	365
,, in German	365
,, in Latin	324
,, the Revised	364
Presbyterianism	120, 342, 350
Proctors in Parliament	296
Prophets	162, 204
Purgatory, S. Patrick's	266, 374
QUERIST, The	387
RATHBREASIL, Synod of	117, 214, 226
Rebellion of 1798	391
Revision of Prayer-book	400-1
Richards, Dean	371
Rome, i.e., a burial-place	96, 97
Roman missionaries	339
Romanesque, Irish	201

INDEX.

	PAGE		PAGE
Ros Ailithir	163	Tisaxon	86
Round Towers	179	Tithes	113, 234
Rubric, the Ornaments	364	,, Impropriate	376, 383
Ruiben	146	,, Composition	394
		,, Commutation	394
SAINTS, who?	34-37	Toleration Act	388
,, daughters of	122	Tonsure, Roman	149
,, sons of	122	Towers, Round	179-181
,, invocation of	71	Trees, Sacred	5
,, Island of	36	Trim, Church of	111
,, attracted to Rome	40	Trinity College	336
Saladin's tenths	262	Turgesius	168, 169
Sardica, Canon of	153	Turlough, King	194, 210
Sarum, Use of	248	Tyrone, Earl of	339, 342
Saul, Church of	256		
Scadinavia	167	ULSTER, Plantation of	356
Schools	56, 159-165	Ultan, S.	69
Scotus, John	83, 84, 174	Undertakers	345
Scriptures	135, 210	Universities, foreign	339, 341
Segéné	118	Union, the	392
Secundinus' poem	12	Usney, Synod of	215, 216
Senán and Canair	67	Ussher	152, 215, 337, 346, 358
Severus, Sulpicius	20, 72, 81		
Sen Patrick	14, 414, 415	VACTROPERITI	148
Sid, The	4	Vergil	101, 106
St. Leger, Sir A.	310, 322	Vernacular writers	281-283, 316
Skelton, Rev. P.	387	Vivian, Cardinal	254
Skelligs	199, 200	Vocabularies	99
Slaves, English	241		
Stokes, Miss	180	WALSH and Leverous	317
Strafford, Lord	352, 353, 372	Warren, Rev. F. E.	132, 139
Stukeley	335	Waucop	306
Submission of chieftains	303	Welsh Bible	360
Sun worship	6	Wesley	384, 387
Swift, Dean	383-386	Western Churches, the	128
Sydney, Sir H.	330	Wetenhall, Bishop	381
Synod of Winchester	192	Whately, Archbishop	385, 394
Synod, the General	397	Whitby, Synod of	132
		Whitefield Synod	118
TERMON-FECHIN	260	Whitherne	61
Termons	126, 147, 170, 284	Wilfrid	82, 84
Test Act, the	373	Würzburgh Glosses	123, 160, 203
Thierry, King	94		
Tigernach, Annalist	196	ZACHARY, Pope	102
Tillemont	13, 16	Zimmer, Professor	10, 24

2 *Paternoster Buildings, E.C., and*
44 *Victoria Street, S.W.*

A SELECTION FROM
Wells Gardner, Darton, & Co.'s
Catalogue of Books.

By the Rev. A. C. AINSLIE, M.A., LL.D., Vicar of Langport.

Instructions for Junior Classes in Sunday Schools.

Fcap. 8vo. Cloth boards. **1s.** each.

A packet of Lesson Leaflets for a class of ten. Price **5s.**

Vol. I. The Story of the Gospels in Fifty-two Lessons.
Vol. II. Fifty-two Lessons on the Acts of the Apostles.

These books are specially designed to help those who have not been trained as Teachers.

By the Most Rev. the ARCHBISHOP OF YORK.

Pastoral Letters and Synodal Charges

Addressed to the Clergy and Laity in the Diocese of Lichfield.
By William Dalrymple Maclagan, Archbishop of York.
Crown 8vo. Cloth boards. **7s. 6d.**

By Lady BAKER.

Friendly Words for our Girls.

Large crown 8vo. Paper, **1s.**; cloth, **1s. 6d.** [24*th Thousand.*

By Lady BAKER—*continued*.

HALF HOURS WITH MY GIRLS.

Being Twenty-six Readings for Sundays. First Series.
Small crown 8vo. Cloth. **2s. 6d.** [*4th Edition.*

LETTERS TO MY GIRL FRIENDS.

Small crown 8vo. Cloth. **2s. 6d.**

MORE HALF HOURS WITH MY GIRLS.

Or Readings for a Village Class. Second Series.
Small crown 8vo. Cloth. **2s. 6d.**

By **C. F. MOBERLY BELL**, Author of "Egyptian Finance."

FROM PHARAOH TO FELLAH.

With upwards of 130 Illustrations from Drawings by GEORGES MONT-BARD. Engraved by CHARLES BARBANT.
Crown 8vo. Fancy cloth boards. **16s.**

With an Introduction by the late **BISHOP OF CARLISLE**.

HOLINESS TO THE LORD.

The Character of the Christian Priest.
Adapted from the French of the ABBÉ DUBOIS for the use of the English Clergy.
Crown 8vo. Cloth boards. **7s. 6d.**

By the Right Rev. the **BISHOP OF LICHFIELD**.

IN COVENANT WITH GOD.

A Book of Instruction on Confirmation.
By the Right Rev. the Hon. AUGUSTUS LEGGE, D.D.
Fcap. 8vo. Cloth boards. **1s. 6d.**

Wells Gardner, Darton, and Co. 3

By the Right Rev. the BISHOP OF MISSISSIPPI.

The World and the Kingdom.

By the Right Rev. Hugh Millar Thompson, D.D.
Crown 8vo. **3s. 6d.** [4*th Edition.*

By the Right Hon. the BISHOP OF RIPON.

Short Outline Lessons for each Sunday in the Christian Year.

By the Right Rev. W. Boyd Carpenter, D.D.
16mo, **8d.**; cloth boards, **1s.**

By the Right Rev. the BISHOP OF WAKEFIELD.

Daily Family Prayer.

By the Right Rev. W. Walsham How, D.D.
Fcap. 8vo, cloth boards, **1s. 6d.**; calf or morocco, **7s. 6d.**
[17*th Edition.*

☞ A Sixpenny Edition, in large type, cloth boards, is now ready. This volume will be found most suitable for Parochial distribution, and is the cheapest book of Family Prayers yet published.

Notes on the Church Service.

Fcap. 8vo. Cloth. **9d.**

Pastoral Work.

Fcap. 8vo. Cloth boards. **2s. 6d.** [3*rd Edition.*

Pastor in Parochiâ.

With the Appendix.

Fcap. 8vo, cloth boards, red edges, **3s. 6d.**; leather limp, **5s.**; calf limp antique, **10s. 6d.** Also morocco plain, and best flexible morocco, red under gilt edges, **12s. 6d.** [15*th Edition.*

By the **Right Rev.** the **BISHOP OF WAKEFIELD**—*continued.*

PLAIN WORDS. First Series.

Sixty Short Sermons for the Poor, and for Family Reading.

Fcap. 8vo, cloth, turned in, **2s.**; cloth, bevelled boards, red edges, **2s. 6d.** Large-type Edition, cloth boards, **3s. 6d.** [49*th Edition.*

PLAIN WORDS. Second Series.

Short Sermons for the Sundays and Chief Holy-days of the Christian Year.

Fcap. 8vo. Cloth, turned in, **2s.**; cloth, bevelled boards, red edges, **2s. 6d.** Large-type Edition, cloth boards, **3s. 6d.** [30*th Edition.*
Vols. I. and II., in one vol. Cloth boards. **4s. 6d.**

PLAIN WORDS. Third Series.

Forty Meditations with a View to the Deepening of the Spiritual Life.

Fcap. 8vo. Cloth limp, **2s.**; cloth, bevelled boards, red edges, **2s. 6d.** Large-type Edition. Cloth boards. **3s. 6d.** [17*th Edition.*

PLAIN WORDS. Fourth Series.

Forty Readings for those who Desire to Pray Better.

Fcap. 8vo. Cloth limp, turned in, **2s.**; cloth, bevelled boards, red edges, **2s. 6d.** [7*th Edition.*
Vols. III. and IV. in one. Cloth boards. **4s. 6d.**

PLAIN WORDS TO CHILDREN.

Fcap. 8vo, cloth limp, turned in, **2s.** Crown 8vo, cloth, bevelled boards, **2s. 6d.** [3*rd Edition.*

POEMS.

Complete Edition. Fcap. 8vo. Cloth boards, gilt edges. **3s. 6d.** Without the Hymns, **3s.** Tree calf, or calf half extra, **7s. 6d.**
[4*th Edition.*

Wells Gardner, Darton, and Co.

By the Right Rev. the BISHOP OF WAKEFIELD—*continued.*

SEVEN LENTEN SERMONS ON PSALM LI.

Fcap. 8vo. Cloth limp, turned in. **1s.**   [13*th Edition.*

TWENTY-FOUR PRACTICAL SERMONS.

Fcap. 8vo, cloth limp, turned in, **2s.**; cloth boards, red edges, **2s. 6d.**
[12*th Edition.*

WORDS OF GOOD CHEER.

Fcap. 8vo, cloth limp, **1s. 6d.** Small crown 8vo, cloth, bevelled boards, **2s. 6d.**

By the Rev. JOHN C. BLISSARD, M.A.

SIDELIGHTS ON REVELATION.

Crown 8vo. Cloth boards. **2s. 6d.**

By the Rev. H. W. BURROWS, B.D., Canon of Rochester.

THE EVE OF ORDINATION.

Fcap. 8vo. Cloth limp. **1s. 6d.**   [3*rd Edition.*

Containing:—Two Meditations before Holy Communion—The Young Clergyman's Dangers and Safeguards—Visiting the Sick—A Few Words on Writing Sermons—An Address on the Day of Ordination.

LENTEN AND OTHER SERMONS.

Fcap. 8vo. Cloth boards. **2s. 6d.**   [3*rd Edition.*

By ALFRED JAMES COPELAND, F.S.A.

BRIDEWELL ROYAL HOSPITAL. PAST AND PRESENT.

A short account of it as Palace, Hospital, Prison, and School, with a collection of interesting Memoranda never before published.
Crown 8vo. **3s. 6d.**

By the **Countess COWPER.**

HELP AT HAND;

Or, What shall we do in Accidents or Illness?
Numerous Illustrations.
Fcap. 8vo, paper cover, **3d.** ; cloth, **6d.** [2nd *Edition*.

By the **Rev. EVAN DANIEL, M.A.**

THE DAILY OFFICES AND LITANY.

Being an Introduction to the Study of the Prayer-Book. Specially designed for the Use of National Schools and Sunday Schools.
Fcap. 8vo, **8d.** ; cloth boards, **10d.** [11*th Thousand*.

THE PRAYER-BOOK.

Its History, Language, and Contents.
Crown 8vo. Cloth boards. **6s.** [14*th Edition*.

DICTIONARY OF THE ENGLISH CHURCH, ANCIENT AND MODERN.

Crown 8vo. Cloth boards. **7s. 6d.**

Edited by the **Rev. P. H. DITCHFIELD, M.A., F.R.Hist.S.**

THE NATIONAL CHURCHES.

I. **GERMANY.** By the Rev. S. BARING-GOULD, M.A., author of "Mehalah," "Germany Past and Present," &c. With Maps. Crown 8vo. Cloth boards. **6s.**

II. **SPAIN.** By the Rev. FREDERICK MEYRICK, M.A., Prebendary of Lincoln. Editor of "The Foreign Church Chronicle." With Map. Crown 8vo. Cloth boards. **6s.**

III. **IRELAND.** By the Rev. THOMAS OLDEN, A.B. With Maps. Crown 8vo. Cloth boards. **6s.**

Arrangements have been made for volumes by the BISHOP OF DELAWARRE, CANON LUCKOCK, CANON MACLEAR, and others.

By the Rev. HENRY T. ELLISON, M.A., Rector of Haseley, Hon. Canon of Christ Church, Chaplain-in-Ordinary to the Queen.

Holy Matrimony.

The Married Life of the Christian Man and Woman.
Fcap. 8vo. Cloth boards. **1s. 6d.** [*New Edition.*

By the Rev. THOMAS FARRAR, Archdeacon of Guiana.

The Christian Ministry.

Crown 8vo. Cloth boards. **4s., 13 as 12.** This volume has been largely used in the Colonies as a Manual for Candidates for Ordination. The present issue has been carefully revised.
4th Edition—Revised and Enlarged.

The Family Lesson-Book.

Being a Selection of Morning and Evening Readings for the Christian Year. Based upon the Church's Lectionary.
Crown 8vo, cloth boards, with silk registers, **1s. 6d.**; leather, **3s. 6d.**

Each reading is complete in itself, and affords a simple subject for meditation. Every Holy-Day will be found to be conveniently noted, and the Readings to correspond with its proper teaching. The cheapest book of the kind ever published.

By Mrs. E. M. FIELD.

The Child and His Book.

Some Account of the History and Progress of Children's Literature in England.
Illustrated.
Large crown 8vo. Cloth boards. **6s.** [*2nd Edition in the Press.*

By Mrs. E. M. FIELD—*continued*.

ETHNE.

Being a truthful History of the great and final Settlement of Ireland by Oliver Cromwell, and certain other noteworthy Events from the Journals of Ethne O'Connor, and of Roger Standfast, Captain in the Army of the Commons of England.

With Etched Title and Frontispiece. Large crown 8vo. Appropriate cloth boards. **6s.** [3*rd Edition.*

By the Rev. JOSEPH HAMMOND, LL.B., B.A.

CHURCH OR CHAPEL?

An Eirenicon.

Crown 8vo, Cloth boards. **5s.**

[3*rd Edition, with Additions and Appendix.*

By the Hon. Mrs. C. HOBART, *née* N. P. W.

THE CHANGED CROSS.

With Outline Illustrations by H. J. A. MILES. Square 16mo. Cloth, bevelled boards, gilt edges. **1s. 6d.**

[20*th Edition.*

By the Rev. EDWIN HOBSON, M.A.

AIDS TO THE STUDY OF THE BOOKS OF SAMUEL.

Fcap. 8vo, cloth boards, 2 vols. **1s. 6d.** each; or 1 vol. complete, with Map, **2s. 6d.**

By the Rev. ARTHUR WILLIAMSON, D.D.

ASPECTS OF FAITH AND RELIGION IN THE SEVENTEENTH CENTURY.

I. THE JANSENISTS.   III. THE QUAKERS.
II. THE QUIETISTS.   IV. THE PIETISTS.

Demy 8vo, cloth boards, **3s. 6d.**

www.ingramcontent.com/pod-product-compliance
Lightning Source LLC
Chambersburg PA
CBHW032002300426
44117CB00008B/870